Midwest Studies in Philosophy
Volume XVII

MIDWEST STUDIES IN PHILOSOPHY

EDITED BY PETER A. FRENCH, THEODORE E. UEHLING, JR., HOWARD K. WETTSTEIN

Many papers in MIDWEST STUDIES IN PHILOSOPHY are invited and all are previously unpublished. The editors will consider unsolicited manuscripts that are received by January of the year preceding the appearance of a volume. All manuscripts must be pertinent to the topic area of the volume for which they are submitted. Address manuscripts to MIDWEST STUDIES IN PHILOSOPHY, Department of Philosophy, University of California, Riverside, CA 92373.

The articles in MIDWEST STUDIES IN PHILOSOPHY are indexed in THE PHILOSOPHER'S INDEX.

Forthcoming Volumes

Volume XVIII 1993 Philosophy of Science
Volume XIX   1994 Naturalism

Available Previously Published Volumes

Volume XII   1987 Realism and Anti-Realism
Volume XIII   1988 Ethical Theory: Character and Virtue
Volume XIV   1989 Contemporary Perspectives in the Philosophy of Language II
Volume XV   1990 The Philosophy of the Human Sciences
Volume XVI   1991 Philosophy and the Arts

Midwest Studies
in
Philosophy
Volume XVII

The Wittgenstein Legacy

Editors

Peter A. French
Trinity University

Theodore E. Uehling, Jr.
University of Minnesota, Morris

Howard K. Wettstein
University of California, Riverside

University of Notre Dame Press ● Notre Dame, Indiana

Published by the University of Notre Dame Press
Notre Dame, IN 46556
Printed in the United States of America

Library of Congress Cataloging-in-Publication Data

The Wittgenstein legacy / editors, Peter A. French,
Theodore E. Uehling, Jr., Howard K. Wettstein.
      p. cm. — (Midwest studies in philosophy : v. 17)
     Includes bibliographical references.
     ISBN 0-268-01394-2
     1. Wittgenstein, Ludwig, 1889–1951. I. French, Peter A.
II. Uehling, Theodore E. III. Wettstein, Howard K. IV. Series.
B3376.W564W565 1992
192—dc20   92-53749
                                               CIP

Midwest Studies in Philosophy
Volume XVII
The Wittgenstein Legacy

Midwest Studies in Philosophy
Volume XVII

Colors, Culture, and Practices

ALASDAIR MACINTYRE

I

It is a remarkable fact that the truth or falsity of a judgment about what color some particular object or surface is is and is generally recognized to be independent of how that color happens to look to the particular person who utters that judgment. Someone looking at an object, who suffers from some as yet unrecognized defect of color vision, or who is looking in visually unfavorable circumstances, may have her or his false judgment about its color corrected by someone blind who has been told what color it is by a reliable informant.

Wittgenstein appears to deny this at one point in the *Remarks on Colour*, when he not only asserted "That it seems so (*so scheint*) to human beings is their criterion for its *being* so" (III, 98), but added that only in exceptional cases might *being* and *seeming* be independent of one another (99). If Wittgenstein meant by this no more than that it is a necessary condition of our color judgments being as they are that, for example, "we *call* brown the table which under certain circumstances appears brown to the normal-sighted" (97), then it would be difficult to disagree. But the use of the word 'criterion', as I shall suggest later, is misleading. For the recognition of a color is not generally the application of a test. In puzzle cases or deviant cases we may of course consult those with certifiably normal eye-sight and perhaps also have been trained in some relevant type of visual discrimination to tell us *how some object looks to them* as a test or criterion of *what color it is*. But this is so only in such exceptional cases. And notice that those who satisfy the required conditions, and therefore are able to provide the needed criterion, had themselves already been tested in respect of their capacity to recognize—without any test or criterion apart from successful recognition—what color the relevant types of objects in fact *are*. They turn out to be, like most of the rest of us, among those for whom in the vast majority of cases the distinction between *what color things or surfaces in fact are* and *what color they seem to be to me here and now* is unproblematic.

This distinction after all is a commonplace. It is unambiguously pre-supposed in such practical activities as those of painters, interior decorators, sign-makers, and students of the physiology of color vision, as well as by ordinary speakers. That this distinction is so widely presupposed does not of course of itself provide sufficient reason for upholding it. But I shall argue that once we have understood the nature of that distinction, we shall also understand that, although the possibility of abandoning it cannot be logically or conceptually ruled out, that possibility is one which it would be empty to entertain. In so arguing I will be unable to avoid engagement with issues whose present canonical formulation we owe to Wittgenstein, to some degree in his discussions of color, but even more in his examination of the possibility of rule-following in action or judgment by a solitary individual. And because the interpretation of what Wittgenstein says is seriously disputed, questions of interpretation will have to be faced.

My initial aim then is to identify the conditions which enable us to ascribe objectivity to color judgments, so that we can understand how we are able to agree to the extraordinary extent that we do in marking the distinction between *what color objects are* and *what color they seem to be to particular individuals in particular circumstances* and what it is that constrains us in so doing and undermines any tendency by an individual to insist upon making her or his own experience of color the sovereign test of what judgments to make. A first such constraint is provided just by the multiplicity of cooperative types of activity participation in which requires that judgments about color should be understood as true or false, independently of the experience of particular individuals.

We, for example, match the colors in fabrics, we design and interpret signals by the use of colors, we identify flags, flowers, and species of birds partly by colors, physicians use skin color in making diagnoses, weather forecasters refer to colors of clouds and skies, scientific instruments use colors as signs, and painters not only use, but extend the range of and the range of uses of colors in ways that not only require a shared vocabulary, but also shared standards of judgment in the application of that vocabulary. Any but marginal disagreements in the use of that vocabulary would render participation in such activities in anything like their present form impossible. But is this not merely a contingent feature of social life as we know it? Could there perhaps be some alternative form of life in which this constraint upon disagreement had been removed? Consider a passage from the *Philosophical Investigations* (II, xi, p. 226) in which Wittgenstein envisages this possibility: "Does it make sense to say that people generally agree in their judgments of color? What would it be like for them not to?—One man would say a flower was red which another called blue, and so on.—But what right should we have to call these people's words 'red' and 'blue' *our* 'color words'?—How would they learn to use these words? And is the language-game which they learn still such as we call the use of 'names of color'? There are evidently differences of degree here."

What Wittgenstein invites us to imagine seems to be a society in which each person names colors without reference to how they are named by others. The more it is that such persons disagree in their naming of colors, the further they are from resembling us in our uses. But it is important that the difference between them and us is not merely a matter of the *extent* of our agreements and disagreements. For there is a second constraint upon our judgments of color, one embodied in a further set of agreements, agreements upon how to explain and thereby resolve disagreements about color, when they do arise. There are four relevant types of explanation to which appeal may be made.

When one person disagrees with another as to what color a particular object or surface is, we may be able to explain the difference in judgment as a result of inviting them to view that object or surface in the same light from the same angle of vision when placed at the same distance from that object or surface. If under those conditions they come to agree in judgment, we shall reasonably conclude that it was a failure to satisfy one of these three conditions which caused them to perceive the color of that particular object or surface differently and so to judge differently. It may be however that even in the same ideal conditions for the perception of color the two still disagree and a next step is to ask whether one of them has not as yet learned to discriminate adequately, at least so far as the color or colors of this particular object or surface are concerned. A failure of this second type of explanation will lead us then to enquire whether one or both persons suffers from some defective form of color vision, that is, is in some way—whether from physiological or psychological causes—color blind. And, if that too turns out not to be the case, then we shall fourthly and finally ask if the disagreement is not about colors themselves, but only about the names of colors, by confronting the two persons who disagree with some standard set of examples of colors and shades of colors, in which a very large number of shades are discriminated and named, so that they may discover, say, whether a particular shade which one calls 'magenta' the other calls 'puce', or, as in Wittgenstein's more radical example whether what one calls 'red' the other calls 'blue'.

What we may well discover in searching for such explanations and resolutions of disagreement is evidence of some past failure on the part of one or more of those who now disagree to have learned how to discriminate and to name colors, either because she or he was not adequately exposed to the standard methods of teaching or because, although so exposed, there was some barrier to her or his learning. The standard methods of teaching and learning about colors are of two kinds. There are those involved in acquiring an elementary color vocabulary, the normal property of any child. And there are those involved in the more specialized education required of those apprenticed within particular practices—in learning how to paint ceremonial masks, say, or how to collect medicinal plants—where a wider range of discriminations is required.

So in one and the same process of learning the uses of the color vocabulary are extended and the abilities to recognize and to distinguish are developed. We learn of course not only ostensively, but also at later stages from descriptions and classifications. Having learnt 'red' and 'yellow', I may have 'orange' explained to me not by some further act of ostension, but as a color intermediate between 'red' and 'yellow', and such a description may enable me to recognize and to name orange. Moreover in learning how to use one and the same vocabulary of colors different individuals often begin the learning process by being introduced to notably different sets of examples. The shade of red which provides my initial paradigm for uses of the word 'red' may be very different from that which provides yours. Nonetheless as we and other speakers extend our range of uses beyond these initial examples, we do so in a rule-governed way which gives evidence of common adherence to one and the same set of linguistic rules in terms of which we order our diverse experiences of color.

What can be learned can of course always be mislearned. But what is mislearned is what can be corrected and it is in subjecting our judgments to correction by others, through admitting the force of one or more of the types of explanation invoked to explain and to resolve our disagreements with those others—particularly when those disagreements threaten our cooperative participation in those shared activities which require agreement in judgments concerning color—that we assent to the distinction between *what color objects are* and *what color they seem to me to be in these circumstances*, and so to standards of truth and falsity in judgments concerning what color objects are.

It is important that it is our common conformity to the established and standard rules governing the use and application of color words in the particular shared language in whose uses we participate which makes it possible for us to make true or false judgments concerning color. And if we misuse color words or if we judge falsely, it is our violation of these standards and rules and not the fact that we have deviated from the consensus of an overwhelming majority of speakers of our language which renders us in need of correction. Because the consensus of that majority is an agreement concerning those particular rules and concepts, any failure in respect of the relevant rules and concepts will also of course be a deviation from that consensus. And certainly were that consensus not to be maintained over an extended period of time, a necessary condition for there being established rules and concepts in this area of discourse would no longer hold. Nonetheless it is not the consensus itself which is normative for our use of color or any other words; what is normative is supplied by the rules and concepts in assenting to which the majority brings that consensus into existence.

To suppose otherwise would be a mistake. For it would make of the customary uses of the majority a particular kind of *criterion* for correct use, a criterion to which appeal could be made to determine correct use and application, independently of an ability to recognize correct uses and applications by oneself or by others. Were there such a criterion, knowing what it is would be one thing and being able to apply it would be quite another. But there is no such criterion and none is needed (compare what Wittgenstein says in *Remarks on the Foundations of Mathematics*, VII, 40 about identity: "For of course I don't make use of the agreement of human beings to affirm identity. What criterion do you use, then? None at all." See also VII, 39). When someone knows how to apply and use color words correctly, and how to recognize correctness and incorrectness in others, there is nothing else remaining for him or her to know, something that would, as it were, provide an extrinsic guarantee. True judgment requires no more than recognition. Yet this claim may be thought to encounter the following difficulty.

If there are rules governing the use and application of color words, then, as Wittgenstein insists, there must be a difference between merely thinking that you have used such words in conformity to those rules, while not having actually done so, and actually having done so (*Philosophical Investigation* 202). But if there is no extrinsic criterion, how is this difference to be established in particular cases? It is established in the same way that disagreement is resolved, that is, by appealing to one or more of the four types of explanation which I sketched earlier. One defends the correctness of one's own judgments first by explaining how one had viewed the relevant object of vision in terms of distance, angle of vision and light, secondly by establishing that one had learned to make the relevant set of discriminations between, say, this shade of purple and that of magenta, thirdly by providing the evidence that one has no form of psychological or physiological color blindness or distortion and fourthly by establishing one's grasp of the relevant set of names of colors. There is nothing further to be done to show that one has reported correctly what color something is rather than having been deceived by how it looks or looked to oneself.

This reply however may generate another objection. For it is obvious that as a matter of historical fact the use of color vocabularies predates an ability to formulate and make any systematic use of some of our commonest explanations of disagreement. Knowledge of the range and types of color blindness and distortion, for example, requires a certain kind of scientific sophistication, not available in all times and places. And true judgments about color antedate catalogues of colors and shades by millennia. Perhaps some aspects of these types of explanatory procedure will have been invoked from some very early stage when disagreements arose over color, but anything like appeal to them in a fully fledged form must occur at a late stage in the history of the rule-governed use of color language.

What this objection brings out is that agreement in the rule-governed use of color-language requires the *possibility* of explanations of these general types being given in more or less fully fledged form. It does not require that any particular competent user of such language should be able to give them in such form. What is necessary is both that such users should be able to distinguish implicitly, if not explicitly, between the question of what color that particular object or surface or light *is* and the question of what color it *seems to me to be* and that in so doing they should recognize implicitly, if not explicitly, that true judgments about color are independent of the point of view of any particular person. In so doing they will be acknowledging that on any particular occasion the standpoint of some other person may be superior to their own in respect of the truth as to some particular judgment concerning color. It is this reference to and regard for the standpoint of other persons which renders our ordinary and normal language of colors inescapably social, one the rules for whose correct use are independent of the standpoint of any particular individual and in this way impose a certain kind of impersonality in judgments concerning color.

The corrigibility and impersonality of our judgments as to what color objects or surfaces are both arise then from the same set of established social agreements which constrain our applications of the color vocabulary. But this is not the only aspect of judgment of color which seems to be inseparable from the social dimensions of the language of colors. Judgments about colors are uttered as speech acts and the intelligibility of a speech-act is a matter of socially shared understandings of what additional information about the speaker has to be supplied or presupposed if a given speech-act is to be construed as an intelligible performance.

Consider the actions of someone who moves around a room judging truly of each object what color it is: "That is magenta," she or he says, and then "That is ultramarine" and "That is emerald green." We can without difficulty imagine acquiring additional information about such a performance which renders it fully intelligible. This is, for example, a child or a foreigner trying out newly acquired English color words to make sure that she or he has got them right. Or perhaps she or he has been suffering from some type of loss of memory and is testing the extent of her or his recovery of memory by naming colors. In each of these types of case the point and purpose of making such color judgments can be discovered, so that the agent's actions can be understood as intelligible in the light afforded by that point and purpose. But suppose instead that when asked what he or she is doing, the person engaged in such a performance has no true reply to offer, except "Judging truly about color." "Judging truly about color" does not by itself without any further point and purpose name an intelligible type of speech-act or indeed an intelligible action of any kind. In what does the unintelligibility of such a performance consist?

Intelligibility of actions in general and of speech-acts in particular has two aspects.[1] An action is intelligible firstly if and insofar as others—socially versed others, that is—know how to respond to it. When such others are baffled by what someone else has just done, because there is no appropriate way of acting in response, it is because they are unable to bring what has been done under some description of a kind which in turn makes it understandable for them—by the standards of everyday life—to act in some particular way. A second feature of intelligible action is that in performing it not only can the agent reasonably expect to elicit a certain range of types of response from others, but she or he can find some point or purpose in doing whatever it is, within the wider range of activities and projects which that agent can recognize as her or his own. To act unintelligibly is not merely to puzzle others; it is oneself to be at a loss about what one is doing in doing this.

These two aspects of intelligibility are closely related. When someone performs an action which she or he finds unintelligible in that context to be doing—walking round the room naming colors, for example—she or he would be unable to say either to others or to her or himself what the point of doing *that then* and *there* was. When someone finds someone else's action unintelligible, that unintelligibility can only be removed by that person's being able to explain what the point and purpose of doing *that then* and *there* was. To say "I am just doing it for its own sake" or "for no particular reason" is not sufficient to remove the unintelligibility. What has to be added is some description which makes doing *that kind of thing* on *appropriate occasions*, whether for its own sake or for the sake of something further, intelligible. If neither of these can be specified, the action will remain unintelligible. If both are successfully specified, the action will have been made intelligible by being assigned a place in the sequence of the agent's actions, so that it can be understood as standing in some specific type of relationship to what precedes it (sometimes not what immediately precedes it) and to what may follow it.

Intelligibility is thus a property of actions in their relationship to the sequences in which they occur, both those sequences of interaction in which agents respond in turn to each other and those sequences of actions which some particular agent moves. For an action to be unintelligible is for it to be uninterpretable, given the context in which it has occurred, in terms of those types of reason, motive, purpose, and intention for which the norms of the shared culture specify certain types of response, either immediately or later, as appropriate or inappropriate. Of course an action may seem unintelligible on occasion to those who observe it only because they lack the necessary information about some particular agent's reasons, matters, purposes, and intentions or about the context in which he is acting. Were that information to be supplied, the action would then be understood as intelligible. But, when all relevant information has been made available, it may turn out that certain actions just are unintelligible. So, for example, if in the course of a conversation between physician and patient, in a darkened room, the physician, between giving a prognosis for the patient's eye ailments and offering nutritional advice, was to interject "The red of the poppies stands out against the cornflowers," his utterance would be at least *prima facie* unintelligible, whereas were the same person commenting on the landscape, while looking out the window together with someone else, the same utterance would be perfectly intelligible.

What I have suggested so far is that our uses and understandings of judgments concerning color are informed by socially established standards of corrigibility, of impersonality, and of intelligibility. And, if this is so, it might seem to follow that participation in and mastery of some socially established language are necessary conditions for any unproblematic use and application of a vocabulary of colors.

Suppose, for example, as some have done, that somewhere there is or was a solitary human language-user, deprived from earliest infancy of the society of other language-users, but her or himself the inventor somehow or other of something that is or approximates to a language. If such a person is to make genuine judgments concerning colors, then it would seem from what has been said so far that they must be corrigible. Yet how could such a solitary and isolated person correct her or himself in respect of judgments of color on the basis of nothing more than her or his own experiences? And if such a person is to make *correct* reports of her or his experiences of color, then it would seem that those reports must be such that any honest reporter would make the same reports of those same experiences, that is, that certain requirements of impersonality would still have to be satisfied. But how could someone restricted to her or his own experiences, and unable to refer to others for any sort of corroboration or correction, achieve such impersonality? And again, since such a person could only be talking to and for her or himself, how could we discriminate in her or his case between the intelligible utterance of a judgment of color from the mere repetition of certain strings of sounds elicited by certain repeated experiences? What would enable us to regard her or his speech acts as intelligible? How then would it be possible for such a solitary and isolated person to satisfy these three conditions conjointly, conditions of corrigibility, and of impersonality of judgment, and of intelligibility of utterance?

These are not mere rhetorical questions. To answer them we need to be able to supply a philosophically adequate account of what kind of language use might be possible for just such an isolated and solitary individual with adequately rich and repeated color experiences. Happily for us, this is an area already explored by Wittgenstein and, even if his account has turned out to be open to rival and incompatible interpretations, it remains nonetheless the best account that we possess so far.

II

Wittgenstein in the *Philosophical Investigations* clearly and unambiguously argued for the conclusion that there cannot be such a thing as a private language, if by that is meant a language not only used by only one person, but composed of expressions referring only to such private objects as her or his sensations. Colors, as we have seen, are not such private objects and so this conclusion has no bearing on my question. What does bear on it is the further conclusion, which some interpreters have ascribed to Wittgenstein, that a single, solitary individual is incapable of rule-following of the kind required for the use of anything worth calling a language.

Wittgenstein wrote: "Is what we call 'obeying' a rule something that it would be possible for only *one* man to do, and to do only *once* in his life? . . . It is not possible that there should have been only one occasion on which someone obeyed a rule. It is not possible that there should have been only one occasion on which a report was made, an order given or understood; and so on. To obey a rule, to make a report, to give an order, to play a game of chess, are *customs* (uses, institutions) . . . " *(Philosophical Investigations* 199). He also wrote that "it means nothing to say: in the history of mankind just once was a game invented, and that game was never played by anyone. . . .Only in a quite definite surrounding do the words 'invent a game' 'play a game' make sense. . . .In the same way it cannot be said either that just once in the history of mankind did someone follow a signpost . . . " (*Remarks on the Foundations of Mathematics* VI, 43).

Everyone agrees that in these and cognate passages Wittgenstein is denying that it could ever be the case that on only one occasion a rule was followed, an expression meaningfully used, a concept given application. The sharpest of disagreements arises over what answer Wittgenstein is taken to have given to the question of whether it could ever be the case that only one person followed a particular rule, used a particular expression meaningfully, or gave application to a particular concept.

Colin McGinn interprets Wittgenstein in *Philosophical Investigation* 199 to be asserting "that if there is just one man then *he* must follow his rules more than once, but if there are many men it can be enough that *each* follows" the rules just once, or possibly not at all, since what are required, on Wittgenstein's view thus interpreted, are many occasions of rule-following, but not necessarily many rule-followers.[2] So when Wittgenstein speaks of 'customs', 'uses', 'institutions', and elsewhere of 'practices', McGinn points out that such words "are never qualified with 'social' or 'community' " and that so to qualify them "is not pleonastic."[3] So his conclusion is that Wittgenstein held that "a sign has meaning only in virtue of being (repeatedly) used in a certain way. *This thesis does not in itself carry any suggestion that meaning is inconceivable in social isolation.*"[4]

McGinn himself goes even further: "Wittgenstein is right to describe rule-following as a practice or custom only in the sense that necessarily rules are things that *can* be followed on repeated occasions, not that necessarily they are repeatedly followed . . . "[5] So neither McGinn's Wittgenstein nor McGinn would presumably see anything conceptually impossible in the notion of an isolated person inventing and using in speech only with her or himself a vocabulary of colors. McGinn imagines someone who, surviving in conditions of complete, solitariness from infancy onwards, later, while still isolated, invents sign-posts and keeps records of the weather,[6] tasks of just the kind for which color discriminations are often employed.

Norman Malcolm has retorted that in constructing his imaginary account of such a person McGinn has failed to recognize that such activities as those involved in inventing sign-posts cannot be carried through except by those who already possess a language, who are already rule-followers.[7] So the notion of an isolated rule-follower does not make sense, "because the idea of a rule is embedded in an environment of teaching, testing, correcting—within a community where there is agreement in acting in the way that is called 'following the rule'. To withdraw that environment is to withdraw the concept of following a rule."[8]

Malcolm goes on to argue that the example of an isolated rule-follower constructed by McGinn presupposes that such a rule-follower already possesses a language, which presumably she or he had had to learn from someone else, so that the example is not after all one of a person inventing a rule-following use in isolation from others.[10] A problem with Malcolm's reply to McGinn is that, if sound and if generalized, it proves too much. For if no one could ever innovate by producing a new rule-following use of language, unless he or she already possessed language, how could language ever begin? If Malcolm's argument is sound, it raises difficult questions about the possibility of a first introduction of language. It is indeed likely that at the very first beginning of language use, whenever and wherever that was, there were behaviors which approximated to language-use before there was genuine rule-following; but there clearly was a time before *any* language and a time when genuine language use had already begun. And how such a transition could have taken place seems puzzling on Malcolm's view. Is McGinn then right on the point of philosophical substance? (Whether it is Malcolm or McGinn who is right as to the interpretation of Wittgenstein is a question which for the moment I leave open.)

The difficulties which McGinn's view confronts can best be brought out by returning to the question of whether or not the three conditions which would have to be satisfied, if a solitary and isolated person were to be held to possess and to be able to use a genuine language of colors, can be jointly satisfied. It will however illuminate what is at stake in McGinn's position if we begin by considering only the first two of these, the requirement that genuine uses of a color vocabulary must be corrigible and that therefore the isolated and solitary person must possess the resources necessary for correcting both her or his misuses of language and own false judgments, and the requirement that judgments about color should be impersonal.

Earlier I connected the need for judgments about color to be corrigible with their impersonality as instances of rule-following. What assures us both in such judgments and more generally that something is a case of actual rather than merely apparent rule-following ("to *believe* one is following a rule is not following the rule" *Philosophical Investigation* 202, as translated by Malcolm) in the making of a particular judgment is, as I noted, that it would be judged to be so by *anyone* with the requisite competence and integrity, no matter what their standpoint. An impartial and impersonal spectator would so judge concerning it. It is only insofar as we accord this impersonal character and a correspondingly impersonal authority to rules that we treat them as *rules*.

In the case of judgments about color the distorting partialities to be overcome are those of perceptual standpoint and the incompetences to be remedied those derived from deficiencies of color vision or vocabulary. With other types of judgment it is other types of partiality and incompetence which have to be identified and overcome from some similarly impersonal point of view. The question therefore is: how is it possible for us to assume a properly impersonal standpoint with regard to our own judgments, both generally and in respect of judgments concerning colors?

If an impersonal standpoint is one that is neutral between the claims and interest of different actual persons, it cannot be the standpoint of McGinn's

socially isolated person. But McGinn could of course reply that the impersonality of rule-following only requires always being open to the *possibility*
of correction by others and that these others need be no more than *possible*
others. McGinn's solitary individual might therefore be able to provide for
these possibilities, even in isolation from all actual others. She or he would
be open to the possibility of self-correction by imagined, possible others, that
is in fact by her or himself, in the imagined role of a possible other. A set
of counterfactuals, specifying how she or he would react, were he or she to
be challenged by others, would be true of her or him. But they could remain
*counter*factual without damaging her or his status as a rule-follower.

What this brings out is the way in which the development of McGinn's
position places continually increasing demands on the conceptual imagination.
McGinn says on an allied point: "I am merely reporting my intuitions of
logical possibility," acknowledges that other philosophers do not share his
intuitions, but asserts that "they are all one has to go on in deciding modal
questions"[11] His position thus formulated seems to entail that between the
contingent impossibilities disclosed by empirical enquiry and purely logical
possibility there is no stopping-place in conceptual investigations concerned
with determining possibilities. That this is false is suggested by reopening the
question of the joint satisfiability by a solitary and isolated language-user of
the three conditions for the use of a language of colors.

Consider first one further aspect of the first, the corrigibility condition.
David Pears in arguing that Wittgenstein may not have rejected the possibility of
a solitary language-user has pointed out that, in actual linguistic communities,
not only do language-users correct their judgments by reference to two "sta-
bilizing resources"—"standard objects and reassuring interlocutors"—but their
use of these resources is such that appeal to one is not independent of appeal
to the other.[12] It is only because and insofar as we suppose that other members
of our community have continued to use the same words of the same objects
that we are able to appeal to their use to confirm or correct our own. And of
course it is also only because and insofar as we are assured that those objects
have continued to possess the properties which make it correct to use those
same words of them that we are able so to appeal. In our normal procedures
the appeal to reassuring interlocutors and the appeal to standard objects stand
or fall together.

With our imagined solitary, isolated person it is quite otherwise. For in
her or his case there are no reassuring interlocutors. So it is not only that
the appeal to standard objects is detached from that to interlocutors, but that
by being made independent it is itself weakened. In this weaker form can it
still provide the required degree and kind of corrigibility? Before I propose an
answer to this question, there is another type of difficulty to be considered.

Any use of a color vocabulary which is more than minimal involves,
as I noticed earlier, the rule-governed extension of the use and application of
color words beyond the situations and the types of situation in which they were
first used; any use of a color vocabulary which achieves intelligible utterance

requires the performance of a certain *range* of intelligible speech-acts in giving expression to judgments about colors. What degree of extension and what precise range I leave open. There is even so a tension between the satisfaction of these two requirements and the satisfaction of the corrigibility condition. For the larger the degree of such extensions of use, and the wider the range of intelligible speech-acts, the greater the need to show and the greater the difficulty in showing that the corrigibility condition is sufficiently strong and adequately satisfied. So an isolated, solitary, speaker capable of only the most limited judgments expressed in a very narrow range of speech-acts would need far less in the way of resources of corrigibility than does a normal speaker in an ordinary linguistic community.

Does this rescue McGinn's thesis from its difficulties? I think not and for a crucial reason. In trying to envisage McGinn's isolated, solitary speaker, whether as a speaker of the language of colors or more generally, we have moved too far away from the actualities of language use, as we know them, to be able to say with any precision or confidence what is possible and what is not. In so contending I am relying upon a very different conception of possibility from McGinn's.

The paradigmatic example of the possible is the actual. As we in any particular type of case move away from the actual in thought, carefully stripping it of its properties one by one we move from imagined cases in which we can clearly say 'Although never actual this type of person, thing or state of affairs is clearly possible', for we can specify with some precision and confidence what would have to be the case for the otherwise merely possible to become actual, through intermediate cases to those in which so much has been stripped away that, although we have not arrived at the limiting case of the logically impossible, we no longer know what to say. And this, I want to suggest, is how we ought to respond to the case of an imagined solitary and isolated user of a language of colors.

Moreover there is some reason to believe that this position on possibility may be closer to that presupposed by Wittgenstein than that of either McGinn or Malcolm. McGinn notes that Wittgenstein asks, but does not answer the question: "Is what we call 'obeying a rule' something that it would be possible for only *one* man to do?" *(Philosophical Investigation* 199), yet goes on to impute an answer to Wittgenstein.[13] Malcolm interprets Wittgenstein's question: "Could there be only one human being that calculated? Could there be only one that followed a rule? Are these questions somewhat similar to this one 'Can one man alone engage in commerce?' " *(Remarks on the Philosophy of Mathematics* VI, 45) by asserting that "just as carrying on a trade presupposes a community, so too does arithmetic and following a rule."[14] So each converts a question into a thesis. But perhaps all that we are capable of when the conceptual imagination has been stretched to this point by this type of case are questions, unanswerable questions. We have no *a priori* resources for going beyond questions to answers and in acknowledging this our original question finds its answer. The concept of a solitary, isolated speaker of language, whether concerning colors or more generally, is neither that of an evidently possible type of person or of an evidently impossible type of person. It is instead a concept whose nature and status is essentially problematic.

Does it follow that all claims which assert or presuppose the possibility or actuality of someone initially isolated from or later somehow disengaged from the shared agreements of a common language, who has or fabricates in its place some language of her or his own, must be rejected? Are stories of infants reared by wolves who come to speak in a language of their own or of philosophical inventors of egocentrically defined phenomenalist languages fables always to be rejected? Nothing so radical follows. What does follow is that the onus is upon those who make such claims to show how and why in these particular detailed circumstances possibilities of which we can make so little when they are articulated only in general terms can be acknowledged. For until the detail has been spelled out, we do not know precisely what it is which we are being invited to declare possible or impossible. Until then we have been provided with insufficient material for our modal intuitions to address. 'An infant reared by wolves who invents a language' does not as yet either succeed or fail in specifying a concept with possible application. Notice that on this view of possibility, to assert that something is possible goes further than to assert that it has not yet been shown to be impossible. To make the former assertion we need to know a good deal more than is required in the case of the latter, in McGinn's example a good deal more about how the presuppositions of individual and solitary language-use are to be supplied. The agreements of shared languages give expression, just as Wittgenstein says, to shared customs, uses, and institutions. An individual who separates her or himself from or is separated from those agreements would have, as McGinn recognizes, to invent her or his own customs, uses, and institutions. But in such invention much more has to be involved than McGinn's fables recognize. My claim is not at all Malcolm's, that such invention can be shown to be impossible. It is that everything that we know about customs, uses, and institutions tells us that in different types of case different and often enough quite complex conditions would have to be satisfied; and that whether they *could* be satisfied in any particular instance needs to be shown for that particular instance. And what holds more generally also holds of questions about solitary and isolated users of a language of colors.

It is at this point that someone may protest impatiently that the examination of these Wittgensteinian arguments has been an irrelevant excursus, a misleading distraction from very different considerations towards which the arguments of the first part of this essay ought to have directed us. In that first part I identified the nature of the social agreements embodied in or presupposed by our uses of language concerning colors. In this second part I have tried to show that those agreements exemplify the constraints of shared social uses, customs, and institutions in just the way that Wittgenstein claimed that they did, that what is true in these respects of the language of colors is what is true of language in general. But, so the objector whom I am imagining will complain, the agreement in use and application of a vocabulary of colors needs to be explained quite differently, in a way that is specific to that vocabulary, namely by an appeal to the scientific facts about color and its perception.

Jonathan Westphal has argued compellingly that "there is a 'general formula' of a certain kind under which the same colours, correlated with different frequencies, fall," a formula according to which what makes yellow objects yellow is "the small amount of blue light *relative to light of the other colours* which they reflect" and "a green object . . . is an object which *refuses* to reflect a significant proportion of red light relative to lights of the other colors, including green."[15] The wavelengths of light, the facts of reflection and of lightening and darkening thus provide a way of defining color. But, so our imagined objector might proceed, the physical facts are invariant, so that what is presented by way of color for perception must be one and the same for all perceivers. The neurophysiology of color perception is also generally uniform. There are of course a small minority of defective perceivers. But given the invariant facts of color perception for the vast majority of persons and the invariant facts of the physics of color, agreement in color discrimination is physically and neurophysiologically determined.[16] And these facts are what underpin and explain agreement in color vocabulary and agreement in color judgment. The social features of such agreement are at best secondary.

Yet if this final conclusion were justified, we would expect to find something approaching complete agreement in color vocabulary not only within particular cultural and social orders, but between different and heterogeneous cultural and social orders. So that our next question has to be: do we in fact find such agreement?

III

Nothing is more striking, so it turns out, than the range of variations and disagreements which are embodied in the different schemes of color identification and classification which are deployed in different languages. So that if we were to conclude from Wittgenstein's or any other arguments—such as the argument from the facts of physics and neurophysiology—that in respect of colors we must speak as all, or almost all other human beings do, we should be mistaken. Indeed my use of the pronoun "we" up to this point has now to be put in question. Like Wittgenstein, like many other philosophers, I have used this pronoun recurrently without ever asking who "we" are. But the "we" of one social and cultural order turns out to speak very differently from the "we" of certain others.

Consider then the range of differences between the languages spoken in different cultural and social orders in respect of the vocabulary of colors. The Dani of New Guinea have only two color words *'mili'* which is used of blacks, greens, and blues and *'mola'* which is used of whites, reds, oranges, yellow, and some kindred colors.[17] In Irish Dinneen's *Dictionary* says of the adjective *'gorm'* that it means 'blue; rich green, as grass; negro tint', as well incidentally as 'noble'. In Tarahumara, an Uto-Aztecan language, *'siyóname'* is used both of what we call 'blue' and what we call 'green'.[18] In the Berber language, Kabyle, *'azegzaw'* is used of blue, green and grey.[19] Berlin and Kay have indeed been able to distinguish eight stages in the development of color vocabularies, ranging from languages, such as that of the Dani, with only two terms, to the eleven terms of contemporary everyday American English or the eleven terms of Zuni and the twelve terms of Hungarian and Russian.

Difference however extends beyond vocabulary. We noticed earlier that, when the learners of some particular color vocabulary are initiated into its use by means of paradigmatic examples, they also, insofar as they are successful learners, acquire a capacity to extend the use and application of the expressions which they have learned to an indefinite range of further examples. To this we must now add that characteristically and generally this extended set of uses includes a variety of metaphorical applications and that agreement in metaphor within any one social and cultural order is as striking as agreement in the use of color words in general. This is obvious and indeed unimpressive when the metaphors are dead metaphors, as when in current English we speak of feeling blue or seeing red. But those metaphors which are alive in a particular language-in-use give expression to a variety of beliefs about identity, resemblance, and relationship which are thus articulated in a way that makes them available for the categorization of objects and properties and happenings. And indeed in such cases the distinction between literal and metaphorical uses is characteristically drawn only from the standpoint of some external observer, in terms of what would be accounted a literal use or a metaphorical use in that observer's language rather than in the language of the observed. So it would be if we as observers, speaking French or English, were so to classify the uses of *'azegzaw'* in Kabyle. And living and powerful metaphors vary, of course, from language to language and from culture to culture, both generally and in the metaphorical uses of color terms.

A third aspect of difference is that of how color words enter into the conceptual organization of experience in combination with other types of expression, so that realities as encountered within a particular culture are categorized in one way rather than another. In consequence colors act as signs of other realities and both the nature of the color vocabulary and the place of colors in the conceptual and categorical organization of experience set constraints upon what kinds of signs they can be. So in the Kabyle language *'azegzaw'*, being used of vegetables and herbs which are eaten green and raw in the spring and of the fodder which feeds the cattle, is associated with spring and with morning and is a sign of good fortune, so that to make a gift of something green, especially in the morning, is to contribute to the good fortune of the recipient.[20] But in other societies green will function quite differently or not at all in their culture's semiotic code.

So here we have a third kind of difference—albeit one closely related to the second kind—distinguishing the ways in which the language of colors is used in some social and cultural orders from that in which it is used in others. It thus seems that we have to relativize the Wittgensteinian thesis about agreement in the use and application of a vocabulary of colors to the languages-in-use of different social and cultural orders. Within each such order agreement in judgments concerning colors is just what that thesis said that it was, an inescapable feature of the use of the language of colors. But differences in color vocabulary, metaphorical extension and categorical organization between different languages-in-use make it the case that the inescapable agreements of one social and cultural order are not the same as the inescapable agreements of certain other such orders. There is not just one language of colors which *we* speak; there are multifarious *we's*, each of whom has its own language.[21]

One response to the discovery of the extent of the differences between the color vocabularies and idioms of different languages has been to attempt to minimize the significance of those differences by suggesting that they have a superficial character. And this would presumably be the response of the objector whom I imagined earlier. The physics and neurophysiology of color vision do indeed, so it is claimed by such an objector, ensure that all, or almost all human beings perceive and discriminate the same spectrum of colors and shades. It is just that in different languages that spectrum is segmented at different points, so that in some languages, for example, there is a single name for the range that includes both blue and green, while in others, as in English, there are two names, one for blue and one for green. But there is an answer to this response. For the facts about differences in color perception and discrimination turn out to be somewhat more complex than this claim is able to allow.

There are, of course, important invariances in color perception and discrimination, due to the uniformities discovered by physics and neurophysiology, and also correspondingly important uniformities in color vocabularies. A range of focal colors, primary and nonprimary, can be identified, which speakers with very different color vocabularies from different social and cultural orders can agree in identifying without much difficulty in a variety of ways; but note at once that even nonprimary focal colors, such as purple, orange, and brown, are assimilated in different cultures with different color vocabularies to different primary focal colors, so that brown will be in one instance assimilated to yellow and in another to black (consider how in neither type of language for very different types of reason would we ask Wittgenstein's question: "What does it mean to say 'Brown is akin to yellow'?" *Remarks on Colour* III, 47). And in cases where two primary focal colors are given a single name, as is sometimes the case with blue and green, there are some cultures in which the paradigmatic example of the color so named, offered by native speakers, will be focal blue and others in which it will be focal green, so that in this type of case difference is not just a matter of the segmentation of a spectrum. The neurophysiology of color vision thus to some significant extent underdetermines the discrimination of color and its attentive perception, and the different color vocabularies of different cultures do seem genuinely to give expression to differences in discrimination and attention which have been embodied in socially established practices.[22]

Moreover in experiments in which speakers of Tarahumara, a language in which, as I noted earlier, *'siyóname'* names a color which includes both what English speakers name 'blue' and what English speakers name 'green', were matched with speakers of English, there were significant differences between the two groups in the performance of a certain type of discriminatory task to which the Tarahumara speakers had been introduced for the first time, differences which the evidence warrants us in ascribing to the difference in color vocabulary. So language itself does at least to some degree determine attention and discrimination and, when in some at least of the languages to which I have referred—*not* including contemporary English or for that matter contemporary Zuni—the particular organization of the experience of color is integrated in some highly specific way into both those metaphorical uses of language which link color to other aspects of experience and that categorical scheme through which, for the speakers of that language, experience in general is organized, the "we" who speak that particular language will in some cases find themselves separated from the speakers of some other alternative languages with their own idiosyncratic integrative schemes by the mutual untranslatability of their languages. For in such cases there will be in their particular language sentences and sets of sentences for which there are no equivalents in some of the others. And the speakers of one of any two such mutually untranslatable languages will use such sentences to make often true, and occasionally false, judgments which cannot be made in the other.

To speak of the partial underdetermination of language by neurophysiological stimulation and of a consequent partial untranslatability may suggest that something like Quine's position is being advanced. But the differences from Quine are crucial. Quine's theses are conceptual. The theses propounded by Lakoff and others are empirical. And the same type of evidence which shows that some judgments about color are underdetermined by the neurophysiological facts also shows that other judgments about color, those concerning the primary focal colors for instance, are sufficiently determined by those facts. So that the relevant issues of untranslatability are not at all those raised by Quine.

What such untranslatability may well seem to warrant is some kind of empirically grounded relativism. If there are alternative schemes of identification and classification embodied in different, sometimes untranslatable languages of color, each with its own standards of correct use and of truth and falsity internal to it, then it may well seem that no question of judging one scheme superior to another can even arise. For the only relevant standards of judgment are those embodied in each scheme. Someone living on the boundary between two radically different cultures with distinctively different languages of color may have to choose which of the two languages to speak, but this will be a choice of standards, not a choice guided by standards. Just this kind of relativistic conclusion is reached by George Lakoff,[23] yet it is the work which Lakoff and such predecessors as Berlin and Kay have done which perhaps undermines a relativist position.

For there is at least one language of colors which seems to receive insufficient attention from Lakoff: his own, that is, contemporary English. And his own language is distinctive, although not unique, in that he is able to translate into it—or, when necessary, to provide explanations which substitute for the work of translation—every language which provides him with his evidence for relativism. Lakoff may perhaps hold that this is irrelevant, since he asserts that the "translatability preserving truth conditions" of two or more languages does nothing to show that the "conceptual systems" to which they give expression are genuinely commensurable, if on any of four other criteria—especially perhaps that provided by the ability or inability of speakers of one language genuinely to understand those of another—those conceptual systems are incommensurable.[24] But this reply would miss the point, which is that what Lakoff through his combination of translation and explanation provides is not only a high degree of translatability, but also of understanding. That is to say, we can as users of the same language as Lakoff understand the uses and applications of the color vocabularies of certain languages the speakers of which lack resources necessary to understand our uses and applications of color words. The relationship of understanding is asymmetrical. Does this in itself show that our language and, to use Lakoff's terminology, our conceptual scheme is superior to theirs? Not at all; for that to be the case we would also have to show that such understanding serves some good, which we can achieve, but of which those with certain types of limited color vocabulary are inevitably deprived.

Yet if this has to be shown might we not simply find ourselves recommitted to relativism, since on Lakoff's criteria it might well appear that different conceptual systems exhibit incommensurable difference and diversity in respect of goods as well as in respect of colors and that by the standards of one such system, for example, that shared by Lakoff and his intended readers, this kind of superior understanding is accounted a good, while by the standards of some other such systems it is not so accounted (Lakoff himself of course says nothing about goods)?

It may well be that nothing can prevent the vindication of this conclusion if the facts of incommensurable difference and diversity are conceded *and* it is also allowed that the only standards to which anyone can appeal in judging what is a good and what is not are the standards embodied in the ordinary language of each particular group, the standards embodied in what Lakoff calls a conceptual system and I have called the language-in-use of a cultural and social order. But it is this latter contention which I now wish to deny.

IV

To what standards may we appeal against those of the particular cultural and social order which we happen to inhabit and whose language we happen to speak? To those of some practice or practices which have grown up within that order and developed to some significant degree its or their independent evaluative standards. The concept of a practice upon which I am relying is that which I introduced in *After Virtue*:[25] practices are forms of systematic human activity, each with its own goods internal to it. Practices develop through time in directions dictated by the conceptions of achievement internal to each, the achievement both of the goods specific to each particular type of practice and of excellence in the pursuit of those goods. Examples of practices are the activities of games, arts, and scientific enquiries, as well as such productive activities as farming, fishing, and architecture. Practices which use, need, and extend vocabularies of color include a variety of natural scientific enquiries, the enquiries of comparative linguistics exemplified in Lakoff's work, and, almost unnoticed in the argument so far, painting. Practices often innovate linguistically and could not progress towards their goals without so doing. How in respect of colors do these innovations relate to the established language-in-use of whatever cultural and social order within which a particular practice is being carried on?

Established languages-in-use are not themselves static. I have so far followed Brent and Kay in speaking of 'the' color terms or 'the' color vocabulary used in some particular language. But their work is meant to teach us lessons about the historical development as well as about the diversity of such vocabularies. And it is clear from their accounts that within many languages-in-use color vocabularies have developed in remarkably uniform and systematic patterns, patterns which reflect the social use of discriminations made possible by the physics and neurophysiology of color vision. Doubtless changes in and the multiplication of discriminatory tasks promote such development in numerous ways. Brent and Kay note that "there appears to be a positive correlation between general cultural complexity (and/or level of technological development) and complexity of color vocabulary,"[26] although they are appropriately cautious about the imprecision of such notions as cultural complexity. One area—and Brent and Kay do not note this—in which such growing complexity is evidenced is in the relationship between the culture in general of some particular order and the development of a variety of practices, as the linguistic innovations required by those practices enrich or displace or otherwise transform the prior vocabularies of the general language-in-use. Consider the relationship of vocabularies of color to examples of the innovative needs of the practice of painting.

The examples to which I am going to appeal are drawn from the history of European painting, but this does not make it improper to speak of 'the' practice of painting. I could as easily have drawn upon the history of, say, Japanese painting. The criteria for the identity of practices are in important respects transcultural. Initially, of course, it is within each practice, as it is situated within some particular culture and as it is developed from the resources afforded by that particular culture, that criteria are developed for what is to be accounted an example of the practice or an extension of it, rather than a corruption or a violation. It was in the light afforded by such criteria that painters in renaissance Flanders and painters in renaissance Italy accorded each other mutual recognition, learned from each other's innovations, and discovered in each other's achievements new standards to be surpassed. It was no different, even if more complex, when a good deal later Japanese painters discovered Western painting, and some time after that Western painters discovered Japanese art, each according to the other the same kind of recognition. It is from *within* the practice of painting in each case that shared standards are discovered which enable transcultural judgments of sameness and difference to be made, both about works of art and about the standards governing artistic practice and aesthetic evaluation. Identity of standards rooted in large similarities of practice provides on occasion common ground for those otherwise at home in very different cultures and societies. They thereby acquire a certain real, if limited, independence of their own social and cultural order. This does not mean that how a practice develops within a particular social and cultural order is not characteristically affected by other features of that order. Nonetheless insofar as a practice flourishes it always acquires a certain autonomy and has its own specific history upon which it draws in developing an institutionalized tradition into which its practitioners are initiated. What those practitioners have to learn are the standards of judgment specific to that particular form of enquiry, including the standards to which appeal is made in reformulating those standards. It is through this learning that abilities to discover, and to justify claims in respect of, new truths and to correct our understanding of what has been hitherto accepted as true are acquired. The acquisition of such abilities and of criteria which enable us to distinguish those who possess them and those who do not is a precondition for according the status of objectivity to the judgments of a practice and the possession of such abilities in painting is characteristically expressed in part in powers of color discrimination.

Wittgenstein asked "Mightn't shiny black and matt black have different colour-names?" (*Remarks on Colour* III, 152). Van Gogh wrote to his brother: "Frans Hals has no less than twenty-seven blacks." Only someone who needed to learn from Hals how to see what Hals saw, by discrimination and attention of the same order, and how to represent as Hals represented, either so as herself or himself to paint or so as to look at paintings with the painter's eye, would so need to distinguish. And if there were a sufficient number of such people engaged in communicating their visual observations, so as to educate themselves further, then they would need an enlarged color vocabulary, with perhaps twenty-seven names for different blacks.

What type of color vocabulary painters need and the range of uses to which they put that vocabulary depends in part upon the tasks specific to different periods of painting. Wittgenstein doubted "that Goethe's remarks about the character of the colours could be of any use to a painter" (*Remarks on Colour*, III, 90). But Turner not only towards the end of his life developed the theoretical conceptions of color, which he had both expounded in his Royal Academy Lectures and put to work in his own paintings, into a critique of Goethe's account, but also produced a visual critique of Goethe's theory in his paintings exhibited in 1843 *Shade and Darkness: the Evening of the Deluge* and *Light and Colour (Goethe's Theory): The Morning after the Deluge Moses writing the Book of Genesis.* Turner had read Eastlake's translation of Goethe in 1840, but he had moved in circles in which Goethe's theory was familiar much earlier, and we can see in the paintings how thinking and talking about colors informed Turner's practice.

Turner's most basic quarrel with Goethe was with the latter's treatment of darkness as nothing but the absence of light (*Farbentheorie* 744). Goethe's thesis that colors are shadows evoked a comment on the margins of Turner's copy of Eastlake: "nothing about shadow or Shade as Shade and Shadow Pictorially or optically."[27] What matters for my present argument is neither the detail of Turner's productive disagreements with Goethe nor who was right, but only that, in developing his own reflections both on the merits and demerits of various paintings and on the natural world represented in his paintings, as an integral part of his own practice of painting, Turner had to develop an understanding of colors in relation to light and darkness, which required the identification of a range of colors and hues, which could not have been achieved without an extended color vocabulary. Not all the discriminations required that there be names for every distinct shade; Turner's range of yellows, for example, outran the then vocabulary of color. But the use of names played an essential part in Turner's reflections. As they did, too, with such later reflective painters as Signac and Mondrian.

There are cultures which are not, as they stand or stood, open to the possibilities disclosed by excellence of achievement in painting, whether that painting is European, Japanese, or whatever. And what debars the inhabitants of such cultures from openness to those possibilities is in part the standards of discrimination embodied in too meagre a vocabulary of colors. Of course the achievement of an enriched and sophisticated vocabulary of colors as part, although only part, of the resources needed for the color discrimination of great painting is always partly the result of the impact of a practice such as painting upon the language-in-use of a particular social and cultural order, rather than its cause. Nonetheless too impoverished a set of practices of discrimination, expressed in a severely limited vocabulary, are signs of a lack of possibility. So the inhabitants of a culture may have to come to recognize that from the standpoint of the goods and excellences achievable only in and through some particular type of practice their culture as it has existed hitherto has to be judged as inadequate relative to certain others. Or they may be unable to recognize this, because their culture cannot for some reason accommodate that particular type of practice. Or again acquaintance with the practice might lead them to deny, from their external point of view, that the goods of the practice can be genuine goods and to exclude the practice from their culture, as representational art has been deliberately and altogether excluded from some cultures.[28] Yet from the standpoint afforded by the practice such a culture will be impoverished. It is perhaps in the capacity to recognize the poverties and defects of one's own culture and to move, so far as is possible, towards remedying it, without in the process discarding that culture in its integrity, that the greatness of a social and cultural order is shown.

Relativism about social and cultural orders thus fails, insofar as the standards provided by practices, such as the practice of painting, can be brought to bear upon their evaluation. The languages-in-use of some social and cultural orders *are* more adequate than those of some others in this or that respect; the vocabularies of color of some social and cultural orders are more adequate than those of some others in respect of the tasks of color discrimination set by the practice of painting. It is not that the color judgments made by the inhabitants of such orders fail in respect of truth, but that the conceptual scheme informing those judgments is inadequate to the realities of color disclosed by the practice of painting and also perhaps to those disclosed by scientific and philosophical enquiries into the nature of color.

There is thus after all a possibility of dissenting from the established linguistic consensus regarding color in our own social and cultural order and the constraints which it imposes upon our judgments of color, not through the kind of idiosyncrasies of linguistic use involved in an individual's using her or his own color words in her or his own way, but through resort to the standards of adequacy and inadequacy provided by the institutionalized norms of some practice. We can of course become aware of the contingency of any particular color vocabulary and of the variety of ways in which it might have been other than it is merely by becoming aware of the range of diversity to be found in different social and cultural orders. But that awareness in itself provides no good reason for judging one vocabulary, or conceptual scheme partially expressed through a vocabulary, superior to another. It is from the standpoint and only from the standpoint afforded by and internal to practices, such as the practice of painting, that questions about the adequacy or inadequacy of such vocabularies and conceptual schemes can be intelligibly posed, let alone answered. And of course what those who participate in the relevant practice characteristically seek to produce, if they radically put in question the vocabulary and conceptual scheme of their own culture, is the achievement of some new consensus with its own new set of constraints upon linguistic use and upon judgment.

Notes

I wish to express my indebtedness to Wilson P. Mendonça and to Philip L. Quinn for criticisms of an earlier draft of this essay.

1. See my "The Intelligibility of Action" and Amélie O. Rorty's "How to Interpret Actions" in *Rationality, Relativism, and the Human Sciences*, edited by J. Margolis, M. Krausz, and R. M. Burian (Dordrecht, 1986).

2. Colin McGinn, *Wittgenstein on Meaning* (Oxford, 1984), 81.

3. Ibid., 78.

4. Ibid., 79.

5. Ibid., 133.

6. Ibid., 196–97.

7. Norman Malcolm, *Wittgenstein: Nothing Is Hidden* (Oxford, 1986), 176–78.

8. Ibid., 178.

9. McGinn, *Wittgenstein on Meaning*, 194–97.

10. Malcolm, *Nothing Is Hidden*, 176–78.

11. McGinn, *Wittgenstein on Meaning*, 197.

12. David Pears, *The False Prison*, vol. 2 (Oxford, 1988), 368–69.

13. McGinn, *Wittgenstein on Meaning*, 80.

14. Malcolm, *Nothing Is Hidden*, 382.

15. Jonathan Westphal, *Colour* (Oxford, 1987), 80–81.

16. For how far this is so see not only Westphal, *Colour*, but also C. L. Hardin, *Color for Philosophers* (Indianapolis, 1988), esp. 155–86.

17. Brent Berlin and Paul Kay, *Basic Color Terms* (Berkeley, 1969), 46–47.

18. Paul Kay and Willett Kempton, "What is the Sapir-Whorf Hypothesis?" *American Anthropologist* 86 (1984): 65–79.

19. Pierre Bourdieu, *Outline of a Theory of Practice*, translated by R. Nice (Cambridge, 1977), 226.

20. Ibid.

21. My argument follows closely that of George Lakoff in *Women, Fire, and Dangerous Things* (Chicago, 1987).

22. See for a summary of the relevant empirical findings Lakoff, *Women, Fire, and Dangerous Things*, 26–30; for the most important items in the literature summarized see Paul Kay and Chad McDaniel, "The Linguistic Significance of the Meaning of Color Terms," *Language* 54, no. 3 (1978): 610–46, and Robert MacLaury, "Color Categories in Mesoamerica: A Cross-Linguistic Study," Ph.D. dissertation, University of California at Berkeley.

23. Lakoff, *Women, Fire, and Dangerous Things*, 334–37.

24. Ibid., 336.

25. *After Virtue*, 2d. ed. (Notre Dame, Ind., 1984), 187–91.

26. Brent and Kay, *Basic Color Terms*, 16.

27. John Gage, *Color in Turner* (London, 1969), 178; for a cogent contemporary development of Goethe's thesis which resolves the puzzles about particular colors posed by Wittgenstein in the *Remarks of Colour*, see Westphal, *Colour*.

28. I owe this example to Philip Quinn.

Primitive Reactions—Logic or Anthropology?

LARS HERTZBERG

Some writers commenting on Wittgenstein's philosophy take a carefree attitude towards the *Nachlaß*. They seem to assume that Wittgenstein's work, at least from the mid-1930s onwards, constitutes a finished whole, and that accordingly any remark by his hand merits equal attention for the light it throws on his philosophy; as if his genius were a natural phenomenon which could not fail to express itself with equal power in all its manifestations. This attitude, however, makes one neglectful of Wittgenstein's own intentions, of the fact that he was actively striving to develop his thought in certain directions, as is made evident by the continual revising and reordering to which he subjected his remarks.

Maybe this attitude is strengthened by an experience many readers of Wittgenstein will have had: in reflecting on some theme which is accorded a brief and, as it may seem, rather open-ended treatment in *Philosophical Investigations*,[1] one may discover that it is discussed much more fully and directly elsewhere (for instance in *Zettel* or in one of the volumes on the philosophy of psychology). Hence it is natural to use the latter texts as a guide to the interpretation of *Investigations*. Now I do not wish to suggest that doing so is in itself a mistake (after all, if Wittgenstein had not wanted those other remarks to be taken into account, he would have probably destroyed them). What I would like to suggest is that appeals made to these other texts should be tempered by reflection on the question: what reason may Wittgenstein have had for not including this or that remark in the collection that he himself, as far as we can make out, came closest to wishing to have us regard as canonical?

Reasons of various sorts may be imagined. Of course, a great many remarks must have been left out simply for the sake of economy: Wittgenstein often tried out various ways of making or illustrating closely related points, and including them all would have made for needless repetition. Then again, he

24

may have left out a remark because he no longer agreed with it or because he thought it misleading in some way. Or his reason for leaving it out may have been stylistic, etc. At other times, however, he may have discarded a remark precisely for the reason which makes it so attractive to commentators searching his texts for slogans: because it was too bold and programmatic, guiding the reader's eyes rather than encouraging him to look for himself.[2] In view of all this, trying to decide what reasons may have been effective in the case of some particular remark not included in *Investigations* should be a healthy exercise for anyone wishing to let the non-*Investigations* writings carry a great deal of weight in his work of interpretation.

I

Wittgenstein wrote in a notebook in 1937:

> The origin and the primitive form of the language-game is a reaction; only from this can the more complicated forms grow.
>   Language—I want to say—is a refinement; 'in the beginning was the deed.' (*CV* p. 31).

This remark, which has received some attention among commentators, has no direct counterpart in *Investigations*. Why is that? Economy does not seem a likely explanation here: the remark makes its point economically enough. A more likely explanation, perhaps, is that Wittgenstein came to find the remark too sweeping. It is a characteristic of his method in philosophy to express points as far as possible by means of examples. Maybe it struck him, when looking for examples of language 'growing from' primitive reactions, that there was no single type of example that could illustrate his point, but rather a variety of cases pointing in different directions. And so he may have thought that there was a deceptive simplicity in the point he had tried to make.

Of course, these conjectures must remain speculative. In this essay, I wish to discuss some of the problems connected with understanding the idea of language as a refinement of primitive reactions. I should make it clear that for me the main interest in discussing what Wittgenstein may have meant is not exegetical but comes from the light it may throw on the philosophical issues themselves. My remarks in this essay will be tentative, a preliminary to a more thorough treatment of the topic.

There are, on the face of it, various ways of looking at the part played by notions of the primitive in Wittgenstein's later writings.[3] In some contexts, it seems, the notion has what might be called a logical sense: here, it seems to indicate the place occupied by a type of reaction or utterance in relation to a language-game. In other contexts, it rather seems to carry a sense that might be called anthropological: to be connected with understanding the place of a reaction in the life of a human being.

What I have called the 'logical' sense could also be described as negative: to think of a reaction, an attitude, etc. as primitive in this sense is to rule out certain types of question concerning it. The point here is to see that something is a foundation, a beginning, and not to seek for any more basic justification or explanation for it. The 'anthropological' sense, on the other hand, seems to be a more positive one. This is so, for instance, when the notion of the primitive is used in connection with the notion of the natural: here the suggestion that a reaction is primitive seems to be a way of saying something about why it occurs by suggesting that it is rooted in human nature.

On either reading, the remark from *Culture and Value* I quoted seems to be connected with certain problems. If the logical reading is assumed, the remark becomes curiously vacuous: it then seems to be saying, roughly, that language starts with its beginnings. But if the remark is to be given a non-vacuous reading, if it is to be taken to say something substantive about the origins of language to the exclusion of certain other possible conceptions, it comes to seem a form of *a priori* theorizing, of the sort Wittgenstein himself was anxious to rule out of court.[4]

A third possibility, however, is that the form of the remark is misleading. Maybe Wittgenstein is not to be understood as putting forward a philosophical principle, but rather as exhorting philosophers to adopt a certain perspective on language and its relation to life. I shall try to pursue this possibility, attempting to give an outline of what I take that attitude to be, and what Wittgenstein's reasons for advocating it may have been. By way of doing this, I shall try to show ways of bridging the apparent gap between the logical and the anthropological understanding of the notion of the primitive.

II

The following remark expresses a well-known theme in Wittgenstein's later philosophy:

> Our mistake is to look for an explanation where we ought to look at what happens as a 'proto-phenomenon'. That is, where we ought to have said: *this language-game is played* (*PI* § 654).

Wittgenstein is persistently arguing against a deep-rooted tendency in our philosophical thinking: the inclination to suppose that the activities we engage in, the forms of language we use, the judgments we make, must have a rational foundation, that they must be rooted in the beliefs we hold, ultimately in the human capacity for thought. This supposition seems to be the common element in a great many different claims that philosophers have tended to advance or to take for granted:

(i)   It would be irrational for us to devote time and energy to some activity unless there were a well-grounded expectation of some useful later result.

(ii) It would be puzzling if we should find other human beings devoting time and effort to activities for which there is no reasonable justification, and we have not properly understood what they are doing until we have succeeded in identifying some external purpose.

(iii) To adopt traditional attitudes or traditional ways of acting for no good independent reason is to submit to the dictates of the arbitrary, and hence a sign of intellectual weakness.

(iv) If we adopt linguistic forms of expression to which nothing in reality corresponds, our use of language will actually lack meaning. (A case of this would be applying the same word to entities or phenomena which are not really the same.)

(v) For someone to accept any judgment without demanding sufficient evidence for it would be a mark of credulity and would expose him to the risk of error.

The idea seems to be that, in all these cases, the place that should be occupied by a reason is left empty, and to go on speaking or acting as before once we have realized this would be imprudent, shameful, or unintelligible. Wittgenstein's point is that this view of things expresses a philosophical illusion, based on a misunderstanding of what it means to have a reason for something. Whether some consideration will or will not count as a reason for the members of a community is ultimately an expression of the kind of life that community lives, of the common standards of argument and criticism adopted in it. To think of reasons in this way is to reject as unintelligible the notion that reality might have the power of determining the forms that human thought and activity in relation to it will take, independently of the ways in which people actually live.

This denial does not entail a commitment to relativism: though we realize that some consideration we find important may not count as a reason with people who live differently from us, it remains open to us to say that it *ought* to count as a reason, and that they are blind to something if they do not see this. What it does mean is that this may entail nothing concerning our chances of actually bringing them around to our view of things. In other words, we must accept the possibility that this may be a sense of 'blindness' which cannot be revealed independently of their failure to see reason as we do. There is no reality that is 'independent' in such a way that it might guarantee convergence.

III

Philosophers may have been kept from realizing the fact that argument and reasoning are dependent on the practices actually adopted in a particular community by their tendency to focus their attention on certain ways of speaking or acting, the rationality of which might be thought to go without saying. On the one hand, certain forms of expression may appear to be self-evidently meaningful, since the reality to which they refer seems unavoidably to confront us in our experience. And on the other hand, certain forms of striving may seem self-evidently reasonable, since they are ultimately concerned with types of experience to which, it seems, no one can fail to give importance.

We can see an expression of these inclinations in the ways philosophers have traditionally discussed the nature of the mind.[5] The issue of the meaningfulness of applying words like 'pain' or 'wish' or 'love', etc. to human beings has been understood as involving an option between the dualist view, according to which the meaningfulness of these terms is provided by the fact that each one of us is acquainted in his own case with the experiences to which they refer, and the materialist view, according to which their meaningfulness is dependent on their usefulness in formulating a theory that will ultimately enable us to explain and predict the movements and physical reactions of other human beings, that is, phenomena with which, it is thought, we are all immediately confronted in perception.

Such inclinations also tend to determine the kinds of answer that are sought to the question of what justifies our dealing differently with people than, say, with physical objects, our attaching particular importance to the feelings and reactions of human beings, as compared with all the other kinds of entities that we encounter. Why, for instance, should we be concerned about the pain felt by other people? (It belongs to the spirit in which this discussion is carried out that it is assumed to be possible, and maybe even necessary, to settle the issue of the meaningfulness of words like 'pain' before we raise the question whether anything justifies the special treatment we reserve for human beings.) Here again, two options seem to be available. On the one hand, it might be thought that our caring for the pain of another is based on our knowing from our own experience how pain feels, and that this knowledge combined with recognizing the other's behavior as a sign of pain presents us with a reason to act.[6] On the other hand, it might be thought that our concern for the pain of others is ultimately grounded in the expectation that benevolent behavior towards others will be reciprocated, or some other belief along similar lines. More generally, on this view the special consideration given to human beings as compared with other kinds of entity is held to be justified by the uncommon powers they have for harming or benefitting us.

Now there are several reasons for rejecting the notion that there might be ways of speaking or acting that are self-evidently rational in the sense presupposed by these views, reasons that I do not have the space to enter into here. Even apart from this, however, a moment's reflection on the actual variety of human relations should suffice to make it evident that all these different views are gross simplifications. The sway they have nevertheless held over the philosophy of mind testifies to the fact that they are grounded in powerful philosophical prejudice. I would argue that they are good examples of the form of thinking that Wittgenstein was trying to counter by drawing attention to primitive reactions.

In a typescript, Wittgenstein wrote (*RPP* I, §§ 915, 917):

it is a help to remember that it is a primitive reaction to take care of, to treat, the place that hurts when someone else is in pain, and not merely when one is so oneself—hence it is a primitive reaction to attend to the pain-behavior of another. . . .

It can be called 'putting the cart before the horse' to give an explanation like the following: we took care of the other man, because going by analogy with our own case, we believed that he too had the experience of pain.—Instead of saying: Learn from this particular chapter of our behavior—from this language-game—what are the functions of 'analogy' and of 'believing' in it.[7]

Here Wittgenstein is urging us to look at our reaction towards another's pain as *independent*, both of our own experience of pain and of other ways of taking note of human behavior. If taking care of the part that hurts when someone else is in pain is a primitive reaction, that means that it is not based on an analogy nor on a calculation (say, on the expectation that he may treat me analogously in the future).

More generally, seeing a way of speaking or acting as primitive means taking note of a feature of the life we live with language. It is a matter of the sort of attention we turn upon it. When a way of speaking or acting is seen as grounded in beliefs or in thinking, this means that it is not regarded as an independent feature of our life, in the way the words we use in speaking about people and the ways in which we relate to them were taken simply to be extensions of our awareness of our physical environment and our interest in the possibilities of using it for the fulfillment of our needs. On the other hand, when some of the ways in which human beings respond to the expression of pain, of thirst or hunger, of joy, grief or anger, of a wish, etc. are regarded as primitive, this suggests a possibility of regarding the *languages* of pain, of thirst, joy, anger, etc., as well as the ways of acting with which they are connected, as existing in their own right, as not only being independent of the ways in which we speak about and act in relation to physical objects and processes, but also as being independent of one another. In other words, it suggests an escape from the notion that there must be a single principle (whether dualist or materialist) by which the meaning of all 'mental' or 'psychological' terms is to be accounted for.

At the same time, seeing a use of language as grounded in primitive reactions involves a rejection of the notion that questions about the meaningfulness of a form of language can be separated from an understanding of the activities connected with it.

Recognizing the rich variety of primitive reactions in human life involves a liberation from the *a priori* forms that we are inclined to impose on our accounts of language and action. The gains from such a liberation are considerable. It enables us to avoid the philosophical problems we encounter in trying to pressure the phenomena into forms where they do not fit,[8] it enables us to escape the impoverished view of human existence that ensues when the rich variety of human relations are forced into a single mold, and it makes us aware of the contingency of the forms taken by human life, of the many ways in which those forms could have been, could be, different from what they are for us.

Though I am here focusing on the ways we speak about people, many of the same points could be made by considering the role of primitive reactions in our learning what a physical object is, or in learning to speak about the properties of objects, about light and darkness, sounds, directions, heat and cold, living beings, the human body, works of art, etc.

IV

Before I proceed to discuss what I called the anthropological sense of the notion of the primitive, I wish to comment on the relation between the 'logically' primitive and the concept of learning. The two passages from *Remarks on the Philosophy of Psychology* quoted above interfoliate the following remark (§ 916):

> What, however, is the word 'primitive' meant to say here? Presumably, that the mode of behavior is *pre-linguistic*: that a language-game is based *on it*: that it is the prototype of a mode of thought and not the result of thought.

The word 'prelinguistic' might easily be misunderstood. The question whether or not some reaction precedes the learning of language is evidently an empirical one, and there seems to be no reason why Wittgenstein should commit himself one way or the other concerning it in this connection. It is evident, however, from what Wittgenstein says in other connections that the suggestion that a reaction is primitive is not meant to exclude the possibility that it may in some sense presuppose learning. Thus, there are primitive, independent reactions of the sort that we are interested in *to* the learning of language, not just before it.[9] In fact, among the most important examples of what I take to be primitive reactions discussed in Part II of *Investigations* are precisely reactions that are only possible *in* a language: seeing aspects, using words in a secondary sense.

Concerning the experience of seeing something as the apex in a triangle, Wittgenstein says, "The substratum of this experience is the mastery of a technique" (p. 208). The point, however, is that the experience is not *part* of the technique we learn. The technique in question presumably consists in doing things like drawing triangles on request, using drawings of triangles for various purposes, etc. The experience of seeing something as the apex is independent of this technique in the sense that having this experience is not a condition for being said to master the technique. Yet someone who has mastered it may spontaneously come to see triangles in this way. And the experience could not be attributed to anyone who had not acquired these (or some other set of) proceedings in which the apex of a triangle plays a part, for in that case we should not know what he meant by the word 'apex'. The experience logically presupposes the routine, but is not logically presupposed by it. Because of this it is a primitive reaction.[10]

V

There is a well-known remark by Wittgenstein on the role of primitive behavior in our learning to use words to speak about sensations (*PI* § 244). His suggestion, what he calls "one possibility," is that "words are connected with the primitive, the natural, expressions of the sensation and used in their place." He goes on to give an example: "A child has hurt himself and he cries; and then adults talk to him and teach him exclamations and, later, sentences. They teach the child new pain-behavior... the verbal expression of pain replaces crying. ..."

Evidently, Wittgenstein uses the words 'primitive' and 'natural' more or less synonymously in this context. The word 'primitive' seems to be used in what I have called an anthropological sense, indicating the place of a reaction in the life of a human being. Primitive, in the sense of natural, expressions are obviously important in our dealings with small children. The normal child will at a very early stage be able to express itself in ways that adults find intelligible, without this being preceded by any kind of conscious effort on the part of those adults. This is not only true of expressions of pain. Adults will respond to some of the child's sounds and gestures as signs of distress, to others as signs of contentment, joy, fright, etc., their response normally consisting in their taking some appropriate action or reacting in some other appropriate way (soothing the child, looking for the cause of discomfort, smiling back, etc.).

What does it mean to call these forms of expression 'primitive' or 'natural'? The answer that may seem at first to recommend itself here is that these terms express a hypothesis: for an expression to be natural, it might be thought, must be a fact about its causal history. On such an understanding, calling an expression primitive or natural would be taken to involve something like this: the behavior was produced by the circumstances through a 'natural' process, not through a process established through learning or some other type of conscious interference. Thus, it may have been due to hereditary mechanisms (perhaps to mechanisms common to all individuals of a similar kind) or to mechanisms developing of their own accord in normal circumstances in any individual of this kind.

This way of regarding the matter would be problematic, however, as should be clear from the following considerations. The relevant hypothesis would have to be one to the effect that what produced the behavior through a 'natural' process was *the pain, the joy, or the fright itself.* Only so could it be understood as a sign of pain or whatever. If the hypothesis were one to the effect that the behavior was 'naturally' produced not by the pain or fright but by some event that might be assumed to be a *cause* of pain or fright, etc.

(such as hurting oneself, hearing a sudden loud noise), this would not link the behavior to pain, since it would not distinguish cases in which the event actually caused pain from cases in which it did not.

If something being a natural expression of pain is a hypothetical condition and hence subject to testing, however, this raises the question: *what* is it to be tested *against*? What could show that something was an expression of pain apart from its being correlated with other forms of behavior that are independently understood to be expressions of pain? If we are to avoid the infinite regress threatening here, we must, it seems, allow that there are cases in which people will respond to human behavior as expressing pain without recourse to empirical evidence.[11] These cases will be the starting point both in teaching the other new ways of expressing pain and in learning to recognize other ways in which pain may manifest itself.

Now I would argue that these responses are to be regarded as primitive in the sense outlined in section I. For a response to be primitive and hence nonhypothetical does not entail that it may not be tentative and subject to revision in the light of later experience, say, after one gets to know someone better. It is simply a response that is not dependent on our knowing (on our remembering and managing to apply) a principle that we could formulate linking behavior of such and such a description to the word 'pain'.

This does not rule out the possibility that such a response may be shaped through a person's experience, say, with being in pain, or with variations in the ways different people express themselves, with the way some particular person expresses himself, etc. What we have to realize, however, is that the lessons taught by experience may take different logical forms. They do not necessarily consist in our learning to apply some proposition to various cases of a certain description; experience may simply shape the ways in which we perceive things. Hence a person's response may be shaped by experience in this sense and still be what I have called logically primitive. This merely means that the person's confidence in his present response ('That man's in bad pain') does not reduce to confidence in any formula he could name ('Whenever they do _____ they're in bad pain'); in other words, his use of the word 'pain' in the case at hand is not merely the extension of some linguistic routine in which the notion of pain plays no part.[12]

The notion of a primitive expression, then, involves a peculiar kind of mutuality or interdependence: regarding something as a primitive expression of pain (in the primary case) is itself a primitive reaction to the expression. In fact, the interdependence goes further: for someone to see another person's reaction as a reaction to the pain expressed by a third party—or by the observer himself—is in turn, in the primary case, a primitive response to that response, or rather, to the situation consisting of the sufferer's expression of pain, on the one hand, and the reaction of the person witnessing that expression on the other hand.

Thus, I may react with pity in seeing a child witnessing another person's pain. Where the pain is my own, on the other hand, someone's compassionate look may give me a sense of relief. And so on. It should be clear that in many cases seeing a form of behavior as a response to another's pain is not to be understood as embodying a hypothesis to the effect that the discovery that someone else is in pain tends to be accompanied by behavior of such and such a description. In applying a hypothesis we are relying on a correlation between phenomena, each one of which can be identified independently of the others. But the elements involved in a situation where someone is responding to another's pain will often not be identifiable independently of that situation. Thus, what enables me to see someone's behavior as a response to pain may only be the fact that I recognize the expression of pain. Or *vice versa*: someone else's response may make me realize that a person is indeed in pain. Or again, it may only be the appropriateness of someone's response to another's behavior that brings it out that it is indeed the other's pain that he is responding to. In such cases, then, it is not as if I brought the pieces together and concluded that the situation is one revolving around someone's pain. Rather, I see the situation under the aspect of pain, and this way of seeing it, as it were, brings the pieces together in this particular way.[13]

These considerations could be taken to show a way in which the gap between what I have called the negative and the positive notion of the primitive may after all be bridged. Giving the case of pain a more general application, it could be suggested that to regard a common way of reacting to the behavior of other people as primitive cannot simply be a matter of regarding it as independent of other ways of speaking or acting. Rather, we must be able to see it as intelligibly connected with the behavior to which it is a reaction; failing this, we would be in no position to tell *what* someone was reacting to, which means that we would not be in a position to see his behavior as a *reaction*. So the notion of the primitive that is relevant here cannot simply be a negative one. And on the other hand, as we have argued, my seeing someone's behavior as an intelligible reaction to the behavior of a third party will in many cases itself be a primitive reaction on my part (in the sense of not involving the application of any empirical hypothesis). To the extent that this is so, then, the harmony between judgments that must obtain if communication is to be possible is one that is ultimately dependent on harmony between human reactions; and this must be a primitive harmony, since to suppose it to be shaped or mediated by a common language would involve a logical circle.

Accordingly, when Wittgenstein speaks about a use of language as having grown from primitive reactions, we would have misunderstood the kind of point he is making if we were to think of this as a case of *a priori* theorizing. He is simply drawing attention to the logical significance of certain facts about human behavior.

VI

The nature of the interdependence between primitive expressions of pain and primitive responses to pain can perhaps be brought out more clearly by considering a distinction between two ways in which a person may express pain: between what might be called intentional and non-intentional expressions. Even when an expression of pain is shaped by learning (as when the child learns to replace the natural expression of pain with verbal expressions) it may still constitute a primitive reaction, in the sense that it is not intentional.

By this, I mean the following. Normally, to think of someone's words or behavior as an expression of pain is to think that the reason he behaves as he does is the pain he is in: he groans, or winces, or touches his leg *because* of the kind of pain he feels, or because he feels it where he does. Now once more this 'because' does not (in the normal case) express a hypothesis or counterfactual conditional of some sort, rather it is itself the expression of a primitive reaction: it expresses the concern we feel about the other's pain. If I express doubt whether his pain is as strong as it seems to be judging by his behavior, by saying "It can't be that bad," I am not making a comparative judgment ("This is how bad it actually is, this much is extra"); my words simply express a different reaction to his behavior (I may be urging him to control himself, or telling someone else not to worry too much).[14]

To the extent to which I regard the other's expression as intentional, however, this means that my reaction to it is not a reaction to someone in pain. In that case, I would not say that he behaves as he does *because of* the pain he is in. Rather, what links this behavior to pain is some intention of his: I may believe, for instance, that he is trying to get someone to notice his pain, or to be deceived into thinking he is in pain, etc. (His pain might be the reason he has that intention, but this is different from the case in which his pain is itself the reason for his behaving as he does.[15]) The possibility of expressing pain intentionally is logically dependent on the existence of non-intentional expressions of pain, hence on primitive reactions to pain. In expressing pain intentionally, one is making use of the existence of those reactions, as in mimicking non-intentional expressions.

This means that the distinction between non-intentional and intentional expressions of pain is bound up with a difference in the grammar of the word 'expression'. When an expression of pain is considered intentional, certain questions arise which do not arise with respect to primitive, non-intentional expressions. For an expression to be intentional means that it involves criteria of success, the criteria in the particular case depending on the nature of the intention. Thus, if I try to simulate pain, I succeed if the person for whom the simulation is intended is actually deceived by it. An actor's portrayal of pain is successful if it is aesthetically convincing. In other cases the level of ambition is more modest: if I am trying to convey that my wife is in pain to a doctor in a country where I do not speak the language, I must succeed in getting him to understand that it is an expression of *pain* that I am giving a performance of, without getting him to think that *I* am the one who is in pain.

Non-intentional expressions do not differ from intentional ones in involving different criteria of success. Rather, it would be out of place to speak about criteria of success in their connection in the first place. With non-intentional expressions of pain, there is not some level of performance to which one must attain in order to qualify as being in pain. People are not told to "scream just a little louder," or "try to make their groans more convincing" to test whether they are really in pain. Though we do pick up non-intentional spontaneous expressions from other people, this does not mean that we are instructed in their use (by being given rules to follow, for instance). The idea of instruction and criticism is ruled out by an understanding of expressions as non-intentional. In a school for actors, on the other hand, there might be training, maybe even rules for the successful portrayal of pain.

The point could also be put as follows: if I make intentional use of an expression of pain and do not succeed in getting others to understand what I mean, this is a failure on my part. But insofar as my expression of pain is regarded as non-intentional, it would be senseless to criticize *me* if others do not notice my pain: if anything, that would be a shortcoming on their part, a failure of attention or sensitivity, say.

VII

On a reading of Wittgenstein which was formerly widely accepted but which seems gradually to be falling into disrepute, the notion of a *criterion* has a crucial part to play in connection with understanding Wittgenstein's views about language in general and about the use of words like 'pain' in particular.[16] By way of summing up our discussion, let us consider the role of this notion. My inclination is to say that it is high time the central status accorded to it in Wittgenstein's thinking be abandoned. The danger is that by speaking about a wide range of linguistic expressions as involving the use of criteria, we will blur over some important distinctions. The reason for this is connected with understanding the role of primitive reactions in Wittgenstein's thinking.

The notion of a criterion seems best at home where there is a question of qualifying for some characterization, coming up to a standard, or the like. Thus, when we are trying to decide whether a person knows or remembers something, or is able to discern something or to figure something out, etc., it is often quite natural to discuss this as a matter of criteria. Here, we might say, to call X a criterion of Y is to say, roughly, that the question of whether something is Y is, or can for the purpose at hand be treated as, the question of whether it is X. ('The question of whether he knows where the railway station is is a question of whether he can drive there from here.') If we do not agree on the relevant criterion in such a context, this suggests that we are talking at cross purposes.

But this kind of treatment seems completely out of place, say, where it is a question of whether someone is in pain, of what he really wants, of whether his love is genuine or not, etc. To understand worries like these is to realize that there is no specific question that they 'boil down to' in any given context. Or rather: to suggest that they boil down to some other question is to express a diminished view of human feelings and wishes. (This is connected with its not

making sense to speak of 'success' in connection with expressions of pain.)
Consider someone who says, "For me, the criterion of whether her love for me
is genuine is her willingness to take care of my laundry." What is important for
him, we would say, is the test of love, not the love itself. Contrast this with the
case of a person for whom the question of the genuineness of someone's love
is important in itself, where there is no other question that could give a more
precise expression to his concern. Analogous considerations can be advanced
in the case of pain. (Suppose a hospital adopted the rule: "The criterion of
whether a patient is in pain is whether he keeps the other patients awake by
his complaints.")

I am not denying that some of the cases in which we discuss knowledge or
memory may have this character too. Thus, a man may consider remembering
his first date with his wife important for its own sake, rather than because he
needs to recall the occasion for some purpose. But cases of the other sort are
more common, and I believe it could be suggested that it is through them that
we first learn the use of words like 'remember.' Now it seems plausible to
think that it is because of differences like these that doubts about 'other minds'
seem to take a stronger hold in connection with feelings, sensation, and the
like than, for instance, in connection with knowledge or memory. The fact that
there is nothing we can point to that would necessarily settle those doubts in
each particular case makes it easier to sustain the notion that they cannot, in
principle, be conclusively settled. But when it is thought that the problem of
other minds can be overcome by invoking the need for criteria in applying
words like 'pain', differences like these get overlooked.

Part of the reason criteria were thought to be important for Wittgenstein's
account of the language of pain was the assumption that there have to be criteria
if a word is to have application. I would suggest, however, that several different
thoughts are being run together here. I take it to be true that, according to
Wittgenstein, for a word to have application there must be room for a discussion
of whether or not two speakers of the language agree in their use of the word. In
other words, a speaker must be able to give grounds for saying that someone
else's way of using it differs from his own. This, in brief, is Wittgenstein's
point concerning the senselessness of a private language. But we should be
clear about what this does not entail. For one thing, even if one can give
grounds they may not be conclusive: some people may be convinced by them
while others are not, so the issue of what constitutes agreement may be to some
extent indeterminate. And secondly, whether or not the grounds are conclusive,
they may not be of a kind that it would be helpful to call criteria. Hence a
word may well have application even if there are no criteria, or no criteria that
all speakers would agree on.

The giving of grounds may, for instance, simply consist in pointing to a
particular example, or in drawing attention to something about that example. In
the case of color words, this is obvious: if I say, "If you call this, red, you don't
mean what I mean by 'red'." I am not appealing to any criterion. But similarly
I may not have any criterion in mind if I say, "If you call that a happy face, you

don't mean what I mean by 'happy'." I may, it is true, draw your attention to something about the face, say, the expression around the eyes. Even so, there are several reasons for refusing to think about that as a criterion. For one thing, even if that is what brings the unhappiness of this particular face home to me and what I think will bring it home to you, a similar feature in a different face might not have the same significance for us. (It might not even be clear what 'a similar feature' would be in a different face. I may be unable to identify it in any way except as the feature which gives this face its unhappy expression.) But quite apart from this, no such feature could be what I *mean* by an unhappy face (or if it were, the expression 'an unhappy face' would just be a description of a certain appearance; it would then have no internal connection with *feeling* unhappy).[17]

The important point is this: in thinking about the use of words like 'pain', 'unhappiness', or 'love' as dependent on criteria we in fact regard the use of those words as merely an extension of some other part of our language. By drawing attention to the possibility that their use might be grounded in primitive reactions we may try to counteract that way of thinking.[18]

Notes

1. I shall be referring to Wittgenstein's texts by using the customary initials: *PI* for *Philosophical Investigations*, *CV* for *Culture and Value*, and *RPP* for *Remarks on the Philosophy of Psychology*.

2. Thus, allowing myself an early quote from the *Nachlaß*, in 1930 Wittgenstein wrote, in discussing the problems involved in writing a foreword: "It is a great temptation to try to make the spirit explicit" (*CV* p. 8).

3. In speaking about the role of the notion of the primitive in Wittgenstein's writings, what I have in mind are certain patterns of thought, not his use of the *word* 'primitive'. In, fact, in the majority of cases in which the word occurs in *Philosophical Investigations*, Wittgenstein seems to be using it in a sense which is different from those that I shall be concerned with here. That sense is a comparative one, involving reference to a form of language or a language-game that is simpler than another and precedes or underlies it (cp. §§ 2, 5, 7, 25, 554). (Consider also the discussion in *Last Writings on the Philosophy of Psychology*, §§ 285–304.) The cases in which I shall be interested, on the other hand, are cases in which there is taken to be a difference in kind (in role or position) between the primitive and the non-primitive.

4. For what seems to me an unequivocally anthropological remark, consider e.g. *Zettel* § 545 (cp. *Remarks on the Philosophy of Psychology* I, § 151):

—Being sure that someone else is in pain, doubting whether he is, and so on, are so many natural, instinctive, kinds of behaviour towards other human beings; and our language is but an auxiliary to, and further extension of, this relation. Our language-game is an extension of the more primitive behaviour. (For our *language-game* is behaviour.) (Instinct.)

5. For a discussion of these issues which I find very congenial, see David Cockburn's essay "Empiricism and the Theory of Meaning," *Philosophical Investigations* 8 (1985), and his book *Other Human Beings* (Houndmills, 1990), especially chapters 4 and 7.

6. Such seems to be the view expressed, for instance, in the following passage:

My knowledge of what somebody wants (let us say, that I should help him out of the fire) sets off in me, granted a humane disposition, a desire to help him out of the fire.

So there are four relevant truths about me in this situation. First, I know how it is for him and that he wants to be helped. Second, I know that if I were in that situation I should want to be helped. Third, I have a preference now, my own person, for being helped in such situations. Fourth, being of a humane disposition, I want to help him. (Bernard Williams, *Ethics and the Limits of Philosophy* [London, 1985], 91).

So if any of these conditions were not fulfilled, I should evidently see no reason for helping the man out of the fire.

7. *Zettel* §§ 540 and 542 correspond closely to the remarks quoted here.

8. An example of this is the need philosophers have felt for trying to account for our ability to use certain words by assuming that we must be guided by some specific inner feeling or experience: e.g., feelings of familiarity or pastness in accounting for memory claims, experiences of volition, etc. (For Wittgenstein, an important case in point seems to have been William James. Cf. his *Principles of Psychology* [New York, 1950], chaps. 16 and 26. But a great many empiricist thinkers, before and after James, could be cited here.) This seems to be the sort of account Wittgenstein has in mind when he writes, in connection with drawing our attention to the way language is used when we confess the motive of an action: "Something new (spontaneous, 'specific') is always a language-game" (*PI* p. 224). Here Wittgenstein is evidently warning us against the idea that we, as it were, 'read off' our motive from some 'specific' experience which constitutes our memory of the motive. The scare quotes around the word 'specific' I understand as an allusion to our inclination to think that if the experience in question is to fulfill the role attributed to it we must be capable of recognizing it on the basis of its quality, and yet if we are asked to say just *how* it feels we would probably be at a loss. (Wittgenstein's discussion of the notion of a feeling of familiarity, *The Brown Book*, pp. 180 ff., is pertinent in this connection. I wish to thank Oswald Hanfling for reminding me of this.)

In *Remarks on the Philosophy of Psychology* (Vol. 1), the same remark occurs in the context of a discussion of what it is to remember a toothache and of the idea that this would have to involve a 'specific' copy of the toothache. The point here, it seems, is to realize that it is a primitive feature of our language that we will say, in a certain range of circumstances, that we remember a toothache: there is nothing further in which this remembering consists. (Cp. also ibid., § 630.)

9. Cp. *PI* p. 218: "The primitive reaction may have been a glance or a gesture, but it may also have been a word."

10. Norman Malcolm has emphasized the role of primitive reactions in the learning of language. Thus, he writes:

Something resembling the primitive reactions that underlie the first learning of words, pervades all human action and all use of language. This is manifested in the way in which people who have received instruction in some procedure (drawing a design, continuing a series of numbers, using a word ...) will, when told to carry on from there, spontaneously go on in the *same* way. It would seem that from the initial instruction those people could branch out in an indefinitely large number of different directions. It is true that they *could*. But they don't! Nearly every one of them will go on in a way that the others will agree is the *same* way. (Norman Malcolm, *Nothing is Hidden* [Oxford, 1986], 152)

Malcolm is obviously making an important point here, though the way in which he puts it might be thought partly misleading, at least where the use of words is concerned. What will count as using a word in the 'same way' is not a matter that can be established independently of the sense of the word. Thus, we might think that a child had not mastered the expression of a wish unless he used it in situations that were quite different from those in which he had first been taught to use it, that is, unless he, as it were, had made this use of words his own. So what is required for someone to be said to have mastered the use of a word might be his using it in what would seem, from a certain point of view, not to be the same way at all. Perhaps Malcolm's point should rather be put in terms of our going on to *make sense* to one another in our use of words.

11. It might be thought that another way of cutting off the regress would be by appeal to analogies with the first person case. However, the problems of this approach are notorious. On this see, for instance, John Cook, "Human Beings" in *Studies in the Philosophy of Wittgenstein*, edited by Peter Winch (London, 1969) or Norman Malcolm, *Problems of Mind* (New York, 1971), 16 ff.

12. On this, cp. *Philosophical Investigations*, pp. 227 f.

13. For a perceptive discussion of related points, see Peter Winch, *"Eine Einstellung zur Seele"* in his *Trying to Make Sense* (Oxford, 1987), esp. p. 143.

14. Cp. the remark by Wittgenstein quoted in note 3, above.

15. The intentional-unintentional distinction, I would suggest, applies to expressions of pain only in special circumstances. And the same is true for other forms of spontaneous expression, such as smiles, laughter, weeping, etc. To call someone's smile or his weeping intentional is to deny that the smile or the weeping is genuine. But this does not mean that in the normal case such expressions are 'unintentional'. We would not call a smile or an expression of pain, say, unintentional unless we thought that someone had a reason for not letting on how he felt.

16. For discussions critical of what were previously commonly accepted readings of Wittgenstein's remarks about criteria, see Cook, "Human Beings," 129–40; Oswald Hanfling, "Criteria, Conventions and Other Minds," in *Ludwig Wittgenstein: Critical Assessments*, edited by Stuart Shanker (London, 1986), 226–38; Malcolm, "Wittgenstein on the Nature of Mind," 138–40.

17. Maybe those who defend the necessity of criteria are not thinking about the sorts of grounds speakers of a language might give. Rather, what they have in mind might be the kind of explanation that an observer would give of what makes agreement among speakers possible. However, it would seem to me to be alien to Wittgenstein's thinking about language to suppose that such explanations can be given once and for all. The question of what makes a use of language possible, if it has any sense at all, would seem to be an empirical question, not one that could be resolved in philosophy.

18. I wish to thank Oswald Hanfling for a number of helpful last minute comments on my essay.

Meaning and Intentionality in Wittgenstein's Later Philosophy

JOHN MCDOWELL

1.

Suppose someone correctly understands the meaning of, say, 'Add 2.' Her understanding must be something with which, if she is aiming to put that understanding into practice and has reached '996, 998, 1000' in writing out the resulting series, only writing '1002' next will *accord*. It seems essential to be able to make this kind of use of notions like that of accord if we are to be entitled to think in terms of meaning and understanding at all. In sections of the *Philosophical Investigations*[1] that have come to be regarded as central, and elsewhere in his later work, Wittgenstein is clearly concerned with difficulties that we can fall into in trying to maintain our hold on this kind of use of notions like that of accord. (See §§198, 201.)

These passages have become increasingly familiar, largely under the impetus of Saul Kripke's celebrated reading of them.[2] Many of the ingredients for a proper reading are now well understood, but I believe that the thrust of Wittgenstein's reflections is often misconceived. The result is that in spite of the recent surge of attention, this part of his legacy is still not widely available to contemporary philosophy. In this essay, I shall offer a brief and dogmatic overview, in the hope that, in the absence of qualification and nuance, the overall lines of a way to place Wittgenstein's later thinking can stand out more clearly.

2.

There is a quite general link between the idea of understanding or grasp of a meaning, on the one hand, and the idea of behavior classifiable as correct or incorrect in the light of the meaning grasped, that is, classifiable as in accord with the meaning grasped or not, on the other. Wittgenstein concentrates on the case of extending a series of numbers in the light of one's understanding of the principle of the series. In that case, given where one has got to in the series, there is nothing but the relevant understanding for one's behavior to accord with or not as the case may be. (The understanding may be of instructions for continuing the series or, in the absence of explicit instructions, simply of the principle of the series.) Contrast the ordinary use of an expression whose meaning suits it for describing the empirical world. Here, if one's utterance is to be correct, it needs to be faithful not only to the meaning of the expression but also to the layout of the empirical world. The series-extension case isolates the way in which grasped meanings in particular give a normatively characterizable shape to the space of options within which behavior is undertaken; so it brings that point into especially clear focus. But the point applies to understanding quite generally.

3.

Suppose we ask: what could someone's grasp of, say, the meaning of the instruction 'Add 2' consist in, given that it would need to bear this normative relation to her behavior?

In order to get the difficulties going, we need to feel the attractions of a certain conception of the region of reality in which we would most naturally look for someone's grasp of a meaning—intuitively, that person's mind. The conception is one according to which such regions of reality are populated exclusively with items that, considered in themselves, do not sort things outside the mind, including specifically bits of behavior, into those that are correct or incorrect in the light of those items. According to this conception, the contents of minds are items that, considered in themselves, just 'stand there like a sign-post', as Wittgenstein puts it (§85). Considered in itself, a sign-post is just a board or something similar, perhaps bearing an inscription, on a post. Something so described does not, as such, sort behavior into correct and incorrect—behavior that counts as following the sign-post and behavior that does not. What does sort behavior into what counts as following the sign-post and what does not is not an inscribed board affixed to a post, considered in itself, but such an object *under a certain interpretation*—such an object interpreted as a sign-post pointing the way to a certain destination.

If we conceive the contents of the mind on the model of sign-posts, considered in themselves, we seem to need a parallel move. It does not matter what item we might at first have been inclined to pick out, from the inventory that we are restricting ourselves to, as a plausible candidate for being what someone's grasp of the meaning of 'Add 2' consists in. Whatever it is, considered in itself it cannot be what we hoped it would be, since it just 'stands there like a sign-post'. What we need is not that item, whatever it was, considered in itself, but that item under the right interpretation.

But now we are in trouble. On our present way of thinking, someone's understanding the instruction, or the principle of the series, would need to involve her putting the right interpretation on something; only so can we get the concept of accord into play, as we need to in order to get the concept of understanding into play. (It does not matter what we suppose she puts the interpretation on: perhaps just the instruction itself as she heard it.) But there is just as much reason for asking what her putting the right interpretation on something could consist in as there was for asking in the first place what her understanding 'Add 2' could consist in. And it is just as plausible that we would need to look for the answer to this second question in a region of reality populated by items that, considered in themselves, just 'stand there' as it was in the case of the original question.

The idea of interpretation seemed hopeful because it promised to enable us to attribute, to items that are in themselves normatively inert, a derivative power to impose a normative classification on items in the world outside the mind—thus bringing into play the application for the concept of accord that seems to be required if the concepts of meaning and understanding are to get a grip. Although no behavior counts as following (acting in accord with) an inscribed board affixed to a post, considered merely as such, nevertheless when such an object is interpreted as a sign-post pointing the way to a certain destination, it is determined that going in a certain direction counts as following the signpost—acting in accord with its instructions for reaching that destination. The hope was that we could exploit this normativity-introducing effect of the idea of interpretation quite generally.

But the hope is bound to be disappointed. As long as the restricted inventory of items we can appeal to, in answering our questions as to what this or that consists in, is in force, the problem that the idea of interpretation was supposed to meet merely duplicates itself. It does not matter what item, from the restricted inventory, we pick as a plausible candidate to be what someone's putting the right interpretation on, say, the heard instruction 'Add 2' (or on anything else) might consist in. Whatever it is, it cannot be what we hoped it would be, since considered in itself it in turn just 'stands there like a sign-post'. We might be tempted to require putting the right interpretation on the item that was supposed to be an interpretation, but that is clearly to embark on a regress, which looks as if it must be hopeless. The item that is supposed to be the right interpretation of the first putative interpretation will shrink in its turn, under the requirement of fitting into the restricted inventory of available items, into something that just 'stands there'. So the very idea of a person's understanding, as something that determines a distinction between behavior that is in accord with the understanding and behavior that is not, comes under threat.

4.

Kripke gives a gripping exposition of this threatened regress of interpretations, and it is beyond question that the regress is one of the ingredients for a proper understanding of Wittgenstein's point.

But Kripke's reading goes beyond identifying the threat and giving it vivid expression. On Kripke's account, Wittgenstein rescues the idea of understanding by abandoning the idea that someone's grasping a meaning is a *fact* about her. According to Kripke's Wittgenstein, as soon as we look for a fact about a person that is what her grasping a meaning consists in, we are doomed to have any appearance that what we pick might be the right sort of fact—specifically that it might have the right sort of normative links with her behavior—crumble before our eyes under the impact of the regress of interpretations. So we should conclude that there can be no such fact. This claim, that there can be no fact in which someone's understanding something consists, is a 'skeptical paradox'. Kripke's suggestion, on Wittgenstein's behalf, is that a 'skeptical solution' can free this 'skeptical paradox' of such devastating implications as that nobody understands anything. The 'skeptical solution' sharply distinguishes something we can have, a story about social practices of mutual recognition and so forth, which can underwrite a conception of correctness in attributions of understanding, from something that the 'skeptical paradox' says we cannot have, a story about facts in which the truth of such attributions would consist.

After the first burst of discussion of Kripke, many readers would agree that this apparatus of 'skeptical paradox' and 'skeptical solution' is not a good fit for Wittgenstein's texts. In §201, Wittgenstein says:

> This was our paradox: no course of action could be determined by a rule, because every course of action can be made out to accord with the rule. The answer was: if everything can be made out to accord with the rule, then it can also be made out to conflict with it. And so there would be neither accord nor conflict here.
>
> It can be seen that there is a misunderstanding here from the mere fact that in the course of our argument we give one interpretation after another; as if each one contented us at least for a moment, until we thought of yet another standing behind it. What this shews is that there is a way of grasping a rule that is *not* an *interpretation*.

This looks like a proposal, not for a 'skeptical solution' to a 'skeptical paradox' locked into place by an irrefutable argument, as in Kripke's reading, but for a 'straight solution': that is, one that works by finding fault with the reasoning that leads to the paradox. The paradox that Wittgenstein mentions at the beginning of this passage is not something we have to accept and find a way to live with, but something we can expose as based on 'a misunderstanding'.

The villain of the piece, Wittgenstein here suggests, is the idea that the notion of accord could be available in the way that we need only by courtesy of an application for the notion of interpretation. And there is no hint that when we try to escape the temptation to think we can get accord into the picture only by appealing to interpretation, we are supposed to be helped by ridding ourselves of the inclination to think of grasp of a rule or a meaning as a *fact* about the person who grasps it. If we can manage to follow Wittgenstein's direction to think of a grasp of a rule (*eine Auffassung einer Regel*) that is not an interpretation, that will ensure that we do not even start on the regress of interpretations. And it will do so in a way that leaves us perfectly at liberty, at least as far as these considerations are concerned, to think of the grasp of a rule that is in question as a fact about the person who enjoys it, if it pleases or helps us to do so.[3]

5.

Kripke's reading of how the regress of interpretations threatens the very idea of understanding turns on this thesis: "no matter what is in my mind at a given time, I am free in the future to interpret it in different ways."[4] This presupposes that whatever is in a person's mind at any time, it needs interpretation if it is to sort items outside the mind into those that are in accord with it and those that are not. There are always other possible interpretations, and a different interpretation, imposing a different sorting, may be adopted at a different time. Considered in themselves, that is, in abstraction from any interpretations, things in the mind just 'stand there'.

This presupposition gives expression to the restricted conception of what a person can strictly speaking have in mind that I mentioned when I introduced the regress of interpretations (§3 above). The presupposition determines that it is only under an interpretation of something in someone's mind that the question can so much as arise whether an extra-mental item accords with that thing. Then the regress of interpretations makes it impossible to privilege an interpretation under which the 'right' extra-mental items count as according with the mental thing we started with, whatever it was. Given the connection between accord and understanding, it follows that whatever is in someone's mind at any time, its being in her mind cannot be what constitutes her understanding something in a determinate way.

Now if the shift from a 'skeptical solution' to a 'straight solution' (§4 above) leaves this presupposition about the nature of possible contents of minds in place, it makes for what looks like only an insignificant divergence from Kripke.

Kripke in effect assumes that the only way someone's understanding something could even seem to be a fact about her would be if one thought her understanding was a matter of her having something in mind. He finds in Wittgenstein an argument, based on the presupposition, to show that a person's having something in mind cannot constitute her understanding something, on pain of the regress of interpretations. And he concludes on Wittgenstein's behalf that a person's understanding something cannot be a fact about her. According to Kripke's Wittgenstein, we must stop conceiving attributions of understanding as candidates for truth in a sense that brings into play facts or states of affairs in which their truth would consist. Instead we must locate a conception of what it is for such attributions to be correct, not involving their being in line with the facts, within an account of a social practice of mutual recognition and acceptance.

If we move to a 'straight solution', we shall no longer suppose it helps to deny that someone's understanding something is a fact about her. But if we leave Kripke's presupposition about the nature of things in the mind unchallenged, we shall still be precluded from supposing that the facts that the 'straight solution' allows us to countenance are constituted by the person's having something in her mind. And then, when we ask what they *are* constituted by, it will be overwhelmingly natural to appeal to the very same sorts of social practices that figure in Kripke's 'skeptical solution', not now as a substitute for saying what fact about the person constitutes her understanding, but as affording an account of what that fact is. On this sort of view, Kripke's error was just to suppose that the only sort of facts about a person that could even be candidates for constituting her understanding something would be facts that consist in her having something in mind. Someone's occupying a suitable social status can be a fact about her. On this reading, her understanding something can be constituted by that sort of fact, without trouble from the regress of interpretations. According to this reading, the way to follow Wittgenstein's instruction to think of "a way of grasping a rule which is *not* an *interpretation*" is to reconceive what sort of fact or state of affairs someone's grasping a rule is. Instead of conceiving it as a state of affairs involving her having something in mind, we should conceive it as a state of affairs involving her occupying a position in a community.

But now it seems a merely notational issue whether we count a story about social recognition and the like, with Kripke, as a 'skeptical solution', replacing any picture of a fact or state of affairs in which someone's understanding consists, or as a 'straight solution', saying in a regress-proof way what the relevant facts or states of affairs come to. The important thing is surely what is common between these positions, namely the idea that to avoid the regress, we must deny that a person's understanding could be her having something in mind.

6.

We get a more radical divergence from Kripke, however, if we suppose that the thrust of Wittgenstein's reflections is to cast doubt on the master thesis: the thesis that whatever a person has in her mind, it is only by virtue of being interpreted in one of various possible ways that it can impose a sorting of extra-mental items into those that accord with it and those that do not.

It is really an extraordinary idea that the contents of minds are things that, considered in themselves, just 'stand there'. We can bring out how extraordinary it is by noting that there is a need for an application for the concept of accord, and with it a threat of trouble from the regress of interpretations if the master thesis is accepted, not just in connection with gasp of meaning but in connection with intentionality in general. An intention, just as such, is something with which only acting in a specific way would accord. An expectation, just as such, is something with which only certain future states of affairs would accord. Quite generally, a thought, just as such, is something with which only certain states of affairs would accord.[5]

Suppose I am struck by the thought that people are talking about me in the next room. The hypothesis implies that only a state of affairs in which *people are talking about me in the next room* would be in accord with my thought. Now the master thesis implies that whatever I have in my mind on this occasion, it cannot be something to whose very identity that normative link to the objective world is essential. It is at most something that *can* be interpreted in a way that introduces that normative link, although it can also be interpreted differently. ('I am free in the future to interpret it in different ways.') Considered in itself it has no relations of accord or conflict to matters outside my mind, but just 'stands there'. The regress of interpretations will then preclude conceiving the thought, considered as something to whose identity it is essential that it is to the effect *that people are talking about me in the next room*, as something I have in my mind at all. What I have in my mind is at most a potential vehicle for the significance in question, in the sort of way in which a sentence, considered as a phonetic or inscriptional item, is a vehicle for a significance that it can be interpreted as bearing.

We can extrapolate from the case of meaning and understanding to philosophical strategies that purport to make this conclusion harmless to the very idea that I might be struck by a specific thought. According to a 'skeptical solution', it was a mistake to think there needed to be a fact to the effect that this is what I think, which would have to be a matter of my having something in mind; instead we should explain the correctness of attributing that thought to me in terms of my occupying a certain position in a social framework. According to a 'straight solution' on the lines of that described in §5 above, a fact to the effect that this is what I think would not have to be a matter of my having something in mind; such a fact can be identified with my occupying a certain position in a social framework. If we supposed that the master thesis was compulsory, that would make us need such contrivances, and the philosophical ingenuity that philosophers have put into elaborating them is certainly impressive.

But when we evaluate the master thesis, it is important not to be side-tracked by a premature admiration for such philosophical ingenuity. The master thesis is not just a piece of common sense which we can sensibly leave unquestioned while we look in Wittgenstein for philosophical contrivances aimed at freeing it of paradoxical implications; or perhaps while we complain, with Crispin Wright, of a 'quietism' that leads Wittgenstein to shirk elaborating such contrivances, although he supposedly reveals problems that require them.[6] The master thesis implies that what a person has in mind, strictly speaking, is never, say, *that people are talking about her in the next room* but at most something that *can* be interpreted as having that content, although it need not. Once we realize that, the master thesis should stand revealed as quite counterintuitive, not something on which a supposed need for constructive philosophy could be convincingly based.

It is surely uncharacteristic of Wittgenstein to leave such a thesis, which is obviously philosophically motivated, unchallenged and work towards or, with a quietism that would evidently be unwarranted in this context, shirk working towards ways of answering the philosophical questions that must look urgent if the thesis is accepted: questions like 'How is meaning possible?' or more generally 'How is intentionality possible?' A more Wittgensteinian lesson to learn from his manipulation of the regress of interpretations is that we need a diagnosis of why we are inclined to fall into the peculiar assumption, crystallized in the master thesis, that makes such questions look pressing. Given a satisfying diagnosis, the inclination should evaporate, and the questions should simply fall away. There is no need to concoct substantial philosophical answers to them. The right response to 'How is meaning possible?' or 'How is intentionality possible?' is to uncover the way of thinking that makes it seem difficult to accommodate meaning and intentionality in our picture of how things are and to lay bare how uncompulsory it is to think in that way.

7.

Wittgenstein's reflections on meaning and understanding bring into prominence an image of meaning as a collection of super-hard rails with which our minds engage when we come to understand anything. It is obvious that this sort of imagery figures in Wittgenstein's texts as a target. We need to see how the tendency to resort to such imagery connects with the threatened regress of interpretations.

The germ of the imagery is clearly expressed in a passage in *The Blue Book*:[7]

> What one wants to say is: "Every sign is capable of interpretation; but the *meaning* mustn't be capable of interpretation. It is the last interpretation."

The effect of the regress of interpretations is that we lose our entitlement to the idea that a grasped meaning imposes demands on a person's behavior. We allow ourselves to think that meaning's demands on behavior must be mediated by an interpretation; nothing else could bring accord and conflict into the picture if we start with something that just 'stands there'. But then we realize that whatever we have hit on as what is to be the mediating interpretation, it is itself something that can be interpreted otherwise so as to make the right bits of behavior count as correct. Now we can no longer appeal to a mediating interpretation to make it intelligible how the space of behavioral possibilities acquires a normative shape. To postulate another mediating interpretation, imposing the right interpretation on the first mediating interpretation, is clearly to embark on a regress. The hardness—the demandingness—of the demands ("the hardness of the logical must", §437) seems to disappear.

Now the right move in response to this is to realize that we ought not to suppose we have to start with something that just 'stands there'. We ought not to suppose that the normative surroundings of the concept of understanding can be in place only by virtue of a role for the concept of interpretation. Contrast the way of thinking expressed in the *Blue Book* passage: this attempts to keep the hardness of the demands, in the face of the softening effect of the regress of interpretations, while leaving unquestioned the idea that the normative surroundings of the concept of understanding can be in place only by virtue of a role for the concept of interpretation. The right move is not even to start on the regress of interpretations, whereas the idea expressed in the *Blue Book* passage is that we can start on the regress but bring it to a harmless stop by conceiving meaning as 'the last interpretation'.

It should be obvious on reflection that we cannot disarm the regress of interpretations like this. There is nothing in the idea that meaning can stop the regress, once we have let it begin, except a recipe for an imagistic pseudo-conception of meaning in terms of super-rigid machinery. It must be self-deceptive to suppose that this is a way to regain an authentic understanding of meaning's normative reach into the objective world.

One thing that is labeled by the word 'platonism', in a contemporary philosophical usage whose relation to Plato we need not consider, is this imagery of super-rigid machinery. As I said, it is obvious that platonism in this sense comes under attack from Wittgenstein.

But the label 'platonism' is also used for various ideas that are simply part of the idea of meaning's normative reach: for instance the idea that the meaning of, say, an instruction for extending a numerical series determines what is correct at any point in the series in advance of anyone's working out the series to that point, so that the meaning yields a standard of correctness for what any calculator or group of calculators does or might do. Putting the idea picturesquely, we can say that the meaning reaches forward in the series ahead of anyone who actually works the series out, and is so to speak already there waiting for such a person, ready to stand in judgment over her performance, at any point in the series that she reaches. The standards of correctness embodied in a grasped meaning are, as Crispin Wright puts it, ratification-independent.

No doubt this kind of picture *may* be an expression of the self-deceptive thinking that seeks to stop the regress of interpretations by conceiving meaning as 'the last interpretation'. But the idea of ratification-independence is in itself just part of the idea of meaning's normative reach, the idea expressed by the relevant use of the notion of accord. The idea of ratification-independence need not come into play in the context of the self-deceptive attempt to let the regress of interpretations begin but come to a harmless stop. In itself the idea of ratification-independence has no connection with the regress of interpretations, over and above the fact that it is part of the general way of thinking that the regress threatens to make unavailable. If the threat posed by the regress is properly disarmed by discarding the master thesis, as opposed to the ineffectual response of conceiving meaning as 'the last interpretation', then ratification-independence, detached from that ineffectual response, can fall into place as simply part of a way of thinking that we are now able to take in our stride. There seemed to be problems about the normative reach of meaning, but since they depended on a thesis that we have no reason to accept, they stand revealed as illusory.

The question 'How is it possible for meaning to reach ahead of any actual performance?' is just a specific form of the question 'How is it possible for the concept of accord to be in place in the way that the idea of meaning requires it to be?' The Wittgensteinian response is not that these are good questions, calling for constructive philosophy to answer them. The Wittgensteinian response is to draw attention to a defect in the way of thinking that makes it look as if there are problems here.

We misread Wittgenstein if we let the elasticity of the term 'platonism' induce us to lump the very idea of ratification-independence (and the like) in with the imagery whose sole point is a self-deceptive attempt to let the regress of interpretations begin but ensure that it does no harm. The effect of lumping these things together is that, on the basis of Wittgenstein's patent hostility to that imagery, we are led to suppose that he finds the idea of ratification-independence (and the like) problematic in itself, regardless of any connection with the regress of interpretations. But we cannot cite Wittgenstein's authority for supposing that the very idea of ratification-independence (and the like) is problematic.

8.

It is often supposed that the concept of *custom* and its cognates figure in Wittgenstein as elements in a constructive philosophical response to questions like 'How is meaning possible?': a response that, according to some readings, Wittgenstein actually gives, and that, according to other readings, he points towards but does not deliver, out of a quietism that must stand exposed as inappropriate by the sheer fact that the questions are supposed to be good ones. I am committed to regarding this as a misreading.[8]

The role of the concept of custom in Wittgenstein's thinking is crystallized in this central text (§198):[9]

"Then can whatever I do be brought into accord with the rule?"— Let me ask this: what has the expression of a rule—say a sign-post—got to do with my actions? What sort of connexion is there here?—Well, perhaps this one: I have been trained to react to this sign in a particular way, and now I do so react to it.

"But that is only to give a causal connexion: to tell how it has come about that we go by the sign-post; not what this going-by-the-sign really consists in."—On the contrary; I have further indicated that a person goes by a sign-post only in so far as there exists a regular use of sign-posts, a custom.

This passage starts by formulating the threat that the regress of interpretations poses to the applicability of the notion of accord. We should avoid the threat by not letting the regress start: by not letting it seem that the concept of interpretation must be in play if the concept of accord is to be secured its application. The passage suggests that we can avoid that appearance by insisting on a bit of common sense about following a sign-post. When one follows an ordinary sign-post, one is not acting on an *interpretation*. That gives an overly cerebral cast to such routine behavior. Ordinary cases of following a sign-post involve simply acting in the way that comes naturally to one in such circumstances, in consequence of some training that one underwent in one's upbringing. (Compare §506: "The absent-minded man who at the order 'Right turn!' turns left, and then, clutching his forehead, says 'Oh! right turn' and does a right turn.—What has struck him? An interpretation?") But if we give this corrective to an over-mentalizing of the behavior, perpetrated by giving the concept of interpretation an unwarranted role in our conception of it, we run the risk that we shall be taken to overbalance in the opposite direction, into under-mentalizing the behavior—adopting a picture in which notions like that of accord cannot be in play, because the behavior is understood as nothing but the outcome of a causal mechanism set up by the training. Such a picture might fit an acquired automatism, in which there is no question of acting on an understanding of the sign-post's instructions at all. This risk, that if we exploit the concept of training to exorcize the idea of interpretation, we shall lose our entitlement to the idea of understanding as well, is averted by adding another bit of common sense, that the training is initiation into a custom.

If the concept of custom figured here as the beginning of a constructive philosophical account of how the meaning of sign-posts, and our understanding of their meaning, are constituted, the custom mentioned would need to be characterizable in terms that do not presuppose meaning and understanding. But the concept of custom can do the work it does here without being capable of being put to that sort of philosophical service. The concept of custom can do the work it does here even if the only answer to the question 'What custom?' is 'The custom of erecting and following sign-posts', or perhaps more specifically 'The custom of erecting and following sign-posts of just this style and configuration'; that is, an answer that, with the talk of following, simply presupposes the supposedly problematic notion of accord. What made the notion of accord seem problematic was the regress of interpretations, and the first move in the passage, the appeal to training, has ensured that we need not begin on the regress of interpretations. The point of the appeal to custom is just to make sure that that first move is not misunderstood in such a way as to eliminate accord, and with it understanding, altogether.

Readers of Wittgenstein often suppose that when he mentions customs, forms of life, and the like, he is making programmatic gestures towards a certain style of positive philosophy: one that purports to make room for talk of meaning and understanding, in the face of supposedly genuine obstacles, by locating such talk in a context of human interactions conceived as describable otherwise than in terms of meaning or understanding. But there is no reason to credit Wittgenstein with any sympathy for this style of philosophy. When he says "What has to be accepted, the given, is—so one could say—forms of life"

(p. 226), his point is not to adumbrate a philosophical response, on such lines, to supposedly good questions about the possibility of meaning and understanding, or intentionality generally, but to remind us of something we can take in the proper way only after we are equipped to see that such questions are based on a mistake. His point is to remind us that the natural phenomenon that is normal human life is itself already shaped by meaning and understanding. As he says: "Commanding, questioning, recounting, chatting, are as much part of our natural history as walking, eating, drinking, playing" (§25).

If one reads Wittgenstein as offering a constructive philosophical account of how meaning and understanding are possible, appealing to human interactions conceived as describable in terms that do not presuppose meaning and understanding, one flies in the face of his explicit view that philosophy embodies no doctrine, no substantive claims. This view of philosophy is what Wright describes as quietism. Wright takes Wittgenstein to have uncovered some good philosophical problems about meaning and understanding. Reasonably enough in view of that, Wright cannot see how a quietistic hostility to constructive philosophy can be warranted: if Wittgenstein reveals tasks for philosophy, he cannot appeal to what now looks like an adventitiously negative view of philosophy's scope to justify not engaging with those tasks. Other interpreters actually credit Wittgenstein with a substantive 'social pragmatist' philosophy of meaning. Wright is less optimistic about what can be found in the texts, which he takes to hold back from substantive philosophy, in line with Wittgenstein's quietistic conception of the nature of philosophy. In Wright's view the texts contain at most a program for the supposedly needed philosophy of meaning. This is to read Wittgenstein in a way that takes note of his disavowal of constructive ambitions, but to make that disavowal a point of criticism, based on the uncovering of philosophical problems that is supposed to be a Wittgensteinian achievement.

Contrast the style of reading I have outlined here. There is indeed room to complain that Wittgenstein reveals a need for something but does not give it, or does not give enough of it. But what we might ask for more of is not a constructive account of how human interactions make meaning and understanding possible, but rather a diagnostic deconstruction of the peculiar way of thinking that makes such a thing seem necessary. It would be good to say something about how the diagnosis should go in detail, but this essay is not the place for that.

Notes

1. *Philosophical Investigations*, translated by G. E. M. Anscombe (Oxford, 1953). Subsequent references not otherwise signaled will be to this work.

2. Saul A. Kripke, *Wittgenstein on-Rules and Private Language* (Oxford, 1982).

3. In any case, a separation of the question whether something is a fact from the question whether some assertoric utterance would be correct seems foreign to the later Wittgenstein; see e.g. §136 on truth. The objection against Kripke that §201 seems to point to a 'straight solution' was made independently and more or less simultaneously by a number of writers, including me in "Wittgenstein on Following a Rule," *Synthese* 58 (1984): 325–63.

4. Kripke, *Wittgenstein on Rules and Private Language*, 107.

5. In passages like §437, Wittgenstein discusses the way intentional concepts like that of wish and thought are affected by versions of the problems about making room for the notion of accord that make for difficulties in our thinking about 'grasping a rule'.

6. This complaint is expressed in several recent writings of Wright's: see, e.g., his "Critical Notice of Colin McGinn, *Wittgenstein on Meaning*," in *Mind* 98 (1989): 289–305, especially at pp. 304–305.

7. *The Blue and Brown Books* (Oxford, 1958), 34.

8. My "Wittgenstein on Following a Rule" is too hospitable to this kind of reading, I now think.

9. I have changed the punctuation in the second paragraph, in a way that brings out what I take to be the dialectical flow of the passage.

MIDWEST STUDIES IN PHILOSOPHY, XVII (1992)

The Dispositionalist Solution to Wittgenstein's Problem about Understanding a Rule: Answering Kripke's Objections

CARL GINET

Wittgenstein's problem about understanding a rule relates to a central preoccupation of his throughout his philosophical life, the question of how it is possible for there to be such a thing as linguistic meaning. How are we able, with our various sorts of signs, to represent or refer to facts or things in the world, and even to nonexistent possibilities? I think Wittgenstein always felt a deep mystery here and in his later work this feeling took the shape of a puzzle that questions the very possibility of meaning. Kripke characterizes this puzzle as "a new form of philosophical skepticism . . . the most radical and original that philosophy has seen to date. . . ."[1]

What is the puzzle? Let us take it that understanding the meaning of a descriptive term or predicate can be thought of as grasping a rule for a certain function whose domain contains all the cases about which it can be asked whether the predicate applies to them and which assigns to each such case one of two values: *applies* or *does not apply*. If one knows what the predicate, 'x is red' means, then one knows a rule for such a function; one knows what determines for any particular member of the domain of visible objects whether or not it satisfies the predicate. To understand the predicate '$x + y = z$' is to grasp a function that assigns a value to every one of the infinitely many different pairs of integers.

For each of us there are enormously many such functions for which we think that we have come to know a general rule that determines the value of the function for every argument to it; and we think we grasp such a thing even though we have not yet explicitly considered all the arguments to the function, even when it would be impossible in principle for us to consider them all. When we do explicitly consider an argument that we have not hitherto considered, we confidently judge that the rule we have all along had in mind dictates such-and-such a value for that argument.

53

Now comes the problem: there are many incompatible rules that agree on all the cases we have hitherto explicitly considered but disagree on this new case. What exactly was it in our mind that determined that the rule we understood was a particular one of these incompatible rules rather than another? To take Kripke's favorite example (7–9): suppose that I have never previously added any numbers larger than 56. When I compute 57 + 68 and confidently get the answer 125, I suppose that this result conforms to the function I have all along meant by the plus sign. But what in my mind could have determined that it was the ordinary plus function that I meant rather than, say, the "quus" function—which is defined this way: x *quus* y equals x plus y if x and y are less than 57, and otherwise it equals 5—*if* I never before considered any numbers as large as 57?

Take a different sort of example. The first time I confront a red patch that is surrounded by an area that is turquoise in color, I confidently judge it to be red and I suppose that my doing so accords with the meaning of 'red' I have long understood. But what that was previously in my mind determined that the rule I intended to follow in applying 'red' was the ordinary one rather than the following one: if a surface area looks like this [pointing to a red surface] *and is not surrounded by turquoise* then call it 'red', but if it does not look like that *or it is surrounded by turquoise* then say 'not red'? The more we ponder such questions, the more it can seem that no sort of fact about me at the earlier time *could* have determined which rule I intended.

But aren't we perfectly familiar with the sort of fact in question? The understanding of a general rule for an "application" function is the sort of thing we often acquire "in a flash." When, watching "Sesame Street," I suddenly see which thing does not "belong," I instantaneously become confident that I could tell for any new thing whether or not it "belongs." I realize, of course, that the general rule I have suddenly grasped is not uniquely identified by the description "a rule that these cases I have so far considered conform to." But, I want to say, I do somehow *have in mind* something that determines the value of the function for all the cases I have not yet considered, for I do understand a general rule that does determine the whole function.

But, says our puzzler, consider. How could there be something in your mind (or anywhere) which, on the one hand, does *not* involve explicitly exhibiting a particular argument and its value, but, on the other hand, does fix it that that pair does belong to the function? How could something that is *not* there in your mind be thus fixed or determined by something that *is* there? Isn't that a remarkable feat? What sort of thing could pull this off? Any ordinary thing we can think of to suggest—a formula that states the rule, a picture of what all the same values have in common—is just an *expression* of the rule that also needs to be understood and thus seems merely to put off answering the hard question: understanding that expression of the rule involves with respect to the symbols involved in *it* the very same sort of grasping of general rules for *their* application that we are asking about.

Wittgenstein uses the term "cube" as an example (*Philosophical Investigations* 139–41). Suppose we try saying that to understand the general rule that determines whether a given visible object is a cube or not is to have in mind a *picture* that shows what anything that deserves the positive judgment must look like. This, too, is just to suggest another way of expressing the rule: "A thing is a cube when it looks like *this*, otherwise it isn't." Wittgenstein asks: what tells me how to apply this to a new case? There are alternative ways in which it is possible to apply it. And one need not have in mind here that the picture may include features (such as color) that are irrelevant to a thing's being a cube. Even if the irrelevant features are ignored, or one's mental picture is indeterminate with respect to them (if that is possible)—even if, *per impossible*, one could contemplate an object that is a cube and that has no irrelevant features, the perfect abstract template—one could, Wittgenstein points out, use a method of comparison different from what we normally think of as determining what counts as *looking like* a thing. (The beauty of Wittgenstein's move here is that it shows that even if Platonic Forms or Lockean abstract ideas were metaphysically possible, they would not do the job that seems to be required.)

There are further suggestions we could try, but it becomes clear that no explanation of how to decide whether a new case comes under the rule is going to be able to avoid this sort of reply from the puzzler. As Wittgenstein puts it (*Remarks on the Foundations of Mathematics* I, 113), "However many rules you give me—I give a rule which justifies *my* employment of your rules"—that is, which justifies an application in a particular case that is different from the one you would make. Concerning any categorical fact we seem able to suggest for the sort of fact that constitutes the grasping of a general rule, the puzzler points out that exactly the same kind of thing could have been in the mind of one who thinks she grasps a general rule but judges a new case differently from the way we would. Thus no such fact can be metaphysically sufficient for having in mind something that fixes the values for hitherto unconsidered cases in one way rather than another. There is no sort of fact that can constitute understanding a general rule as we need to think of it, as something that somehow "contains" the values for all the cases it does not explicitly exhibit. "This was our paradox: no course of action could be determined by a rule, because every course of action can be made out to accord with the rule" (*Philosophical Investigations* 201).

In explaining how this conclusion is reached, we have focused on examples of functions that we can identify only by general rules and not by enumeration. But this is not essential. The same problem can be generated for small finite functions that we can give by complete enumeration and that we must initially learn from a complete enumeration. The alphabetical ordering of the letters of our alphabet can be thought of as a function of 25 ordered pairs: <'a', 'b'>, <'b', 'c'>, etc. We know the alphabetical ordering when we know this function and we learn all the ordered pairs in it by enumeration. Typically, when I speak of the alphabetical order of the letters and mean this function, I do not have the whole thing exhibited in my mind. And yet on those occasions I mean that very function and not some other. How do I do it? How can anything short of exhibiting the whole alphabet to myself constitute my then meaning that order rather than some other?

The crux of the problem is that one does not have all of a number of things *explicitly* in mind at a time when one does, as one wants to say, have them all in mind *implicitly*—by having in mind a rule or just the thought, "Yes, I know what all that is." How can anything be in my mind *only implicitly*? How can anything short of actually having a particular thing present to my mind constitute having that particular thing "in mind," meaning it, rather than something else instead? Meaning seems typically to entail my being somehow in contact with things that I do not then have explicitly in mind. The problem is that, when we ask what sort of current fact about me could put me in contact with those absent things, no sort of fact seems capable of doing the job.

That is the problem. What is the right response? Kripke (66–67) divides the possible ways of trying to deal with the problem into two kinds: straight solutions and skeptical solutions. A straight solution tries to make intelligible some kind of fact or other that, it alleges, *is* capable of doing the job that needs to be done. A skeptical solution concedes that no kind of fact can meet the demand and says that we must therefore reinterpret all of our talk that seems to imply the mysterious containment of absent cases in such a way that it no longer has that implication. Kripke attributes to Wittgenstein a skeptical solution, but he also considers and criticizes several straight solutions, usually claiming to be expounding Wittgenstein's criticisms of them. The solution I find most appealing is the straight solution that Kripke spends the most space criticizing (22–37). He calls it *dispositionalism*.

The dispositionalist's idea is that the sort of fact that can do the job we want done is a *counterfactual conditional* fact. Roughly, the idea is that what I meant or intended at a particular time dictated a certain result for a case that was not then before my mind if it was true of me then that I *would* have reacted in an appropriate way to the case if I *had* then considered it: I had at the time a *disposition* to react appropriately in the relevant circumstance.[2] My meaning at a given time a certain function by a sign I used then was my having then a multiplicity of dispositions to assign the various values of the function to its various arguments, each disposition in the set determining one of the ordered pairs in the function. Any later claim I make that a particular ordered pair belongs to the function I then meant is correct or not according to whether or not the corresponding disposition is a member of that set of dispositions I then had. It is this counterfactual conditional sort of fact that provides an intelligible way of clarifying the sense in which my present state of meaning or intending can "contain" something, even a great many things, that are not presently before my mind.

At *Philosophical Investigations* 195, Wittgenstein puts in quotation marks what he is tempted to say—"But I don't mean that what I do now (in grasping a sense) determines the future use *causally* and as a matter of experience, but that in a *queer* way the use itself is in some sense present"—and responds:

"But of course it is, 'in *some* sense'! Really the only thing wrong with what you say is the expression 'in a queer way'." A bit earlier, at 187, Wittgenstein remarked:

> When you said "I already knew at the time ... " that meant something like: "If I had then been asked what number should be written after 1000, I should have replied '1002'."

Perhaps dispositions provide a *non*-queer way in which all the uses (applications) are present at one time.[3] The dispositionalist says that, if the reach to the absent cases strikes us as something very "queer" and "mysterious," that is because we are looking for what constitutes it in the wrong "dimension." We are thinking of it as a *categorical* fact rather than as one expressible only in the subjunctive, a counterfactual conditional fact.

Let me now be more specific about the content of these counterfactual conditionals. According to the dispositionalist, the fact that I meant a certain application by a certain term I used at a certain time is (for a basic class of cases: more on this qualification later) the fact that there was true of me a counterfactual conditional for each ordered pair in the application function that I meant, that is, for each truth of the form 'the application function I meant assigns this value to that argument'. As a first shot, it is natural to think of this conditional as having something like the following form:

> If I had been asked whether the rule (application function) I meant (understood) assigns this value (*applies* or *does not apply*) to that argument, I would have answered that it does.

But this is too crude. It makes the presence of the disposition depend on whether or not I would hear and understand the question asked, and whether or not I would be able or motivated to respond, and it should not depend on such things. For if it did, then it would not be plausible for the dispositionalist to claim (as I think the dispositionalist must claim: more on this point later) that I can later know that the disposition was there simply by remembering it, in the same direct way that I can know what a past intention of mine was. So let us refine the form of the counterfactual conditional to read as follows:

> If I had *considered the question* whether the rule I meant assigns this value to that argument *and given a relevant and sincere response to it*, my response would have been that it does.

The antecedent and consequent here do imply that I understand some meanings and hence some rules of application. But this is not objectionable, for the dispositionalist's purpose of giving a non-mysterious fact that contains decisions on the absent cases. What the puzzler wants contained and claims cannot be contained are *judgments* about the absent cases. To explain satisfactorily how these *can* be contained we do not need to reduce them to something of a non-intentional nature.

My object in the remainder of this essay is to defend the dispositionalist idea against Kripke's objections to it. I divide these into three.

1. The objection on which Kripke spends the most space (22–25, 37) is that the dispositionalist account leaves out the *normative* aspect of a rule. A collection of dispositions gives us a function only as a mere collection of ordered pairs. But the functions meant by the plus symbol and by descriptive words generally are not *arbitrary* collections, but are bound together by a rule. A set of dispositions determines the function *only extensionally*, whereas there is something more when there is a rule we grasp. There is a *reason* why the function includes just the pairs it does. Kripke suggests (23) that the mere truth of a counterfactual conditional about me cannot make the response it says I would give *"justified* in terms of instructions I gave myself, rather than a mere jack-in-the-box unjustified and arbitrary response."[4]

This normative aspect of a rule is certainly something that dispositionalism must get into the picture if it is to provide an adequate solution to the puzzle; and nothing I have said so far brings it in.[5] The challenge to the dispositionalist is this: You have given us a disposition, a counterfactual conditional, for *each* ordered pair in the function; but you have not given us anything that makes this *collection* of dispositions *nonarbitrary*, determined by a general rule, as must be the case for the application functions determined by the meaning of "plus" and by the meanings of most of our descriptive terms.[6]

It seems to me that the first thing the dispositionalist should say in order to provide the account needed here is this: a subject's meaning a function involves understanding it to be determined by a rule *if* (but not only if) the subject is disposed to recognize some non-trivial expression of the rule as correctly stating the rule determining the function the subject means. Such a disposition is surely always present, for instance, in the case of meaning addition by "+"; one who knows what addition is is disposed to recognize as correct some description of some procedure for finding the sum of any two numbers. There is, for instance, the sort of procedure we all learned in school when we got beyond single digit numbers, that of "roughly, writing one numeral under the other (preserving the order of digits and aligning on the right), adding zeros on the left of the shorter number to make both numbers the same length (when necessary) and then adding corresponding digits by referring to the table, carrying 1 and entering only the right digit when the table gives a two-digit answer."[7]

Of course, this raises the question of what the subject's understanding of the *expression* of the rule consists in and how *that* determines (contains) all the values of the function. And one must admit that, if the subject's understanding of the various terms in the expression of the rule is unpacked in terms of her having further dispositions to recognize expressions of rules that determine *their* application functions (e.g., a rule she knows for addition involves reference to *counting* and she knows a rule that determines when *that* term is correctly applied), then the same question arises, *until* we get to terms such that the subject's grasp of a rule that determines their applications does not require explanation in that way (in terms of a disposition to accept some informative expression of a rule for how to apply the term) but can be explained in some other way.

We must get down to what might be called a *brute level* of rule grasping where, as Wittgenstein puts it, justification comes to an end—that is, there is no more justification *in terms of further expressions of rules.*

There do seem to be terms such that, although the application function is not arbitrary, one would be at a loss to describe any general procedure for finding the application value given the argument, or at any rate it would not seem to be crucial to one's understanding the term, to one's knowing how to apply it correctly, that there be something one would recognize as an informative expression of the rule one follows. Cases in point would, I think, be "*x* is red," "*x* is hot," "*x* is sweet," "*x* is shrill (in sound)," "*x* contains an edge" (applied to visual fields), "*x* is the same in color as *y*," "*x* has the shape of the numeral *3*," "*x* feels warmer than *y*," "*x* sounds higher in pitch than *y*"—terms for directly sensed properties and relations.

The application of the term is nonarbitrary—indeed, it is rule-governed in the sense that *it is always the same thing that makes it correct to apply it*—but one's grasp of what makes all the cases the same in the respect one means by the term need not be expressible in other terms in any informative way. (Of course, one can always use or invent a synonym for the term in question or say, "They are all the same in the respect I mean"). In such cases one's grasp of a rule for applying a term does not (at any rate need not) consist in one's being disposed to recognize some informative definition of the rule, but just in one's being disposed to apply the term correctly to particular cases. As Wittgenstein says in *Philosophical Investigations* 201, "there is a way of grasping a rule which is *not* an *interpretation*, but which is exhibited in what we call 'obeying the rule' and 'going against it' in actual cases." This way of grasping a rule, which is *exhibited* in appropriate judgments about particular cases, could be just one's possessing dispositions to make such judgments.

But, one still wants to ask, what is it in such cases that makes all the applications one is disposed to make *correct*, in accord with a single rule? Taking a clue from some of Wittgenstein's remarks,[8] one might try to get nonarbitrariness into a collection of dispositions by putting into the consequent of the conditional something about the subject's *attitude* toward her response, producing the following:

> If I had considered the question whether or not the rule I meant assigns this value to that argument and given a relevant and sincere response to it, then I would have responded that it does *and I would have regarded this response, not as a new decision made for this case, but as just doing the same thing I have done (or would do) for other arguments where I assign the same value.*

Here the consequent of the conditional specifies a two-part response: a judgment about the case and an attitude toward that judgment, the attitude that this judgment is not an arbitrary *decision* for just this particular case.

But, of course, that attitude toward the judgment implies something about the content of the judgment, namely, that what the subject is judging is that the term applies (or does not apply) *for the same reason* it does (does not) in *other* cases and that this reason has to do with the nature of the case. So we might make this explicit in the consequent of the conditional, producing the following:

> If I had considered the question whether the rule I meant assigns this value to that argument and given a relevant and sincere response to it, then I would have responded that it does and I would have regarded this response, not as a new decision made for this case, but rather as a *judgment that there is present in this case that which makes it right to assign this value (or there is absent in it that whose absence makes it right to assign this value) and it is the same thing that is present (absent) in any other case to which it is right to assign this value.*

Note that the proposition that the subject makes (or would make) a judgment naturally expressible in the terms suggested here does not imply that the subject *does* grasp any rule that determines positive and negative cases, that makes the collections nonarbitrary. For it is possible for the subject to be disposed to make judgments with this content that are all false, to be under an *illusion* that she goes by a rule in judging whether or not the term applies, to *think* she grasps a general rule (and to have the dispositions to back up this thought) when she in fact does not. This means that the dispositionalist has not completed the required task for these brute level cases. We still need a noncircular account of what distinguishes *really* grasping a general rule in these brute level cases from only thinking one does.

Before pursuing that question, let me introduce one more refinement of the content of the counterfactual conditional that I think the dispositionalist should make. The *antecedent* should include something about the subject's being adequately informed about the particulars of the case being judged. We want to rule out the possibility of the subject's giving the wrong judgment or "don't know" because of her having a false impression of, or being ignorant about, crucially relevant elements in the case. So the standard-form counterfactual should, finally, be something like this:

> If I had considered the question whether or not the rule I meant assigns this value to that argument, *been fully aware of all relevant particulars of the case*, and given a relevant and sincere response to the question, then I would have judged that there is present in this case that which makes it right to assign this value (or there is absent that whose absence makes it right to assign this value) and it is the same thing as is present (absent) in any other case to which it is right to assign this value.[9]

Now, our question is: What distinguishes pseudo-rule-following from the real thing? The real thing is where the rule-follower's dispositions are not an arbitrary collection but are all correct because they are in accord with a single rule and the subject has the dispositions because she grasps that rule. What distinguishes this from a case where a subject is disposed to react as a genuine rule-follower would (that is, a large set of counterfactual conditionals of the sort most recently specified are true of her) but there is in fact no rule which makes all those dispositions correct, with which they all accord, and so the subject has only a delusion of following a rule?

Two rather different sorts of possible answers come to mind. (1) The *community agreement* answer: the dispositions constitute genuine following of a rule if and only if other subjects in a suitably defined community would, after suitably defined training, have the same dispositions. (2) The *objective property* answer: there is a property that is present in all the cases on which the subject is disposed to make the positive judgment, and absent in all those on which she is disposed to make the negative judgment, and the subject is disposed when suitably placed to recognize the presence or absence of that property.

The first answer is nominalist, subjectivist, anti-realist with respect to the properties or universals our discerning of which many have thought (and it is natural to think) is the basis for our application of descriptive terms. The second answer is realist, objectivist about properties or universals. Can dispositionalism choose the second sort of answer? I do not see why not. As far as I can see, dispositionalism does not need to be nominalist about universals in order to achieve its aim. What dispositionalism aims at is to provide a non-mysterious fact about the subject that has the property of "reaching to" or "containing" all the absent cases covered by the rule the subject grasps. This is the feature of understanding a rule that puzzles us (and the feature that the puzzler says is impossible). What dispositionalism offers is a set of counterfactual conditional facts, each dealing with a different absent case. I cannot see any incompatibility between, on the one hand, offering that answer to that question and, on the other hand, taking seriously and literally the idea that what the grasped rule dictates is that the term applies to just those cases that have a certain objective property in common.

To say that a property is *objective* is to say that it is (or can be) possessed by things independently of any subject's dispositions to classify particular cases. The property could still be there *in* things even if there were no subjects capable of classifying things or there were none who noticed or discerned this property. Even if no entities with minds ever existed there nevertheless might exist various shapes in common to many objects. Even if no one ever discerned or thought of it, there could exist in things the property of being negatively charged.

On an objective, realist view of properties, the problem dispositionalism addresses (and proposes to solve) could be put this way: How can a present fact about the subject collect just the actual *and possible* instances of *this* property rather than those of some other property, since all that the subject can have before her mind at one time, in the way of positive and negative instances, is a small number of cases which are also positive and negative instances, respectively, of a great many other properties? What constitutes the subject's *picking out* the right property, her grasping the particular respect of resemblance, that the term stands for? It seems that no *occurrent* phenomenon can do the trick. "Fastening attention on the right property" does not pick out an occurrent phenomenon that does it, because no matter what occurrent, nondispositional phenomenon you suppose answers to this description, it is possible for someone to be the subject of the same sort of occurrence and *not* be attending to the right property.

The dispositionalist comes to the rescue with her conjunction of counterfactual conditionals as the only sort of fact about the subject that can collect all the absent cases needed to select the right property uniquely. The dispositionalist can characterize the reaction to which the subject is disposed as that of *recognizing the same property* in each case. The reaction is *correctly* so characterized only if the subject is disposed to have the appropriate reaction (specified in the standard-form counterfactual conditional we arrived at above) to every *possible* case where the property is in fact present. The mark of the subject's recognizing the right property, of her reaction's being based on recognizing the right property, need not be any occurrent, nondispositional phenomenon, but can be just the dispositions to the appropriate reaction in all the possible cases that do instantiate the property. The presence of those dispositions in a particular case of her actually reacting in the way we have specified make it the case that she is then reacting to the right property.[10]

2. A second difficulty for dispositionalism that Kripke raises is this: if what I meant were a matter of what I was *disposed* to do, then I could not have the sort of direct memory knowledge of what I meant that I surely do have. Kripke asks:

> Am I supposed to justify my present belief [as to what I meant] in terms of a *hypothesis* about my *past* dispositions? (Do I record and investigate the physiology of my brain?) Why am I so sure that one particular hypothesis of this kind is correct . . . ?(23)

And later he affirms:

> The idea that we lack 'direct' access to the facts whether we mean plus or quus is bizarre. . . . Do I not know, directly, and with a fair degree of certainty, that I mean plus? . . . There may be some facts about me to which my access is indirect, and about which I must form tentative hypotheses: but surely the fact as to what I mean by 'plus' is not one of them! (40)

With this latter claim—that I do have direct memory knowledge of my meaning intentions, that for me they are not hypotheses—I could not agree more. But the claim implicit in the earlier passage—that, if what I meant were a matter of what I was disposed to do, then I would have to form *hypotheses* about what my disposition was, based on evidence as to what a certain counterfactual condition would have caused some mechanism in me to produce—seems to me to be wrong, to reflect too narrow a view about counterfactual conditionals, about their truth-conditions and how they can be known or justifiably believed to be true. I do know some past tense counterfactual conditionals about myself as directly, by memory, as I know what some of my categorical conscious states were. Suppose I said the words 'the ordering of the letters' and thereby meant the alphabetical ordering of all the letters of the alphabet (rather than, say, a misspelled word that I had earlier referred to with that same phrase). A few moments later I can (normally) simply, directly *remember* not only that I said those words, but also that I meant by them the function <'a', 'b'>, <'b', 'c'>, . . . etc. And I can also simply *remember* that if I had then considered the question, I would have thought that the function I meant includes the pair <'f', 'g'>. I can directly remember that a certain counterfactual conditional was true of me. That is, we allow a *memory* impression with that content to justify me in claiming to know the truth of such a counterfactual.

Compare one's knowledge of the truth of a subjunctive conditional that expresses one's *conditional intention*: in normal circumstances when I assert, "If the telephone were to ring now, I would answer it," I am not making a hypothesis about myself. And when I *remember* having had such an intention, I am not making an hypothesis about my past self: I know simply on the basis of memory that the conditional was true.[11] Consider some more examples.

(1) In *Philosophical Investigations*, I, 576, Wittgenstein discusses the state of *expecting* something.

> I watch a slow match burning, in high excitement follow the progress of the burning and its approach to the explosive. Perhaps I don't think anything at all or have a multitude of disconnected thoughts.

For several moments before the explosion occurs I have been expecting to see an explosion very soon. When I do see an explosion I regard it as the sort of thing I was expecting. That is part of my reaction to it, my attitude toward it. Wittgenstein would, I think, call this reaction a *criterion* of the fact that I was expecting an explosion. But my state of expecting an explosion was there *before* I saw the explosion and reacted to it. And its having been there is quite independent of whether or not I ever do actually react in that way to an explosion: it would still have been there if something had prevented the explosion at the last second or if I had been killed instantly by a bolt of lightning a couple of seconds before the explosion. So there must have been some fact about me entirely there before the explosion that is sufficient to make it the case that I was then expecting just that sort of thing. What sort of fact could this have been? It need not be that I had in my mind any sort of image or description of an explosion. As I think Wittgenstein means to suggest in the remarks just quoted, I could have been expecting an explosion without having in mind any sort of representation of one. Nor is it plausible to suggest that, if I did have in mind some image or description of an explosion, that by itself would be *sufficient* to make it the case that I was expecting an explosion.

What then? It seems to me very natural and compelling to say that what made it true of me that I was at a given past moment expecting an explosion is the subjunctive conditional fact that, if an explosion had occurred just then I would have had a reaction to it expressible by 'This is the sort of thing

I've been expecting'. When the explosion actually occurs I know with direct certainty that *this* is the sort of thing I have been expecting. But to know this, it seems to me, *is* to know that I *would* have had the same reaction *if* an explosion had occurred at some earlier point during the period I have been expecting it.

(2) I am working at home and I think, "I need to take this book to the office with me today." Later when I get to the office, I do not have the book: I forgot to stick it in my briefcase. But I am sure that, *had* I thought of it when I was packing my briefcase, or when I was leaving the house, I *would* have stuck it in. This is a fact about my past of which I can be as certain as I am of the fact that I did form the intention earlier to bring the book. I am no more forced back to mere hypothesizing in the one case than in the other.

In such cases, there is a marked and profound contrast between the way I am justified in believing the counterfactual conditional about myself and the way I can be justified in believing a similar conditional about someone else. Forming a belief about what another person would do, or would have done, *is* to form a hypothesis (based perhaps on my knowledge of their past behavior, or perhaps on the assumption that the other person is very much like me) in a way that my belief about what *I* would do, or would have done, is *not* a hypothesis. The contrast here strikes me as quite as great as the contrast between the way I can know about my own past conscious states and processes (sensations and the like) and the way I can know about those of others.

I conjecture that behind Kripke's assumption that one's beliefs about one's past dispositions must be hypotheses[12] there lies something like the following reasoning:

(a) It is a necessary condition of the truth of the counterfactual conditional about me that there was some *categorical basis* for it. (That is, there were independent[13] intrinsic[14] properties of me that would causally explain why the condition or occurrence described in the antecedent would produce the occurrence described in the consequent, that would be sufficient for the truth of the counterfactual conditional.)

(b) If (a), then I could not know that the counterfactual conditional was true of me without knowing that there was some categorical basis for it.

(c) I could know that there was a categorical basis only as an hypothesis (that is, something confirmed for me by evidence as to what specific sorts of mechanisms there are in me or by evidence as to how I and others like me have reacted in similar situations in the past).

(d) Therefore, I could know that the conditional was true of me only as an evidence-based hypothesis (and not in the sort of direct way I have memory knowledge of my recent past experience or have knowledge of my current intentions).

Of the three premises here, (c) alone seems quite acceptable: at any rate, I shall not question it. (b) seems doubtful. It is not the case in general that one must know everything entailed by what one knows. For many instances where *p* entails *q*, one may know *p* without knowing *q* if one fails to know that *p* entails *q*. Is this such a case? I find it difficult to address this question, since I doubt that in this case *p does* entail *q*.

That is, I doubt (a), that the existence of a categorical basis *is* a truth-condition for every sort of counterfactual conditional. In particular, I doubt that it is a truth-condition for the sort of conditional that the dispositionalist account of meaning needs or for the sort illustrated in my recent examples. And it appears that Wittgenstein eventually had doubts about this, too. In notes written in 1937 he says:

> Think of two different kinds of plant, A and B, both of which yield seeds; the seeds of both kinds look exactly the same and even after the most careful investigation we can find no difference between them. But the seeds of an A-plant always produce more A-plants, the seeds of a B-plant, more B-plants. In this situation we can predict what sort of plant will grow out of such a seed only if we know which plant it has come from. Are we to be satisfied with this; or should we say: "There *must* be a difference in the seeds themselves, otherwise they *couldn't* produce different plants; their previous histories on their own *can't* cause their further development unless their histories have left traces in the seeds themselves."?
>
> But now what if we don't discover any difference between the seeds? And the fact is: It wasn't from the peculiarities of either seed that we made the prediction but from its previous history. If I say: the history can't be the cause of the development, then this doesn't mean that I can't predict the development from the previous history, since that's what I do. It means rather that we don't call *that* a 'causal connection', that this isn't a case of predicting the effect from the cause.
>
> And to protest: "There *must* be a difference in the seeds, even if we don't discover it", doesn't alter the facts, it only shows what a powerful urge we have to see everything in terms of cause and effect.[15]

In *Zettel* 608 this example of the seeds is introduced with

> No supposition seems to me more natural than that there is no process in the brain correlated with associating or with thinking; so that it would be impossible to read off thought-processes from brain-processes. I mean this: if I talk or write there is, I assume, a system of impulses going out from my brain and correlated with my spoken or written thoughts. But why should the *system* continue further in the direction of the center? Why should this order not proceed, so to speak, out of chaos?

In *Zettel* 609 he says

> It is thus perfectly possible that certain psychological phenomena *cannot*

be investigated physiologically, because physiologically nothing corresponds to them.

And in *Zettel* 610 he comments, "If this upsets our concept of causality then it is high time it was upset." Commenting on Wittgenstein's example of the seeds, Budd (1984, 311) supposes that an A-plant seed and a B-plant seed fail to germinate because of lack of water and says

> All the same, we can truly say of the one seed that if it had been watered it would have become a plant of kind A, and of the other that if it had been watered it would have become a plant of kind B. And we can truly say this even though there was no intrinsic, nonrelational difference between the physical states of the two seeds and they were in identical circumstances. . . . Wittgenstein sees no difficulty in the supposition . . . that counterfactual differences need not be based in intrinsic, nonrelational differences . . .

If Wittgenstein did indeed think that counterfactual conditionals could be true without a categorical basis, and if he thought that ascriptions of understanding and meaning could be cashed in terms of such counterfactual conditionals, then Wittgenstein thought that, as Budd puts it (313), "the condition of someone who suddenly understands how to continue a series [or means or intends or expects a certain thing] need not be distinguished from that of someone who does not understand [or mean or intend or expect] . . . either by (i) something that was present to or went through his mind but which was not present to or did not go through the mind of the other person . . . or by (ii) the condition of his mental apparatus." I am inclined to agree with Wittgenstein's remarks, as Budd interprets them, and therefore I am inclined to think, with respect to the argument I attributed to Kripke, that there is no compelling basis for premise (a) or, therefore, for the conclusion (d).

Is there an *argument* against the claim that the truth of a counterfactual conditional always entails a categorical basis? It is notoriously difficult to argue for the denial of an entailment, but one can make the following points.

What argument is there *for* the entailment? The entailment is not self-evident and until we are given a convincing argument for it we should hesitate to believe in it.

If a categorical basis were entailed, this should be reflected in our intuitions. Concerning Wittgenstein's hypothetical example of the seeds, for instance, we might (if the entailment held) be expected to feel intuitively compelled to deny that it is even in principle possible that (i) it is true of an A-plant seed but not of a B-plant seed that, if it had been watered, it would have grown into an A-plant, and (ii) there is no intrinsic difference between the seeds that would causally explain why the counterfactual conditional holds for the one but not for the other. But I find myself quite willing to allow that, however much I might initially resist believing both of those things to be actually true, it is nonetheless possible that they should be: if I were confronted with all the facts of Wittgenstein's example, it would seem to me reasonable, not incoherent, to begin to suspect that both things are true.

Consider another example, a variant of one Wittgenstein gives in *Philosophical Investigations* 666. Suppose there are two people in the situation of simultaneously having a toothache and hearing a piano being tuned and both say, "It will stop soon." A short time later one says that if she had been asked what she meant by "It" in that remark, she would have said that she meant the toothache, and the other says that if she had been asked she would have said that she meant the piano tuning. If I know that both speakers speak sincerely then I have a basis for confidently accepting both of those counterfactual conditionals that would not be undermined by my finding that there was no relevant, independently ascertainable intrinsic difference between the two people at the time the conditionals are about, *nor* any relevant difference in their histories prior to that time, that would explain why the one conditional holds for the one person and the other holds for the other person. Though there *may* have been such differences, why *must* there have been? My intuitions about such cases do *not* reflect any sense that the counterfactual conditional simply cannot be true unless there existed independent conditions that would explain why, if the antecedent had been true, then the consequent would have been true.[16]

If this does not demonstrate that a counterfactual conditional does not entail the existence of a categorical basis, it at least shows that one can fail to know that there is such an entailment. And that is enough to open up the possibility of knowing a counterfactual conditional to be true without knowing that there is a categorical basis for it. So I think the dispositionalist has a viable response to Kripke's objection that if meaning intentions were a matter of dispositions then one could not know one's own meaning intentions with direct certainty (as we do) but could only hypothesize about them. The dispositionalist can respond that the objection incorrectly assumes the truth of premises (a) and (b) in the argument above.

3. The two remaining objections that Kripke makes (26–32) I will consider together because I think there is a move the dispositionalist can make that deals with both difficulties at the same time. They are difficulties the dispositionalist faces in trying to explain our understanding of computable functions like addition. One problem is that there are numbers so large that I lack the capacity to consider them and, therefore, it seems to make no sense to suppose that I am disposed to respond in any determinate way if I should consider them; yet the function I mean by "plus" determines sums for those very large numbers, too. The other problem is that people are sometimes disposed to make systematic *mistakes* in computing sums; yet what they mean by addition is not different from what is meant by people who are not disposed to make those mistakes: they mean the standard function, not some bizarre function that includes what would be incorrect results on the ordinary understanding.

Regarding the first problem Kripke asserts (26–27) that

not only my actual performance, but also the totality of my dispositions, is finite. It is not true, for example, that if queried about the sum of any two numbers, no matter how large, I will reply with their actual sum, for some pairs of numbers are simply too large for my mind—or my brain—to grasp.

How is it that "some pairs of numbers are simply too large for my mind— or my brain—to grasp"? In the sentence following the one just quoted, Kripke suggests that there are numbers that would take too long to mention—one would die of old age first. Couldn't a suitable notation help with this difficulty? We could use exponents, special names for very large numbers ("googol"), and have special rules for adding numbers expressed in these special ways. Are there any integers so large that special notation and techniques could not make it possible to add two of them in a reasonable length of time?

Kripke's likely response to this would be that it misses the point of the objection. The point is that there are numbers so large that *I am not now conversant* with notation and techniques that would make me able even to mention them, much less add them; therefore, my *current* dispositions and capacities with respect to doing sums do not reach beyond some finite limit. That does seem right. We need to find a better response to this too-big-numbers objection.

Suppose we grant that it is a feature of the addition function that, although we grasp it and frequently mean it by what we say, we do not have dispositions, of the sort we specified, for all the arguments to it. That is, for some trio of integers x, y, and z such that $x + y = z$ it is beyond my capacity to consider the question whether $x + y = z$ and therefore the counterfactual conditional 'If I had considered whether $x + y = z$ and...etc., I would have judged that it does' is not true of me: it is either false or lacks a truth value altogether. There are two important points to note.

First, this feature of the addition function is *not* a feature of every function we mean by a descriptive term we use, not even every one that is defined on an unlimited set of actual and possible cases and determined by a rule. There are application functions for meaningful descriptive terms where no case to which the function applies is more difficult to consider, as far as one's cognitive capacities are concerned, than any other. For color terms, shape terms, 'one side of the visible rectangle is longer than the other', 'the note changed pitch downward', and the like the too-big-numbers sort of problem just does not arise.[17]

Second, those application functions where this problematic feature (of cases too "big" to consider) *is* present will always be ones such that a person means the function by a term if *and only if* the person knows some correct and informative definition of a rule for the function. That is, the person is disposed to recognize as correct some correct expression of the rule and the person possesses understanding of the terms used in that expression sufficient to enable her to understand it. For *these* sorts of functions, having a capacity to understand some correct expression of the rule and a disposition to recognize it as correct when understood is a necessary as well as sufficient condition of meaning the function. Whatever dispositions to respond to questions about particular applications of the addition function a particular subject may have or lack, this capacity and disposition to recognize a correct general definition of addition is the overriding criterion of whether or not the subject grasps or means the appropriate rule and function.

These points suggest a different and less crude dispositional account of meaning such functions and rules from that which Kripke seems to be considering, one to which his criticism does not apply. The account is that understanding a term to mean an unlimited function determined by a rule is always either a case of the sort where the cases-too-big-to-consider feature is not present or it is a case where the understanding is built on the basis of dispositions to recognize correct definitions plus understandings of the terms of the definitions.

Let me elaborate. Consider the case of meaning the addition function by the plus symbol, where, I have claimed, the overriding criterion of a person's meaning this is her knowing some informative correct definition of the function. With respect to the subject's understanding of each term in that definition, either this condition of her knowing some correct definition of the term is satisfied for it, too, or it is not. If it is satisfied then she must understand the terms of some correct definition of *this* term. If it is not satisfied, then it must be a case (such as that of understanding a color term) where the criterion of whether she grasps the appropriate rule is just her having the appropriate dispositions with respect to all the actual and possible cases to which the rule applies.

This second sort of understanding a rule for the application of a term is what I earlier called the "brute level" way of doing so. And the distinction between the first and the second sorts of understandings is, to borrow Wittgenstein's words, the distinction between a way of grasping a rule that *is* an interpretation and a way that "is *not* an interpretation, but which is exhibited in what we call 'obeying the rule' and 'going against it' in actual cases" (*Philosophical Investigations* 201).

A higher level sort of understanding unpacks into various understandings of terms in expressions of rules, at least some of which may also be higher level understandings. This unpacking continues until brute level sorts of understandings are eventually reached: there is a hierarchy of understandings built up by understandings of rule expressions, or definitions, on a foundation of brute level sorts of cases where understanding a rule is not a matter of understanding an expression of it (not a matter of understanding a definition of the term).

The unpacking of any particular higher level understanding can be represented by a downward branching tree. However many branches the tree has, they all eventually terminate in brute level understandings of terms, where, for any case in the domain of the application function, there is no difficulty about S's having the capacity to consider it. For example, among the many brute level understandings at the base of my understanding the rule for adding two numbers quoted earlier from Graeme Forbes would, perhaps, be sets of dispositions to recognize marks as instances of the numerals "0" through "9," to recognize when two numeral marks are in vertical alignment, and the like.

The dispositionalist thesis is, then, that understanding the meaning of a term is always either a brute level case or else a higher level case for which such an understanding tree can be constructed on the basis of brute level cases. This dispositionalism avoids Kripke's objection regarding the addition function (and the like) that, for any person who does understand and mean the function, there are arguments to the function beyond the capacity of that person to consider. This dispositionalism admits this point, but says that its dispositional account of grasping the addition function does not require that every argument to it be within the grasper's capacity to consider. It requires this only for rule-graspings of the brute level sort, and for these every argument to the function is such that there is no difficulty regarding the subject's having the cognitive capacity to consider it.

This dispositionalism avoids equally well, I think, the other objection mentioned above (presented by Kripke, 28–32), which is based on the fact that people can have dispositions to make *systematic errors* in calculating sums even when they correctly understand what addition is and do mean the right function by "+" (similarly for other functions). Thus there might be someone of whom are true a great many counterfactual conditionals of our prescribed form, where the antecedent has him considering a pair of numbers as argument for the plus function and the consequent has him giving the wrong value for the sum. This might be so *despite* his correctly understanding what addition is—as evidenced by, say, his being able to give a correct informative general account of it—because, for example, he is disposed to forget to carry when calculating the sum of numbers longer than two digits. Our dispositionalism can allow that such dispositions to make errors in applying terms are compatible with correct understanding of them, provided that they occur for terms that are at levels in the structure of one's understanding that are above the brute level. At those higher levels there is a criterion of one's correctly understanding the application rule that overrides one's dispositions to make erroneous judgments in particular cases, namely, one's understanding a correct definition of the term (which entails possessing an understanding tree for it that goes down to brute level dispositions).

On the other hand, there do seem to be terms with respect to which there cannot be both systematic errors in application and also correct understanding of the term. If I am disposed to errors in judging the application of "red" to particular objects when I have optimal visual awareness of them, then I do not grasp the correct rule for applying "red." There is not available another explanation of my errors that is compatible with my grasping the correct rule: I simply do not understand the meaning of that term. I think the same goes for any of the terms for which one can grasp a rule of application without knowing any informative expression of the rule. These are the brute level cases on which, says our dispositionalism, all understanding of application rules must be built.

On this theory, the explanation of what a person's understanding of a particular rule or meaning consists in depends on where it is in the structure of a person's understanding. If it is above the brute level then it will consist partly in the person's understandings of other rules or meanings. The account tells us how every grasping of a term's meaning can be given a finite analysis that does not appeal to her understanding of this term's meaning (though, if the understanding in question is not at the brute level, it will appeal to the person's understandings of other terms' meanings). And, most important for the problem we have been concerned with, it does not appeal to any mysterious state that "contains" all the applications in an unexplained way. For each particular understanding of a term's meaning, the sense in which it does contain all the applications is explained in terms of a tree of understandings which has at its terminal nodes sets of dispositions to apply or withhold terms in particular cases.[18]

Notes

1. Kripke (1982), 7; all references to Kripke are to this work.
2. I always use 'disposition' to refer to the counterfactual conditional fact itself, never to a categorical fact that is its causal basis (if there is one).
3. It cannot be said, however, that there is conclusive evidence that dispositionalism was Wittgenstein's own solution to his puzzle. I do doubt that his solution was the "skeptical" one that Kripke (chapter 3) attributes to him.
4. Note that this objection applies only to cases where the application function I meant is a collection of ordered pairs that is, in fact, not arbitrary, but determined by a general rule. It is the general rule that determines the function and makes nonarbitrary, justifies, the inclusion of each ordered pair. In cases where the function I mean by a term is in fact arbitrary and not determined by a general rule—as, for example, the function we usually mean when we speak of the alphabetical order of the letters of the alphabet—the question Kripke is raising here does not apply; for here there is not the sense that all the different assignments of value to argument are justified by a single rule.
5. But we have already made some significant progress with the puzzle. Dispositions show how a fact about me now can reach an object or state of affairs not present to me now and thus provide a non-queer sense in which my present state of meaning (intending) a certain application function can "contain" all the applications not presently before my mind.
6. To try to help make clear how insufficient a merely arbitrary collection of dispositions must be, Kripke introduces (on p. 24) the example of the star symbol. He writes:

> Assuming determinism, even if I mean to denote *no* number theoretic function in particular by the sign '∗', then to the same extent as it is true for '+', it is true here that for any two arguments m and n, there is a uniquely determined answer p that I would give. (I choose one at random, as we would normally say, but causally the answer is determined.) The difference between this case and the case of the '+' function is that in the [latter] case, but not in the [former], my uniquely determined answer can properly be called 'right' or 'wrong'.

And he comments in a footnote to this passage:

> I might have introduced '∗' to mean nothing in particular even though the answer I arbitrarily choose for '$m ∗ n$' is, through some quirk in my brain structure, uniquely determined independently of the time and other circumstances when I am asked the question....What I will not say is that my particular answer is 'right' or 'wrong'

in terms of the *meaning* I assigned to '∗', as I will for '+', since there is no such meaning.

The example is not spelled out as fully as one would like. What *is* the question about "*m* ∗ *n*" to which I am disposed to give an answer? If it is "What is the value of 68 ∗ 57?", why shouldn't my response be simply, "I don't know; the star means nothing to me"?

Kripke wants the case to be one where (1) it is plausible to suppose that I am disposed to come up with a number when asked the question (whatever it is) about any instantiation of "*m* ∗ *n*"—so my dispositions determine a function on all pairs of integers—but (2) my having this collection of dispositions does *not* constitute my understanding the star symbol to *mean* that function (or anything else). Perhaps both conditions are satisfied if the question I am disposed to respond to with a value is "What value do you (now) arbitrarily choose to assign *m* ∗ *n*?" The word "arbitrarily" needs to be in the question or, otherwise, my response is likely to be "How am I to decide what value to assign?"

If this is the sort of case Kripke has in mind, then the dispositionalist might be tempted to deal with it by saying that the counterfactual conditionals involved here are importantly different from those the dispositionalist posits in the case of meaning the addition function by "+". For an "application" of "∗" the conditional would read: "If I had been asked to arbitrarily choose a number to associate with '68 ∗ 57', I would have chosen 125." For an application of "+" the conditional (as I most recently formulated it) reads: "If I had considered whether the value assigned to '68 + 57' by the function I mean by '+' is 125 and had given a relevant and sincere response, I would have said that it is." In the difference between these, the dispositionalist might say, lies the difference between *meaning* a function in the one case and failing to do so in the other.

It is fairly clear what Kripke's response to this move should be. It is to image a person who has an unlimited set of dispositions to respond to star symbol pairs, each of which dispositions is specifiable by *the sort of counterfactual conditional the dispositionalist gives for the plus symbol*. Such a thing is possible. Now, one of two things must hold of such a person. (1) Her set of dispositions is an arbitrary collection and not determined by her grasp of a rule; in that case, despite the nature of the reactions she is disposed to have, it is doubtful that her having that set of dispositions constitutes the subject's meaning something by the sign. Why should we think that merely having all those dispositions is meaning that completely arbitrary function? (2) Her set of dispositions is *not* arbitrary but is determined by the subject's grasp of a rule, in which case the dispositionalist still owes us an account of this latter, crucial aspect of the matter; we need not only the collection of dispositions, but also some non-mysterious fact about the subject that makes them all in accord with a single rule she grasps.

7. Forbes (1984), 224. The table referred to is one which gives the sums of all pairs of single digits. To carry 1 is to add 1 to the digit heading the next column to the left, unless (a) that digit is 9, in which case one changes it to 0 before adding that column and caries 1 to the next column to the left of it, or (b) there is no column to the left, in which case one adds a leftmost place to the sum and puts 1 in it.

8. *Philosophical Investigations*, 219 (first and next-to-last sentences), 223, 225, 231–32, 238.

9. It should be noted that, for simplicity's sake, we are ignoring the fact that among the relevant sorts of responses to which the dispositionalist needs to posit dispositions in brute level cases is "This is not a case to which that question applies," which are needed to handle cases for which the application function determined by the rule is not defined. And we are ignoring the fact that for vague terms (which may include all empirically descriptive terms) there are needed dispositions to respond in certain appropriate cases with "That is not a clear case either way; it's on the borderline."

10. And a case of pseudo–rule-following will be one where there is no property in common to all the possible cases to which the subject is disposed to have the specified reaction.

11. On this issue of whether one can know such counterfactual conditionals about oneself in the direct sort of way, it is not clear that Wittgenstein always sides with me rather than with Kripke. On p. 142 of the *Brown Book* Wittgenstein seems to take Kripke's line on how I know these conditionals about myself: they are hypotheses my confidence in which should be based on observation and experiment (and, presumably, well-confirmed theory about how things work). In the same passage, Wittgenstein appears to doubt the view Kripke and I share, namely, that I do know with direct certainty, and not merely as a hypothesis, what my meaning intentions were.

12. And, perhaps, behind Wittgenstein's remarks on p. 142 of the *Brown Book*.

13. Independent because the sort of disposition we are concerned with could itself be regarded as an intrinsic property.

14. We are concerned here only with cases where the truth of the counterfactual conditional about me is *not* guaranteed by properties of things external to me.

15. Wittgenstein (1976), 410.

16. Some may say that, however it may be with the conceptual requirement, we in fact have plenty of reason in what we know about how nature works to be justified in being confident that the truth of any contingent counterfactual conditional about a macroscopic object supervenes on the microphysical properties of the object and its circumstances, and, hence, that the truth of any counterfactual conditional of the sort we are concerned with does have a categorical basis. Perhaps so, but if we substitute this claim for (a) in the reasoning I attributed to Kripke, then the revised premise (b) looks very doubtful indeed. (b) becomes: If in fact the truth of any such counterfactual conditional does have a categorical basis, then I could not know that it was true of me without knowing that there is a categorical basis for it. I see no more reason to suppose that this is so than to suppose that one must know that sensations supervene on brain processes in order to know that one feels pain.

17. To be sure, for a perceptible object remote from the subject, or one not actually in existence, it may be that it would be *practically* impossible for the subject to perceive the object in the way required by the antecedent of the counterfactual conditional (one cannot easily get rocks on Mars within one's field of view, one does not have the resources to manufacture certain chemical compounds). But this is not the sort of difficulty regarding the subject's mental capacity to consider them that Kripke cites for very large numbers. One still knows quite well what it would be like to have a good look in good light at rocks now lying on the surface of Mars or to have a good look at a certain chemical concoction that has not been and never will be created. The counterfactual hypothesis that one does these things has definite truth-conditions which do not entail one's having any *cognitive* capacities one now lacks.)

18. I have discussed the issues in this essay in several courses at Cornell and have received a lot of help with them from people attending those courses. I am grateful to Sydney Shoemaker for a number of helpful comments.

References

Budd, Malcolm. 1984. "Wittgenstein on Meaning, Interpretation and Rules." *Synthese* 58: 303–23.

Forbes, Graeme. 1984. "Skepticism and Semantic Knowledge." *Proceedings of the Aristotelian Society* 85: 223–37.

Kripke, Saul A. 1982. *Wittgenstein on Rules and Private Language.* Cambridge, Mass.

Wittgenstein, Ludwig. 1956. *Remarks on the Foundations of Mathematics.* Oxford.

———. 1958. *The Blue and the Brown Books.* Oxford.

———. 1958. *Philosophical Investigations.* 3d ed. New York.

———. 1967. *Zettel.* Oxford.

———. 1976. "Cause and Effect: Intuitive Awareness." *Philosophia* 6: 409–25.

MIDWEST STUDIES IN PHILOSOPHY, XVII (1992)

On the Paradox Kripke Finds in Wittgenstein

ARTHUR W. COLLINS

1. "THE WITTGENSTEINIAN PARADOX"

Let us contemplate Kripke's now famous "quus" function.[1] Addition is a function of two arguments. This is "plus." Quus is also a function of two arguments. For every pair of numerical arguments, quus has a value, which Kripke calls their "quum." For some arguments the values of the two functions are the same. In particular, (*a* quus *b*) = (*a* plus *b*) for all pairs of arguments of which neither is greater than 56. But for all other pairs, the quus function has the value 5. Kripke has us assume that 56 is the largest number a subject *K* has encountered in computing what *K* has been calling "the plus function." Kripke has tailored the quus function to agree with the plus function in all the cases that *K* has already calculated and to differ from the value of the plus function for all the other cases. Now *K* has to try to prove to a "bizarre skeptic" that his performance in getting "57 + 68 = 125" coheres with his past practice. In particular, *K* has to rule out the possibility that when he "added" in the past, he was actually computing the quus function and that in his past use of "plus" he intended and referred to the quus function.

A detailed exposition of *K*'s failure to meet the challenge illustrates the "skeptical paradox" that Kripke ascribes to Wittgenstein. Since a person's extension of the use of a word to a new case is in significant ways like the extension of the computation of a function to new arguments, the paradox explained concerning the quus function also indicates the impossibility of defending a claim that a person's present use is determined by his antecedent understanding of the meaning of a word. By ascribing this skeptical paradox to Wittgenstein, Kripke unifies a great portion of the *Philosophical Investigations* and, in particular, he brings together the discussions of private language and the discussions of arithmetical functions, the formulas that express them, and our ability to compute them for new arguments. No doubt these themes are rightly brought together.

The prospect for this as the basis of a discussion of Wittgenstein's ideas, however, will seem severely limited to anyone who recognizes that Wittgenstein certainly does not propound this or any other skeptical paradox in the *Philosophical Investigations*. I do not believe that it would repay the time and effort needed to show definitively that this is so and, therefore, that Kripke's interpretation of Wittgenstein is off the mark. Actually Kripke's essay is interesting as an articulate example of the kind of thinking about mathematics and philosophy of mind that Wittgenstein *does* oppose. In consequence, Kripke's work can help to make Wittgenstein's difficult and obscure lines of thought more accessible. That will be the topic here.

Concerning Kripke's general claim that Wittgenstein does present a skeptical paradox, I will make only the following point: The very passage (*Philosophical Investigations* I, §201, quoted as text for the explication of which Kripke invents the quus function, is a passage that expressly *rejects* the idea of a paradox in our ability to follow rules. Kripke quotes

> This was our paradox: no course of action could be determined by a rule, because every course of action could be made to accord with the rule. (7)[2]

Kripke says that his essay "will attempt to develop the 'paradox' in question" which "is perhaps the central problem of *Philosophical Investigations*." In fact, Kripke's book consists mostly of this development together with a "skeptical solution" for it, again attributed to Wittgenstein. But the passage quoted actually continues thus:

> The answer was: if everything can be made out to accord with the rule, then it can also be made out to conflict with it. And so there would be neither accord nor conflict here.

And the rest of §201 completes the rejection of the mentioned paradox identifying it as a "misunderstanding."

Kripke introduces the quus function as though it at least fits and illustrates the paradox that Wittgenstein mentions and immediately rejects at §201. In fact, the quus function does not even illustrate "our paradox" as described, but, instead, it introduces a quite different idea. The skeptic does not challenge K's representation that K had followed the rule (function) expressed by "plus" on the ground that any action (any value) would do just as well as 125 for the value of "57 + 68 = ?" Were that the bizarre skeptic's challenge, which it would be for the paradox Wittgenstein mentions, then 5 would do as well as 125 as the relevant value *of the plus function*. There would be no need to invent a quus function.

Taking up a stance that is completely out of touch with the paradox of §201, Kripke's skeptic concedes without a murmur that 125 is the unique value of the plus function for those arguments. The skeptic introduces *another* function (rule) which he also assumes to determine unique values unproblematically, and challenges K to defend his claim to have computed the plus function rather than the now-described quus function in the past. That the functions do have unique values for arguments is not questioned at all by Kripke's skeptic, nor by Kripke himself,[3] for that matter, but this is precisely what is questioned in the paradox Wittgenstein introduces and then sets aside in §201.

There are, no doubt, ways of looking at the problem the skeptic sets for K in Kripke's exposition so that it seems to cover pretty much the same ground as the paradox mentioned by Wittgenstein. To the extent that this is so, it may not matter much whether one challenges the idea that functions *determine* unique values or challenges the idea that one can defend the claim to have computed this rather than that function, where both are *conceded* to determine unique values. It seems to me that what difference there is between these two exotic challenges is connected with a conception of the nature of mathematics concerning which Wittgenstein really is skeptical. I have in mind especially the idea that a numerical function is, in some sense, *all there* already, utterly insulated from human thought and, thereby, from all skepticism. This idea makes it seem that in calculating we are tracing over something that is already done. Although we have created mathematics, it seems as though the infinite values of a function already exist and are, as though, *given.*

Indeed, Kripke does extend this kind of ideal status to mathematical facts explicitly. He says in a number of places that the value 125 is, without any doubt, the value of the plus function for the given arguments, and that this is simply a fact of arithmetic. It is clear that Kripke's skeptic is utterly unskeptical about the arithmetical facts.

Given Kripke's point of view, a certain overhaul of the paradox that Wittgenstein at least mentions in §201 becomes inevitable. In his conception of the mathematical facts, Kripke has actually ruled out the paradox that Wittgenstein does describe in §201. Kripke cannot entertain the idea that any value at all can be made out to cohere with the rule (function) *plus* for the arguments 57 and 68 since he *takes it for granted* that *that* function can only have the value 125. Thus, for Kripke, if he is to illustrate a skeptical challenge for the words "57 + 68 = 125" at all—if, that is, he is to indicate that 5 may be the right value for K to give—he has to make the issue turn on the possibility that K has been computing and, to be consistent, ought now compute, another function which K calls "plus" but which is not plus at all.

I have already said that the paradox of §201 is set aside at once, so I do not want to create the impression that Wittgenstein offers a paradox but a different one from that which Kripke ascribes to him. That would be so if §201 were part of a Wittgensteinian propounding of "our paradox." It is not. Wittgenstein is not trying to urge that, paradoxically enough, other values than 125 would be as defensible for these arguments of the plus function. It is worth noting, however, that Wittgenstein does question the idea that the infinite values of a function are in some sense already there without any reference to or reliance on human computing activities. Wittgenstein draws our attention to but does not endorse the view that, in calculating, we merely trace over steps which are, as though, already taken. A familiar form of the issue here concerns the concept of the actual infinite which Wittgenstein opposes, for example, in the discussion of the expansion of π (§516) and the discussion of Cantor's diagonal argument in the *Remarks on the Foundations of Mathematics* II, §9.

In his reliance on the mathematical facts, Kripke seems to accept a form of the idea that the steps are, as though, already taken, the values being, in some sense, given. Of the statement that there is a unique sum for every pair of integers, Kripke says that "it is an assertion about infinitely many instances" (105). This may illustrate the way in which Kripke's thinking about mathematics is rooted in conceptions that Wittgenstein wants to question. At one point, Kripke comments on Wittgenstein's remark: "Finitism and Behaviorism are quite similar trends. Both say, but surely all we have here is. . . . Both deny the existence of something, both with a view to escaping from a confusion."[4] In the course of the discussion, Kripke not only rejects the finitist's scruples about infinity, he also appears to ascribe the rejection to Wittgenstein.

> Finitists regard the infinitistic part of mathematics as meaningless. Such opinions are misguided: they are attempts to repudiate our ordinary language game. (107)

But it is not at all clear that Wittgenstein would agree, and if he would, to what extent he would agree, that the extension of discourse about mathematical matters to infinite domains is guaranteed by ordinary language. Is there an ordinary use of mathematical concepts of infinity at all? Just consider that the mathematical assertion: "An infinite set can be mapped onto a proper subset of itself," was long called "Galileo's paradox" because it affronts common sense. Close to the passage that mentions "our paradox" and thus inspires Kripke to look for a Wittgensteinian paradox, Wittgenstein himself distinguishes between the expression "and so on," which he says can be just an abbreviation, and the expression "and so on *ad infinitum*" which cannot be an abbreviation. He adds

> The fact that we cannot write down all the digits of π is not a human shortcoming, as mathematicians sometimes think. (§208)

Kripke, on the other hand, cites, it seems with approval, the Platonist's emphasis on "the non-mental nature of mathematical entities," and as a consequence of the recommended adoption of this emphasis he can say

> there is no problem—as far as the present considerations go—as to how the addition function (taken, say, as a set of triples) contains within it all its instances, such as the triple (68, 57, 125). This simply is in the nature of the mathematical object in question, and it may well be an infinite object. (53–54)

Such views, which Kripke assumes to be common ground in contemplating the nature of mathematical rule-following, keep him from seeing the stance

Wittgenstein really adopts and lead him to impose alien goals on Wittgenstein's text.

Finally, we might confirm these preliminary reflections by noting that the paradox Kripke ascribes to Wittgenstein does resemble "our paradox" of §201 to the extent that the grounds Wittgenstein offers for rejecting "our paradox" seem to apply as well to the paradox Kripke generates with the quus function. If we could never establish which of two different functions we had been computing in the past then there would be no question of having computed one rather than the other function. There would be no fact of the matter to be skeptical about. Kripke seems to arrive at this perspective himself, but he perseveres with the development of the paradox and credits its discovery to Wittgenstein as a great achievement. In contrast, Wittgenstein concludes in §201 that, since the so-called paradox would mean that "there would be no such thing as accord or conflict," we have to reorganize our thinking about what conforming to a rule is. Wittgenstein does not say that we face anything paradoxical, but instead that

> What this shows is that there is a way of grasping a rule which is *not* an *interpretation*, but which is exhibited in what we call "obeying the rule" and "going against it" in actual cases.

In these remarks I do not want to suggest that it is easy to interpret Wittgenstein's views on any of these matters. But, whatever Wittgenstein's views are, the gap between them and Kripke's reconstruction is pretty conspicuous. In the remainder of this discussion I want to consider the "skeptical solution" Kripke finds Wittgenstein offering for the skeptical paradox with which he credits Wittgenstein. Once again the point will be to show that Kripke's thought is very firmly rooted in an outlook that Wittgenstein is trying to challenge. It is as though Wittgenstein fails to draw Kripke's attention to what he really questions so that Kripke finds in his writing a view that would be reasonable for someone with Kripke's outlook but a view that is actually quite incompatible with the main tendencies of Wittgenstein's thought. In the context of the skeptical solution, it is Kripke's deep adherence to ideas in the philosophy of mind that derail his interpretation of Wittgenstein.

2. THE "SKEPTICAL SOLUTION"

I do not have enough to say about the details of the skeptical solution to justify an elaborate exposition of it. The gist of what Kripke offers depends upon a contrast between a "straight" solution and a "skeptical" solution to the paradox. A straight solution would proceed by

> pointing out to the silly skeptic a fact he overlooked, a condition in the world which constitutes my meaning addition by "plus." (69)

A skeptical solution is one that agrees that

> there is no such fact in either the "internal" or the "external" world. (69)

Then Kripke centers his effort on the contention that Wittgenstein's skeptical solution involves the shift from truth conditions to assertibility conditions. The solution then explicates the assertibility of something that seemed irrevocably threatened by the skeptical paradox. What is it that is rescued? What performance is secured by appeal to assertibility, even if we have to let go our aspirations to truth? Plainly, the assertibility conditions that are going to do the job will condition the assertibility of exactly what the paradox has jeopardized. That is, the solution gives assertibility conditions for saying things like

(A) Jones, like many of us, means addition by '+'. (86)

In other words, the solution is tailored to meet the skepticism interpreted in terms of what function K has referred to and intended by the word "plus." The provision of assertibility conditions is, as explained by Kripke, not supposed to apply, for example, to saying things like

(B) 57 + 68 = 125.

No theory of assertibility conditions is offered for the latter because no skepticism has been entertained about the latter. Kripke's discussion of assertibility is certainly replete with Wittgensteinian themes. Assertibility derives from practices, it is grounded in the social, not in the mental, it is unaffected by the fact that we reach a level where "we act unhesitatingly but *blindly* (87)." In contrast, concerning (B), we can presumably assert it because, as Kripke has already indicated "This much is a theorem of arithmetic." The skeptical solution is supposed to explicate contexts where we speak "without justification" but not "wrongfully" as Kripke says (87). Surely, "That's just a theorem of arithmetic" will qualify as a justification, so the arithmetical facts, unchallenged by Kripke's paradox, are also undefended by his solution.

Once again, I have to be careful not to give the impression that Wittgenstein does extend a theory of assertibility as a solution to skepticism about assertions like (B) and that Kripke is mistaken in confining his solution to statements like (A). It is the case that if §201 were to express a "Wittgensteinian paradox" as Kripke says, a solution to it would have to extend to (B), since only Kripke's unjustified overhaul of "our paradox" has confined our attention to assertions like (A). But Wittgenstein has not put forward any paradox and, as a consequence, does not offer assertibility conditions as a feature of any solution to a paradox.

The specific assertibility conditions on which Kripke proposes that we rely are themselves another clue to the gulf that separates his thinking from that of Wittgenstein. First, Kripke considers the case of an individual acting in isolation, and this is a parallel for the idea of private use of language that Wittgenstein does investigate at length. Kripke says

All we can say, if we consider a single person acting in isolation, is that our ordinary practice licenses him to apply the rule in the way that it strikes him. (88)

It does not take a bizarre skeptic to doubt that our practice does any such licensing. The idea of such a license violates the very idea of action *in isolation*. The case of the person acting in isolation ought to mean the case of solipsistic rule-following. If we consider this case at all, we consider it from within. The "we" becomes editorial, and *there are no others* to license *our* practice. If Kripke does not mean solipsistic isolation, his license for a solitary performance will counsel the last bank teller to add as he pleases when everyone else has gone home for the day. In any case, in spite of his willingness to license lonely adders, and presumably because the license he envisions is so permissive, Kripke thinks that the notion of being guided by a rule "can have *no* substantive content" for the performances of such persons (89).

The real work of the assertibility conditions as a solution to the skeptical paradox is directed to the case of people doing arithmetic "while interacting with a wider society" (89). Surprisingly enough, the remarkable latitude granted to persons in isolation is not restricted in order to secure conformity in a social setting. On the contrary, that he is inclined to respond in a certain way "entitles" a subject to assert what he does assert in public just as it does when he is on his own. This is all there is to the assertibility condition. There is no other source of a person's title to respond to questions like those the skeptic has pressed on *K*. Kripke simply adds that, in the public case, this entitlement does not guarantee that others will not "correct" a speaker's response.

> Jones is entitled . . . to say "I mean addition by 'plus'," whenever he has the feeling of confidence—"now I can go on!"—that he can give correct responses in new cases; and *he* is entitled, again provisionally and subject to correction by others, to judge a new response to be 'correct' simply because it is the response he is inclined to give. (90)

Jones may make his assertions with a measure of trepidation since he stands to be corrected, but this is not a further assertibility condition since it cannot be met without first making an assertion and then seeing whether others correct it. Anyway, Kripke does not offer the correction process as a constituent of the concept of assertibility deployed here. He says, that is,

> The assertibility conditions that license an individual to say that on a given occasion, he ought to follow his rule this way rather than that, are, ultimately, that he does what he is inclined to do. (88)

The arbiters of correctness in this conception of the skeptical solution merely compare what Jones says with what they are inclined to say themselves. When you stop to think about Kripke's account of assertibility conditions, no one is ever offered an outlook that is an advance over the one proposed for the single person acting in isolation. All I ever have to go on is what I am inclined to say. That is all that my teachers and those that may correct me are relying on when they speak. Even if I am corrected, I can always hope that someone else will come along to correct that "correction" and give me the comfort of a majority. Though there is a distant whiff of Wittgenstein's thinking in all this, it has gone seriously wrong.

A tiny point offers us a way into the problem. Kripke momentarily forgets the terms of his own skepticism in the exposition just rehearsed, and, when he forgets, he writes as though this is supposed to be a solution for the paradox Wittgenstein actually mentions at §201. I mean he forgets that he has said it is not the arithmetical assertions that are at stake here. For instance, Kripke contemplates a child learning addition, and having his arithmetical statements corrected by a teacher (89). But to what is this relevant? There is no problem, according to Kripke, about the arithmetical facts, and the child has no freedom about them, whether acting in isolation or with others. Kripke seems to be reminded of the nature of the skepticism he has officially introduced when he proposes that an apparent wrong answer by a child might lead the teacher to say that the child must be computing some other function (89). Then he adds at once that this comment by a teacher is not literally very likely. Kripke ignores the response by a teacher that is entirely natural and highly probable, namely, "No, that is not the sum of those two numbers." He ignores this, pretty obviously, because he does not think there is any paradoxical leeway about what the sum of two numbers is. The only skeptical question that is relevant here is supposed to be "How do you know that you didn't mean quus by 'plus'?" The teacher's improbable comment at least addresses that issue.

But again on the next page Kripke momentarily extends the skeptical solution to include assertibility conditions for theorems of arithmetic. For the teacher to judge that the child's arithmetical answer is the correct answer means "that the teacher judges that the child has given the same answer that he himself would give" (90). At this point, it is not just claims about past use of the word "plus" but claims about the value of the plus function for proposed arguments that are placed in setting of answers we are inclined to give and "corrections" we are inclined to make. Theoremhood is, for the moment, forgotten. The very same thing happens in the next paragraph already quoted when Kripke offers the confidence that "now I can go on!" to give " 'correct' responses in new cases" in explanation of the inclination-test for assertibility. There is no question of *a feeling of being able to go on* in identifying one's past intentions with the use of 'plus'. Being able to go on does not have any sense for that kind of assertion and only makes sense when it means "go on to get correct answers for new cases of *the one* function I have been trying to learn." But this is not the issue that generated the need for a skeptical solution according to Kripke. He has slipped into an extension of skepticism to arithmetic.

The full-scale extension of the skepticism and the solution to include the assertion of arithmetical facts is clear in this:

> *Smith* will judge Jones to mean addition by 'plus' only if he judges that Jones's answers to particular addition problems agree with those *he* is inclined to give, ... (91)

If the theorems of arithmetic are available at all, why will Smith not judge Jones to mean addition if that interpretation of Jones's 'plus' makes arithmetical theorems of Jones' responses to new cases? Why will Smith merely compare inclinations with Jones when the arithmetical theorem is at hand?

Of course, it might be surmised that Kripke always meant to extend his theory of assertibility conditions to B-type assertions such as "57 + 68 = 125," and that I am just wrong in saying that he confines skepticism to assertions of the A-type. This is, however, quite inconsistent with Kripke's express and nearby contention that Wittgenstein's paradox raises no questions about "the addition function" but only about "what function 'plus' (as I use it) denotes (82)." Furthermore, the whole story about "quus" would be extraneous, and an indefensible rigamarole, if the skeptical problem and the need for a solution were supposed to include assertions like (B).

In sum, we are forced to conclude that, considered in itself and not as an interpretation of Wittgenstein, this solution to a skeptical paradox is a pretty chaotic affair. To this we have to add notice of the fact that the idea that, when doing arithmetic, we are responding as we are inclined; and that we are entitled to our responses because we are inclined to make them; and that corrections are merely comparisons with contrary responses that spring from contrary inclinations in others; and that this works out reasonably well because our inclinations are similar to the inclinations of others—in short, the whole theory of assertibility advanced by Kripke as a skeptical solution to a paradox— is wrongly ascribed to Wittgenstein.

This is particularly clear in connection with the central role Kripke gives inclination in the "solution" he gives Wittgenstein. For Wittgenstein considers a complex sequence of cases that more or less resemble people doing what they are inclined to do. Thus

§232. Let us imagine a rule intimating to me which way I am to obey it; that is, as my eye travels along the line, a voice within me says: "*This* way!"—What is the difference between this process of obeying a kind of inspiration and that of obeying a rule? For they are surely not the same. In the case of inspiration I *await* direction. I shall not be able to teach anyone else my 'technique' of following the line. Unless, indeed, I teach him some way of hearkening, some kind of receptivity. But then, of course, I cannot require him to follow the line as I do.[5]

Then at §233 Wittgenstein goes on to imagine training people to follow rules by this method of inspiration as "training in a sort of arithmetic." Calculating would be a "kind of composing," as each adept listened to an inner command and obeyed it. Then Wittgenstein actually anticipates pretty much the very theory that Kripke would like to burden him with in the next paragraph:

§234. Would it not be possible for us, however, to calculate as we actually do (all agreeing, and so on) and still at every step to have a feeling of being guided by the rules as by a spell, feeling astonishment at the fact that we agreed? (We might give thanks to the deity for our agreement.)

It goes without saying that Wittgenstein is not claiming that this is how things actually stand and that §234 does not express a theory of assertion-entitlement via assertibility conditions. These imaginings help to remind us that we would be rightly astonished if we all acted on bare inclinations and then, in our performances, we were in harmony with one another. Furthermore, if I were only voicing what I was inexplicably inclined to say, I would hardly feel "confidence" that I am able to go on with the series, for this confidence has to mean confidence that I will be right, not confidence that others will *miraculously* agree. If our mere inclinations regularly agreed I would have to be astonished. I could not be confident and also astonished.

When he presents the fantasy of training children in this kind of "calculation" at §233, Wittgenstein reminds us that we do not train children to follow an inner voice, or to respond as they feel inclined. Such a training is imaginable but it would not be anything like learning how to add. It sounds as if Kripke has got himself to a position where it seems to him that there could be nothing else to teach children.

3. KRIPKE AND THE CARTESIAN PHILOSOPHY OF MIND

Kripke makes much of not being a behaviorist, and of Wittgenstein not being one either. Kripke thinks that something inner must constitute *meaning this by that*. His conviction is so great that he is able to accept an extraordinarily disappointing constitution for meaning addition by "plus" rather than no constitution at all. For that is what blind response based only on inclination is. It is *something* to fill the Cartesian bill, however inadequately. The theorist begins by trying to articulate some failsafe inner determinant that will secure, not only his arithmetical performance, but the calculator's memories about what functions he was calculating in the past and what he meant by his words. All this, according to the view Kripke sees in Wittgenstein, is a failure. Kripke is left with an eerie feeling that nothing means anything. Then, in desperation, quite reminiscent of the catastrophic skeptical slide that precedes the *cogito*, Kripke hits upon a residual undefeated inner mental item. I am to stand up to all comers but only with the modest fact that I am inclined to say what I do say. This is the only title I can have, so I am to invoke it.

Actually, this is not *like* the *cogito*, it is part and parcel *of the cogito*. Descartes establishes not merely that he exists but that all his mental contents are as he takes them to be. He is warmed as though by the fire. His beliefs are as he finds them. He does indubitably will to avoid errors, as he thinks he does. Last, but not least, he is inclined to say "2 + 3 = 5" although, since he knows he may be in the grip of an evil demon, he allows that even this simple arithmetical assertion may give voice to an error. Like Kripke, Descartes also appreciates that this inclination is no reason for supposing that 2 + 3 does equal 5. The mystery of conformity of our inclinations with the inclinations of others, and, for that matter, with arithmetical truth (if such there be) is not dispelled by this skeptical solution. Descartes invokes God in explaining this mystery, while Kripke does not explain it at all.

But why do I propose this Cartesian analogy? Does Kripke's thinking actually embody Cartesian assumptions in any serious way? To approach this question I would like draw attention, first, to the concept of behaviorism, and behavioral criteria for meaning addition by "plus" and like matters. Kripke very properly dismisses the frequently heard view that Wittgenstein himself is a behaviorist and Kripke correctly says that Wittgenstein proposes no behavioral criteria in the spirit of the analytical behaviorist projects that have been sketched in our times. But there is much reason to think that Kripke equates the repudiation of behaviorism with the retention of a Cartesian outlook. For example, Kripke describes the alleged posture of Wittgenstein's skeptical paradox as follows:

> the way the skeptical doubt is presented is not behavioristic. It is presented from the "inside"....Wittgenstein's challenge can be presented to me as a question about *myself*: was there some past fact about me—what I meant by plus—that mandates what I should do now? (15)

Similarly, Kripke stresses throughout that the skeptical paradox is not generated by looking at public evidence for a user's past intentions in using "plus."

> So whatever "looking into my mind" may be, the skeptic asserts that even if God were to do it, he still could not determine that I meant addition by "plus". (14)

It is this attitude, Kripke believes, that gives Wittgenstein's skepticism a power it would not have if it were a mere exercise in behaviorist dogma. In short, Kripke rightly thinks that Wittgenstein is not going to appeal to behavioral criteria, in case an inner meaning-constituting reality is not discovered. It is actually this point that leads Kripke to impute a skeptical paradox to Wittgenstein in the first place, and this point also determines the contour of the solution that Kripke finds for Wittgenstein. For, once the issue of a behavioral criterion for meaning is set aside, and, I repeat, Kripke is right to think Wittgenstein does set this aside, then if an inner mental reality that manages to *constitute* my meaning addition by "plus" does not exist, we face, *Kripke supposes*, a dire skeptical paradox. For we plainly do mean things by our words, meaning demands an inner constitution, and yet there is nothing in us that even God could find to constitute meaning. Thus, as a condition for satisfying the skeptical challenge Kripke says an answer

> must give an account of what fact it is (about my mental state) that constitutes my meaning plus not quus. (11)[6]

Since Kripke thinks Wittgenstein, as a non-behaviorist, is himself convinced that meaning demands an inner mental constitution, and since he correctly reads Wittgenstein as showing in the most imaginative and varied sequence of discussions that no such inner constitution can exist, he ascribes a skeptical paradox to Wittgenstein. One would have to agree that this combination of views would be a devastating crisis for anyone holding them. But, as a matter of fact, Wittgenstein does not see the makings of a paradox here because he surmises from the outset that "my meaning addition by 'plus'" cannot have and does not need an inner constitution any more than it can have or needs a behavioral constitution.

One of the profundities of Wittgenstein's thinking is that he recognizes that philosophies of mind like behaviorism and the various forms of materialism are actually transformations of Cartesian assumptions into another key, one might say. We philosophers, Wittgenstein thinks, are sympathetic to dispositional and materialistic reconstructions of the fact about me in virtue of which I mean *this* by *that* because we are wedded to the initial Cartesian conviction that there *must be* such a constitution. If I mean something, or intend something, or believe something, or remember something, then there must be some reality that constitutes my meaning, intending, believing or remembering what I do. If we repudiate the Cartesian immaterial soul, then we must turn to the brain, or to a dispositional constitution. Wittgenstein does not go along with this extremely common pattern of thought that generates the schedule of alternatives in contemporary philosophy of mind. His rejection of it does not take the form of skeptical paradox found when we are convinced that there is no such inner fact. Throughout, *Philosophical Investigations* is trying to show that the familiar philosophical search for such an inner constitution is a complex of mistakes and false assumptions and misapplied pictures. In a complex variety of ways we are tempted to posit inner mental events and realities and then, mistaking the nature of the difficulties that arise, we try to re-identify the posited realities as physical items in the brain, or as behavioral dispositions.

At §308, a passage that Kripke himself quotes at length, Wittgenstein makes it clear that the preliminary, seemingly innocent, assumption that mental things must have an inner constitution, an assumption made before we are aware of doing any philosophical theorizing, is a "conjuring trick" that leaves us shopping among hopeless "theories" about our psychological concepts. Because Wittgenstein sees, as Kripke knows he does, that no inner constitution for meaning and believing is feasible he is prepared to

> deny the yet uncomprehended process in the yet unexplored medium. And now it looks as if we had denied mental processes. And naturally we do not want to deny them.[7]

This looks like a paradox to Kripke. He thinks that we do not want to deny mental processes because we believe so firmly that there are and must be such processes and that a dire outlook threatens if we cannot find them. Commenting on §195, where Wittgenstein is exploring our elusive and rather magical thought that *all the values* of a function are present to the person who grasps it already "in a *queer* way," Kripke says

Before we hear Wittgenstein's skeptical argument, we surely suppose—
unreflectingly—that something like this is indeed the case. Even now I
have a strong inclination to think that this is indeed the case. (52)

So, in Kripke's estimate, Wittgenstein's potent case against the inner constitution simply creates a tension with the still potent conviction that there must be
these inner realities. Thus, a paradox is engendered.

But this is not what Wittgenstein means at all. He means that it looks as
if we have to deny that people mean anything because nothing can constitute
meaning something. Wittgenstein's reason for not wanting to deny that people
mean anything is just that it is obvious that people do mean things. Wittgenstein
himself is quite comfortable denying that meaning *this* by *that* is constituted by
something existing in or happening in the person who means *this* by *that*. Thus

What we deny is that the picture of the inner process gives us the correct
idea of the use of "to remember." (§305)

Kripke's solution adheres to his Cartesian presumption. Although we do
not find much of an inner process, and in spite of the terribly disappointing
account of meaning that we are able to salvage, we do salvage the inclination to
respond in a particular way. The subject's inclinations are presented as residual
facts about his mental life. In saying this, I take it for granted that "being
inclined to respond thus" is a concept of a mental episode and not a disposition,
as this concept is employed by Kripke. For one thing, his explanation of the
skeptical paradox has itself examined in great detail and rejected definitively all
efforts to replace an inner-constitution account of meaning with a dispositional
account. It would be a travesty to resolve the paradox at the end by putting
forward another dispositional view for which no special considerations are
argued. Furthermore, in his elaboration of the solution, Kripke seems to include
the plainly episodic "now I can go on!" feeling as part of the inclination.[8] We
might say that the inclination to respond is a reportable propositional attitude
and not merely something that can be read-off from the response that the subject
in fact makes.

In reflecting on the skeptical solution when it is baldly stated, it will
be tempting to think that this cannot be what Kripke has really articulated
and ascribed to Wittgenstein. Kripke's own summary statement is better than
anything that I could provide to frustrate this temptation.

Wittgenstein thinks that these observations about sufficient conditions
for justified assertion are enough to illuminate the role and utility in our
lives of assertion about meaning and determination of new answers. What
follows from these assertibility conditions is *not* that the answer everyone
gives to an addition problem is, by definition, the correct one, but rather
the platitude that, if everyone agrees upon a certain answer then no one
will feel justified in calling the answer wrong. (112)

This remains a wholly unworkable "solution." What agreement we find in our inclinations has to be mere coincidence if we accept the account Kripke gives us. We have to remember that no subject is justified in asserting a statement about his past meaning or a determination of a new answer on the ground that that is the statement or answer others give. Agreement or disagreement emerges by comparing what various subjects are entitled to assert when they follow their unaided inclinations. The inner reality of inclining to assert that . . . is doing all the work of constituting the speaker's title to assert that. . . . Of course, Kripke would be closer to Wittgenstein if he did try to connect assertibility with what others actually *agree to assert*. Something like this would, for example, be a suitable analogy for Wittgenstein's very convincing showing that two men could not play a game of chess even if they sat in front of a board that looks right and even if they had the right sequence of inclinations to move pieces. This could not be a chess game in the absence of the existence of the game of chess as a social institution and practice (§200). Similarly, an appeal to the performances of others would fit with §242:

> If language is to be a means of communication there must be agreement
> not only in definitions but also (queer as this may sound) in judgments.

The social locus of meaning and participation in a shared practice as a condition for the possibility of meaning are major themes in Wittgenstein's *Philosophical Investigations*. In some sense, it is, I believe, more or less certain that these suggestions are in the right direction, and the old Cartesian thinking that Kripke still hopes to exploit will prove permanently sterile. In his skeptical solution, Kripke gives inner realities (inclinations) a feeble and unconvincing role in connection with his essentially Cartesian theory of meaning.

In any case, Wittgenstein has not provided a theory of meaning, nor has he shown clearly that we should not expect such a theory. All these matters remain in the air in spite of Wittgenstein's revolutionary ideas, and perhaps partly because those ideas are still for the most part ignored. A very small number of philosophers have tried to develop them since the initial set-backs that the over-extended Wittgensteinian claims of the 1950s received at the hands of Donald Davidson and others. So the fact that Kripke does not really go along with Wittgenstein's general tendency of thought—not in the philosophy of mathematics, and not in the philosophy of mind—does not mark his views as evidently untenable. The deep divergence of basic attitudes, which seems not to be appreciated by Kripke, is responsible for the fact that he wrongly ascribes a skeptical paradox to Wittgenstein and then a very unconvincing solution for that paradox.

Notes

1. See Saul Kripke, *Wittgenstein: On Rules and Private Language* (Cambridge, Mass., 1982), chap. 2. "The Wittgensteinian Paradox," which I am using in quotation marks as a heading, is Kripke's title for this chapter.

2. Numbers in parentheses, such as "(7)" here, are page reference to Kripke, *Wittgenstein: On Rules and Private Language*. Numbers preceded by "§" in parentheses are references to numbered sections of Wittgenstein, *Philosophical Investigations* I.

3. "The addition function—as Frege would emphasize—yields one precise value for each pair of numerical arguments. This much is a theorem of arithmetic" (82).

4. Wittgenstein, *Remarks on the Foundations of Mathematics* II, §61.

5. The last clause here seems to indicate, and very properly it seems to me, that, if we were to follow rules by such inspiration (or by Kripke's *inclination*), Wittgenstein thinks that the concept of "correcting" the performance of others would lose its applicability. Kripke's striking combination of a permissive license to mere inclination followed by authoritarian *correction* of the resulting assertion sounds like a good formula for softening up prisoners in preparation for political brain-washing, but it does not sound like a plausible picture of what actually happens in teaching and learning arithmetic, and then making and correcting arithmetical assertions.

6. Another manifestation of this assumption that meaning demands a mental constitution is presented in a discussion of the possibility that a sophisticated *ceteris-paribus* understanding of dispositions might succeed against the skeptical challenge while "crude and literal" notions of a disposition fail. Kripke sets aside this proposal on the ground that it appeals to counterfactual circumstances in which I would be able "to carry out my intentions with respect to numbers larger" than can I actually deal with.

> Such a counterfactual conditional is true enough, but it is no help against the skeptic. It presupposes a prior notion of my having an intention to mean one function rather than another by "+". It is in virtue of a fact of this kind about me that the conditional is true. But of course the skeptic is challenging the existence of just such a fact; his challenge must be met by specifying its nature. (28)

Readers familiar with his *Naming and Necessity* (Cambridge, Mass., 1990), will recall that Kripke believes that the considerations he raises about the mind-brain identity thesis make that thesis counterintuitive and encourage a Cartesian dualist outlook, although he confesses to seeing difficulties for this position, too. In a note, he concludes, not that Cartesian dualism appears to be refutable, but that we have no clear concept of a "soul or self" (155n). In many places in *Naming and Necessity* Kripke assumes that there are inner mental realities without worrying about the problems of the concept of the soul or self needed to house them. These mental things figure in the articulation of reference-fixing devices. I have in mind concepts such as "sensation of pain," "sensation of heat," "sensation of yellow" and "visual impression" for example, of the sort that yellow things ordinarily cause us to have. The casual adoption of these concepts exemplifies Kripke's natural gravitation toward posited inner realities which will have to be "mental" if materialist identifications of them fail, as Kripke plainly thinks they do. Of course, Kripke shares this propensity to think in terms of inner realities needing to be identified one way or another with most philosophers of mind, and, in particular, with the materialists that he discusses. Wittgenstein stands out as one thinker who is explicitly critical of this widely shared Cartesian attitude.

7. *Philosophical Investigations* I, §308.

8. See the already quoted passage (90) on the teacher's judging of the child's answer. Either the feeling is included with an episodic inclination to give a certain response, or Kripke means to include the particular response in the feeling as the response about which the subject has confidence.

Intelligibility, Imperialism, and Conceptual Scheme

S. L. HURLEY

There is a kind of conceptual relativism that claims, among other things, that it is possible that there are different groups of minds such that the groups are unintelligible to one another. This claim is implied by forms of relativism that hold that conceptual schemes may be strongly incommensurable, for example, so that its role in such forms of relativism is relevant to evaluation of the claim. However, it is the claim that it is possible that there are groups of minds that are unintelligible to one another, rather than relativism *per se*, that is the subject of this essay. Not all positions that involve this claim deserve the title of relativism; relativists add remarks such as: there is no such thing as making sense, period, or absolutely, so that we can say of the practices of some other group that they do not make sense; making sense is relative to conceptual scheme, which may vary radically among groups; their practices may well make sense, relative to their own scheme of things; it is not for us to judge, since we are not part of that group. And so on.[1] This familiar type of general relativistic position is parallel to other more local versions of relativism, such as those that hold right and wrong not to be absolute, but relative to evaluative scheme, which again may vary radically among groups, so that different groups may be unintelligible to one another just in respect of the evaluative point of their practices rather than in respect of making sense more generally.

It is not clear whether Wittgenstein would have endorsed the claim that it is possible that there are groups of minds unintelligible to one another. He wrote:

> one human being can be a complete enigma to another. We learn this when we come into a strange country with entirely strange traditions; and, what is more, even give a mastery of the country's language. We do not *understand* the people. (And not because of not knowing what they are saying to themselves.) We cannot find our feet with them.[2]

He also wrote:

> if anyone believes that certain concepts are absolutely the correct ones,
> and that having different ones would mean not realizing something that
> we realize—then let him imagine certain very general facts of nature to
> be different from what we are used to, and the formation of concepts
> different from the usual ones will become intelligible to him.[3]

To understand the relationship between these remarks and their bearing on
Wittgenstein's position with respect to the above claim, we could consider the
relationship between the intelligibility of the formation of concepts different
from the usual ones and the intelligibility of a group of people who use those
concepts.[4] We might also consider the relationship between such remarks as
these and his critiques of solipsism and of the notion of a private language.[5]
In this essay I will be pursuing issues closely related to these issues emerging
from Wittgenstein's work, but will be doing so primarily on the merits rather
than as a matter of interpretation.

1. INTELLIGIBILITY: ABILITY VS. CAPACITY.

Let us approach the claim at issue by considering the notion of intelligibility.
I take intelligibility to be a relation such that x is intelligible to y if and
only if y has the capacity to understand x. Applied to groups of minds, one
group of minds is intelligible to another if and only the latter has the capacity
to understand the former. "Understanding" between groups is shorthand for
understanding, on the part of some members of one group, of many concepts,
beliefs, desires, and other propositional attitudes of members of the understood
group; it involves understanding that they have minds by understanding their
minds, as opposed to merely believing or allowing or supposing that they
have minds, without understanding their minds. This sense of *understanding*
focuses on propositional attitudes rather than qualities of experience, on the
assumption (which I cannot examine here) that it is possible to have the relevant
concepts and to understand what someone believes or desires, for purposes of
intelligibility, even if one does not understand everything about what it is like
for him or her to have that belief or desire.

We should distinguish two notions, which I will call *capacity* and *ability*.[6]
There is a sense of *possibility* in which something has the *capacity* to do
something if it is *possible that* it does the thing in question, even if it does not
have the ability to do it. However, if something is able to do something, then
it is possible that it does it in this sense, and so it has the capacity to do it. So,
in the sense of *possibility* I want for capacity, ability to do entails possibility
and hence capacity, but capacity and its associated sense of *possibility* do not
entail ability. More is required for ability than capacity: I have the capacity to
speak Chinese, and it is possible that I speak it in the corresponding sense of
possibility, since if I were to have the opportunity to study it and were to invest
the necessary resources in studying it, I would be able to speak it. But I am

not able to speak it as things are. If it is now possible that I am able to speak Chinese in a few years' time, say, then I have the capacity to speak Chinese.

The sense of *possibility* needed for capacity as I intend it obeys the S4 rule that possible possibility entails possibility.[7] (This rule is common to the modal logics S4 and S5. If the modality in question were an S5 modality, we could add that possibility of doing implies necessary possibility of doing as well; the accessibility relation is transitive in S4, both transitive and symmetric in S5. It will be important in what follows not to conflate these features of the accessibility relations of certain standard semantics for modal operators with corresponding features of the intelligibility relation itself.) Because ability to do x entails possibility that x is done (but not vice versa in the sense of *possibility* required for capacity), possible ability to do x entails possible possibility that x is done, which entails possibility that x is done (given the S4 rule), which entails capacity, though not ability.[8]

Intelligibility as I used it to characterize a kind of relativism inherits these properties of *capacity*. One group of minds is intelligible to another if and only if the latter has the capacity to understand the former. If it is possible that the latter acquire the ability to understand the former, even though it does not currently have the ability, then it has the capacity to understand the former. (Note that I am not claiming at *this* point that intelligibility *per se* obeys the modal reduction rule, so that the intelligibility of intelligibility would amount to intelligibility, or the possibility that a understands the possibility that b understands c would amount to the possibility that a understands c. It is rather that the component modality of intelligibility does so, in the manner of *capacity*: the possible possibility that someone understands amounts to the possibility that he understands. More on the relation between these two claims follows.) Mere lack of ability to understand, as opposed to lack of capacity to understand, would not serve to characterize an interesting sense of relativism; it is simply obvious that many groups are not able to understand one another, just as it is obvious that I am not able to speak Chinese. The fact that we are unable to understand a certain group unless, for example, we learn a new language, but reasonably do not wish to invest the time or resources necessary to do so, hardly gives rise to an interesting or controversial relativism.

It is not obvious how limits could be placed on the *cost* of acquiring the ability to understand by the notion of capacity; one group may sensibly and correctly decline to invest the resources needed to acquire the ability to understand another without losing the capacity to understand the other. Moreover, the notion of capacity does not seem to require that the possibility of acquiring the possibility of understanding be under the *voluntary control* of members of a group of minds; in certain cases of capacity it may depend on various natural or social contingencies (including perhaps Wittgenstein's "very general facts of nature"). For example, it may be possible that members of a group of minds discover methods of artificially sensing energy patterns that members of another group of minds perceive directly, such that if they did discover and develop these methods, they would be able to understand the other group. It may not be under the voluntary control of the first group whether or not they discover these methods, even if they try to do so. But so long as it is possible that they discover the methods, it cannot be said, in the 'in principle' sense relevant to the characterization of relativism, that the first group lacks the capacity to understand the second, or that the second group is fundamentally unintelligible to the first. Bad luck with respect to such a contingency does not make for unintelligibility in principle in a sense that would characterize an interesting or controversial relativism; it is simply obvious that bad luck with respect to various contingencies may preempt ability to understand. At present I see no principled way of distinguishing among such contingencies with respect to the claim in question so as to avoid its trivialization.

Does this mean it may be possible that the first group acquires the ability to understand the second merely by persisting, so to speak: merely by waiting for evolution to take its course and gradually bestow upon members of it the ability to understand? The opposite danger of trivialization may lurk if we have to regard ourselves as intelligible to all our evolutionary ancestors. To get an interesting sense of relativism, we need a sense of intelligibility that is neither too demanding (for example, by requiring ability instead of capacity), so that the denial of intelligibility becomes trivially true too close to home, nor too undemanding, so that it becomes trivially false too far from home. The background condition for present purposes that avoids the latter danger, however, is that we are concerned with intelligibility to groups *of minds*: we could not be intelligible to single-celled creatures or embryos, which are not minded at all. Whether we are intelligible to higher animals is left an open question by our stipulations, as it should be; it turns on whether they are minded and on whether a path of possibilities of understanding exists from them to us (which may be an *a posteriori* question).[9]

The notion of intelligibility may seem to have overtones of epistemic possibility, which involve doctrines that rely on it in charges of verificationism. We can, however, disown these overtones. The possibility of understanding a group as minded is not the epistemic possibility that they are minded; it is not a possibility that they are minded, *for all we know*. Rather, it is a *metaphysical possibility that* they be understood by us; we may not know that it is possible that we understand them, or we may falsely or irrationally or self-servingly believe it is not possible. Metaphysically, intelligibility may not be independent of mindedness—may not be independent, that is, of the mindedness of understand*ers*, as in the previous paragraph but one, or of the mindedness of the under*stood*, as in this paragraph.

2. THE IMPORTANCE OF WHY THE "WE" DISAPPEARS

Suppose one wanted to deny the claim I began by drawing attention to, which can be referred to as *the strong claim*. That is, one wanted to deny that it is possible that there are groups of minds such that each group is unintelligible to the other; that is, such that each group lacks the capacity to understand the other; that is, such that it is not possible that either group acquires the ability to understand the other. It would follow from this denial that for any pair of groups of minds, at least one of the pair must have the capacity to understand the other; I will sometimes refer to this denial of the strong claim as *the weak counterclaim*. A *weaker claim* would merely be that it is possible that there are groups of minds such that one group is unintelligible to the other; its denial would make the *stronger counterclaim* that any pair of groups of minds must be mutually intelligible. The weak counterclaim I concentrate on is open to the issues about the transitivity of intelligibility, which I discuss below, suggested by an argument of Mark Johnston. The strong counterclaim raises issues about the symmetry of intelligibility as well. I will return to this below. Again, the *understanding* that is in question is understanding that the others have minds in the sense of understanding their concepts, beliefs, desires, etc., not merely in the sense of believing or allowing or supposing that they have minds without understanding them. According to the counterclaims, groups of minds could not be individuated by mutual failure of the intelligibility relation, and there could not in this sense be radical incommensurability of understanding between groups of minds or of conceptual schemes. Making sense could not be relative to conceptual scheme.

For ease of reference, where "—I—" stands for the relation of intelligibility, we have:

Strong claim: $\Diamond \exists x \, \exists y \, (-x I y \,\&\, - y I x)$
Weak counterclaim: $\Box \forall x \, \forall y \, (x I y \lor y I x)$
Weak claim: $\Diamond \exists x \, \exists y \, (-x I y \lor - y I x)$
Strong counterclaim: $\Box \forall x \, \forall y \, (x I y \,\&\, y I x)$.

Donald Davidson quips: "Kuhn is brilliant at saying what things were like before the revolution using—what else?—our post-revolutionary idiom."[10] Someone denying the strong claim could add the opposite point: groups of pre-revolutionary minds had the capacity, though perhaps not the ability, to understand groups of post-revolutionary minds, because it was possible that the former acquire the ability to understand the latter, e.g., by working up to and precipitating a revolution. Thus intelligibility would not fail merely on account of revolutionary shifts of paradigm. Even if the pre-revolutionary group had in fact declined or failed for one reason or another to precipitate the revolution, so long as it was possible that they do so and thereby to acquire new abilities to understand, there would be no lack in principle of capacity to understand and hence no failure of intelligibility.

It might be objected that, given the broad sense I have given to *capacity* and *intelligibility*, it is difficult to see how groups of minds could be individuated. How could one group of minds be different from another in the relevant sense, if even possible evolutionary or other involuntary developments in abilities may serve to unify a group? Perhaps I have trivialized the denial of the strong claim after all by not permitting any contingencies that might affect the abilities to understand possessed by a group of minds to change it into a different group, so long as there is a possible path from one set of abilities to understand to another set. But this, I reply, is precisely part of the substantive point of this denial: there is no principled basis for distinguishing among groups so long as there is such a path. This is just another way of describing an aspect of the view in question: the 'we' disappears, to borrow a phrase from Jonathan Lear,[11] because all groups of minds are part of us, not in the sense that other minds are squeezed into our mould, so to speak, but rather in the sense that *we* are stretched. In defending this substantive point, we have the responsibility of making out a sense of intelligibility that can be used to express the view in question coherently; trying to meet this responsibility is not the same thing as trying to make the substantive claim true by stipulation.

Notice the difference between the use to which I put the notion of the disappearing "we" and that to which Jonathan Lear puts it in discussing Wittgenstein. Lear, pursing a transcendental interpretation of Wittgenstein, considers the relationship between the Kantian "I think" and the Wittgensteinian "we are so minded" and argues that the latter is by itself empty and that there is no empirical explanation of who "we" are. The "(for us)" ultimately cancels out, "for we come to see that being one of 'our' representations is all that there could be to being a representation." "The concept of being minded in any way at all is that of being minded as we are."[12] Lear seems here to be interpreting Wittgenstein as assimilating the notion of being minded to that of being minded as we are, whereas in a sense I am pointing out the possibility of the reverse assimilation, that of being minded as we are, or being intelligible to us as minded, to being minded.

Notice also the way in which the possibility of reversing the direction of assimilation provides a response to some of the points Barry Stroud makes in commenting on Lear's views on Wittgenstein. Stroud asks the important question, "Is there something in the very concern with the 'psychological' itself that forces or even inclines us to ignore or deny the distinction between something's being so and its being thought to be so?" However, in arguing that idealism underwrites the disappearing "we," he seems to assume the same direction of assimilation as does Lear. "If idealism is correct and our ways of thinking 'constitute' the way things are, there will be no difference between examining our ways of thinking and examining the way things are." Why, he asks, should our fear of being imprisoned in our way of thought with no guarantee of its legitimacy dissolve if we found it essential that thought be like our thought? That would still be something on the side of thought, something subjective, not objective. Idealism bridges that gap by holding the things we think about to be constituted by the fulfillment of the conditions of our thinking; legitimation turns on *why* the "we" has disappeared; idealism is the only answer to the problem of legitimacy.[13] If we apply these considerations to the concern with the psychological itself, the relevant gap is between being minded and being intelligible to us as minded. The idealist way of bridging that gap is by assimilating being minded at all to being intelligible to us as minded. Idealism about mindedness gives rise to various problems, both on the merits and as interpretation of Wittgenstein, which I cannot discuss here.[14] But the reverse assimilation, which I am drawing attention to, provides another way of bridging the gap and explaining why the "we" disappears, one which Stroud seems to overlook. (In fact I do not wish to endorse *reversing* the direction of assimilation so much as to deny *both* one-way directions of assimilation in favor of an interdependence claim. I will return to this point in commenting on Thomas Nagel's interpretation of Davidson, below.)

3. SOLIPSISM AND CONCEPTUAL IMPERIALISM

Consider the general group of arguments against solipsistic and Cartesian conceptions of the mind made familiar by Wittgenstein, Strawson, Davidson, and others. Such arguments lead to variants of the view that mindedness cannot be an essentially private matter but rather is in some sense an essentially public and/or social matter. We can express this generic anti-solipsistic type of view by means of *the constitutive claim*: a thing has a mind if and only if it is in principle possible that there is a group of minds to which it is understood as minded; by which I mean, that is, if and only if the thing is in principle intelligible as minded to some possible group of minds with some member not identical to the thing itself. This gives a moderately weak interpretation to the anti-privacy claim, in that the understanding group need not actually exist. Suppose a wolf-child or a Robinson Crusoe happens to be the sole survivor of a nuclear accident. He does not run afoul of the constitutive claim because of his contingent solitude. This interpretation accommodates views to the effect that the target of Wittgenstein's private language argument is not the solitary language user but the essentially private language of the kind put forward by the solipsist, which, necessarily, there is no one else who understands.[15]

Now it is at least not obvious that the denial of solipsism entails the denial of relativism. For similar reasons, the constitutive claim does not entail even the weak counterclaim. The intelligibility of any mind to some possible group of minds is consistent with the failure of all pairs of groups to be characterized by a relation of intelligibility in one direction or the other. Indeed, it is often supposed that such a constitutive claim can happily go along with, if not support, the strong claim I characterized earlier with respect to different groups of minds, and an associated form of relativism; some might interpret Wittgenstein's later work to combine these two positions.[16] With respect to this possible combination of views, it is worth asking whether the conception of mind as public and/or social reflected in the constitutive claim provides a basis for stopping somewhere between one mind and all minds, so that even if there could not be a single essentially isolated mind, there might be isolated groups of minds not in principle intelligible to one another.

I will not be addressing the latter question directly. However, suppose that the sense of *intelligibility* involved in the constitutive claim is the same as that I have been characterizing above, so that the possibility involved in the constitutive claim is metaphysical, not epistemic, and obeys the S4 rule.

Combined with this conception of *intelligibility*, the anti-solipsistic constitutive claim can support the counterclaims by disarming a certain objection to them, the objection from imperialism.

It is sometimes thought that one of the advantages of relativism is toleration of deviance. It may be feared, more specifically, that the counterclaims I have set out may lead to the most profound form of imperialism, to a tendency to dismiss forms of life we cannot understand as not minded at all. Strictly speaking, only the strong counterclaim might have this consequence, since the weaker form could allow that we might be unintelligible to another group of minds, even if they were intelligible to us, or vice versa. Only the strong counterclaim insists that a mutual intelligibility relation holds for all pairs of minds. So we could respond to the objection by insisting on the distinction between the weak and strong counterclaims. But the line of thought I want to indicate would disarm the objection at a more fundamental level, if it succeeds, and does not rely on this distinction.

Consider the anti-solipsistic constitutive claim, that a thing is minded if and only if it is possible that there is a group of minds to which it is understood as minded. If this claim is itself supposed to be necessary, then it entails the following: it is possible that a thing is minded if and only if it is possibly possible that there is a group of minds to which it is understood as minded. Then it is also possible, in the S4 sense, that there is a group of minds to which it is understood as minded, hence, by the constitutive claim, it is minded. We have got from the possibility that a thing is minded, to its being minded.[17]

Because of the way in which intelligibility ties possibility and understanding together and the way in which the constitutive claim ties understanding and having a mind together, the possibility of there being a group of understanding minds as a separate condition seems to fall out. Far from intolerantly or imperialistically ruling out too many possible forms of mental life as not minded at all, this position permits great liberality with respect to mindedness: all possible minds are minds. Given the constitutive claim and S4, however, the possibility of there being a group of minds to which a thing is understood as minded is involved in the determination of what counts as a *possible* mind to begin with—as well as what counts as a mind. Since the sense of possibility involved in the notion of intelligibility and the constitutive claim is not epistemic, the degree of liberality of the position with respect to mindedness will depend on the account given of the metaphysical possibility in question and in particular the metaphysical possibility of understanding. I cannot here try to give a general account of metaphysical possibility, but I have tried, above, to motivate liberalism with respect to the metaphysical possibility of understanding. Given the breadth of intelligibility, then, even given the strong counterclaim, the link between the possibility of being understood as minded and being minded begins to looks less worrying: it always will be possible that there is a group to which another is understood as minded in the relevant capacity sense whenever it is possibly possible. This is a very weak condition:

in virtue of what would it ever be *impossible* that it be possible that there is such a group—impossible, for example, that the group of minds 'we' are in acquires the ability to understand under any conditions—*unless it were just the absence of mind to be understood?* The 'we' disappears given the counterclaims as here made out, not because others are ruled out of existence, but because the 'we' and our capacities to understand (along with everyone else's—but this is redundant!) are accommodating of mental life to its far reaches, well beyond our abilities to verify.[18]

It might be objected, first, that it is precisely because the sense of possibility in question is not epistemic that we should still be worried. Even if no metaphysically possible minds are ruled out by the counterclaims, too many epistemically possible minds may be, and we may not be very good at discerning metaphysical possibilities. However, this is an epistemic worry, not a metaphysical one; the danger here is not one of ontological imperialism about mindedness, but one of making mistakes. But why should even the strong counterclaim have a tendency to encourage such mistakes? We are not told by it that if, as far as we know, they are not minded, then they are not minded. We are rather told that we have the metaphysical capacity to understand them if and only if they are minded. The counterclaims justify no less caution about mistakes with respect to our capacities than about mistakes with respect to their mindedness itself, given the way it links them together.

It might be objected, secondly, that the constitutive claim is in tension with a position that is antirelativistic in the sense that it employs one of the counterclaims and the conception of intelligibility I have described. It might be assumed that the constitutive claim aims to give an account of having a mind that takes intelligibility to be the independent and better understood term, one in terms of which we can verify the presence or absence of mind. But intelligibility as conceived here, at any rate, may in turn depend on the presence or absence of mind, in that mindedness may ultimately determine what it is possible to understand as minded, so that intelligibility cannot function as the independent term in any kind of reduction. There is no necessity that the constitutive view include any reductive or verificationist aspirations or any version of a conception of intelligibility as the independent term in relation to mindedness. It may rather include the view that intelligibility and mindedness are mutually and constitutively interdependent, in the way characterized by the combination of the constitutive view and the conception of intelligibility in question.

4. IDEALISM ABOUT MINDEDNESS AND THE THIRD DOGMA

Here we return to the issue raised above in relation to the interpretations of Wittgenstein by Lear and Stroud. There I suggested that, in considering why the 'we' might disappear, we consider assimilating intelligibility to us as minded to mindedness rather than the other way around; but in fact we need not endorse a one-way assimilation or reduction at all—not in either direction. The notion of the interdependence of intelligibility and mindedness provides the qualification promised above.

Similar issues arise with respect to interpretations of Donald Davidson's views. As I understand him, Thomas Nagel attributes a view of intelligibility as the independent term in relation to reality to Davidson, in arguing against Davidson in chapter 6 of *The View from Nowhere*. Nagel seems to use the term *capacity* in the way that I have stipulated *ability* to be used, when he says that "There are plenty of ordinary human beings who constitutionally lack the capacity to conceive of some of the things that others know about," such as blind and deaf persons.[19] Of course the choice of labels is somewhat arbitrary; I would admit that the blind and deaf lack the *ability* to conceive of colors and sounds respectively, but deny that they lack the *capacity* to do so in any principled sense relevant to my purposes here, even though it may not be within their own powers to achieve such abilities. But of course nothing turns on the choice of labels. Nagel regards Davidson, as well as Wittgenstein, as an idealist, where the common element of various forms of idealism is a "broadly epistemological test of reality."[20] By contrast, I suggest that Davidson's rejection of what he calls the third dogma of empiricism treats mind and world symmetrically; at least there is no *more* reason to regard the rejection as idealist than as realist. In rejecting the third dogma he rejects as ultimately unintelligible the dualism of world, or its immediate reflection in brute experience, waiting to be conceptualized or organized, on the one hand, and conceptual scheme or organizing system, on the other hand. In shorthand, he provides a view of the mind and the world as constitutively interdependent. I have suggested elsewhere that his position is not a kind of idealism or verificationism because it sees the mind as world-laden as much as vice versa. He denies that we understand the notion of truth independently of that of translation, for example, but he also adopts a strong version of externalism about content and includes in his conception of charity, which constitutively constrains interpretation, what he calls "norms of correspondence" as well as "norms of pattern."[21]

We could think of the alternative conception of intelligibility indicated three paragraphs back and adopted here as a particular application of the rejection of the third dogma. That is, we are here considering a rejection of the third dogma as applied to that special aspect of the world, mindedness: if mind and world are inextricably engaged with one another, they do not cease to be when the aspect of the world in question is mind itself. Hence the interdependence of intelligibility and mindedness should not come as a surprise. What keeps this kind of anti-relativist position from being a kind of idealism or anti-realism about mindedness is a parallel kind of externalism about intelligibility: the dependence runs from intelligibility to mindedness as much as vice versa.

5. FROM THE INTRANSITIVITY OF INTELLIGIBILITY TO CONCEPTUAL SCHEMES?

In "The Very Idea of a Conceptual Scheme," Davidson argues that translatability should be taken, not as a criterion of identity for conceptual schemes, but as a condition of languagehood. Failure of translatability cannot tell us that members of another group have a different conceptual scheme, but only that they have not got language at all. To pursue the more general version of this argument, about explanation in terms of meanings, beliefs, and desires: interpretability should be taken, not as a criterion of identity for conceptual scheme-cum-scheme of values, but as a condition of rational mental life. If it is wrong to suppose that uninterpretable forms of life express intentions, beliefs, desires at all, then conceptual relativism is impossible: there is just *the* conceptual scheme, within which rational mental life exists. By the same token, there is no neutral external point of view on the world, or on unconceptualized experience, from which to relativize, from which uninterpretable forms of life can be regarded as nevertheless having an alien conceptual scheme; there is no such neutral content to the general idea of rational mental life. As already mentioned, Davidson rejects the distinctness and mutual independence of conceptual scheme and what it organizes, or, for short, of mind and world. Truth cannot be relative to conceptual scheme if the duality between scheme and reality cannot be sustained. Interpretation of forms of life as minded is possible, when it is, and not radically underdetermined, because it is subject to constitutive constraints, including both substantive and formal norms, which provide the background of agreement that makes disagreement about a common subject matter possible. Other minds must share with us various specific beliefs about the world with which we are both in causal contact, various specific conceptual contents, various specific standards of formal rationality, and various specific values, if they are to have title to rational agency and hence to disagree with other rational agents about some of these matters. (Of course, this cannot mean that if other minds inhabit a very different physical environment from our own—one in which certain very general facts of nature are different, as Wittgenstein puts it—say on another planet, we somehow magically share their beliefs about their physical environment, with which we are not in contact. It is rather that we would, under the right conditions, which may include having perceptual capacities adapted to that different environment, share those beliefs. Davidson cannot charitably be interpreted to be offering us a transcendental deduction of the impossibility of extraterrestrial mental life.) What is more, partial failure of interpretability, Davidson holds, provides no more basis for relativism than does total.[22]

It is sometimes said that this kind of argument against conceptual relativism can be undermined by an appeal to a series of overlapping sets of practices or forms of life, such that each is interpretable by its neighbor, but the interpretability relation fails of transitivity. Recast in my terminology, the issue would be one about the transitivity of the intelligibility relation. Mark Johnston, in lectures, has given a version of this objection to Davidson's position about translatability and conceptual scheme. He argues from premises, the first three of which he takes to express Davidson's own views, to the conclusion that there can be alternative conceptual schemes. I here try to generalize Johnston's argument to make it applicable to issues about the interpretability and intelligibility of forms of life in general, as opposed to translatability and language use in particular, but he would not necessarily endorse this version of it:

1. Suppose conceptual schemes are individuated as held by classes of inter-interpretable forms of mental life. So if there are two forms of mental life that are not inter-interpretable, then alternative conceptual schemes are possible.[23]
2. It is sufficient for a form of life to be a form of mental life that it is in principle interpretable as such by another.
3. Significant, though not complete, overlap in contents of beliefs and desires is a necessary condition for interpretability.
4. Significant, though not complete, overlap in contents of beliefs and desires in the presence of other empirically realizable conditions can be sufficient for interpretability.
5. Now imagine a sequence of forms of mental life such that each successive group's attitude contents substantially overlap with those of its predecessor (the overlap in each case is sufficient for interpretability) and such that there is no overlap in attitude contents between the first and the last groups. For simplicity, let us assume the series has three members, though nothing will turn on this assumption; it could be much longer.
6. Given 3, the first and the last forms of mental life in 5 are not inter-interpretable.
7. Therefore, there can be alternative conceptual schemes.

I think there are some problems with putting the argument this way. First, as mentioned earlier, Davidson cannot charitably be supposed to hold that if other minds inhabit a very different physical environment from our own, we must somehow magically share their beliefs about their physical environment, with which we are not in contact. Rather, the point about overlap in attitudes being a necessary condition for interpretability must be liberalized and conditionalized; it is that either we do or *we would*, under the right conditions, share many beliefs; we are to include the beliefs we *would have were we* in the different environment, with appropriately different perceptual abilities, etc.[24]

Moreover, the above way of putting the argument seems to suppose that attitude contents are determined and identified independently of interpretability. But for Davidson significant overlap in attitude contents is a necessary condition of interpretability not in the sense that, unless the overlap independently holds, interpretation is not possible; rather interpretation determines, constitutively, not epistemically, attitude contents to the extent they are determined and establishes the overlap, as it must, in order to be possible at all. Agreement in attitude is, as it were, transcendentally determined by the possibility of interpretation; it is not simply an independent necessary condition of interpretation. The attitude overlap is not constitutively independent of interpretability; his is a version of what I called above the constitutive view about intelligibility and minded-ness. (Recall that in defending the dependence of intelligibility on mindedness earlier I was not denying the dependence of mindedness on intelligibility, but asserting their *mutual* dependence or *interdependence*, in a version of third-dogma rejection.) As Davidson emphasizes, there is no sharp line between a difference in concept and a difference in belief; we cannot, on his premises, treat relations among beliefs as independent of relations among concepts. So, to reflect Davidson's views on attitudes and interpretability, we would have to rephrase the argument, in particular the third and fourth premises, in terms of a series of overlapping relations of interpretability (or, to shift to my terms, intelligibility) to begin with rather than inferring the latter from an overlapping series of attitude contents. Otherwise, at any rate, the argument will not be one from premises that express Davidson's views on attitudes and interpretability.

In "On the Very Idea of a Conceptual Scheme," Davidson responds to the idea of an intransitive series of interpretability relations (though not to Johnston's objection in particular) by questioning the supposition that the relation holds between members of the second and third groups in the series (let us assume we are part of the first form of life). The supposition that a member of the second form of life tells us so would merely raise the question of whether we had correctly interpreted him. That is, our interpretation of "interpretation" for the second form of life as indeed meaning *interpretation* may be brought into doubt if it is not possible that we interpret the third form of life. A parallel question would arise about our interpretation of any non-linguistic 'interpretation'-behavior of the second form of life. This response seems to go along with the conception of interpretability as an intransitive relation, rather than the transitive ancestral[25] of such a relation. The result is, in the imagined case, to restrict the interpretability relation.

6. CAPACITY AND THE TRANSITIVITY OF INTELLIGIBILITY: MORE ON WHY THE "WE" DISAPPEARS

But rather than restricting the interpretability relation by bringing into doubt the assumption that it is possible that the members of the second form of life interpret the members of the third, let us grant that assumption for the sake of argument and try another way of responding, which employs a *capacity*-notion rather than an *ability*-notion. Consider what the relationship may be between (1) the transitivity or otherwise of the interpretability relation itself and (2) the points made earlier about the way in which the component modality of intelligibility obeys the S4 reduction rule. Of course we should not confuse (1) with (2), but it may be possible to argue explicitly for (1) from (2). Let us ask: could it really not be possible that members of the first group interpret members of the third if we assume it is possible that they interpret members of the second and that it is possible that members of the second interpret the members of the third?

At the risk of possible distortion, let us cease to distinguish between interpretability and intelligibility; any results we achieve must be thus qualified and should not be regarded as interpretation of Davidson's position but rather as related speculation. Recall the S4 logic of the component modality of *capacity* and *intelligibility*: if it is possibly possible to understand, then it is possible, in the sense of *capacity*, to understand; possible intelligibility is intelligibility. We may thus have the capacity to understand though we lack the ability. The question becomes: what is the relationship between this point about the component modality of the concept of intelligibility, and the transitivity or otherwise of the intelligibility relation itself? We evidently cannot just help ourselves to the transitivity of intelligibility itself on the basis of the point about the component modality. But how does the possibility that the first group understands the second group, including the latter's possibility of understanding the third, bear on the possible possibility, hence the possibility, that the first group understands the third? If we could argue that the intelligibility to the first group of the intelligibility of the third group to the second itself makes for the possible intelligibility of the third group to the first, then we will have secured the transitivity of the intelligibility relation. Cashed out, this issue is: could it be possible that a group of minds understands that it is possible that a second group understands the third group, without it being possibly possible that the first group understands the third group? To ask this is to return, in effect, to a version of one of the questions from Wittgenstein I raised at the beginning of this essay: what is the relationship between the intelligibility of the formation of concepts different from ours and the intelligibility of the group that uses those concepts?

Either the second group actually does understand the third, or it is possible that they understand the third but they do not in fact. Consider the case in which it is not only possible that the second group understands the third, but it actually does; then it has beliefs about the third group's beliefs, desires, concepts, etc. Thus, the whole set of the beliefs of the second, which *ex hypothesi* it is possible that the first largely understands, includes beliefs about the beliefs, desires, concepts of the third.

The first critical step in the needed argument is this: If it is possible that the first largely understands the beliefs of the second, which include beliefs about the beliefs, etc. of the third, then surely it is at least possibly possible that the first understands the beliefs of the second about the beliefs, etc., of the third, even if the first lacks the present ability to do so. The holism of propositional attitudes supports the assumption that any member of a set of beliefs, which it is possible that the first largely understands, is itself such that it is possibly possible that the first understands it. The web of inferential relations among all the attitudes in the set of the attitudes of the second group suggests that if, for example, it is possible that the first group acquires further inferential abilities, which seems a plausible assumption, then it may be possibly possible that they understand the beliefs of the second group about the beliefs of the third. Or perhaps additional information about the world would be needed as well as further inferential abilities.

For example, possible technological developments might provide the first group with new information about the world which might be accessible to the second group perceptually and which provides the second group with the ability to understand the third group, an ability the first group as it is lacks. Given the inferential web formed by the propositional attitudes of the second group, possession of the new information might provide the first group with the inferential ability to understand the beliefs of the second about the beliefs of the third that they previously lacked the ability to understand. Imagine a color-blind Edwin Land discovering, as the color-sighted Land did, a device that can accurately predict judgments by the color-sighted of the phenomenal color of patches of variously colored surface areas under varying lighting conditions by running over these surfaces and computing the relative lightness of the patches in long, medium, and short wavelengths. Color-blind art students could then use the new understanding this technique gave them to work their way into understanding the attitudes of color-sighted art historians about the attitudes of a third group, impressionist painters, as expressed in exchanges among painters of the period, etc., which the students were previously unable to understand. (Recall that I am working with a sense of understanding that falls short of understanding of everything it is *like* to have a belief such as a color belief.)

If possible possibility entails possibility, then it follows from this first step that it is possible that the first understands the beliefs of the second about the beliefs, etc., of the third. It would not follow from this first step of the argument that it is possible that the first group understands all members of a set of beliefs it is possible that they largely understand, since claims of the form "it is possible for all x that ... " do not follow from claims of the form "for any x, it is possible that.... " (This is worth noting, since it would beg the question against the Johnston-derived argument at issue to make the stronger assumption.) But now we may ask, as the second step of our argument: how could it be possible that the first understands the beliefs of the second about the beliefs, etc., of the third without it *eo ipso* being possibly possible—with similar reference to the right, including counterfactual, conditions—that the first understands the beliefs, etc., of the third? Recall that we are assuming at this point that the second group actually does understand the third, so the possibility of radical error, even if it were otherwise admissible, is not relevant here. It is hard to see what else the possibility of the first group's understanding of the beliefs of the second about the beliefs, etc., of the third could consist in. Thus, if the second group actually does understand the third, then the possibility of the first group's understanding of the second does support the possible possibility of the first's understanding the third, hence the possibility of the first's understanding the third.

But what if it is not the case that the second group actually does understand the third, but merely the case that it is possible that they understand? That, after all, is all we are entitled to assume, since we are concerned with whether the possible understanding of *possible* understanding of *x* amounts to possible understanding of *x*, not merely with whether the possible understanding of understanding of *x* amounts to understanding of *x*. If the second group does not actually have beliefs about the beliefs, etc., of the third, it would seem that we cannot use the argument of the preceding paragraph. But perhaps we can use a kind of conditionalized version of the preceding argument that appeals to the role of possible beliefs in different possible circumstances in understanding. If it is possible that the second understands the third, then the second *would* have beliefs about the beliefs, etc., of the third under some possible conditions even if the second does not, as things stand at present, understand the third. If it is possible that the first understands the second, then it is possible, given what has already been said about different possible circumstances (above and in note 24 below), for the first largely to understand a set of attitudes that includes not just the actual beliefs of the second, but also what the second would believe under a variety of possible conditions. That is, there is no reason to exclude from the set of beliefs and possible beliefs of the second that, *ex hypothesi*, it is possible that the first largely understands, the subset of possible beliefs of the second about the beliefs, etc., of the third group.

Now repeat the first step of the previous argument, which depended on the possibility of the first group obtaining further inferential abilities or new information which connected inferentially with their prior understanding of the second group: any member of the whole set of the beliefs and possible beliefs of the second, which *ex hypothesi* it is possible that the first largely understands, is something that it is similarly reasonable to assume that it is possibly possible that the first group understands, even if they lack the present ability to do so. It follows that it is possibly possible that the first group understands the possible beliefs of the second about the third's beliefs, etc., or what the second would believe about the beliefs, etc., of the third under certain possible conditions. Hence it is possible that the first understands what the second would believe about the beliefs, etc., of the third, under certain possible conditions.

But, again, the second step goes, how could it be possible that the first understands what the second would believe about the beliefs, etc., of the third, under certain possible conditions, without it being possibly possible—with similar reference to the right, including counterfactual conditions—for the first to understand the beliefs, etc., of the third? Again, it is hard to see what else the possibility of the first group's understanding of what the second group would believe, under certain possible conditions, about the beliefs, etc., of the third might consist in. So, even if the second group does not actually understand the beliefs, etc., of the third, but only would do so under certain possible conditions, it seems that the possibility of the first group's understanding of the second again supports the possible possibility of the first group's understanding the third, hence the possibility of the first group's understanding of the third.

Very schematically, the structure of the argument looks like this (where "$\Diamond 1U2_3$" reads "it is possible that the first group understands the beliefs of the second group about the third"):

step 1: $\Diamond 1U2$ & $\Diamond 2U3 \longrightarrow \Diamond \Diamond 1U2_3$, $\Diamond 1U2_3$;

step 2: $\Diamond 1U2_3 \longrightarrow \Diamond \Diamond 1U3$, $\Diamond 1U3$.

The route has been tortuous, but in fact it does seem plausible in the end to go from possible understanding of possible understanding to possibly possible understanding, hence to possible understanding. Given what it is to understand, the way in which understanding itself involves possibility, and the holism of the mental, we can use the noted features of the sense of *possibility* that provides a component of the notion of intelligibility, or possible understanding, to support the transitivity of the intelligibility relation. (Intelligibility, on this reading, is properly taken to be the ancestral of the connectedness relation it is in effect taken for in the Johnston-derived argument.)

This response to Johnston's objection reiterates the expansive, as opposed to restrictive, interpretation of the disappearing 'we', suggested above in connection with the interpretation of Wittgenstein. It is not inconsistent with Davidson's response, but indeed could form part of a dilemma rebuttal to the objection. Either it is right to suppose it is possible that the second group understands the third, in which case my argument applies, or it is not, as Davidson suggests. But, by allowing that the intelligibility, or interpretability, relation is transitive, we disarm objections to the effect that the disappearing 'we' claim is unattractively conservative and/or imperialistic. On the present reading of intelligibility, just the opposite is the case: we are held *capable* of understanding a great deal more than we may actually understand or be able to understand, hence capable of communicating, disagreeing, and deliberating with members of a much wider range of forms of life than those with whom we may at present be able to communicate, disagree, and deliberate. When the range of possible understanding for us is taken to include possibly possible understanding, the scope for secure complacency is narrowed and that for challenging self-determination is widened. We can be none too sure of what we are not capable of understanding.

I began by querying the relationship between the intelligibility of the formation of concepts different from the usual ones, when very general facts of nature are different, as Wittgenstein puts it, and the intelligibility of a group of people who use those concepts. I end by suggesting that the distinction will not take too much weight.[26]

Notes

I am indebted to Mark Johnston for many friendly discussions of the topic of this essay, although I think I can safely say that he does not agree with the positions I take. I am also indebted for helpful comments to John Campbell, Gerald Cohen, Ronald Dworkin, Justin Gosling, Derek Parfit, Christopher Peacocke, Joseph Raz, Ralph Walker, and Timothy Williamson. Thanks are also due to the Humanities Council and the Philosophy Department of Princeton University for support of this work in its early stages during my tenure of a visiting research fellowship at Princeton.

1. Conceptual relativism of the kind I have in mind is characterized, for example, by Donald Davidson in "On the Very Idea of a Conceptual Scheme," in *Inquiries into Truth and Interpretation* (Oxford, 1984), 183ff: "Conceptual schemes, we are told, are ways of organizing experience. . . . There may be no translating from one scheme to another, in which case the beliefs, desires, hopes and bits of knowledge that characterize one person have no true counterparts for the subscriber to another scheme. Reality itself is relative to a scheme: what counts as real in one system may not in another."

2. Ludwig Wittgenstein, *Philosophical Investigations*, translated by G. E. M. Anscombe, (Oxford, 1958), 233.

3. Wittgenstein, *Philosophical Investigations*, p. 230.

4. For a discussion of Wittgenstein that touches on this point, see Barry Stroud, "Wittgenstein and Logical Necessity," in *Wittgenstein: The Philosophical Investigations*, edited by George Pitcher (New York, 1966). See also Barry Stroud's criticism of Jonathan Lear in "The Allure of Idealism," *Proceedings of the Aristotelian Society* supplementary volume 58 (1984): 243–58, at p. 255. Lear interprets Wittgenstein to show that there is no concept of being other-minded; Stroud interprets Wittgenstein to acknowledge such a concept.

5. For a discussion of Wittgenstein that touches on this question, see Thomas Nagel, *The View from Nowhere* (New York, 1986), 105–109. I will return to Nagel's views on Wittgenstein and on Davidson below.

6. Compare Georg Henrick von Wright, *Norm and Action: A Logical Inquiry* (London, 1963), 50.

7. See, e.g., G. E. Hughes and M. J. Cresswell, *An Introduction to Modal Logic* (London, 1968).

8. A natural sense of responsibility in certain cases is tracked by the notion of capacity rather than that of ability (though I do not suggest the notion of responsibility applies wherever that of capacity does). For example, I may be responsible for driving safely when I have the capacity but not the ability to drive safely: I may not be able to drive safely because I am not wearing my sun glasses, it is a very bright day, and my eyes are very sensitive to bright light; but I have the capacity to drive safely because it is possible (though perhaps inconvenient) that I acquire the ability to drive safely by stopping, finding my glasses or buying a new pair, and putting them on.

9. Perhaps in some cases the development by some members of a group of a capacity to understand some other group into an ability to understand the other group will involve the loss of the members' previous ability to understand the first or 'home' group. It would not follow that their capacity to understand their home group was lost. But it might be the case that while they had the capacity to understand each group, they did not have the capacity to understand both together, because the abilities were somehow incompatible. This branching-path possibility is one I do not address in this essay.

10. See Donald Davidson, "On the Very Idea of a Conceptual Scheme," in *Inquiries into Truth and Interpretation.*

11. See Jonathan Lear, "The Disappearing 'We'," *Proceedings of the Aristotelian Society*, supplementary volume 58 (1984): 219–42.

12. Ibid., 229, 232–33.

13. See Barry Stroud, "Allure of Idealism," 244, 248, 250, 256–57.

14. For a discussion of some of them, see Paul A. Boghossian, "The Rule-Following Considerations," *Mind* 98 (1989): 507–49, at p. 547. See also Nagel, *View from Nowhere*, 26, and of course Stroud, "Allure of Idealism."

15. See and compare G. P. Baker and P. M. S. Hacker, *Wittgenstein: Rules, Grammar and Necessity* (Oxford, 1985), 171–79; G. P. Baker and P. M. S. Hacker, *Scepticism, Rules and Language* (Oxford, 1984), 41ff, 78, 80; Colin McGinn, *Wittgenstein on Meaning* (Oxford,

1984), 191ff; on a related point, see the crucial footnote on p. 99 of P. F. Strawson's *Individuals* (London, 1959).

16. For a possible example, see Thomas Nagel, *View from Nowhere*, 105-106.

17. Here I am indebted to suggestions made by Timothy Williamson, though in a different context; I do not suggest he would agree with the arguments I make here.

Here is the inference spelled out for an arbitrary a, where 'M' stands for '. . . is minded'; 'G' stands for '. . . is a group of minds such that there is at least one mind in this group not identical to a', and U stands for '. . . understands . . . '. I do not represent the logical structure within the predicate 'G' because it does not affect the inference.

(1) $\Box(Ma \longleftrightarrow \Diamond \exists x(Gx \;\&\; xUa))$

(2) $\Diamond Ma \longleftrightarrow \Diamond \Diamond \exists x(Gx \;\&\; xUa)$

To prove (1) entails (2), first show (1) contradicts (3), then show (1) contradicts (4).

(3) $-(\Diamond Ma \longrightarrow \Diamond \Diamond \exists x(Gx \;\&\; xUa))$
(4) $-(\Diamond \Diamond \exists x(Gx \;\&\; xUa) \longrightarrow \Diamond Ma)$

Contradiction between (1) and (3):

from (3): $\Diamond Ma \;\&\; \Box \Box \forall x(-Gx \;\vee\; -xUa)$

In world 1, we have:

from (3): Ma
from (1): $Ma \longrightarrow \Diamond \exists x(Gx \;\&\; xUa)$
                 $\Diamond \exists x(Gx \;\&\; xUa)$
from (3): $\Box \forall x(-Gx \;\vee\; -xUa)$

In world 2, we have:

from world 1: $\exists x(Gx \;\&\; xUa)$
                        $Gk \;\&\; kUa$
from world 1: $\forall x(-Gx \;\vee\; -xUa)$
                        $-Gk \;\vee\; -kUa$

Contradiction between (1) and (4):

from (4): $\Diamond \Diamond \exists x(Gx \;\&\; xUa) \;\&\; \Box -Ma$

In world 3, we have:

from (4): $-Ma$
from (1): $Ma \longleftrightarrow \Diamond \exists x(Gx \;\&\; xUa)$
                 $-\Diamond \exists x(Gx \;\&\; xUa)$
                 $\Box \forall x(-Gx \;\vee\; -xUa)$
from (4): $\Diamond \exists x(Gx \;\&\; xUa)$

In world 4, we have:

from world 3: $\exists x(Gx \;\&\; xUa)$
                        $Gj \;\&\; jUa$
from world 3: $\forall x(-Gx \;\vee\; -xUa)$
                        $-Gj \;\vee\; -jUa$

The above shows that (1) entails (2). Then from (2) and $\Diamond Ma$, we can derive:

$\Diamond \Diamond \exists x(Gx \;\&\; xUa)$

and via S4 this entails:

$\Diamond \exists x(Gx \;\&\; xUa)$

which, given (1), entails:

Ma.

18. Compare Bernard Williams's on a related view of Wittgenstein's: "If they are groups with which we are in the universe, and we can understand that fact (namely, that they are groups with a language, etc.), then they also belong to 'we'" (*Moral Luck* [Cambridge, 1981], 160). Compare also Jonathan Lear, "The Disappearing 'We'," and Barry Stroud, "The Allure of Idealism." I seem here to be advocating a version of what Thomas Nagel describes as a 'desperate measure' in his discussion of Wittgenstein in *View from Nowhere*, 105–106.

19. Thomas Nagel, *View from Nowhere*, 95; see also 24.

20. Ibid., 91.

21. See Donald Davidson in "A New Basis for Decision Theory," *Theory and Decision* 18 (1985): 87–98, at p. 92. For elaboration see my *Natural Reasons* (New York, 1989), Part I, esp. chapter 5 section 4; I offer a related interpretation of Wittgenstein.

22. See various essays in his *Inquiries into Truth and Interpretation*, and also in his *Essays on Actions and Events* (Oxford, 1982).

23. Note that the antecedent of this conditional seems to characterize what I am calling the weak claim, which asserts merely the possibility of one-way failures of intelligibility, rather than of the mutual failures alleged by the strong claim. The weak claim rules out the strong counterclaim, which requires intelligibility to be symmetric. But since the weak claim does not entail the strong claim, it does not rule out the weak counterclaim, which has merely to resist the kind of intransitivity Johnston claims, not to defend symmetry as well; symmetry could fail while transitivity holds. Since transitivity rather than symmetry is at issue in the Johnston-derived argument, we should here focus on defending the weak counterclaim against Johnston's argument and abstract from the further symmetry issue with respect to mutual intelligibility raised by the strong counterclaim.

24. See also David Lewis, "Radical Interpretation," in his *Philosophical Papers, Volume 1* (New York, 1983), 112. Lewis explains that a principle of charity constrains the relationship between the agent as a physical system (described in terms of bodily movements and the like, not yet in terms of his intentional actions) and the attitudes we ascribe to him: he "should be represented as believing what he ought to believe, and desiring what he ought to desire. And what is that? In our opinion, he ought to believe what we believe, or perhaps *what we would have believed in his place*; and he ought to desire what we desire, or perhaps *what we would have desired in his place*. (But that's only our opinion! Yes. Better we should go by an opinion we don't hold?)" [My emphasis.]

25. For an informal account of the notion of an ancestral relation, see John Perry, "The Problem of Personal Identity," 3–30, in *Personal Identity*, edited by J. Perry (Berkeley, 1975), at p. 17.

26. I have not addressed issues about whether either the accessibility relation for the component modality of possible understanding or the intelligibility relation itself is symmetric; transitivity without symmetry is not ruled out. That is, I have not addressed the difference between the weak and strong claims; I have attacked the latter, and *eo ipso* defended the weak counterclaim, but have not tried to attack the weak claim or defend the strong counterclaim. Nor, as noted earlier, have I considered the possibility that makes trouble for appeals to ancestral relations in accounts of personal identity, namely, intransitivities based on branching paths. In responding to the Johnston-derived argument, I have merely argued that iterated overlapping local differences do not, at least on one plausibly motivated understanding of the modality of intelligibility, add up to a difference in conceptual scheme.

Wittgenstein on Understanding

WARREN GOLDFARB

Wittgenstein's treatments in the *Philosophical Investigations* of the cognitive or intentional mental notions are evidently meant to persuade us that, in some sense, understanding, believing, remembering, thinking, and the like are not particular or definite states or processes; or (if this is to say anything different) that there are no particular states or processes that constitute the understanding, remembering, etc. Such a dark point desperately needs clarification, if it is not to deny the undeniable. For surely we may (and Wittgenstein does) speak of a *state* of understanding, or of thought-*processes*; surely when one understands—understands a word, a sentence, or the principle of a series—one is in a particular state, namely, the state of understanding the word, sentence, or principle. Now Wittgenstein sometimes puts the point more specifically, speaking of "a state of a mental apparatus" (§149), or, with respect to understanding, of "a state which is the *source* of the correct use" (§146), as that which he wishes to deny. But clearly these denials, though they sound somewhat less paradoxical, are equally in need of elaboration.

However Wittgenstein's point is clarified, though, there is an objection that will inevitably be made, an objection claimed to arise from a scientific viewpoint. The objection asks: isn't Wittgenstein here usurping the place of empirical inquiry? Is it not possible that empirical science—neurophysiology, in particular—will find specific states and processes that will fill the bill, as far as understanding, believing, remembering, etc. are concerned? And so, whether or not there are definite states or processes of understanding is something that we will discover. That there are such can certainly be entertained as a scientific, empirical hypothesis, and its consequences discussed. To preclude such an outcome *now* is just to claim that we shall never obtain certain sorts of results in future neurophysiology. But then Wittgenstein is simply making a bet on the future course of science or else he is engaged in a priori anti-science, denying a priori that certain projects could bring results, and hence they ought not even be investigated empirically.

For brevity I shall call this objection, that Wittgenstein is simply ruling out something that science could discover, the "scientific objection." I mean it to be narrowly based on envisaged possibilities of results in neuroscience and thus *not* to be the charge that Wittgenstein fails to leave room for the discoveries of psychology, or cognitive science, or psycholinguistics, or some as yet unknown science of the mind. The latter charge has been made frequently since the publication of the *Investigations*, but it is not so much an objection to a specific point of Wittgenstein's as a denial of all of Wittgenstein's philosophy of mind. Much in the *Investigations* is devoted to exposing the conceptual confusions that would be involved in a "science of the mind"; in any case, any such science would *presuppose* just the picture of mental states or processes and the whole notion of a mental apparatus that Wittgenstein is concerned to undercut. In contrast, the scientific objection as I am imagining it exploits the unarguable status as empirical science of neurophysiology and the independence from psychology of the conceptions of state and process that it employs. Consequently, the objection requires detailed attention to what Wittgenstein is saying or denying about intentional notions, and so can function to elicit clarification of Wittgenstein's dark point about states or processes.

The scientific objection is, it seems to me, a most natural one, and for that reason powerful. And it puts Wittgenstein in a poor (and stereotypical) light: as a philosopher, making ungrounded empirical claims or, worse yet, a philosopher trying a priori to deny the progress of science, like a late Scholastic refusing to grant the coherence of the Copernican conception or an Idealist "proving" the impossibility of Einsteinian physics. Indeed, the charge that Wittgenstein is ruling out certain empirical possibilities a priori is doubly damaging against a philosopher whose major concern is to fight against a priorism, to demolish pictures of how things must be, to expose "preconceived ideas to which reality *must* correspond" (§131).

A common view of Wittgenstein takes his response to such an objection to proceed by noting that a physiological state would be "hidden"; it would not reflect central conceptual features of our notion of understanding (or believing, thinking, etc.). No such state would have conceptual links to correct responses and the other criteria of understanding; but the transparency of those links is essential to our concept of understanding. In short, the point is that no physiological state has the "grammar" of understanding. Hence, Wittgenstein is taken to urge, understanding cannot be conceptually constituted by any such state.

Although there are passages in the *Investigations* that suggest this response, to my mind it fails to capture Wittgenstein's thought. The response requires a general and sharp distinction between conceptual and empirical, between criterion and result of investigation. Wittgenstein does not have the resources to make this distinction; in fact, the distinction is of a piece with the a priorism that he wishes to attack (see §79, last paragraph). That is, the response requires a form of essentialism which I do not believe Wittgenstein accepts.

Moreover, the response leaves it open that understanding, although not "conceptually" constituted by a neural state, might be "empirically" constituted by one.[1] This underreads Wittgenstein's conclusion. Thus the suggested response does too little. Yet it is not totally off the mark, for Wittgenstein does think that the identification of any state of understanding would have to bear some conceptual burden. His conclusion will be that, in some sense, "nothing is hidden." But this is meant to result from detailed considerations of the notion of understanding, not to be assumed more or less as a premise, as an unargued feature of his methodology.

The notion that Wittgenstein dismisses or ignores questions of "empirical" identity also reinforces the view of him as simply anti-scientific. Now we do know that Wittgenstein was distrustful of the claims of science and its role in contemporary culture. He makes this quite explicit when he expresses his opposition to "the spirit of the age" in the Foreword to the *Philosophical Remarks*, and the theme is repeated elsewhere in his work, both early and late. Some have gone on to ascribe to him a hostility to or belittling of projects aimed at scientific explanation, of such proportions as to depict him as simply dogmatic and blinkered. Bernard Williams, for example, complains that Wittgenstein's general practice and teaching serve to "stun, rather than assist, further and more systematic explanation," and offers as illustration a story about Wittgenstein used by Georg Kreisel in 1960 as evidence for Wittgenstein's hostility to legitimate scientific explanation.[2] The story bears repeating. Imagine a child, learning that the earth is round, asking why then people in Australia don't fall off. I suppose one natural response would be to start to explain about gravity. Wittgenstein, instead, would draw a circle with a stick figure atop it, turn it upside down, and say "Now *we* fall into space."

Now I myself do not find the story emblematic of an attitude against science, or of a desire to "stun'" further explanation. In fact, I think it shows Wittgenstein being highly insightful. For he is examining the source of the child's question, in the concepts with which the child is operating. Given those concepts, an appeal to gravity can do nothing but mislead: the child will take it that the antipodal people are upside down, but they have gravity shoes, or glue, or something similar, that keeps them attached to the surface of the earth; as for us, we are right side up, so the problem does not arise. What Wittgenstein's trick does is precisely to expose the conceptual confusion in the way the child is thinking of up and down (cf. §351). Once the child sees the relativity in the notions of up and down, she may then go on to ask, "Well, why don't all these objects—us, the Australians, and the earth—go careening around independently?" or perhaps, "Then why do objects fall down rather than up?" At that point, explaining gravity might well be in order; the child is now prepared to appreciate it correctly.

The lesson, of course, is general. It is central to Wittgenstein's teaching that the conceptual underpinnings to a felt need for explanation must be scrutinized, for what it is, exactly, that wants explanation may only become clear through such an investigation. This does not make him anti-scientific.

It does make him anti-scientistic, against the smug and unexamined assurance that what wants explanation is obvious, and that scientific tools are immediately applicable.

For Wittgenstein, it is characteristic of the notions that figure in philosophical problems—prominently, mental concepts and linguistic concepts like meaning—that a structure is imposed on them, without grounding in the ordinary use of these notions and without being noticed, when they are taken to be amenable to certain explanatory projects. (Much work in the *Investigations*, on my view, is precisely devoted to getting us to notice, to see that there is a place at the start of philosophizing, where this imposition happens.[3]) Hence, only through clarification of what the legitimate questions are can proper sense be made of the applicability of science. A scientistic viewpoint ignores this need for clarification. As a result, for Wittgenstein scientism is just as misguidedly metaphysical as traditional, more transparently a prioristic, approaches.

I am depicting Wittgenstein as thinking that conceptual work must be done before the question of the applicability of science should be raised. Now it is also true that whatever empirical, scientific results may legitimately be foreseen or hypothesized after that work is done are of little interest to Wittgenstein. He seems to believe that what is really at issue in a philosophical question will be answered, or dissolved, by the conceptual work, and not touched by science. That is, science is simply not of use in dealing with the sorts of problems with which he is concerned. But this broad characterization can be misleading. Wittgenstein is not being dismissive; he is not urging a distinction between questions of the mind vs. questions of the heart. Nor is he saying that in doing science we are talking about different things; he would have had little patience with Eddington's "two tables" and with Goodman's different worlds (although the latter claim may be thought controversial). Moreover, as I mentioned above, I do not believe that he wishes to rely on a sharp distinction between conceptual and empirical, that is, a Fregean divide between logic and analysis on the one hand and "mere" psychology and physics on the other. Rather, Wittgenstein operates case-by-case. For each philosophical question we treat, we are to tease out what we are aiming for, or what we think we are aiming for, and then to come to see how our objectives will not be served by a scientific investigation; and we are to recognize how the inclination to look to science for answers elides or ignores so much as to suggest that a philosophical picture is at work.

This point is made in §158, the one explicit appearance in the *Investigations* of something like the scientific objection. Here he suggests that, although the objection says that the scientific investigation may come out either way, that it is only a scientific hypothesis or conjecture that such-and-such a process or state will be found, at bottom the objector is being moved by an a priori demand that things *must* turn out a certain way. The claim of a modest empiricism is mere lip service.

With respect to understanding, the point might be phrased thus. Wittgenstein asks us to look in detail at the range of our practices relevant to an ascription of understanding. We find an enormous variety of considerations that can enter, a dependence on context that is impossible to describe accurately by any general rules, a lack of uniformity in mental accompaniments. In individual cases we have stories to tell to justify our ascriptions, but there is no uniform feature that pulls the various cases together. It is just this that can drive us to think there must be some final item behind the phenomena that grounds each ascription, that is what the ascription is an ascription *of*; we feel that without this the ascriptions would be arbitrary (cf. §146). If it is at such a juncture that the scientific objection is voiced—if the objector is saying, even though our ascriptive practices now show no uniform features, "that's only because we have too little acquaintance with what goes on in the brain and the nervous system" (§158)—then the roots of the objection in a priori demands that something unitary and definite must ground the ascription are evident.

If we accept this diagnosis, then the scientific objection is undercut for its attractive empirical stance—its appearance of making only the modest claim that things might turn out either way, we might or we might not discover an appropriate neural state—is seen to be a pretence. The objection thus loses its scientific cachet and, with that, its particularity as an objection. It becomes just a restatement of a picture of what *has* to be there. Wittgenstein's work is meant first and foremost to free us from such pictures. If this is done, it will also free us from the desire to object in this way.

In sum, Wittgenstein's first reaction to the scientific objection is to examine when we are inclined to bring it up and for what particular purpose. And then he asks whether we are sincere in our empiricist stance or rather whether we see a "must" creeping into our language. If so, then what is operative at bottom are a priori demands on the mental notions.

Such demands are the focus of Wittgenstein's investigations of mental concepts. Through his treatment of them we can develop themes concerning the scientific objection that are more general than the reaction or diagnosis just canvassed. If his investigations succeed, we shall lose the idea of the specific particular process or state that is the understanding, along with the idea that we need such a thing. But then the question will arise of what the progress of science was supposed to have provided, according to the objection. That is, Wittgenstein's investigations are to have the effect of making entirely obscure what could be scientifically discoverable that would *be* the mental state-or-process of understanding—since, if you will, there is nothing for it to be; there is no role for it to play.

In Wittgenstein's considerations, I see two predominant strands, perhaps separated only at the cost of some distortion. The first concerns how the state is conceived to operate. The idea under scrutiny is that the state of understanding is the source from which flow the manifestations of understanding; Wittgenstein asks whether we have any conception of the "flowing from," any conception of what we are asking of the state when we take it as issuing in, determining, fixing, what counts as a manifestation of the understanding. The second strand concerns the range of things the particular state or process is supposed to do. Here the strategy involves examining the topography of understanding and manifestations of understanding in varieties of circumstances; it entails the laying out of particular cases which is part of what Wittgenstein calls a "grammar investigation."

Let me start with the first strand. The definite state of understanding that Wittgenstein wants to deny is meant to be the state that, in and of itself, in some way determines everything that counts as a manifestation of that understanding. Wittgenstein argues that this notion is confused. It is based on a misconstrual of the models we have, in which samples, pictures, formulas, standards, and so on, can issue in or determine or fix the characterizations of items.

In order to pass from "disguised nonsense to . . . patent nonsense" (§464), an example less abstract than understanding might be helpful. I shall present one from cognitive science which illustrates Wittgenstein's point vividly. Several years ago I was intrigued to read a newspaper item with the headline "Mental Tuning Forks Noted in Perfect Pitch."[4] It began:

> New evidence has been found that people with perfect pitch, the ability to recognize a note that they hear without having the identifying pitch sounded beforehand, use a special set of mental tuning forks other people lack. The findings suggest that those forks let them distinguish between pitches by recognizing each tone.

I could not tell from this what mental tuning forks were, but that would presumably emerge from the empirical evidence for the claim. The evidence turned out to be as follows. There is a certain brain wave, called P300, which has been claimed to be associated with memory (the researchers also said the P300 was a measure of "brainpower"). Subjects with perfect pitch, when asked to identify the pitches of tones played to them, have a small or absent P300 brain wave, whereas those without perfect pitch had larger P300. The cognitive scientists took this to mean that the latter were reaching into memory "in order to compare what they heard with a remembered standard." The *absence* of P300 in subjects with perfect pitch was the sole evidential basis for the claim of mental tuning forks.

The argument seems to be this. Those who use memory use it for a "remembered standard." Those with perfect pitch do not use memory. Therefore they must have a standard not in memory; thus, mental tuning forks.

Tuning forks! Are they sounding all the time? If so, what a cacophony! How does the subject know which fork's pitch to pick out of the cacophony when confronted with a tone to identify? If they are not always sounding, how does she know which one to sound when confronted with a tone? And if she sounds one, and it is too low, what tells her that it is too low, what gives her instructions as to which fork to sound next? Does she have internal ordered pairs of tuning forks which give her the standards for "higher" and "lower," so that she may compare her tuning forks with the tone she heard? But how does that help since she still has to compare the tone with a member of the ordered pair?

I admit that the expression "mental tuning forks" occurred only in a newspaper article, not in the research report published in the journal *Science*.[5] The latter was more restrained and concluded, "subjects with this skill have access to permanently resident representations of the tones, so they do not need, as the rest of us do, to fetch and compare representations for novel stimuli." "Permanently resident representations" here are the tuning forks of the newspaper article, the standards not in memory. But clearly the same questions arise about such representations, even without the picturesque language.

Real tuning forks give us the means to identify pitches, but they do so because we have the practices and abilities to use them. The internal standard is supposed to give us the means to identify items, but without practices and abilities, for the internal standard is also meant to operate by itself, in a self-sufficient manner. (If it were not, it would be otiose: why not settle for practices and abilities themselves? It hardly adds explanatory value to say, instead of "She can recognize that as middle C," "She has a permanently resident mental tuning fork at middle C and can recognize when a tone is the same as that.") In short, the internal, mental determinant is imagined on the model of external standards, but in the absence of the surroundings that make the standards into standards. This is how the model is misconstrued.

The case of "mental tuning forks," despite its foolishness, is similar to more serious ones. The questions that point out the misconstrual here are congruent to the third-man type arguments Wittgenstein invokes with respect to samples (§74), signposts (§86), mental pictures (§139), and rules (§198). The same move is made in construing understanding: the notion of the self-sufficient state is just the notion of an "internal representation" that legislates all the individual uses. It is just the idea that recognition *must* involve comparison to a standard. Wittgenstein's point is to expose its incoherence.

Here, however, the scientific objector has a retort. Once physical science is in play, causal notions become available. Thus the incoherence can be avoided: what is being imagined as being in principle discoverable is not some confused notion of standard or representation, but a physical state that will *cause* the manifestations of understanding.

Now the notion of cause can seem inapposite at this juncture, that is, as that which will *first* give sense to the determination by the understanding of what counts as a manifestation of the understanding. None of its ordinary (scientific) surroundings are in place (cf. §169). The notion of the standard that legislates the uses, one might think, would have to be given first; only then the scientific or scientifically inclined would urge an empirical investigation to see how this works. Wittgenstein's attack is on this prior notion. For this reason, I think, Wittgenstein tends not to take seriously the idea of using causal notions. His interlocutor at §195 says "I don't mean that what I do now (in grasping something) determines the future use *causally* and as a matter of experience, but that in a *queer* way, the use itself is in some sense present," and Wittgenstein agrees that causal notions are not at issue.

Nonetheless, one might want to examine more closely what the imagined causal location is. Any relation between understanding and manifestation has little of the invariability that a straightforwardly causal relation would entail. I do not produce manifestations of my understanding at all times: I may not want to, I may be bored, I may make a mistake, I may have misheard what you said, I may be making a joke or pulling your leg. Thus any causal story has now to bring in other factors, e.g., my "belief that you asked thus-and-so," my attentiveness, my "desire to manifest my understanding correctly," and so on. In order to establish some hint of lawlike regularity, each of these other factors now must be imagined to be scientifically discovered as distinct, definite particular states, presumably *independently* of the state of understanding. Clearly we have little clue as to how such states will be identified. After all, these factors have been specified so far only in circular fashion, via the assessment of the behavior as a manifestation of correct understanding. The point here is to show how much is glossed over in the retort, how little we have a grasp on what we are meant to be imagining.[6]

Yet another reaction to the objector's recourse to causal relations is grounded on what I called the second strand in Wittgenstein's efforts to undermine the notion of a particular state or process as constituting understanding. That strand concerns the range of practices relevant to ascriptions of understanding. I have been talking, simplistically, of "manifestations of understanding," as if all that were involved were correct uses of the understood word. But in fact a major part of Wittgenstein's considerations are to get us to see the enormous variety of features that play a role in our ascriptions of understanding or lack of understanding, and the dependence of these on particularities of the context in which the ascription is made. There is no short repertoire of behavioral manifestations; there is enormous play in what understanding can be said to come to or not in different circumstances; an ascription of understanding can rely on features of the subject far beyond the immediate manifestations. Different performances are required of new learners and old hands; character traits, mental states—of all kinds, intentional, emotional, and perceptual— and personal history of the subject can be relevant. Special circumstances of considerable intricacy can affect an ascription of understanding. (To use Wittgenstein's well-chosen example on p. 59 of the *Investigations*, think of the cases in which it would be legitimate to speak of an interruption of understanding. More generally, one might reflect on the very different ways in which mistakes can affect ascriptions, for example, of the ways we distinguish between errors arising from carelessness and errors arising from misunderstanding.) In short, the differences that can emerge in circumstances are overwhelmingly complex and inhomogeneous; different cases of understanding may have little in common.

Wittgenstein exploits considerations along these lines in many ways in his general attack. The variegation and lack of uniformity make clear how far any unitary state or process is from what we observe in the cases of understanding, and thus emphasizes the leap made in postulating such a "hidden" state or process. Any of the features that play a role in an ascription of understanding would have to be construed as evidence for this hidden state. But our grasp on the state-evidence model is cast into doubt by the variability of what and when any particular feature functions as evidence. For we lack any conception of how the state is connected to just the particular things that matter in a particular context. If we say that in each particular case there is some particular connection, then all we are saying is that the particular circumstances justify me in my ascription; the *one* state drops out. But what conception can we have of a general connection that issues in such variability? It begins to look as if in each instance the state must include, in some sense of include, something answering to any feature that could possibly arise in any circumstance; this is a notion of internal standard gone wild. It also looks as if the state has to be able to take account of all possible circumstances. But that is not a well-defined totality. In some circumstances, indeed, we might not know how to ascribe understanding; we might just not know what to say.

These are ways, more and less subtle, in which the range and variegation of our practices might be exploited at a stage in the argument when it is still open what the relation of a putative state to the manifestations could be; when, that is, we are still talking of the "as yet uncomprehended process in the yet unexplored medium" (§308). If, however, we return to the scientific objection, with its envisaged brain states and processes and its recourse to physical causation as linking state and manifestation, the upshot of that range and variegation is fairly straightforward. They show that we have little grasp of how to identify what is at issue in the brain. For it becomes hard to see how we could even begin to pick out the jobs that the supposed particular brain state was meant to do, that is, to say what causal role qualifies the state to be the state of understanding. If the objector is saying that we could in principle discover that which biochemically causes us to behave in ways that a person who understands does, to this we can now point out that the latter is simply not definite enough: there is no surveyable checklist of such behaviors, and inclusion of any particular behavior will depend on a not circumscribable range of features of the situation and on the person's particular circumstances and history. Again, what we are imagining in talking of a brain state identified as the understanding by its causal location, becomes entirely unclear.

A somewhat different cast can be put on the consideration of our practices as follows: the things which we count as behavior associated with understanding are not grouped together by any scientific unity; we have no grasp on the collection in scientific terms. When we talk about manifestations of understanding, we are seeing, or conceptualizing, the behavior through the concept of understanding; it is only that concept that links them together. Wittgenstein seems to be exploiting this in *Remarks on Philosophy of Psychology I*, §§903–906 (= *Zettel*, §§608–611):

§903. No supposition seems to me more natural than that there is no process in the brain correlated with associating or with thinking; so that it would be impossible to read off thought processes from brain processes. I mean this: if I talk or write there is I assume, a system of impulses going out from my brain and correlated with my spoken or written thoughts. But why should the *system* continue further in the direction of the center? Why should this order not proceed, so to speak, out of chaos? . . .

§904. It is thus perfectly possible that certain psychological phenomena *cannot* be investigated physiologically, because physiologically nothing corresponds to them.

§906. The prejudice in favor of psychophysical parallelism is a fruit of primitive interpretations of our concepts. . . .

That is, if we look at all of the things that we call manifestations of understanding, we find no physical or physiological regularity in them. Hence there is no reason to expect a physical systematicity in understanding. If you eliminate all the mental notions, what are you left with by way of the data? What you have left to do the science on is very little indeed.

The note Wittgenstein is here sounding has a Quinean ring. In fact, I do see a confluence between the two at this point. If one restricts oneself to the austere language of the physical sciences (which is the rightful home of the notion of cause that the objector is trying to exploit), then the data are very thin: you have people's movements and emissions of noises of various sorts (it would already be illicitly interpreting the data to say there are actions and there are words being spoken). In that, you do not see understanding at all. But then there exists little reason to think there will be a scientifically discoverable state that will group together just the right things under the concept of understanding. This is "merely" a plausibility argument, although I think a rather strong one. But it can serve to undercut the scientific objection in an additional way as well. Part of the force of the objection, part of the reason one might think to look for the brain state that causes manifestations of understanding, is simply a Laplacean view that everything we do is caused. But what is caused, in that sense, is behavior in the most physicalistic sense. If you have applied the Laplacean picture to notions like the understanding, then what you have done has inflated the data. You have a mere metaphysical insistence rather than anything that comes from a scientific worldview.

The point underlines what I have been implicitly suggesting all along: that the inclination to think that science might discover an appropriate state rests on an accession to a picture of the mental apparatus, of definite states and processes of some sort; given those states and processes, questions can then be framed of whether they can be tied down physically. If, on the contrary, the only apparatus assumed is physical, then upon scrutiny it becomes clear how little conception we have of what is supposed to be discovered.

There is an objection to all of these points, though. Surely, it will be said, one can—without acceding to any overblown ideas of the mental—imagine the discovery of a physical state that a person is in if and only if that person, say, understands a particular word; a state that is merely *coextensive* with understanding, with no further structure presumed. However, this is far less clear than it might seem. For what Wittgenstein emphasizes—the nonuniformity of our criteria for understanding and their intertwining with much else in our physical, social, and mental lives—represents differences from the models we have of states and processes in physical science. The features we rely upon in finding general properties of or structures in, e.g., physical substances, features that lead us to call them natural kinds and that allow us to generalize from one sample to another, are lacking. Thus it becomes unclear how anything we discover in some cases in which we would ascribe understanding could be justifiably generalized to all cases. There are, in a sense, too many singularities.

Perhaps that should be the end of the matter, but one might feel inclined to indulge the objection, and to suppose (for the sake of argument) that we can carve out some class of cases that *is* tractable enough from the standpoint of physical science to support inductions, yet broad enough to be interesting. Now suppose further that we discover a physical state common to all cases within this class that are cases of understanding. Is this a discovery of a state of understanding? There is in Wittgenstein's considerations a suggestion that, even if we can make sense of being able to identify some physical features of the brain somehow linked with cases of understanding, then anything that we could discover would be at best concomitants of understanding and not what the understanding itself is. "For even supposing I had found something that happened in all those cases of understanding,—why should *it* be the understanding?" (§153).[7]

The difficulty here lies in making this point out without returning to the "grammatical" argument I am concerned to avoid, and thereby imputing some form of essentialism to Wittgenstein. Obviously, were we to discover that, in some tractable class of cases, an understanding of the word "eleemosynary" goes along with a disposition to blink upon hearing the word, then we have discovered an accompaniment of understanding, not anything we would identify with the understanding itself. The blinking has no connection to those things that are importantly involved in understanding, e.g., correct usage and the ability to explain the word. Hence the discovered disposition seems extrinsic to understanding, a mere accidental concomitant, rather than anything we would be inclined to call the state of understanding.

Clearly then, any brain state, if it is not to be dismissed as a mere accompaniment of understanding, would have to be suitably connected to the features that we rely upon in our ordinary ascriptions of understanding: it would have to be identified by way of the manifestations and practices. So, in the end, more than a bare coextensiveness claim is needed. But then once again the considerations elicited by Wittgenstein's investigation of the nature of our ascriptive practices come into play; here they serve to show that anything isolable enough and general enough to be usable for the identification of a particular brain state could reflect little of the range of our practices.

Consequently, it can be argued, any state that is so identified would have a tenuous claim to being the state of understanding that the scientific objector claimed to envisage.

To argue this, to elaborate the requirement that the brain state be linked to criteria of understanding, we should look closely at the work the scientific objection was supposed to do. We must evoke or uncover specific character- izations of what the state that is the understanding itself is wanted for, what work the isolation of such a state is meant to do. For example, suppose that one takes the understanding itself to be needed in order that there be a principled distinction between a mistaken usage (given this understanding of the word) and a different understanding, that is, any possible different understanding. That would demand that the state be connected in some way to *all* correct usages, that is, all correct possible uses. For if it had connection to only a subset of them, then the state would be indistinguishable, by itself, from the different understanding which would issue in only the correct uses in that subset. If we continue to think of "connection" here to be causal, we then have the demand that the state causally produce all correct further responses. This is just the demand Kripke puts on such states in his book, and he argues persuasively that it cannot be met.[8]

The demands we would impose for a state's being more than a mere ac- companiment of understanding, it now appears, depend on what we expect from the identification of a "state of understanding." This is, I think, corroborated by consideration of an intermediate case. Ignoring numerous difficulties and obscurities, let us suppose we can imagine the discovery of a brain state that is common, within some tractable class of cases, to those who understand the word "table' and that is identified by causal links to correct usages in just a few straightforward cases and links confrontations with paradigmatic tables.[9] In this imagined case, are we to call the state the understanding or merely an accom- paniment of understanding? My reaction is to echo Wittgenstein's remark: "Say what you choose, as long as it does not prevent you from seeing the facts" (§79). Whether or not one claims the identification, what is important to note is how little by way of further enterprises are supported. Precisely because the state lacks connection to important features of understanding, it provides no basis for claims about the "structure" of the understanding and little notion of the content of what is understood. It does not even have links to straightforward verdicts about tables and non-tables beyond the paradigmatic few, and thus does not intrinsically rule out other possible different understandings. As a result, the connections between understanding and content that are crucial to any philosophical, cognitive, psychological, or semantic theorizing are absent.

The lesson is that once we reflect on any particular task, philosophical or mentalistic, that the discovery of a state of understanding was to do, the paucity of features that could be built into a specification of a brain state will make such a state look too little like the understanding "itself." Given what we wanted from a definite, particular state of understanding, what we can imagine discovering scientifically will not suffice.

Clearly, though, the success of this line of argument will rest to a considerable extent on Wittgenstein's more basic strategies to show the inaptness of definite state or process characterizations of understanding. That is, one has to undermine a picture of the mental apparatus at the start, and emphasize the intricacy, connectedness, and nonuniformity of our practices of ascription, so as to make clear how different this is from the case of mechanisms in the physical world. The scientific objector always has examples from the physical sciences in mind. We discovered the internal constitution of ammonia, after all; what we discovered was not an "accompaniment" of ammonia, whatever that would mean. To this we ought respond: understanding is not like ammonia. Wittgenstein's investigations are meant to bring us to see how different the cases are. The surroundings that make "What is ammonia" a question, the same question as "What is the structure of ammonia," are absent for "What is the understanding of 'table',," or worse yet, "What is the structure of the understanding of 'table'." Wittgenstein's aim is to get us to reflect on differences that make the latter question so peculiar.

Notes

An abridged version of this essay was published under the title "Wittgenstein, Mind, and Scientism" in the *Journal of Philosophy* 86 (1989): 635–42. I am indebted to Steven Affeldt, Louise Antony, Burton Dreben, Edward Minar, Angel Oquendo, and Thomas Ricketts for helpful discussions and suggestions.

1. The terminology comes from Paul Horwitch, "Critical Notice: Kripke: *Wittgenstein on Rules and Private Language*," *Philosophy of Science* 51 (1984): 168.

2. B. Williams, "Wittgenstein and Idealism," *Understanding Wittgenstein, Royal Institute of Philosophy Lectures, vol. 7*, 1972–73, edited by G. Vesey (London, 1974), 91; G. Kreisel, "Wittgenstein's Theory and Practice of Philosophy," *British Journal for the Philosophy of Science* 11 (1960): 238–52.

3. See my "I Want You to Bring Me a Slab: Remarks on the Opening Sections of the *Philosophical Investigations*," *Synthese* 56 (1983): 265–82.

4. "Mental Tuning Forks Noted in Perfect Pitch," *Los Angeles Times*, March 25, 1984.

5. Mark Klein, Michael G. H. Coles, and Emanuel Donchin, "People with Absolute Pitch Process Tones without Producing a P300," *Science* 223 (March 23, 1984): 1306–09.

6. Here, in talking about the causal efficacy of presumed understanding states, we are in the neighborhood of Saul Kripke's arguments in *Wittgenstein on Rules and Private Language* (Cambridge, Mass., 1982). Kripke emphasizes the infinitude of potential responses and the finitude of those anyone could actually make, given human limitations. In my "Kripke on Wittgenstein on Rules" (*Journal of Philosophy* 82 [1985]: 471–88), I noted that the point could be turned aside, at least at first blush, by one who believed that neural science could discover both competence states and "interfering" states that prevent the competence from being fully exhibited. My point now is meant to show how the latter is a woeful oversimplification; for the problem is not simply a matter of not giving all the responses. The extent of the responses is not the issue. Rather, the giving of responses can be thought of as a causal upshot of states only once a vast variety of other putative states are brought into play, involving many areas of the person's psychic economy. This renders the notion of locating the understanding state (the competence state) much less clear than a simple separation into competence and interference would depict it.

7. It should be noted, however, that in §153 Wittgenstein is discussing *mental* processes that may accompany understanding; it is the picture of a mental apparatus that is at issue.

The considerations he adduces in this and contiguous paragraphs do not, I would think, apply *tout court* to our present question concerning physical states.

8. Kripke, *Wittgenstein on Rules and Private Language*.

9. I suggest this scenario in my "Kripke on Wittgenstein on Rules," 478; I am now far more doubtful that the scenario is coherent. The notion of finding a state that *causes* usage is highly questionable, as I argued above. There are further problems with the identifiability of the state as "the same" in different people.

Persuasion

PETER WINCH

I ought to be no more than a mirror, in which my reader can see his own thinking with all its deformities so that, helped in this way, he can put it right.[1]

1. *TRACTATUS LOGICO-PHILOSOPHICUS*

Wittgenstein stated very clearly and forcefully in various contexts in the *Tractatus* that his aim was not to put forward any philosophical theory and that, indeed, to try to settle the difficulties that concerned him there in terms of a theory would show decisively that one had failed to understand the nature of those difficulties. He writes for instance in the "Foreword" that one cannot draw a line to mark the limit of intelligible thinking, as that would mean being able to "think" what lies on both sides of the line, and therefore to think what is unthinkable. And so, he concludes, the line must be drawn within language, that is, we must observe a limit to what can be expressed, since everything that lies beyond such a limit will be "simply nonsense" ("*einfach Unsinn*"). In other words, we must simply learn to recognize nonsense for what it is and avoid it. And so the only correct philosophical method, he writes at the end of the book (6.53), would be to say nothing except what is sayable, to wait until someone tries to say something metaphysical, and then show that person that certain signs in his or her sentences had not been given any meaning.

The *Tractatus* tries to show that the real nature of the distinction between sense and nonsense is obscured by pervasive misunderstandings about the nature of logic. These misunderstandings have a common pattern: they all involve attempts to supply some "basis" for logic, whether in the form of structural features of reality, axioms, principles of inference, psychological features of the human mind, arbitrarily introduced "logical constants," or whatever. Against any such view the *Tractatus* insists (5.473) that "Logic must look after itself."

Crucial here is Sheffer's demonstration that the generally accepted logical connectives are all definable in terms of iterated negation. For Wittgenstein this had an importance that went far beyond systematic elegance. It seemed to show how logic is involved from the beginning in the nature of what it is to say, or think, that something is the case.

A proposition, or thought, according to the *Tractatus*, draws a line between all possible states of affairs; on one side of the line lie those states of affairs that make the proposition true, on the other side of the line lie all the rest: all circumstances in which the proposition is false. The possibility of the operation of negating flows directly from this essential feature of propositions. To negate a given proposition *p* is simply to reverse the truth values on either side of the line. What makes *p* true makes *not-p* false; what makes *p* false makes *not-p* true.

Repeating the operation has the same result. What makes *not-p* true makes *not-not-p* false, what makes *not-p* false makes *not-not-p* true. In other words *p* and *not-not-p* are equivalent.

If all this is correct and if all logical connectives can be fully accounted for in terms of iterated negation, it seems that logic indeed does flow in its entirety simply from what is essential to a proposition or thought. Logic, then, *can* "look after itself." In view of this, it is not surprising that Wittgenstein's new start in philosophy in the early 1930s began with a thorough-going criticism of these assumptions, especially that concerning the relation between the results of a single negating operation and those of repeating that operation. I shall return to this criticism shortly.

Tractatus 6.613, basing itself on the considerations I have lightly sketched, reads: "Logic is not a theory, but a mirror image of the world." The question I now want to raise is whether this conception of logic is one that does enable Wittgenstein to play the role he aspires to in my opening quotation.

Sections 5.621 to 5.633 of the *Tractatus* claim that there is no such thing as the thinking subject; the subject does not belong to the world, but is a limit of the world. The relation of the subject to the world is compared to the relation of the eye to the visual field. Nothing in the visual field allows one to conclude that it is seen by an eye; the eye is not *part* of the visual field.

Suppose someone were to object to this that one can in a sense see the eye—by looking in a mirror. To this Wittgenstein might have replied that nothing that one sees when looking in a mirror shows that it has anything to do with *seeing*.[2] The possibility of such a response shows, I think, that what concerns Wittgenstein here is not so much the eye as a physical organ as *the power of seeing*. This is not something that can be seen—even in a mirror.

According to the very persuasive interpretation developed by James Conant and Cora Diamond,[3] the *Tractatus* as a whole is to be understood as a demonstration of someone's succumbing to the philosophical temptation to talk nonsense. We are not supposed to *understand* the sentences of the *Tractatus*—since they are nonsense they express nothing to be understood; we are however supposed to understand Wittgenstein—to understand what he is doing in producing these senseless expressions. That is to say, we are to understand the *Tractatus* as an object lesson in what *not* to do. It is to be the mirror in which we see our own temptations *and recognize them as temptations to be avoided.*

But if our power of seeing were such that everything we saw were deformed, we could not detect the deformity by looking in a mirror, since what we saw there would be as deformed as everything else.[4] Correspondingly, even if I am shown my thinking with all its deformities, I shall not recognize them as deformities. If the *Tractatus* is right in saying that "I am my world," there is hardly even any sense in suggesting that I might recognize my world as a deformed one; that I might see that the sentences I have such a strong disposition to utter are senseless.

Do not think that what you have just read is a mere *jeu d'esprit*. The reaction I have described is after all precisely that of that majority of readers who have taken the *Tractatus* for a more or less straightforward essay in metaphysics. More importantly, the argument of the *Tractatus* itself is infected with just such a fundamental deformity, as Wittgenstein himself, in the 1930s, came to recognize. This brings me back to iterated negation.

2. ITERATED NEGATION IN *PHILOSOPHICAL GRAMMAR*

I said earlier that, in *Tractatus*, the requirement imposed by "Logic must look after itself" is that logic must rest on no "assumptions": given the *Satz*, everything else follows inexorably. Hence too, the consequences of repeating the operation of negation cannot rest on any assumption. If, in negating *p*, I have arrived at *not-p*, in which the truth-values of *p* are reversed, then, in negating *not-p* in its turn, I reverse *its* truth-values too in arriving at *not-not-p*. And were I to protest and ask what would happen if I refused to accept this result, the *Tractatus* would speak to me as Lewis Carroll's Achilles spoke to the Tortoise and say: "Then Logic would take you by the throat and *force* you to do it!.... Logic would tell you 'You can't help yourself' "—once you have accepted that if *p* is true, *not-p* is false, then you *must* accept that *not-not-p* is true. "So you've no choice, you see."[5] Lewis Carroll of course wanted to show that this pervasive conception of "logical compulsion" is a myth, and this is precisely the conclusion Wittgenstein comes to in the following very important discussion:

> "This paper is *not* black, and two such negations yield an affirmation."
>
> The second clause is reminiscent of "and two such horses can pull the cart." But it contains no assertion about negation; it is a rule for the replacement of one sign by another.
>
> "That two negations yield an affirmation must already be contained in the negation that I am using now." Here I am on the verge of inventing a mythology of symbolism.
>
> It looks as if one could *infer* from the meaning of negation that "~ ~ p" means p. As if the rules for the negation sign *follow from* the

nature of negation. So that in a certain sense there is first of all negation, and then the rules of grammar.

It also looks as if the essence of negation had a double expression in language: the one whose meaning I grasp when I understand the expression of negation in a sentence, and the consequences of this meaning in the grammar.[6]

It is misleading then to say that the grammatical rules we follow are determined by the meaning of the signs we are using. It would be nearer the truth to say that the rules determine the meaning of the signs. Furthermore, as is made progressively clearer in the spectacular development in Wittgenstein's thinking that ensued in the years following the composition of the material in *Philosophical Grammar*, while we may characterize the grammatical, or logical force, of a rule by saying that its application in a certain context *determines* a certain result, to say that *we*, who have learned the rule, are *determined* by it to get that result is to say something of quite a different sort. It is an observation belonging to our "natural history," about the normal effect on human beings of subjecting them to a certain sort of training.[7]

The big change in Wittgenstein's thinking in the 1930s does of course involve abandoning the conception of logic which gives rise to such difficulties. Instead of thinking of logic as a feature, or consequence, of "representation as such," he abandons the whole idea of "representation as such" and introduces the conception of an indefinite diversity of "language games" which do not necessarily have anything in common and which provide the context in which people understand each other and make inferences.

This language game just *is* like that. And everything descriptive of a language-game is part of logic.[8]

This opens up the possibility of an entirely new methodology. Instead of exploring the limits of sense from within one all-embracing logical network, Wittgenstein is now in a position to *compare* one language game with another. What we are shown in the mirror is something we can put alongside other possibilities. The situation is the one described in a different context in the following:

God may say to me: "I am judging you out of your own mouth. You have shuddered with disgust at your own actions, when you have seen others do them."[9]

But of course there are new problems.

3. "A NORMATIVE SCIENCE"

These problems are introduced in a passage in *Philosophical Investigations* which is, I believe, pivotal for the whole argument of the book.

F. P. Ramsey once emphasized in conversation with me that logic was a 'normative science'. I do not know exactly what he had in mind, but it was doubtless related to what only dawned on me later: namely, that in philosophy we often *compare* the use of words with games and calculi which have fixed rules, but cannot say that someone who is using language *must* be playing such a game.—But if you say that our languages only *approximate* to such calculi you are standing on the very brink of a misunderstanding. For then it may look as if what we were talking about were an *ideal* language. As if our logic were, so to speak, a logic for a vacuum.—Whereas logic does not treat of language—or of thought—in the sense in which a natural science treats of a natural phenomenon, and the most that can be said is that we *construct* ideal languages. But here the word "ideal" is liable to mislead, for it sounds as if these languages were better, more perfect, than our everyday language; and as if it took the logician to shew people at last what a correct sentence looked like.

But all this can appear in the right light only when we have become clearer about the concepts of understanding, meaning and thinking. For then it will also become clear what can mislead us (and did mislead me) to think that anyone who utters a sentence and means or understands it is operating a calculus according to strict rules.[10]

It is clearly Wittgenstein's intention in this passage to avoid anything like the conception of logic expressed by Lewis Carroll's Achilles. On the other hand he also clearly recognizes the importance of the idea that we may correct our thinking by appealing to standards we find in logic. The problem is how we can have the latter without the former. At first sight Wittgenstein's treatment of this problem looks distinctly lame: he writes that "we often *compare* the use of words with games and calculi which have fixed rules." But we shall naturally want to ask why we make one comparison rather than another; and what *authority* such an object of comparison may have, if we have to deny it the status of an "ideal."

One source of our dissatisfaction is addressed in some remarks about the dogmatic exaggerations Wittgenstein finds in Oswald Spengler's claims about "family resemblances" among different manifestations of a given "cultural epoch."

Spengler could be better understood if he said: I am *comparing* cultural epochs with the lives of families: within a family there is a family resemblance, though you will also find resemblances between members of different families; family resemblance differs from the other sort of resemblance in such and such ways, etc. What I mean is: we have to be told the object of comparison, the object from which this way of viewing things is derived, otherwise the comparison will constantly be affected by distortions. Because willy-nilly we shall ascribe the properties of the prototype to the object we are viewing in its light; and we claim "it *must always* be. . . ."

This is because we want to give the prototype's characteristic features a foothold in our argument. But since we confuse prototype and object we find ourselves dogmatically conferring on the object properties which only the prototype necessarily possesses. On the other hand we think our view will not have the generality we want it to have if it is really true only of the one case. But the prototype ought to be clearly presented for what it is; so that it characterizes the whole discussion and determines its form. This makes it the focal point, so that its general validity will depend on the fact that it determines the form of discussion rather than on the claim that everything which is true only of it holds for all the things that are being discussed.

Similarly, the question always to ask when exaggerated dogmatic assertions are made is: What is actually true in this? Or again: In what case is that actually true?[11]

The decisive conception here is that "we want to give the prototype's characteristic features a foothold in our argument." Spengler thought to achieve this by, as it were, supposing the prototype to be directly drawn from reality itself. But this is precisely to do what Wittgenstein objected to in the conception of a "normative science": a confusion between the relation of logic to thinking and that of a natural science to a natural phenomenon—as though logic dealt in "ideals" the existence of which we *discover*. As an alternative Wittgenstein asks us to think of the object of comparison as a sort of "measuring rod" and hence as something which gives our reasoning in this instance its form—in the way in which the form of a piece of reasoning about the dimensions of a room is determined by the kind of measure we are using: a meter rule, say, or a yardstick. There is a remark in *Philosophical Investigations*, which is in fact adapted from the discussion of Spengler in *Culture and Value*:

For we can avoid distortion, or emptiness, in what we assert only insofar as we present the prototype as what it is, an object of comparison—a measuring rod, so to speak; and not as a prejudice to which reality has to correspond. (The dogmatism into which we so easily fall when we philosophize.)[12]

How much, we may ask, does this achieve? The emphasis on the *form* of the argument does give the argument in question a certain "generality," as Wittgenstein expresses it. That is, we are not to think of the argument as arbitrarily constructed just for this particular occasion. It exhibits a *pattern* that has a use, or can be given a use, elsewhere in our practices and lives. So, we may say, the source of the argument's authority is to be sought *in our practice*. It will depend on how important such a form of reasoning is within our practices, on how important those practices themselves are in our lives, and so on.

This point certainly plays a substantial role in Wittgenstein's thinking. For instance:

You could attach prices to thoughts. Some cost a lot, some a little. And how does one pay for thoughts? The answer, I think, is: with courage.[13]

It is striking and important that he uses an "ethical" concept *courage* here in discussing an apparently "logical" question. It takes courage to call in question familiar ways of thinking, to take seriously the idea that we are not *compelled* to think in accustomed ways, that there are other possibilities. It is not just that this is likely to be, as a purely internal matter, psychologically strenuous, though that is certainly not to be taken lightly, but that to strike out on new intellectual paths is also prone to bring us into conflict with other people, to expose us to the prospects of long, difficult argument, disruption of friendships and relations with collaborators, or worse.

4. PERSUASION AND ARGUMENT

All this, however, may still give the misleading impression that accepting or rejecting a particular form of argument is just a matter of choice. And this is by no means universally, or perhaps even commonly, the case. Achilles' conception of "logical compulsion" is certainly a confused one; but the phenomenon of finding an argument "compelling" is still a real one; and what I have so far been saying hardly does it justice.

Consider the following remarks:

> My own thinking about art and values is far more disillusioned than would have been *possible* for someone 100 years ago. That doesn't mean, though, that it's more correct on that account. It only means that I have examples of degeneration in the forefront of my mind which were not in the *forefront* of men's minds then.[14]

There are several relevant points here. In the first place, some of the examples of "degeneration" Wittgenstein has in mind may not even have existed a hundred years earlier, or—for one reason or another—may not have been available for the thinking of people living then. Moreover, Wittgenstein is not suggesting that he himself has *chosen* to have such examples at the forefront of his own mind. And in general, though it would be wrong to say that such matters are never a matter of choice, they are clearly not always so in any obvious sense. Certain examples may force themselves upon one for a wide variety of reasons: reasons not always easily, if at all, fathomable. Furthermore, though Wittgenstein insists that his own thinking is not "more correct" because it takes certain examples as paradigmatic of degeneration, he does not think that there is anything *wrong* with it, just because he finds himself unable to get away from these examples.

It is true that a large part of Wittgenstein's philosophical practice consists in attempting to break the hold of certain "pictures" on our thinking, pictures to which we may be obsessively attached and which in a real sense imprison us. It is this aspect he alludes to in the following remark:

> A man will be *imprisoned* in a room with a door that's unlocked and opens inwards; as long as it does not occur to him to *pull* rather than push it.[15]

But on the other hand we have the following, which might be read as a warning given by Wittgenstein to himself.

> It is true that we can compare a picture that is firmly rooted in us to a superstition, but it is equally true that we *always* eventually have to reach some firm ground, either a picture or something else, so that a picture which is at the root of all our thinking is to be respected and not treated as a superstition.[16]

In one of his Cambridge lectures on the "foundations of mathematics" Wittgenstein had tried to bring out differences between mathematical calculations and experiments. Alan Turing, who was in the audience, resisted Wittgenstein's arguments and, at one point in discussion of the lecture, said that the difference between Wittgenstein and himself lay in the fact that they were using the word "experiment" in two different ways. Wittgenstein opens Lecture XI by taking up and rejecting this interpretation of the disagreement. The way in which he characterizes the argument that follows is itself revealing. He does not say he is going to prove Turing wrong. Rather, he insists on the *persuasive* character of what he is about to attempt.

> ... I think that if I could make myself quite clear, then Turing would give up saying that in mathematics we make experiments.[17]

He then asks how it is that the misunderstanding between him and Turing is so difficult to clear up and compares the issue between them to the way in which he, Wittgenstein, would respond to a remark of Hilbert's:

> "No one is going to turn us out of the paradise which Cantor has created."
>   I would say, "I wouldn't dream of trying to drive anyone out of this paradise." I would try to do something quite different: I would try to show you that it is not a paradise—so that you'll leave of your own accord. I would say, "You're welcome to this; just look about you."

Let us now consider what Wittgenstein takes the importance of his type of inquiry to be. Here the following remark is important:

> One of the greatest difficulties I find in explaining what I mean is this: You are inclined to put our difference in one way, as a difference of *opinion*. But I am not trying to persuade you to change your opinion. I am only trying to recommend a certain sort of investigation. If there is an opinion involved, my only opinion is that this sort of investigation is immensely important and very much *against the grain* of some of you.

I think it is clear that the importance of the inquiry directly depends on the fact that it tends to go so much "against the grain." And this brings me to an important passage from the "Lecture on Freedom of the Will." Wittgenstein had been trying to show how one source of philosophical difficulties about free will is the fact that comparison with certain very special kinds of case tends to dominate our thinking about human action. Wittgenstein's own discussion is in terms of a somewhat bizarre invented example, but it will suffice for our purposes to think of cases of post-hypnotic suggestion, where people may be convinced that they are freely choosing what they do, but where we (at least think we) know better.

> We are comparing the case of a human being with those special cases where we *would* say that a man was determined: where we would say that he thought he was deciding freely, but was actually compelled. Why should anyone be inclined to compare ordinary cases with such a very special case?
>
> When sometimes I have looked frantically for a key, I have thought: 'If an omniscient [*sic*] is looking at me, he must be making fun at [*sic*] me. What a joke for the Deity, seeing me look when he knows all the time.' Suppose I asked, Is there any good reason for looking at it in this way?
>
> Must you look at looking for something in this way? No. But it is one of the most important facts of human life that such impressions sometimes force themselves on you.[18]

When Wittgenstein calls this one of the most important facts of human life, I do not think he is simply thinking of the role of such impressions in generating philosophical puzzlement. It is, e.g., essential to the "matter of course" way in which we operate with a world picture.

The importance of the role of pictures "at the root of all our thinking" is followed up most systematically perhaps in *On Certainty*. Consider especially §167. Lavoisier, when he makes an experiment, does not wonder whether, conditions being the same on another occasion, the result would be the same. He regards the experiment as establishing a certain result which he is willing to apply in the future. He does not decide to do this because he can give a reason for doing so. (And as the difficulties philosophers have had over induction show, convincing reasons may be hard to come by.) The fact of the matter is that this is not an issue for Lavoisier, the question does not arise. As Wittgenstein puts it, he has inherited a certain "world picture" which is "the matter of course foundation of his inquiry and as such is not expressed."

It might be thought that the next task should be to formulate some criteria for distinguishing between a picture that is "at the root of all our thinking" and one that is a "superstition." However, that would be a mistake. The distinction is of its nature a shifting one and will depend on the particular context. One might say: whether a particular picture is superstitious or not is not an inherent character of the picture, but a matter of how we are tempted to use it. We shall just have to investigate, in the particular case, whether the way we are using a picture is leading to confusions.[19]

5. CALCULI WITH FIXED RULES

I now come to what is perhaps the most important point of all in what I want to say. The thought I have just tried to express, so basic to Wittgenstein's philosophizing, that "we always have to reach some firm ground," is itself a powerful picture that can easily lead us into confusions. This is the theme that Wittgenstein alludes to in the last paragraph of *Philosophical Investigations* I, § 81:

> But all this can appear in the right light only when we have become clearer about the concepts of understanding, meaning and thinking. For then it will also become clear what can mislead us (and did mislead me) to think that anyone who utters a sentence and *means* or *understands* it is operating a calculus according to strict rules.

The calculi that Wittgenstein clearly has mainly in mind here are those of the formal logician. These are in any case particularly important in the context of his discussion. For though, in a remark from *On Certainty* I have already quoted, Wittgenstein says that "everything descriptive of a language-game is part of logic," one may well be disposed to think that logic must have another, more fundamental, part which sets limits to what is and what is not a possible, or at least acceptable, language game. This final stronghold of the conception of logic as a normative science is one that Wittgenstein also wishes to reduce. I believe that his treatment of this issue contains the most radical part of his thinking.

Wittgenstein's *Philosophical Grammar*, Part III, contains an important discussion of the concept of generality and, more particularly, of the part it plays in logical inference. Among the problems that he addresses here is one which is another form of John Stuart Mill's problem in *A System of Logic*: whether syllogistic reasoning involves a *petitio principii*. I will start with a brief discussion of Mill.

Consider the syllogism:

All men are mortal
Socrates is a man
Therefore, Socrates is mortal.

Traditionally, the validity of such an inference has been thought to rest on the fact that the major premise asserts something of each individual member of a certain class, while the minor premise asserts that a certain individual is a member of that class. Mill poses the following dilemma: to read the syllogism in this way is to treat the major premise as a sort of abbreviated conjunction. Either Socrates is included as one of the conjuncts or he is not. If yes, then we are indeed entitled to assert that Socrates is mortal; but we can hardly speak here of an "inference," since we are doing no more than repeating in different words something we have already asserted. If no, then we are indeed, in the syllogism, moving to a new conclusion, but the move must be an invalid one on this traditional conception, since nothing has been said about Socrates' mortality.

More serious yet, Mill argues, if an inference is supposed to be a move from the known to the unknown and if the quoted syllogism is supposed to display such a move, we must ask how I have arrived at the major premise. I may be able to answer by citing a certain, perhaps very large, number of individual cases of human beings whose mortality I have confirmed empirically. Let us suppose the major premise is a conjunction of all these cases. If it is to play its traditional role it must still be explained how it enables me to make assertions about other cases I have not empirically confirmed.

> The error committed is, I conceive, that of overlooking the distinction between the two parts of the process of philosophizing, the inferring part and the registering part, and ascribing to the latter the functions of the former. The mistake is that of referring a person to his own notes for the origin of his knowledge. If a person is asked a question, and is at the moment unable to answer it, he may refresh his memory by turning to a memorandum which he carries about with him. But if he were asked, how the fact came to his knowledge, he would scarcely answer, because it was set down in his notebook: unless the notebook were written, like the Koran, with a quill from the wing of the angel Gabriel.[20]

Mill's own conclusion is that there is no such thing as logical inference as understood by traditional logicians; all inference is from particular to particular. Frank Ramsey thought that Mill overlooked the fact that "we think in general terms,"[21] and Wittgenstein's treatment of similar problems also seeks to retain the notion of generality in its account of logical inference. But, where Ramsey had sought to do this by reinterpreting the major premise as a "variable hypothetical," the direction taken by Wittgenstein is importantly different. His treatment is closely connected with the problems about "exact rules" raised in my last section.

> If I say to someone, "Stand roughly here!"—cannot this explanation function work perfectly well? And cannot others fail too?
> "But isn't the explanation inexact?"—Certainly, why shouldn't we call it inexact? But let us just understand what "inexact" means! For it doesn't mean "unusable." And let us consider too what we call an "exact" explanation in contrast to this one. Perhaps drawing the boundaries of an area with a chalk-mark? But then it at once occurs to us that the mark has breadth. So a colour boundary would be more exact. But then does this kind of exactness still have a function, isn't it an idle wheel? And besides, we haven't settled what is to count as crossing this sharp boundary, how, with what instruments, this is to be established.[22]

To make the link between these discussions consider the following "syl-logism." Someone says to me: "Stand roughly here;" I think to myself: " 'Here' in this context means Position^1, Position^2, Position^3, *or* ... Position^n. So I will

stand at Position[3]; then I shall have obeyed the order." Of course one can
imagine circumstances in which one *would* reason like this; but it would be
pure mythology to suppose that some such reasoning must take place *whenever*
anyone obeys such an order. The thinking which may lead to such a mythology,
goes something like this.—If I obey such an order by standing in some definite
place, then both the person giving the order and I obeying it must have *meant* or
understood the order as including that place; and the same goes for *any* of the
places standing in which would constitute obeying the order. The "syllogism,"
therefore, simply analyzes what is involved in this *understanding* or *meaning*.
     Wittgenstein rejects such an account root and branch.

> I should like to say that in the sentence "There is a square in the circle"
> there is no mention at all of the particular place.[23]

We have to look in a quite different direction to understand the "generality"
involved in such cases.

> "How do you know he is in the room?" "Because I put him in there and
> there is no way he can get out."—Your knowledge of the general fact
> that he is somewhere in the room has, then, the same multiplicity as this
> reason.

This "multiplicity" has various dimensions, among which is the fact
that this reason is an example of a pattern that is constantly repeated in our
lives.[24] The *authority* of such a reason too, one can say, derives from the
indispensable role, or roles, played by similar reasons in countless aspects of
our lives, rather than from the (purely mythological) content, that is ascribed
to such propositions by traditional logicians. I believe it is the picture of such
a "content" that Wittgenstein is mainly referring to when he writes:

> A *picture* kept us imprisoned. And we could not escape from it, since it
> lay in our language, which seemed just to repeat it to us inexorably.[25]

6. MEANING AND UNDERSTANDING

Verbs like "to mean" and "to understand" have been conceived in philosophy as
expressing psychological activities or states. This conception is connected with
the above-mentioned "picture," which involves a certain way of representing
human beings' relation to logic. Logic is thought of as a kind of mechanism with
which human beings connect themselves when they think. Mill's discussion of
syllogistic theory for instance leans heavily on the question: What can possibly
be before our minds when we understand the major premise of a syllogism?
And we have seen that in the *Tractatus*, too, a very central role is played by the
idea that in negating a proposition we are inexorably committed to a certain
interpretation of iterated negation.
     In *Philosophical Investigations* Wittgenstein is at pains to argue that
"meaning," "understanding," etc. do not express *psychological* concepts at all,
but *logical* concepts. This belongs to his discussion of *logic*, not to a philosophy

of mind. To see how it is to be understood, consider an example. Suppose I am trying to convince a fellow Englishman that Britain should be willing to join a European federation. I say to him: "But you agreed with me a short while ago, when I said that all Europeans belong together in a single state". He objects: "Yes, but I didn't know that you meant to include the British in 'European'." I say: "Yes, of course, that's what I meant."

At the time of my earlier remark I need not have so much as asked myself whether, in saying "Europeans," I meant to include the British. I would justify my present reply quite differently. Perhaps I would remind my friend that Great Britain is after all already a member of the EC, that a great deal of our present conversation only made sense insofar as we were regarding the British as Europeans, and so on. In other words in saying "Of course that's what I meant" I am, as Wittgenstein sometimes puts it, making "a logical determination." I am trying to clarify what our argument really amounts to. My reference to what I *meant* with those words belongs to the *logic* of the argument; it is not a piece of information about my past state of mind.

How is this point connected to the belief "that anyone who utters a sentence and *means* or *understands* it is operating a calculus according to strict rules"? I think it comes to the following. To speak logically, one rightly thinks, is to subject oneself to a certain discipline. Hence, if I have said something, it is not permissible for me later to interpret my words quite arbitrarily (à la Humpty Dumpty). And, one wants to ask, how can I *actually have meant* something definite when I spoke, unless at that time there was some actual meaning (some "psychical process of meaning")? This question has to be taken seriously; and Wittgenstein does so. He shows, however, that it is not to be answered in the way its formulation suggests but, as it were, in quite another dimension.

7. JUDGMENT

In my imagined conversation the acceptability of my claim to have *meant* such and such by what I said is a matter for *negotiation* between us. Each of us will have to ask what is to be gained and what lost by a certain outcome. All kinds of imponderable may have to be taken into consideration: e.g., the honesty and sense of responsibility of the participants, what is the most important thing at issue in the argument, etc. Such questions cannot be answered by any "calculation," they demand judgment, a kind of judgment that may bring ethical qualities into play—including courage.[26]

Towards the end of *Philosophical Investigations*, Part II, xi,[27] there are some important and disquieting remarks about the indeterminacy of the judgments we make about each other (and, indeed, about ourselves). For instance:

Is it possible to learn knowledge of human beings. Yes, some can learn it. Not, however, by taking a course in it, but through '*experience*'.—Can someone else be one's teacher? Certainly. He gives one the right *hint*. This is what 'learning' and 'teaching' look like here.—What one learns is not a technique; one learns good judgment. There are rules too, but they do not form a system and only someone with experience can apply them properly. They are not like rules of calculation.

The most difficult thing here is to express the indeterminacy properly and without distortion.

Wittgenstein is not here *simply* differentiating between concepts of one sort—those expressing human states of mind—and others—such as mathematical concepts. Of course, this is part of his intention. But we should be missing what is perhaps most important in the discussion if we stopped there. For his whole argument—I almost said: the argument of his whole book—aims to show that human language is somehow embedded in such "judgments." Whatever may be the subject of our discourse, the possibility always exists that we shall have to evaluate the real attitude of the *human being* with whom we are conversing (or whose words we are reading).

Think, for example, of the two scientists who in 1990 claimed to have produced a thermo-nuclear fusion reaction "cold" in the laboratory. Naturally, sound scientific knowledge and strict logic were necessary to evaluate this claim. But something else was needed too: a sound understanding of human beings, including an ability to judge their ethical qualities as well as their scientific and "logical" abilities.

A related power of judgment is required in deciding on one's own argumentative strategies. The question may always arise how I can honestly go about convincing just *this* person of something. An argument which would be completely appropriate and rigorous in some circumstances may elsewhere be pure sophistry. The nice English expression "blinding with science" alludes to this possibility.

This again is, of course, not to deny that logical calculi can play an important role in maintaining argumentative discipline. It is to say that this role presupposes such an understanding of human beings and their ethical attitudes. For it is within such a context that they have their application.

Notes

1. *Culture and Value* [1931], p. 18ᵉ. The bracketed dates in references to *Culture and Value* refer throughout to the date of composition of the quoted remark. The superscript "ᵉ" refers to the English translation of the *en face* German/English text.

2. It is important in this connection to realize that the *Tractatus* is not concerned with epistemology, but with a kind of "phenomenology." See the opening sentences of *Philosophical Remarks*.

3. See Cora Diamond, "Throwing Away the Ladder: How to Read the *Tractatus*" in Cora Diamond, *The Realistic Spirit, Wittgenstein, Philosophy, and the Mind* (Cambridge, Mass., 1991); James Conant, "Throwing Away the Top of the Ladder" in *The Yale Review* 79, 3.

4. For a similar point made in connection with the problem of anti-semitism, see *Culture and Value* [1931], 20ᵉ.

5. Lewis Carroll, "What the Tortoise Said to Achilles," *Complete Works* (London, 1939).

6. *Philosophical Grammar*, Part I, II, p. 53. Wittgenstein returns to this question in *Philosophical Investigations* I, § 547ff.

7. See *Philosophical Investigations* I, § 189. The confusion between these uses of "determine" pointed out here is of course perpetrated by Achilles in the Lewis Carroll

episode; more recently by Saul Kripke. (See my *Trying to Make Sense*, [Oxford, 1987] 54–63.)

8. *On Certainty*, § 56.

9. *Culture and Value* [1951], p. 87ᵉ.

10. *Philosophical Investigations* I, § 81.

11. *Culture and Value*, p. 14ᵉ. I have slightly revised my own published translation.

12. *Philosophical Investigations* I, § 131.

13. *Culture and Value* [1946], p. 52ᵉ.

14. *Culture and Value*, p. 79ᵉ.

15. *Culture and Value* [1942], p. 42ᵉ.

16. *Culture and Value* [1949], p. 83ᵉ.

17. *Wittgenstein's Lectures on the Foundations of Mathematics, Cambridge, 1939*, edited by Cora Diamond (Hassocks, 1976), 103.

18. See the journal *Philosophical Investigations*, vol. 12, No. 2, April 1989. The text is from notes of Wittgenstein's lecture taken by Yorick Smythies.

19. There are some good examples in Wittgenstein's remarks about Bunyan's religious imagery and about the idea of predestination in *Culture and Value*.

20. J. S. Mill, *A System of Logic* II, II, § 3.

21. F. Ramsey, "General Propositions and Causality," *Philosophical Papers* (Cambridge, 1990).

22. *Philosophical Investigations* I, § 88.

23. *Philosophical Grammar*, Part II, II, § 5.

24. For a fine treatment of this subject, see Rush Rhees, "Questions on Logical Inference," *Understanding Wittgenstein, Royal Institute of Philosophy Lectures 1972/73* (London, 1974).

25. *Philosophical Investigations* I, § 115.

26. This much was clearly seen by Hobbes who of course was also much exercised by the possible sources of discipline in human communication. In a passage which might be given more attention than is customary he notes that there are people who will keep their word not out of fear of external sanctions but because of

a glory or pride in appearing not to need to break it. This latter is a generosity too rarely found to be presumed on, especially in the pursuers of wealth, command, or sensual pleasure; which are the greatest part of mankind. (*Leviathan*, chapter 14)

27. *Philosophical Investigations*, 227.

There is No Such Thing As Addition

PETER VAN INWAGEN

I will present an argument for the conclusion that there is no such thing as addition and explain why I think that this conclusion is not so obviously absurd that we could not possibly accept it. I shall argue for the latter conclusion by drawing an analogy between my conclusion and the conclusions of certain arguments for the non-existence of things we are naturally inclined to believe in.

The argument I shall present is inspired by Saul Kripke's discussion of the "quus" paradox in *Wittgenstein on Rules and Private Language.*[1] I will not discuss the question whether Kripke's arguments are in any sense Wittgenstein's arguments.[2] I will not discuss the question of the relation of the argument of the present essay to Kripke's arguments. I will discuss none of the relevant secondary (or tertiary, or whatever) literature. Finally, I will not discuss the question whether my Kripke-inspired argument applies to non-mathematical language—it *is* an argument about language—or whether there is some feature of mathematical language (its explicitly infinitary nature, for example, or its absolute precision) that restricts the application of the argument to mathematical language.[3]

I have to anticipate a certain reaction to the position I am arguing for. Recall Mark Twain's response to the question whether he believed in infant baptism: "Believe in it?—I've seen it done!" There is, of course, such a *human activity* as addition: I've seen it done. It is not this human activity that I am denying the existence of. I will begin by getting clear about what it is that I am denying the existence of. I am denying the existence of a certain abstract object, a certain mathematical object called 'addition' that is supposed to bear some intimate semantic relation to the "plus" sign. (It is supposed to be denoted by it or expressed by it or whatever the proper term is.)

Here is a picture of elementary mathematics—the arithmetic of the natural numbers[4]—that most of us have. (Or, if we do not have just this picture, we probably have something very much like it; enough like it that the differences are probably not going to matter very much.)

There is an infinite set of objects called natural numbers. (Infinite but small: each of its subsets that is not the same size as the set itself is finite.) Every natural number measures the size of various finite sets, and every size a finite set can have is measured by (exactly) one of them. As to "sizes": the empty set has the smallest size, and if x and y are finite sets, then y has the next larger size after x's just in the case that the members of x can be put into 1–1 correspondence with some of the members of y, with just one member of y left over.

These conditions define an ordering of the natural numbers in terms of size (that is, in terms of the sizes of the sets whose sizes they measure), an ordering usually expressed by 'greater than' or 'larger than'. On this ordering there is a least natural number, the one that measures the size of the empty set, and, for each natural number, there is a unique natural number that is the next larger, and, for each natural number but the least, that number is the one that is the next larger after some number.

No doubt many of us have a more filled-in picture of the natural numbers than this, but this will do to go on with.

Now let us define the notion of a *binary operation on* the natural numbers in the usual way: a binary operation on the natural numbers is any function that is defined on all ordered pairs of natural numbers, and whose value for any argument is a natural number. A binary operation on the natural numbers— hereinafter, a binary operation—is an infinite "machine" that has the following property: when you feed it a natural number and then feed it another (the order in which you feed it the numbers can make a difference), it gives you a single natural number back. (The nature of the machine is such that it is in a sense "already determined" what number you will get back when you feed it any two numbers in order. Binary operations x and y are assumed to be identical if they would always give you back the same "output" for the same "input." (That assumption is, of course, automatically satisfied if 'function' is understood in its set-theoretical sense, as, I suppose, it always is these days.)

Set theory tells us that, on the assumptions we have made about the natural numbers, there are a vast number of binary operations on them, a number vastly *larger* than the number of the natural numbers themselves. There are, in fact, c binary operations, as many as there are subsets of the set of natural numbers, or as many as there are real numbers. (Consider only those binary operations whose values are restricted to 0 through 9. Imagine a well-ordering of all the ordered pairs of natural numbers—say, Cantor's well-ordering of the fractions. Then each real number defines a distinct operation on pairs of natural numbers: the operation that takes the nth pair in the well-ordering and gives you the number that occurs in the nth place in the decimal expression of that real number.)

One of these operations, of course, is addition—provided that there is such a thing as addition. It is the operation that assigns to any two numbers their sum. Another is Kripke's "quus" operation:

$x \oplus y =_{df} x + y$ if $x, y < 57$, and
5 otherwise.

And there are, as I have said, lots more.

Is the picture I have painted, the picture of the natural numbers and the binary operations on them, a correct picture? Do such things actually exist? Well, if the picture is not correct, then it is hard to see how there could be any such thing as addition—the mathematical object, not the human activity—for the only understanding we have of this object is as a part of this picture: addition is one among the binary operations on the natural numbers. Let us therefore simply *assume* that the standard picture is correct. Let us assume that there are all these natural numbers and all these binary operations on them. What I shall try to show is that none of these binary operations is addition. If that thesis could be established, it would follow easily that there is no such thing as addition—for, if there were such a thing, it would be one of these objects.[5]

I will try to show that addition is not one of the binary operations by attempting to show that the English word 'addition' is not a name for any of them. If this semantical thesis could be established, it would follow that none of the binary operations was addition—for if one of the binary operations were addition, the English word 'addition' would be a name for it. Or, if you prefer indicative conditionals: if one of the binary operations *is* addition, then the English word 'addition' *is* a name for it. After all, the antecedent of this sentence ('One of the binary operations is addition') is an English sentence, and it expresses a truth only if the English word 'addition' names a unique binary operation. And if 'addition' does name a unique binary operation, the binary operation it names is addition. So, if the antecedent of the conditional is true, its consequent ('The English word "addition" is a name for it'[6]) is also true.

Some people I have discussed this argument with have expressed reservations about it. It may therefore be worthwhile to discuss the following parallel argument:

— The English word 'Socrates' is not the name of a human being;
— If the English word 'Socrates' is not the name of a human being, then no human being is Socrates;
— If there is such a person as Socrates, then he [or ' . . . then Socrates'] is a human being;
  hence, There is no such person Socrates.

This argument is certainly valid. Its first premise, of course, is false, but the question that interests us is whether someone who accepted it would be committed to its conclusion—that there is no such person as Socrates. Let us leave out of account everyone who does not know that Socrates is (if he exists) a human being.[7] We are thus restricting our examination to those who would accept the third premise. (Accepting the third premise corresponds to accepting the thesis that if there is such a mathematical object as addition, it is one of the binary operations on the natural numbers.) Now, what about the second premise, which, I believe, is the one that is most likely to arouse suspicion. Must one accept this premise? It is certainly possible to imagine someone who rejects the proposition expressed by the sentence written out above. Suppose, for example, that Jane is entirely unfamiliar with any language other than her native tongue (which is not English), and that the customary (and only) name for Socrates, according to the conventions of her native language, is a word that looks and sounds nothing like 'Socrates'. If the second premise of the above argument were translated into Jane's language—that is if the English sentence that I have used to express that premise were translated into Jane's language— she might well decline to accept the proposition expressed by that translation. And if she believed, for some reason, that the English word 'Socrates' was not the name of a human being, she might even *reject* that proposition. And that proposition is just the second premise of the argument.

But this is beside the point. I do not maintain that the English sentence

If the English word 'Socrates' is not the name of a human being, then no human being is Socrates

expresses a necessary truth. I maintain only that it expresses a *truth*. And I do not maintain that this truth can be seen to be a truth by just anyone who understands just any sentence that expresses it. I maintain only that an English speaker can see that *this sentence* expresses a truth, and can see that it expresses a truth without knowing whether 'Socrates' is the name of a human being. And doesn't the sentence

If the English word 'addition' is not the name of a binary operation, then none of the binary operations is addition

also express a truth? And can't we see that it expresses a truth without knowing whether 'addition' is the name of a binary operation? Certainly no English speaker would want to use the following English sentence to make an assertion:

One of the binary operations is addition, but the word 'addition' is not a name for it.

That would be a pragmatic contradiction, exactly parallel with using

There was such a person as Socrates, but the name 'Socrates' does not refer to him

to make an assertion.[8]

Our argument so far has been for the conclusion that if 'addition' is not a name for a binary operation, then there is no such thing as addition. Let us now turn to the promised argument for the conclusion that the word 'addition' denotes no binary operation.

If this word does denote a binary operation, which one does it denote? The answer seems obvious enough. In fact, we have already given it: the one that operates on any natural numbers x and y and yields their sum, $x + y$. And there is no doubt that this answer is correct—*provided* that the sign '+' that occurs in this answer has the following property: it picks out (or whatever the most felicitous semantical term may be) a unique binary operation. Provided that this symbol, this little piece of human language, is such that when one learns its meaning or its use, *what* one learns determines a unique binary operation, determines for *every* pair of natural numbers a unique natural number.

Is this the case? Is this what happens when one learns the meaning of '+'? Well, what do we learn when we learn the meaning of '+'? We learn

— An algorithm, a mechanical rule for manipulating bits of notation. There is, however, no particular algorithm that we have to learn. When we add (on paper, as opposed to in our heads or using a calculator), we use an algorithm that manipulates Arabic numerals, and the Romans, appropriately enough, used one that manipulated Roman numerals.[9] One could learn the meaning of '+' in a way that involved learning the Roman algorithm rather than the one we are familiar with. (Even a "physical" algorithm—an algorithm comprising instructions for the manipulation of mere counters, physical objects that lack semantical properties—would no doubt do. Kripke has discussed an algorithm of this sort: to compute the sum of x and y, count out x pebbles into a pile; then count out y pebbles from a different source into a second pile; then shove the two piles together into one pile and count the pebbles in that pile; the result is the the sum of x and y.[10] In the sequel, however, I shall assume that algorithms manipulate strings of symbols.) When we are taught whatever algorithm it is that we are taught, we learn that there is no limit on the length of the strings of notation to which it can be applied. (Perhaps we are taught this "implicitly," simply by never being told that there is a longest string to which the algorithm can be applied.)
— An explanation of what the algorithm is *for*. We learn that the manipulable strings of notation represent numbers, and we learn what numbers they represent, and we learn that if you take the string representing the number of the A's and the string representing the number of the B's and manipulate them as the algorithm tells you to, you will get a string representing the number you would arrive at if you counted the A's and then turned to the B's, and, without starting over, continued your counting till you had got through the B's.
— Some conventions that pertain to the *public* nature of '+'. We learn that others use this sign and that they have the right to dispute one's sums. We learn conventions governing disputes about whether the algorithm yields a particular string in a particular case. (As with

the algorithm itself, there is no particular convention that has to be adopted. One society might have a "sum czar" who is the ultimate arbiter of such matters. In another, more democratic, society, several people might be asked to apply the algorithm in the disputed case, and the dispute settled by the vote of the majority.)

— Various abbreviations and shortcuts. Unlike Humpty-Dumpty, we do not need to resort to the actual use of an algorithm to compute the sum of 364 and 1. *Fortunately*, we do not have to resort to the actual use of an algorithm to compute the sum of 2,000,000 and 2,000,000. And we know without computing the sum of 568,242,924 and 63,077,510 that this sum is considerably greater than ten.

These things, it seems to me, are the things we learn when we learn the meaning of '+'. Quite possibly, one could learn the meaning of '+' without learning all of these things, but learning all of them would certainly be sufficient. (We shall presently examine a suggestion to the effect that it would be possible to learn the meaning of '+' without learning any of them.) There may be things that you can learn about the addition of natural numbers that are not included in this list—things you could learn from a mathematician, for example—but I take it that an accountant who has not learned any of these esoteric facts about addition does know the meaning of '+'.

Is learning this much enough? Can it be that the sense that one who has learned these things is able to attach to '+' is sufficient to enable this sign to pick out a particular one of the c binary operations? I shall argue that it is not. My argument will be presented in the form of philosophical reflection on an imaginary situation. The case I shall examine is inspired by and partly modeled on some cases Kripke imagines in the course of his development of the "quus" paradox. But my case is different in various important respects from any of Kripke's cases. (And, unlike Kripke, I use the case I imagine as the basis for a philosophical argument that I endorse for a conclusion that I accept: that there is no such thing as addition.) Nevertheless, Kripke's influence will be evident throughout the remainder of the essay. Many of the points I shall make he has made. I shall not in every case take note of this.

Here, now, is the imaginary situation.

One day in the far future we meet the Arcturans. We get to know them, or we think we do, and we learn their language—or, at least, we are satisfied, on the basis of our experience of our linguistic interaction with them, that we have learned their language. The Arcturans have a system of notation that we believe is isomorphic to our mathematical notation. (This belief is grounded in our examination of the use they make of that notation and in what we think they are saying to us in Arcturan concerning their use of it.) In particular, we believe that their sign '∗' corresponds to our '+'.

Now the philosophical reflection. We begin with some definitions. Let us say, first, that a natural number is *Enormous* if it is so large that in no possible world does any human being or any Arcturan refer to it or to any larger natural number. This definition is not devoid of application. There are Enormous numbers. (And, of course, if any numbers are Enormous, most of them are.) If you are doubtful about this, consider some largish natural number—say, ten raised to the following power: ten raised to the fortieth power, which is known as Skewe's Number.[11] Reflect on the fact that almost all numbers *smaller* than Skewe's Number are such that in no possible world does any human being or Arcturan refer to them.[12] It is, of course, true that for each such number we can refer to *larger* numbers: to Skewe's Number itself, to its successor, to its square, and so on. But almost all natural numbers must be such that they *and all greater natural numbers* are "referentially inaccessible" to us. (If Jane spends the whole of her life speaking the name of a single number, piling exponent on exponent, and factorial on factorial—let us imagine that she follows the most efficient possible strategy in respect of using the time that she has available to her to name the largest possible number[13]—when she has gasped her last, and the number-name that is her life's work is, perforce, complete, it will still be true that almost all natural numbers are larger than the one that name denotes.)

Now let us say that two or more distinct binary operations are *inaccessibly divergent* if, for some Enormous number n, they take the same value for every pair of arguments both of which are less than n. And, finally, let us call a particular binary operation inaccessibly divergent if that operation and addition are inaccessibly divergent. We should note that if the standard picture is correct, there are inaccessibly divergent operations; there are, in fact, c of them.

Let us now ask why it is that we should suppose that '✱' expresses addition rather than one of the inaccessibly divergent operations? (If we were able to refer to one of the inaccessibly divergent operations—refer to it individually—we could ask why we should suppose that *that* is not the operation the Arcturans mean by '✱'. But we are not able to refer to any individual inaccessibly divergent operation; if we were able to refer to one of them, we could refer to a certain number as the least number such that the result of applying the operation to that number and some other number differed from the sum of those two numbers; but this number is one that is by definition referentially inaccessible to us.[14])

It is tempting to think that an appeal to behavioral dispositions may help us with this question. It is an attractive thesis that what we mean by '+', and what the Arcturans mean by '✱', is fixed by our, and their, dispositions with respect to the use of these symbols. No doubt this is at least a part of the truth, perhaps a very large part. But it does not seem that an appeal to behavioral dispositions will be of much use to anyone who is worried about how to reply to our question, for our, and the Arcturans', dispositions do not have the capacity to differentiate among the inaccessibly divergent operations, or to distinguish between addition and any of the inaccessibly divergent operations. The following analogy may help us to see the importance of this point. Consider your pocket calculator.[15] It has a '+' key. We normally suppose that, if it is in proper working order, it computes a *sum* when you enter a number, press the '+'

key, enter another number, and, finally, press the '=' key. But the dispositions of your calculator are finite. In fact, any of us can "outrun" them, because any of us can provide answers to addition problems that there is no way even to instruct your calculator to perform. If your calculator is like mine, it will not "take" a number larger than 99,999,999, and that is the largest number it will give as output. If you set it the problem '99,999,999 + 1 =', you will get a signal telling you that you have outrun its capabilities. Still, we are inclined to say, the calculator computes a *segment* of the addition operation, one defined by length-limitations on arguments and values when these numbers are expressed in decimal notation. But consider the operation "shaddition":

$x \# y = x + y$ if $x + y \leq 99,999,999$
5 otherwise.

What makes it the case that the calculator computes a segment of addition, and not a segment of shaddition? There are, I think, only two possible ways to respond to this question.

First, one might say that the calculator *does not* compute a segment of addition, or at least not of addition alone. What it computes is a segment of c different operations—of which, of course, shaddition is one—and it does not favor any one of them over the others. Hence, addition is in no way uniquely embodied in the calculator. The '+' that occurs on one of the keys of the calculator is strictly speaking a mislabeling, at least to the extent that its presence on that key implies that the key bears some "special" relation to addition, some relation that it does not also bear to infinitely many other binary operations. It may, of course, be a harmless, and, indeed, a very useful mislabeling, given our interests.

Secondly, one might say that the calculator does compute a segment of the addition operation, and that this is a *conventional* truth. Since it is true prior to the establishment of any convention that addition is the only operation of any interest to us, such that the part of the calculator activated by the '+' key embodies a segment of that operation, we adopt a convention to the effect that our calculator embodies a segment of addition, and the convention *makes it true* that the calculator embodies a segment of addition and of no "competing" operation. But a physically identical calculator produced by another species with other interests might embody a segment of one of the competing operations.

Can we say anything analogous to either of these things about the Arcturans and their symbol? It certainly does not seem to be at all plausible to say anything in any way analogous to the "conventionalist" account of the symbol inscribed on the calculator. We cannot say that there is a convention in force that '✳' represents addition and that that convention makes it true that '✳' represents addition. For who would establish the convention? Not the Arcturans: they would need to have some sort of prior grasp of addition to establish the convention, a grasp that existed independently of convention. And if they had that, there would be no need to appeal to convention to explain the fact that one of their symbols referred to addition. Not we human beings: if we were to say this, we should be committed to saying that before we met the Arcturans they *did not* mean addition by '✳', and that if we had never met them they would never have meant addition by '✳'. It is, moreover, absurd to think that the Arcturans would need the help of another species to refer to or mean a particular binary operation by one of their symbols. If they needed such help, shouldn't *we* need the help of another species to mean addition by '+'? I suppose one *might* say that God had some sort of interest in the Arcturans' having a symbol that meant addition, and that *He* had established a convention to the effect that the Arcturans meant addition by '✳'. But I doubt whether anyone, theist, atheist, or agnostic, would be pleased with this solution to the problem, despite the long tradition of appeals to God to help philosophers out of epistemological and metaphysical holes they have dug for themselves.

What about the other possibility? Suppose we say that the Arcturans *do not* use addition, and that our translation of '✳' is, strictly speaking, a mistranslation, albeit a harmless and useful one? But if the Arcturans do not mean addition by '✳', then, surely, they do not mean any binary operation by this symbol. (Would anyone seriously maintain that they meant one of the others?) And if this is true of the Arcturans, it should also be true of us: our symbol '+' does not pick out one of the *c* binary operations defined on all the natural numbers. To suppose that we could refer to a particular binary operation and they could not would be speciesism at its worst. The Arcturans and we are essentially equivalent in our abilities to refer to mathematical objects, and their dispositions and behavior in relation to '✳' differ in no important way from our dispositions and behavior in relation to '+'. If, therefore, their use of '✳' does not pick out a particular binary operation, neither does our use of '+'.

The lesson of our visit to the Arcturans would seem to be that if behavioral dispositions are all we have to go by, we do not mean a particular binary operation by '+'. (It is important to remember that by "dispositions" we do not mean simply *individual* dispositions, dispositions of this or that person to get answers using an algorithm. As Kripke has pointed out,[16] a theory that explained an individual's grasp of '+' entirely in terms of that individual's dispositions to use that sign would imply that no one could ever use '+' *incorrectly*, for one's answer to a question posed using the symbol '+' must inevitably be in accord with one's dispositions as regards the use of that symbol. Rather, we mean dispositions—centered on, but not exhausted by, dispositions to use an algorithm to come up with strings of symbols in certain circumstances— embodied by or in the whole community of human '+'-users.) Dispositions, even the dispositions of an entire population, will not provide an answer to the question, 'How is it that human beings or Arcturans mean a particular binary operation by '+'?' simply because there are infinitely many binary operations that are consistent with the dispositions of an entire species to use '+' or '✳' and which share an initial segment with addition (if, indeed, there is such an operation as addition) that runs right out to the Enormous numbers.

But if dispositions will not provide an answer to our question, what will? What else *is* there, after all?

It is tempting to try to explain how it is possible to mean a particular binary operation by '+' by means of an appeal to the concept of *going on in the same way*. (Perhaps it is only at this point that a truly Wittgensteinian theme enters the discussion. A major theme in *Philosophical Investigations* is the idea that we learn the meaning of a word by learning a rule for its use—whether by being shown instances of the correct application of that word, or by being given a general description of the way the word is used—and our *having* learnt the meaning of the word consists in our applying the rule in novel situations in the same way as the way we were taught.) When we learn an algorithm for addition, one might argue, part of what we learn is that the algorithm is to be applied in the *same* way, no matter how large the numbers to which it is applied. Let us look at an example that illustrates how this seemingly rather commonplace observation might be thought to be relevant to our problem. Let us pretend that we enjoy a God's-eye view of the natural numbers, and that in consequence we are able to consider a particular inaccessibly divergent operation, *ddition. (The pretense of a God's-eye view is not essential to our argument; we could avoid this pretense by quantifying over inaccessibly divergent operations.) If we can pretend to a God's-eye view of the natural numbers, we can pretend that we are able to imagine a being who is actually capable of computing s*ms in some significant segment of that prodigiously remote arithmetical region in which *ddition and addition diverge—"the divergent region," I shall call it. We are to imagine that this being does his s*ms just as we do our sums: by applying an algorithm to strings of symbols (he uses decimal notation, just as we do) that represent numbers; but *he* is capable of the algorithmic manipulation of strings that represent the Enormous numbers that inhabit a significant segment of the divergent region. And let us suppose that this being is also capable of doing *sums* in that part of the divergent region. Now (the argument commences) this being would be aware that he had to apply a different algorithm to do s*ms in the divergent region from the one he applied to do sums, and (the argument continues) he would be aware that when he was doing sums he was applying the very same rule that we arithmetically puny human beings have devised to compute what we call sums—the only difference being that he was applying it to strings of symbols whose length we could not so much as conceive.[17] He would see that he was applying the *same algorithm* in the divergent region that we apply to the minuscule numbers to which we have access. Hence (the argument concludes), our instructions for the use of '+' do rule out *ddition, and all other inaccessibly divergent operations, as possible interpretations of '+'.

Will this do?

Let us examine the notion of "going on in the same say." Here is a well-known case from Wittgenstein.[18] I teach someone a rule for continuing a sequence of numbers by displaying five or six numbers that I describe as the first few terms of the sequence: 2, 4, 6, 8, 10.... Later, I am surprised to discover that in the vicinity of the number 1000, he continues the sequence like this: ... 996, 998, 1000, 1004, 1008, 1012. ... I take him to task for "not going on in the same way." He replies that he *is* going on in the same way. And why should he not make this reply? There are an infinite number of sequences having the initial segment 2, 4, 6, 8, 10 ..., and he is certainly writing out some of the members of one of them—of *lots* of them—and is in that sense "going on in the same way." And what other sense of 'going on in the same way' is there?

It may, of course, be true, it *is* true, that what my pupil does is unnatural, so unnatural, so contrary to the nature of human beings, that it could occur only in the imagination of a philosopher. But when we say this, we are making a statement about what one might call our natural history.[19] And we are *not* making a statement about any of the following things:

— the intrinsic, mathematical features of the finite sequence 2, 4, 6, 8, 10.
— the intrinsic, mathematical features of any of the *c* omega-sequences of natural numbers of which this finite sequence is an initial segment, including the one I "intended" when I gave him instructions for continuing a sequence (always assuming that there exists an infinite sequence that is the one I intended).
— what is explicitly represented in one's mind when one is told, "Now I'm going to teach you a rule for continuing a sequence: 2, 4, 6, 8, 10. Just go on like that."

The same points would, of course, apply if I had supplemented my instructions with the words, "As you can see, the rule is: Each term of the sequence is 2 greater than the previous member," or with the words, " ... the rule is: $t_k = t_{k-1} + 2$." For suppose I *had* given these supplementary instructions, and my pupil nevertheless went on in the way imagined by Wittgenstein. I say, "I said that the rule was 'add 2'." He replies, "I *was* applying the rule 'add 2'." Why should he not have interpreted the form of words 'add *n*' as conveying the instruction that you and I would convey by using the words 'add *n* if the previous term is less than 1000; otherwise add *2n*'? Only our natural history rules this out. And our natural history must mean our natural dispositions as regards interpreting instructions for continuing a sequence. But how can these natural dispositions force upon us *one* member of the set of all omega-sequences of natural numbers as the sequence that is determined by the instructions I gave my pupil, if they are impotent to distinguish among the members of a vast subset of this set? It would seem that they could do no more than rule out of court sequences with certain initial segments (including, of course, all those having initial segments consistent with the terms of the sequence developed by my unnatural pupil). A similar question can be asked about addition: How can our natural dispositions tie our meaning for '+' down to *one* member of the set {addition, the inaccessibly divergent operations}—assuming that there is such a set—when these dispositions are impotent to distinguish among the members of this set? And we have seen the answer to this question: they cannot.

When, therefore, we talked about a being who was capable of computing sums in the divergent region, and when we said that he would see that when he was doing this he was not using the algorithm that we human beings learn when we learn the meaning of '+', it is hard to see what we could mean. We described his noetic state, the content of his mind, in these words: 'He would see that he was applying the *same algorithm* in the divergent region that we apply to the minuscule numbers to which we have access.' But these are *our* words. They are words in *our* language. And if there is nothing that can fix the sense in which we use the words 'applying the same algorithm in the divergent region', then the words we have used to describe the state of mind of our imaginary being do not make sense. And what could fix the sense of these words? Not what is present in our mind when we are taught the meaning of '+'. Not our natural history. And what else is there?

One possibility that has no doubt occurred to some readers is that the set {addition, the divergent operations}—"the addition set," let us call it—does indeed exist, and that exactly one of the operations belonging to this set has a certain intrinsic, mathematical property, a property that belongs to it independently of the accidents of notation and the procedures that are laid down in particular addition algorithms, a property that somehow renders the one operation belonging to the addition set that possesses it salient to the human mind (and no doubt to the Arcturan mind, and to all the minds of any beings who are not vastly more complex than we) and that this is the operation that we mean by '+'—that it is in fact *addition* that has this feature. (It would have to be addition, of course. To suppose that the addition set existed and that some *other* operation was its single salient member would be to fall into pragmatic contradiction.) What might this property be? Well, such words as 'simplicity' and 'straightforwardness' and 'non-arbitrariness' suggest themselves. And, indeed, it seems to me that *if* there is such a thing as addition, then this must indeed be such a property. The only difficulty I have with this suggestion is that I can think of no reason for believing that there is such a property for addition to have—other than the fact that if addition exists there must be such a property and addition must have it. As to 'simplicity' and the other candidates for terms that might actually denote a property whose possession would make one member of the addition set salient to the human mind, it is not at all clear to me what it means to apply these terms to mathematical objects in themselves. Surely, I want to say—in some moods, anyway—simplicity must be a feature of notation, or of the procedures laid down in the statement of an algorithm, or must be relative to our capacities for constructing mental representations of mathematical objects. Well, couldn't this last idea be of use? Perhaps only one member of the addition set—addition, of course—is one that we are able to represent. If this is so, however, it must be so in virtue of some intrinsic feature, or combination of features, of the operation. And what reason have we *a priori* for thinking that there is such a feature and that exactly one member of the addition set has it?

Let us try something else.

It will perhaps have occurred to some readers that it may be possible for us to bring some of our general mathematical knowledge about addition to bear on the problem. It may be argued that we can distinguish between addition and the divergent operations owing to the fact that there are mathematical properties, ones we can specify, that addition does not share with various of the divergent operations.[20] Consider, for example, the fact that the sum of any number and the number 1 is the successor of that number—the next-larger number. A moment's reflection will reveal that the corresponding relation does not hold between just any divergent operation and the successor operation. And if we consider *all* of the relations that addition bears to the successor operation, it is clear that we can use these relations to specify addition. (After all, addition can be defined in terms of the successor operation.) But this argument presupposes that the operator 'the successor of' picks out a unique *unary* operation on the natural numbers, and there would seem to be every reason to think that 'the successor of' is in the same boat as '+'. If we are indeed unable to specify a unique binary operation on the natural numbers to be the operation expressed by '+', why should we be able to specify a unique unary operation on the natural numbers to be the operation expressed by 'the successor of'? It is a trivial exercise to show that for every axiomization of the arithmetic of the natural numbers, there exist models that interpret '+' as a divergent operation and on which all of the axioms come out true. Such models, of course, will have to reinterpret other items in the vocabulary of the language of arithmetic as well—items like 'the successor of'. (When I say that this is a trivial exercise, I mean that it is a trivial exercise provided that the arithmetical symbols we use in proving the existence of these models really do pick out operations and relations defined on all of the natural numbers.)[21]

These remarks are likely to met with considerable resistance. Perhaps this resistance could be articulated in the following words. "There is, surely, something very queer about the notion that we do not grasp the successor operation. We understand the notion *next larger than* quite independently of any ability we may happen to have to use an algorithm for turning a string of symbols that represent a given number into a string that represents the next-larger number. And, when you think about it, this fact seems to undermine your whole argument. Since addition can be defined in terms of the successor operation, it follows that the question whether we pick out a unique operation by the word 'addition' can be answered (and answered Yes) quite independently of any considerations involving our natural history or our dispositions to generate determinate strings of symbols by the use of an algorithm."

This is a point eminently worthy of consideration, but it does not really involve the successor operation, or not in any essential way. If our grasp of the successor operation essentially involves the mastery of a mechanical procedure for replacing the last digit in a string of digits (and the next-to-last, if the last is replaced by '0', and the next-to-next-to last if the next-to-last is replaced by '0', . . . , and prefixing the string with a '1' if the first is replaced by '0'), [22] then our earlier arguments about addition would appear to apply to the successor operation with little modification. The critic, however, has argued that we have a grasp of the successor operation that does not require the mastery of an algorithm—we simply *understand* the concept "next larger than." But I would ask the following question. When we look inward and try to examine this grasp, what do we find? What do we find, that is, besides a sense of the mastery of an algorithm? What do we find besides a sort of vague, all-purpose mental representation of a string of digits "of any length" (a representation that is focused, as it were, on the final two or three digits in the string), together with a conviction that we could "in principle" apply "the algorithm" to "that string," a conviction that we know how to start and that the task, however long, will never confront us with anything that is not covered by the rule we have mastered?

What we find, I think, is set-theoretical, or at least belongs to some intuitive mode of mathematical thought that mathematicians have used the concepts of set theory to put into rational and systematic order. What we find has as an essential component the idea of the size of a set. And this idea depends on the idea of two sets' being in one-to-one correspondence. An explicit definition of the successor operation will also involve the idea of a number's *measuring* the size of a set.[23] (Moreover, an explicit definition of addition in terms of the successor operation requires the apparatus of set theory.) But we can give a definition of addition on the natural numbers in set-theoretic terms without bothering to mention the successor operation. Let us therefore apply the essentials of the above argument "directly" to addition, without bothering to mention the successor function.

Quite independently of any algorithm for computing the sum of two numbers, and prior to the establishment of any system of axioms intended to capture some class of arithmetical truths (the "direct" argument runs), we understand the *concept* of addition. Let us embody this understanding in an *explicit definition* of '+':

> For all numbers x and y, $x + y$ is the unique number that measures the size of any set S that satisfies the following condition: There are two sets whose intersection is empty and which are such that x measures the size of one of them and y measures the size of the other, and S is their union.[24]

Do we not, in providing this explicit definition of '+', specify the operation that this operator expresses?

This is unsatisfactory. In giving this definition, we assume that there is a binary operation (expressed by 'x measures the size of y') that is defined on all of the natural numbers and on all of the members of some suitably vast set of sets. And we could obviously carry out an argument with respect to *this* operator that was sound if and only if our earlier argument with respect to '+' is sound.

But might it not be that we "just understand" the idea of a number's measuring the size of a set? This suggestion seems to me to have much less initial plausibility than the suggestion that we "just understand" the idea of a next-larger number or even that we "just understand" addition. The initial plausibility of supposing that we "just understand" these two concepts is, to my mind, simply a consequence of their familiarity. The concept of a number's measuring the size of a set is somewhat less familiar, and I, at any rate, do not feel nearly as strong a "pull" in the direction of supposing that I "just understand" it. It seems to me, on reflection, that my understanding of the concept of a number's measuring the size of a set is based on certain procedures that I have learned to apply—such as counting the members of what I intuitively understand to be a set, or putting the members of two sets into one-one correspondence by drawing lines on paper or in my mind, or establishing a rule that associates every member of one set with some member of another. The idea that a mastery of these procedures (even if it were a "social mastery," embodied in the whole community of users of 'measures the size of') would enable us to pick out a unique relation to be the one that is expressed by 'x measures the size of y' would seem to face difficulties exactly analogous to the difficulties faced by the idea that the mastery of certain procedures enables us to pick out a unique binary operation to be the one that is expressed by 'the sum of x and y'. The possibility remains, however, that we can "bypass" these procedures and define 'measures the size of' in terms of some concept or concepts that we "just understand." If we could do this, it would show that a mastery of these procedures was not really essential to our understanding of 'measures the size of'. I know of only one way in which such a definition might be attempted: to cease to regard numbers as *sui generis* objects that measure the sizes of sets, and to regard them as special sets. If we do that, we can provide a definition of 'measures the size of' in entirely set-theoretical terms. If we do that, however, there will be no point in carrying on our argument in terms of 'measures the size of', for, once the natural numbers have been identified with certain sets, we can define addition on the natural numbers as a set-theoretic operation "directly," without having to make use of the concept of a number's measuring the size of a set. We may, therefore, just as well turn once more to a "direct" argument: An argument to the effect that an appropriate set-theoretic reduction of the arithmetic of the natural numbers would enable us to specify the operation denoted by 'addition' by using set-theoretical concepts that we "just understand."

In a way, the philosopher who appealed to a reduction of arithmetic to set theory to specify the operation denoted by 'addition' (and who believed that this was the only way to evade the above line of argument against there being such a mathematical object as addition) would be conceding that there was no such thing as addition. For it is obvious that if any mathematical object is uniquely addition, that object had already been determinately picked out by the thoughts and activities of human beings by, say, the end of the eighteenth century. And it is also obvious that nothing people had thought or done in 1800 or earlier favored any one of the set-theoretic reductions of arithmetic (even one of the now-available ones) over any of the others. But the proponent of a set-theoretic specification of addition might well grant this point, at least for the sake of argument, and speak as follows: "Even if there is *now* no such thing as addition, there could easily come to be such a thing. More exactly, it could come to pass that the word 'addition' stood for a particular operation that had all of the features that we wanted an operation denoted by this word to have. To bring about this eventuality, we should have only to establish a convention to the effect that 'addition' denoted the appropriate operation in one of the available set-theoretic reductions of the arithmetic of the natural numbers. The obvious fact that establishing such a convention would not be worth the trouble shows that the non-existence of addition should not trouble us very much."

Now one might argue about whether this speech was a relevant or an evasive reply to the point to which it is addressed. But I want to say something about it that is unrelated to this question.

Either the set-theoretic universe—at least, say, something like the Zermelo-Fraenkel universe—exists or it does not. If it does not exist, then no set-theoretic reduction of arithmetic is possible. If it does exist . . . well, we know how many alternative models there are for any axiomatic set-theory. That is, we know this if we know that we can informally specify the features of these models using naive set theory. But what gives us the right to suppose that our naive understanding of 'ϵ' enables us to pick out a particular one of the many relations that hold between objects and sets? What gives us the right to suppose that we "just understand" set membership? Not, surely, the informal explanations of set membership in the first few pages of Halmos; not our memory of what was in our minds when we first read these pages; not our knowledge of our natural history.[25] Or not unless there is something wrong with our arguments about '+'. If these arguments were wrong, then we do not need to appeal to set-theoretic reduction to evade them, and if there was nothing wrong with them, then set-theoretic reduction will not, in the last analysis, evade them, for similar arguments will show that 'ϵ' does not express a unique relation, not even a unique relation defined on the universe of some tame set theory like Zermelo-Fraenkel.

It would seem that there are no other accounts than those we have examined of how it might be that 'addition' designates a particular one of the binary operations on the natural numbers. It would seem, therefore, that the word 'addition' does not designate a particular one of the binary operations on the natural numbers. It would seem that there is no such thing as addition.

This does not, of course, mean that people never add. As I said, I've seen it done. What the argument of this essay shows, if indeed it succeeds in showing anything, is that the human activity called addition cannot be regarded as the application to a few very small numbers of a procedure that determines uniquely an operation that is defined on all of the natural numbers. But if this reflection shows that accountants have nothing to fear from the argument of this essay, what does it show about pure mathematicians? What about those professionally interested in statements like 'Addition is commutative' and 'There are infinitely many numbers that can be expressed in more than one way as the sum of two cubes'? Doesn't the conclusion of our argument entail that the kinds of things they say are radically defective and that they should therefore just stop saying them? (And, of course, if our argument shows that number theorists should close up shop, the same practical consequence would follow for, say, specialists in the theory of non-linear partial differential equations.)

I do not believe that the argument of this essay does entail this practical conclusion (that mathematicians should just stop doing what they have been doing), but I cannot say why. I cannot say why because I do not have an adequate philosophical understanding of mathematics, and I expect no one else does, either. (Indeed, I wonder whether anyone has an adequate philosophical understanding of anything.) But I will not simply leave the matter there. Here is what I will do. I will outline two "nihilistic" philosophical arguments whose conclusions are very strongly analogous to my conclusion about addition, and I will offer some reflections on the practical consequences of accepting them. My reflections convince me that although the situation of pure mathematics is hopeless, it is not at all serious.[26]

The first argument. Suppose we accept, as many able philosophers do, the following very strong principle of mereological summation: any things whatever have a mereological sum. If we do, we are faced with a problem discovered (as far as I know) by Peter Unger and called by him "the problem of the many."[27] Let us take as an example the chair I am sitting on as I write. Assume for the sake of argument that this chair exists. The chair is obviously "made of" elementary particles: if it exists at all, it must be the mereological sum of certain elementary particles. Let us call the elementary particles that compose the chair "the particles." Now let us pretend that we are able to refer to one of the particles, and let us call it 'X'. Consider the mereological sum of "the particles other than X." This object is numerically distinct from the sum of the particles. But the sum of the particles and the sum of the particles other than X are indistinguishable (by us, at least). There is simply no way in which any phrase in a human language could attach to one of them rather than the other. (The fact that we, in the context of the present argument, are apparently able to use phrases that refer to each of these mereological sums is due to our assumption that the chair exists and is the sum of certain elementary particles, and to our pretense that we are able to refer to a particular elementary particle that is a part of the chair.) Therefore, there are two equally good candidates for the office "referent of 'this chair'." And a moment's thought will show that there are not only two such candidates, but a vast—although finite—number of candidates. But the words 'this chair' could refer to something only if there were a thing that was somehow the *one best* candidate for the office "referent of 'this chair'." We must therefore conclude that the phrase 'this chair' does not refer to anything, and that there is therefore no such thing as this chair.[28]

The second argument. Suppose we accept, as many able philosophers do, the thesis that time is structured in a way suggested by the real number line. If time is indeed so structured, then particular instants of time, the correlates in the structural analogy of points on the real line, are very elusive things, so elusive that no one has ever referred to one of them. And it follows from this that no one has ever referred to a particular hour, day, year, decade, century, or millennium. (For it seems inevitable to suppose that—on the "real line" model of the structure of time—if there is such a thing as the seventeenth century, it is a thing that stands to individual instants of time as a bounded interval on the real line stands to individual real numbers. And if one can refer to a bounded interval on the real line, then one can refer to an individual real number: for example, the number that is either the smallest number in that interval or the largest number smaller than all of the numbers in that interval. Similarly—on the real-number-line model of time—if the description 'the seventeenth century' actually denoted something, then one could single out the moment of time that was either the earliest moment in the seventeenth century or the latest moment earlier than all moments in the seventeenth century.)

Each of these two arguments is certainly valid. If the strong principle of mereological summation is correct, no one ever refers to a chair or to any other physical object. If time is structured like the real-number line, no one ever refers to a century or any other stretch of time. But even if the premises of the two arguments are true, it does not follow that no one ever pulls up a chair or knows the date. Nor does it follow that there is anything wrong with making assertions that have the form of quantifications over artifacts or calendar years; it does not follow that there is anything wrong with saying, "Some of her chairs are very good nineteenth-century copies of Chippendales," or "The world population has been growing faster in every successive decade of the twentieth century." (Imagine the World Health Organization deciding to cancel a project that was premised on the assumption that the world population had been growing faster in every successive decade of the twentieth century, owing to the discovery that, since time is structured in a way analogous to the real number line, there are no such decades as "the 1930s" or "the 1950s". Imagine, for that matter, a philosopher deciding not to regard time as structured in a way analogous to the real number line, since that way of regarding time, if accepted by the World Health Organization, would force that august body to cancel any project premised upon the existence of happenings in successive decades of the twentieth century.) These things do not follow, I would suppose, because (given the premises of the two arguments) the propositions expressed by the quoted sentences do not really entail the existence of uniquely specifiable artifacts or periods of time. How to understand the propositions expressed by the quoted sentences without supposing that they entail the existence of such things are difficult philosophical problems for the advocates of those two premises. I do not know how they should go about trying to solve them. What I would do in this sort of situation, however, is to try to improve my philosophical understanding; I would not even consider any suggestion to the effect that I should speak or act differently when I was conducting the business of everyday life.[29]

Notes

1. Saul Kripke, *Wittgenstein on Rules and Private Language: An Elementary Exposition* (Cambridge, Mass., 1982).

2. I use the phrase 'Kripke's arguments' to refer to certain arguments that occur as parts of Kripke's text. The following statements from *Wittgenstein on Rules and Private Language* should be kept in mind. "Primarily I can be read, except in a few obvious asides, as almost like an attorney presenting a major philosophical argument as it struck me. If the work has a main thesis of its own, it is that Wittgenstein's sceptical problem and argument are important, deserving of serious consideration" (*ix*). "In the following, I am largely trying to present Wittgenstein's argument, or, more accurately, that set of problems and arguments which I personally have gotten out of reading Wittgenstein. With few exceptions, I am *not* trying to present views of my own; neither am I trying to endorse or to criticize Wittgenstein's approach" (9). "I suspect . . . that to attempt to present Wittgenstein's argument precisely is to some extent to falsify it. Probably many of my formulations and recastings of the argument are done in a way Wittgenstein would not himself approve. So the present paper should be thought of as expounding neither 'Wittgenstein's' argument nor 'Kripke's': rather Wittgenstein's argument as it struck Kripke, as it presented a problem for him" (9).

3. Cf. Kripke, *Wittgenstein on Rules*, 19–20. I find Kripke's argument on these pages plausible but not indisputable.

4. I shall use the term 'the natural numbers' to express the concept more properly expressed by 'the non-negative integers'—that is, I shall include 0 among the natural numbers. I do this because that is the concept I want to have a handy name for, and 'the non-negative integers' is cumbersome.

5. The argument of this essay could be looked on as a dilemma: Either the standard picture is correct or it is not; if it is not, there is no such thing as addition because there is no suitable candidate for the office of addition; if it is correct, there is no such thing as addition because (for reasons that will transpire) there are many equally good candidates for this office, many candidates tied for first place; therefore, there is no such thing as addition.

6. Or, if you like, 'The English word "addition" is a name for addition'.

7. This category would include at least those who have never heard of Socrates. It is an interesting question in the philosophy of proper names whether someone could have "heard of" or could "know about" Socrates, but *not* know that Socrates is a human being. It is not, however, a question we need consider.

8. It may be that there are philosophers who will want to say that if the word 'addition' does not denote a particular binary operation (or any other particular object), then this word is meaningless, or has only a partial or incomplete meaning, one it shares with 'subtraction' and 'division' and all other words that purport, falsely, to denote particular binary operations. This position might be appealing to some because of its close analogy with certain popular views about the meanings, or lack thereof, of proper names that are without denotations. If this view if right, I should rephrase my conclusion as 'The word "addition"—insofar as it is supposed to name a mathematical object—is meaningless'. The words of my title would then have to be regarded as a loose way of expressing this semantical thesis. This conclusion is close enough to mine that I have no desire to argue with those who would prefer it to mine—just as a classical atheist might have no desire to argue with the logical positivist who contended that, strictly speaking, one should not say, "There is no God," but rather, "The word 'God' is meaningless."

9. Or so it seems reasonable to believe, although there is no direct historical evidence for this. At any rate there *is* a very simple addition algorithm that works by manipulating Roman numerals. (See M. Detlefsen, D. K. Erlandson, J. C. Heston, and C. M. Young, "Computation with Roman Numerals," *Archive for History of Exact Sciences* 15, no. 2, (1976): 141–48.)

10. Kripke, *Wittgenstein on Rules and Private Language*, 15. Since the point is not a sensitive one, I have described the physical algorithm in a natural but misleading way: I

have talked as if an algorithm takes *numbers*, and not numerals, as its input and output. Strictly speaking, I should not have said, e.g., 'count out *x* pebbles into a pile'; I should have said something like 'make a pile of pebbles by placing pebbles one at a time on a previously bare surface, saying the names of the numerals in numerical order starting with '1', one numeral for each act of placing, till you reach the *x*th numeral; then stop'.

11. Skewe, a student of Littlewood, showed that the primes do a certain thing (a thing that it was known that they did somewhere) before they exceed that number. I have read somewhere that this is the largest finite number ever to occur in a mathematical proof.

12. Or so it seems to me. But some people I have talked with are inclined to dispute this thesis. They argue that one can refer to any number, given world enough and time. As to "world enough," I have heard the suggestion that, for any natural number, there is a world that contains human beings and exactly that number of, say, atoms. In a world containing *n* atoms, one could use the phrase 'the number of atoms' to refer to *n* even if one had no other way to refer to *n*. It will do for my purposes to weaken 'in no possible world' to 'in no possible world that has the same laws of nature and is of about the same size as the actual world'. As to "time," one could obviously refer to any natural number given enough time. Let us, therefore, build into our definition of 'Enormous number' some extravagant time-limit on acts of reference to numbers: a thousand years or a million years or what you will. (Perhaps I should also add to the definition the qualification 'by the use of their own unaided natural powers' to rule out cases of divine aid.) I do not believe that any of these qualifications is really necessary. I believe that I could easily name a finite number that exceeds the number of atoms that exists in any possible world, and I doubt whether, for every *n*, there is a world in which a human being (or a multitude of human beings, working in cooperative succession across many generations) spends *n* years speaking the name of a single number, and I doubt whether there is any possible world in which God helps us to refer to numbers that we could not otherwise refer to. But nothing of any substance turns on whether I am right in these convictions.

13. Since there are only a finite number of strategies aimed at naming the largest possible number in a given number of "moves," or at least only a finite number of such strategies that it is humanly possible to learn, then, assuming that any two strategies can be compared as to efficiency, there must be a highest degree of efficiency possessed by any strategy.

14. What about the description, 'the least number such that some inaccessibly divergent operation and addition diverge on that number'? Does this description not refer, paradoxically, to a referentially inaccessible number? The resolution of this paradox (its similarity to the Richard paradox is, I believe, superficial) turns on the fact that 'Enormous', and, therefore, 'inaccessibly divergent', are vague predicates. As a consequence, the above description, like 'the shortest tall man', does not refer to anything. The fact that 'inaccessibly divergent' is not a sharply defined predicate is of no relevance to the question of the validity of the argument in the text.

15. The pocket-calculator analogy is borrowed from a lecture Kripke delivered at Cornell University in the mid-1980s. I can no longer remember the point Kripke was making by means of this analogy, and I cannot be sure which of the details of my development of the analogy are his and which are my own inventions. The "conventionalist" explanation of the correctness of interpreting the '+' key of the calculator as expressing addition, and the impossibility of appealing to convention to explain how it is that human beings mean *plus* by '+', certainly have their origin in Kripke's lecture, but I cannot remember much about the form his discussion of convention took. What follows in the text could be a faithful reproduction of what he said or a radical distortion or anything in between.

16. Kripke, *Wittgenstein on Rules*, 28–32.

17. He might even go so far as to say that when he computed s*ms in the divergent region, he was in some important sense applying a *different algorithm* from the one he applied when he computed s*ms in those regions in which addition and *ddition coincide. He might say that in the "coincident" regions he computed s*ms simply by applying the

addition algorithm, and that he had to apply what was really a different algorithm in the divergent region. He might say that the so-called algorithm for *ddition was really two algorithms, and that its only unity derived from the fact that the two algorithms came in the same package (so to speak), a package that also contained a sheet of instructions to the effect that the user was to apply one of them within a certain range of arguments and the other in the complement of that range. He might say that, if one insisted on calling this amalgam of two algorithms "the *ddition algorithm," one should say that at a certain point there is a "bend" in the *ddition algorithm (*cf.* Simon Blackburn, "The Individual Strikes Back," *Synthese* [1984]). But the argument does not require us to suppose that he would say any of these things.

18. *Philosophical Investigations* I, § 185.

19. This use of the phrase 'our natural history' is suggested by Wittgenstein's use of the phrase at such places as *Philosophical Investigations* I § 25 and *Remarks on the Foundations of Mathematics* I § 63. But, as far as I know, Wittgenstein never applies 'our natural history' specifically to our natural tendency to apply a rule in certain ways in cases that were not thought of while we were learning the rule.

20. Cf. *Wittgenstein on Rules and Private Language*, p. 16, n. 12.

21. Ibid. Kripke points out that this argument applies not only to the specifically mathematical items in the language of elementary arithmetic (the items that receive semantical assignments in the specification of a model), but also to the purely logical items in the vocabulary of that language, items such as the universal quantifier and the identity-sign. These, too, can be reinterpreted.

22. Or if it essentially involves our mastery of some procedure equivalent to this one, without essentially involving any particular procedure.

23. Something like this: For any number x, the successor of x is the unique number that measures the size of any set S that satisfies the following condition: for any y belonging to S, x measures the size of $S - \{y\}$.

24. I am grateful to Michael Kremer for saving me from an embarrassing quantifier error in this definition.

25. *Cf.* David Lewis, *Parts of Classes*, including an Appendix by John P. Burgess, A. P. Hazen, and David Lewis (Oxford, 1991), 29–31. Lewis's book is in part an argument for the conclusion that set theory can be reconstructed using only a concept that we "just understand": parthood. Lewis shows that membership can be defined in terms of 'part' and 'singleton of'. He shows how to use Ramsey techniques to eliminate 'singleton of'. Finally, in the Appendix, the authors show how to apply the required Ramsey techniques without quantifying over relations or other set-theoretical objects. A discussion of the question whether Lewis's reconstruction of set theory could be used to refute the argument of the present essay would raise questions that I cannot address here. Here are three: If parthood has the features that Lewis's reconstruction requires, is it evident that we "just understand" this notion? No one has ever actually understood the sentences of set theory to mean what the corresponding sentences of Lewis's reconstruction mean; what is the relevance, if any, of this fact for our argument, which turns on what people actually have meant by mathematical sentences? Suppose that there were a race of beings who conducted all of their mathematical reasoning in the terms provided by Lewis's reconstruction, and who had never known any other way of doing things; if these beings were to study a human text on elementary mathematics, wouldn't they agree with me that there was no such thing as addition—in more or less the way that a nineteenth-century mathematician would agree with Berkeley that there were no such things as infinitesimals?

26. I believe that someone said this about the economy of Hungary in the 1930s.

27. Peter Unger, "The Problem of the Many," *Midwest Studies in Philosophy* 5 (1980): 411–67.

28. This argument can be stated much more compactly as follows: If there were such a thing as the chair, it would be possible to refer to the set whose members are the elementary

particles that compose the chair; but it is impossible (for a human being, at any rate) to refer to a particular set of elementary particles—or at least to a particular set that is of anything like the size that the set of all of the particles that compose the chair would have to have. The force of the compact argument, however, is best appreciated by one who has gone through the longer argument in the text.

29. Many of the ideas in this essay were developed in response to the arguments of Paul Hrycaj's doctoral dissertation, *An Essay on Saul Kripke's "Wittgenstein on Rules and Private Language"*, which I supervised. Drafts of the essay were read to departmental colloquia at California State University, Northridge, Cornell University, Franklin and Marshall College, New York University, Notre Dame University, Queen's University, the University of California, Santa Barbara, the University of California, Riverside, and the University of Rochester. I am especially grateful for help and comments from José Benardete, John Bennett, David Braun, Anthony Brueckner, Marian David, Richard Feldman, Michael Kremer, Henry Laycock, David Lewis, Colin McGinn, Alvin Plantinga, Alex Rosenberg, Glenn Ross, Nathan Salmon, Roy Sorensen, Cindy Stern, Peter Unger, Ralph Wedgwood, Howard Wettstein, Edward Wierenga, Takashi Yagisawa, and C. M. Young.

Quietism

NICK ZANGWILL

1. METAPHILOSOPHICAL PESSIMISM

Metaphysics—the enquiry into the constitution of reality—seems like the very crown of philosophy. What could be more exciting, more important, and more substantive than the pursuit of such a discipline? The majority of philosophers have been content to assume that metaphysics is a viable enterprise; they have held various metaphysical views and engaged in metaphysical arguments. But there has always been a small but persistent maverick minority of philosophers who have cast aspersions on the whole undertaking. Metaphysics, they tell us, cannot be what it seems. There is something desperately wrong at the heart of the discipline. The jewel is a fake; it is in fact worthless glass. Philosophers make a lot of noise about metaphysics, but perhaps there are really no genuine metaphysical issues—only a lot of bogus hot air. Perhaps metaphysics is a meaningless tale told by idiot philosophers—full of sound and fury, signifying nothing. These pessimistic philosophers may have been few, but they rank among their numbers no less than Wittgenstein, the positivists, and perhaps Kant. So the attitude is to be taken seriously.

Despite the importance of the metaphilosophical issue about whether metaphysical issues have content, the sad fact is that philosophers with the pessimistic metaphilosophy hardly ever give much argument for their attitude. The attitude is usually held with a dogmatism far outstripping that of any metaphysician! Argument is needed because metaphysical issues *seem* to make perfect sense. Asking whether there are numbers or times does not seem very different from asking whether there are yeties or flying saucers. And asking whether there is a genuine property of goodness or causal efficacy does not seem so different from asking whether there is a genuine property of simultaneity or lunacy. It is just that the categories that interest metaphysicians are wider and more fundamental than these others. The burden of proof lies with the metaphilosophical pessimist.

There is one philosopher who has recently provided a pattern of argument which might be employed so as to yield such a pessimistic result. This philosopher is Simon Blackburn, and the pattern of argument is what he calls 'quasi-realism'.[1] Blackburn himself does not endorse the pessimistic metaphilosophical conclusion—although he thinks that quasi-realism achieves much else. He does endorse considerable methodological caution: giving content to metaphysical issues may not be as simple as it seems. However, we may find that we can use Blackburn's argument to establish more than its progenitor desires or thinks can be achieved.

2. THE TWO FACES OF QUASI-REALISM

In recent years, one relatively clear sort of metaphysical debate has had the following structure: to begin with, we isolate some disputed range of judgments—moral, causal, modal, probabilistic, scientific, or whatever. The 'realist' holds two theses: (1) that the disputed range of judgments is 'cognitive'. A cognitive judgment is one whose role is to represent a realm of facts or states of affairs as it is, a cognitive judgment aims to be true in virtue of the fact or state of affairs which it represents. And (2) that there really are some facts or states of affairs answering to the disputed judgments. There is a thesis about the mind and a thesis about the world. Let us call someone who denies both these claims a 'non-realist'. (In fact, (2) can be denied without (1), and then we have an 'error theory'.[2]) In the sorts of areas just mentioned, non-realism tends to take a particular form. Non-realism must do more than just deny (1) and (2); it must provide some positive account of the nature of the judgments. 'Projectivism' is the view that the disputed judgments express non-cognitive mental states, such as emotions, desires, habits, or expectations; but the projectivist also holds that such non-cognitive states are *spread* or *projected* onto the genuine facts and states of affairs. So we come to speak and think as if there were an extra layer of properties in the world. When we think in terms of morality and causality, we are projecting our attitudes and expectations onto the natural and acausal world. (Some areas of thought might be realist while others are projectivist. As Michael Dummett has emphasized, it makes no sense to be a realist or anti-realist, period; one can only be a realist or an anti-realist about some subject matter.) Such debates between realism and projectivism—about morality, causality, modality, or probability—look perfectly genuine.

The immediate practical problem, however, is how to *tell whether* our thought in some area is realistic or projectivistic. We need some *criterion* for determining when we are dealing with a range of thought whose *raison d'être* is that of matching facts. Now, what Blackburn calls 'quasi-realism' is the attempt to earn for the projectivist the right to think in ways which might be thought to be the preserve of the realist. For example, perhaps a projectivist can turn around and agree with the realist that the disputed sort of truth does not depend on what we think. Or perhaps quasi-realism can explain the way the disputed commitments occur unasserted in indirect contexts, such as the antecedent of conditionals. Quasi-realism tries to capture, on behalf of the projectivist, the features of ordinary thinking which a realist might naively propose as symptomatic of realism.

This is one face of quasi-realism; let us call it 'criterial quasi-realism'. The second face of quasi-realism is its more radical potential for undermining the very difference between realism and projectivism. This sort of quasi-realism is not concerned with features which are allegedly *symptomatic* of realism, but with the very thesis itself. Here, the quasi-realist's ambition is not just to capture mind-independence and other such features, so that we can no longer tell whether or not our thought is realistic. The ambition is to undermine the content of the whole debate. This sort of quasi-realism attempts to show that realism about some subject matter (and equally, its opposite) is *meaningless, not false*. The conclusion would be that there is no distinction which can be drawn between what we cognize in the world, and what we project onto it. Blackburn calls this pessimistic metaphilosophy 'quietism'. Let us refer to the pattern of argument which is supposed to establish this conclusion as 'quietist quasi-realism'. (There seems to be no immediately obvious reason why one should be a 'quietist' *tout court*; for example, one could be a quietist about moral philosophy, but a 'loudist' in the philosophy of science.) Blackburn takes this aspect of quasi-realism furthest in his "Truth, Realism, and the Regulation of Theory." For this reason I find this essay the most interesting and disturbing of all his various discussions of quasi-realism. In this essay, Blackburn puts the radical conclusion to which quasi-realism might lead us like this:

> I begin to doubt whether familiar ways of characterizing debates in the theory of truth—realism vs. instrumentalism, and so on—actually succeed in marking out interesting areas of dispute. (p. 353)

> There are certainly images and perhaps attitudes to our discourse within a field which seem to be associated with realism, but I shall argue that unless these are given some concrete employment they represent not so much subjects for decision as for nostalgia. (p. 353)

> our problem all along has been to determine whether a distinctive attitude really is associated with realism, and so far we have nothing but similes and images to gesture towards it. (p. 367)

This is obviously reminiscent of Wittgenstein's cynical metaphilosophical pronouncements. If quasi-realism makes good, it turns out that both the realist and the non-realist have only succeeded in producing disguised nonsense.

In this essay, I want to argue that we need not worry too much about the prospect of realism debates dissolving before our eyes. Irrespective of any views we might have about the success or lack of success of criterial quasi-realism in protecting projectivism by capturing features which are allegedly symptomatic of realism, quietist quasi-realism is no threat to the genuineness of realism debates. Quietist quasi-realism can be blocked. Even if there are no easy answers and metaphysical debates are not easy to decide, metaphysical debates have content.

3. REDUNDANCY

Quietist quasi-realism aims to capture, on behalf of the projectivist, the very thoughts which a realist and a projectivist previously agreed were sufficient to assert or to deny realism. Take morality: the thoughts over which realism and projectivism agree to differ are 'There are moral facts' or 'There are moral states of affairs'. It seems as if one side is saying something controversial and substantial which the other side is denying. Quietism will threaten if quasi-realism can show that the very notions of a moral *fact* or *state of affairs* can be appropriated by projectivism. Perhaps a projectivist has a perfect right to utter such locutions as 'There are moral facts' or 'There are moral states of affairs'.

How can a quasi-realist trap facts and states of affairs?

By now, most philosophers must have heard the news that the mere use of the truth-predicate is no big deal. It does not signal anything of earth-shaking metaphysical import. Given that a moral projectivist says that attitudes such as being for or against something are expressed in the indicative sentence form 'X is good', it is no monumental extra step to add 'And that's true'.[3] 'Truth theory', with all its insights into logical form, could follow naturally. Redundant truth is cheap.

Now if a projectivist can have a redundant notion of moral *truth*, a projectivist can also have a redundant notion of moral *facts* and *states of affairs*. What, after all, is a fact or state of affairs? It is the possession, by an object or event, of a property. But that seems to be neutral between whether the property is a real or a projected property. The moral projectivist, for example, should be expected to endorse saying things like 'It really is a fact that killing the innocent for fun is wrong'; and the causal projectivist should be expected to endorse saying things like 'Striking matches really causes fire, and that's a fact'. The fact that we say that there is a certain sort of fact or state of affairs does not imply any metaphysical commitment. (Perhaps this sounds better with 'facts' than with 'states of affairs', but this might be an accident of English.) The difficulty is to tell the difference between real and projected facts and states of affairs.

If a metaphysician cannot appeal to facts or states of affairs as categories which indicate reality, existence, or what is in the world, then what else? There seem to be no words left with which to frame a metaphysical thesis.

The availability of a redundant notion of facts and states of affairs seems to cause the ground to drop away from beneath the feet of the squabbling metaphysicians. However, I think we do not reach this quietist conclusion quite so quickly. The problem is that if talk of facts and states of affairs amounts to so little, then it is unclear why we go in for it. What is the point of such talk? (The same goes for the notion of truth.) Quasi-realism must not merely explain why moral or causal projectivism *can* go in for talk of facts or states of affairs, but also why it *does* and why it *should*. We do not talk of comic facts and states of affairs in the way that we are prone to talk of moral and causal facts and states of affairs. So what is it which is special about morality and causality which explains why we not only can but do employ this locution? A redundancy theory of facts or states of affairs might tell us about the *semantics* of talk about facts and states of affairs, but not its *pragmatics*. If redundant talk of truth, facts, and states of affairs is cheap, why do we not deploy such talk more widely? The suspicion will be that we deploy these notions in just those areas where we are committed to realism. Thus the redundancy point does not have the immediate quietist consequence that it initially seems to have. If we are to embrace quietism, we need more argument.

4. QUIETISM AND THE INTERNAL READING

The following strategy seems to me to be the most likely to succeed. For any sentence which we might naively think expresses a metaphysical claim, the quasi-realist must find a *non-metaphysical* or *internal reading* of it. It needs to be shown how the moral projectivist can assert 'There are moral facts' but so that the sentence does not mean what it means when the realist asserts it. Blackburn employs such a strategy when dealing with features which appear to be *symptomatic* of realism. For example, according to Blackburn, 'mind-independences'—the idea that moral truth does not depend on our moral judgments—expresses a disapproval of people who need beliefs about people's attitudes to things in order to form their own attitudes to things.[4] Similarly, I suggest that quietist quasi-realism could hold that 'There are moral facts' expresses an approval of people who hold certain strong attitudes. We might express moral *fervor* by standing up and shouting 'It really is a fact that killing the innocent for fun is wrong', striking the table with our fists as we do so. The bare claims 'There are moral facts' or 'There are moral states of affairs' are given an 'internal' non-metaphysical reading to which a projectivist can assent. A quietist quasi-realist might say that it is good to feel strongly about things— or about *some* things at any rate. Moral projectivism can assert that there are moral facts, meaning that we should be prepared to endorse or reject various things, rather than project the value 'neutral' onto them. The sentence 'There are moral facts' is interpreted as expressing a substantive moral view, not a piece of meta-theory. Since a moral or causal fact or state of affairs is nothing but an object ar event which possesses a moral or causal property, enthusiasm can be expressed in terms of facts or states of affairs. But the property which is in part constitutive of the fact or state of affairs is a projected property.

Similarly, a causal quasi-realist might say that it is good to have well-entrenched expectations; and we could express this by speaking of causal facts. Even comedy provides an example: one might say 'Things really are funny after all', not expressing a commitment to comic realism, but expressing the fact that one had regained one's sense of humor. The general idea is that the sentences 'There are *F* facts' and 'There are *F* states of affairs' express *enthusiasm* for thinking in *F* terms. Commitments in an area are *emphasized* with the notions of fact and state of affairs. This explains why a projectivist might go in for fact and state of affairs talk—the problem of pragmatics that we noted above.[5]

We should note that this general strategy should work with equal success the other way round. Blackburn could just as well take the sentence 'There are *no F* facts' and attempt to find a sense in which the realist can *assent* to it. Someone who rejects the sentence 'There are *F* facts' or 'There are *F* states of affairs' might be expressing a dismal *lack* of enthusiasm for thinking in *F* terms. Perhaps a moral realist could be found asserting that the world is a morally desolate, dull, uninteresting, neutral place. We can imagine a context in which *both* a projectivist *and* a realist could be found, *either* asserting *or* denying the words 'There are moral facts' in an internal sense.

If this is all on the theoretical cards, then both the realist and the projectivist have the problem of finding the words in which to say exactly what it is that the realist is asserting and the projectivist is denying. If the projectivist can have facts and states of affairs or if the realist can deny them, then the ground on which both realism and projectivism stand has indeed dropped away. We can no longer phrase what the very difference between them is supposed to be. So it seems that there is no genuine meaningful issue after all. 'Quietism' has turned out to be correct.[6]

5. A HOLISTIC OBJECTION

It will be objected that in giving these sentences an internal reading, we are changing their original sense, and that is unfair. But one cannot just *assert* that the sense is being changed. It needs to be argued. Otherwise the internal reader can reply that the objection is question-begging. Why *do* we tend to think that even though there is one sentence, 'There are moral facts', we can distinguish two senses—one metaphysical and the other internal or substantive? Why are we tempted to think that those who say 'There are no comic facts' or 'There are no colors in the ultimate fabric of the world' are indulging in metaphysics rather than expressing a dull sense of humor or poor vision?

One argument for a difference in sense is this. Consider the sentence 'There are moral facts'. As already noted, both a projectivist and a realist might be found either asserting or denying this sentence in an internal sense. However, the *reasons behind* these assertions would be quite different from those which lie behind their use when intended in a metaphysical sense. The *place* of the judgment in the holistic scheme of commitments would be very different on the two readings. Both a realist and a projectivist might say 'There are no moral facts' as an expression of despondency or 'angst'. And they might both support what they say in a Pascalian vein, saying, "Don't you see how insignificant humanity is in the infinite vastness of the universe. Everything we create will be destroyed. Human life is unbearably short and filled with unavoidable and, what is worse, avoidable suffering. Life is miserable." This would plainly be a substantive, negative, and pessimistic value judgment on life, and not a piece of meta-theory. And both the realist and the projectivist might say the words 'There are moral facts', expressing a sense of the vividness and importance of moral issues, citing some ethically inspiring text. Or we might express optimism, saying, "Don't you see how wonderful it is to be alive? Can't you see what a privilege it is, considering that the chances against our existence were enormous? Life is challenging, exciting. There is so much beauty, love, and friendship. It is silly to sit around moping." On a metaphysical reading, these sorts of considerations would be irrelevant. Instead, we find arguments such as John Mackie's queerness arguments, Blackburn's supervenience argument, explanatory arguments, and arguments from motivation and dilemmas. When they express substantive, internal claims, the supporting considerations are quite different from those which are advanced when they express metaphysical claims. This makes it plausible that the two readings of the one sentence give us two quite different meanings. Quietist quasi-realism is trying to capture for the projectivist what realists and projectivists profess to be disputing. To do that, quasi-realism must capture not only the mere sentence 'There are moral facts' but also the considerations which each side thinks support its view. A splash of holism about meaning comes in handy here. The considerations advanced in support of the claims are so radically different that it is plausible that what is being supported by such considerations is also radically different. So the quasi-realist internal reading fails to capture what the realist *means* by uttering the words 'There are moral facts'. The quasi-realist needs to capture not just the words which the realist emits, but also the sense of what the realist professes to assert. To stay in business, the quasi-realist must not simply change the subject while mouthing the same sounds.

This looks like a good objection. At one time I seduced myself with this holistic objection to quietist quasi-realism. I have come to see my folly. The quasi-realist has a powerful reply. The thrust of the objection is that the internal reading fails because we can separate two different senses. The reply to the objection is that it begs the question by assuming that there *is* a metaphysical sense of 'There are moral facts' in the first place. To assume this, however, is to assume that there is a viable realism issue and that quietism is false. Perhaps the *only* sense which can be given to 'There are moral facts' is the internal substantive sense. If so, the reasons and arguments advanced in favor of the metaphysical sense or its negation are in fact bogus reasons and arguments. Quietist quasi-realism is still in business.

6. BLACKBURN AND EXPLANATION

Blackburn has argued that the point beyond which quasi-realism cannot trespass is a certain *explanatory* claim. He writes:

> But surely we do have a serviceable way of describing the debate, at least as far as it concerns evaluations and morals. It is about explanation.

The projectivist holds that our nature as moralists is well explained by regarding us as reacting to a reality which contains nothing in the way of values, duties, rights and so forth; a realist thinks it is well explained only by seeing us as able to perceive, cognize, intuit, an independent moral reality.[7]

[For the projectivist] moral 'states of affairs', above all, play no role in causing or explaining our attitudes, their convergences, their importance to us.[8]

[Hume] is merely explaining our normal sayings, our normal operations with the concept, in terms of the reaction we have, after exposure to a reality which exhibits no such features.[9]

Many philosophers fail to see the shift away from *analysis* which Blackburn's appeal to explanation involves. For example, in his review of *Spreading the Word*, Crispin Wright objects:

Once the quasi-realist has earned himself the right to a truth predicate, must not the projectivist sulk in silence unless he can *somehow* distinguish that predicate from the one which is characteristic of genuinely factual statements.[10]

Truth is a semantical notion; semantics is about meaning; and meaning is what gets analyzed. But when we seek to explain, we may take up a standpoint *external* to that which is being explained (since we would be concerned with its causal *relation* to other things). That there is no difference between realism and projectivism, as far as truth or meaning are concerned, leaves open the possibility that there is an explanatory difference. Blackburn thinks that we can isolate a distinctively realist sense of fact or state of affairs just when the invoking of such facts or states of affairs plays an explanatory role with respect to our judgments about them. This, he thinks, is something that only a realist can admit. After all, surely only something real can be a cause or an effect. The non-existent is peculiarly impotent! Blackburn's idea is that when a philosopher says that there exists a certain sort of fact, we should look to see whether such facts are endowed with causal-explanatory weight—in particular, with regard to our judgments about them. If they are, the philosopher is a realist, if not, the philosopher is a non-realist of some variety. Such an explanatory story is something which quasi-realism cannot emulate for the scope of quasi-realism is limited to semantic considerations. This causal-explanatory story can be used to define a distinctively realist conception of fact: only a realist endows facts with a causal role with respect to our judgments. This is Blackburn's line of reply to quietism on behalf of both projectivism and realism, and it would be his reply to Wright's unfair accusation that if quasi-realism succeeds, the projectivist must "sulk in silence." Explanation plants the metaphysician's feet back on solid earth.

7. RESUSCITATING BLACKBURN'S QUIETIST PHASE

Now, in his 1980 essay "Truth, Realism, and the Regulation of Theory," Blackburn was far more circumspect about the explanatory idea. In that essay, he raised difficulties for its application. This is what made that essay so radical. Since then, these doubts have not resurfaced in his writings. In *Spreading the Word*, for example, the explanatory answer to quietism is put with no recognition that it may have difficulties.[11] But I cannot see that Blackburn has anywhere disposed of the interesting worries that he raised back in 1980.

In that essay, Blackburn considers as a distinguishing mark of *Real* Realism:

> (RR) It is because opinion is caused, perhaps indirectly, by the fact that p, that it converges on p. (p. 367)

He says that this seems to work well in that it categorizes Hume's account of morality and causality as non-realistic (pp. 367–68). (I discuss this claim below.)

Blackburn mentions in passing the following objection to the explanatory idea:

> one might wish to have the same attitude towards the reality of the future and the past yet believe that only past states of affairs play a causal role in generating opinion. (p. 368)

This is surely not a severe problem. Blackburn admits that the relevant causal relations may be *indirect* (p. 369). For example, the immediate cause of our beliefs about other minds is just other behavior, but the other minds themselves play a causal role further back in the causal chain. And if we admit that the causal relations can be indirect, then we can also admit cases of 'common causality'. Beliefs about future events are caused by the past events which also cause the future events about which we have beliefs. But this triangle recurs. Past 'futures' are among the causes of present opinions about the future, together with the assumption that the 'present future' will behave like 'past futures'. So beliefs about the future present no fundamental problem for the explanatory criterion of genuine facthood.

Blackburn's more interesting problem for the explanatory criterion is this:

> it may be possible to [accept (RR)] without being a realist. It would mark a necessary but not sufficient condition of realism. The problem arises if a test is made to determine whether our attitude is one of real realism or not, when the opinion or theory that we are testing *itself* makes causal and explanatory claims. (p. 368)

And a dozen lines latter:

> [(RR)] has no part to play in detecting a realistic attitude towards the most interesting theories: those such as our view of the external world, or the existence of the past or other minds, where to hold the theory is *ipso*

facto to hold a certain explanation of our opinions. Not all theories have this kind of involvement with their own meta-theory—first-order morals does not, for instance. (p. 368)

I shall argue that this is the wrong way round: the appeal to explanation *fails* to block quietist quasi-realism in cases like that of morality and causality; but it *succeeds* in the cases of the external world, the past, and other minds.

8. MORALITY AND CAUSALITY

If thinking in causal-explanatory terms is *part* of our ordinary way of thinking in an area, then quasi-realism might be able to mimic this way of thinking, without real facts or states of affairs. According to projectivism, we project our reactions onto reality. But so long as we conceive of the reality on which we spread our reactions as having causal powers, we can also think of the spread property as causing and being caused. Given the idea that we project a property onto a reality which is causally efficacious, we can then go on to capture the idea that the projected property is also causally efficacious. So once quasi-realism can capture the idea of the independent standing of a property, the apparent causal efficacy of these properties is also within reach. And if we can think of the spread property as standing in causal relations, we can also think of it as standing in causal relation to our judgments. For example, funniness is very plausibly a projected property. Yet it is not uncommon to credit funniness with causal efficacy. Comedians *make* people laugh. In thinking of funniness as projected, a projectivist can also capture its apparent causality. And moral quasi-realism can admit that people corrupt others and that they inspire others with their example. This is not meta-theory but ordinary moral wisdom. Quasi-realism can and should allow that we think that good and evil are causally efficacious and that we think of ourselves as causally sensitive to them.

In a sense, of course, for a moral projectivist, moral facts play no causal-explanatory role. As we noted previously, what does not exist has a hard time causing anything. But on a projectivist account, we can talk as if moral facts play a causal-explanatory role. The problem is to tell when we talk as if moral facts play a causal-explanatory role because they really do play such a role. We need to spot the difference between genuine explanation and 'quasi-explanation'—between causation and 'quausation'.

At any rate, it is clear that any very simple appeal to explanation fails to exclude projectivism about morality and causality. Blackburn's appeal to explanation cannot quieten the quietist in such areas. Moral and causal quietism are still alive and kicking.[12]

9. EXTERNAL WORLD, PAST, AND OTHER MINDS

The conflict between realism and projectivism is the form that metaphysical debate takes in many areas. But metaphysical debate arises rather differently when we come to the external world, the past, and other minds. Here the question about the world is not so much whether these things exist at all, but whether they *transcend* some undisputed reality. For example, the question about the external world is whether the external world is anything over and above my sense experiences. And the question about my judgments about the external world is whether they aim to represent anything beyond my sense experiences. There is a similar structure with the past and present memories and traces, and with other minds and other behavior.

The realist holds that the controversial facts transcend the uncontroversial facts and that we represent them as transcending the uncontroversial facts. However, the realist about *these* subject-matters (unlike, say, mathematics) also holds that the controversial and uncontroversial facts stand in *causal relation*. The realist thinks that the uncontroversial facts are our causal *evidence* for the controversial facts. Present memories and traces are evidence for the past because they are caused by the past; other behavior is evidence for other minds because it is caused by other minds; sense experience is evidence for the external world because it is caused by the external world.

On the other hand, the non-realist in these areas believes that the controversial facts are nothing over and above the uncontroversial facts. So they cannot stand in causal relation. The non-realist believes that there is no external world which transcends experience, no past which transcends present memories and traces, and there are no other minds which transcend other behavior. Typically, the non-realist also has a thesis about our thought: that our cognition of the controversial facts does not aspire to reach beyond the uncontroversial facts. The non-realist view of the controversial judgments is that the controversial judgments are disguised uncontroversial judgments. The non-realist option in these areas is 'reductionism'. A strong reductionist theory is that the meaning of statements about the external world is analyzable in terms of sense-experiences. The same holds with the past and memories and traces, and with other minds and bodily behavior. A weak form of reductionism, however, merely requires that we know that whenever a controversial statement is true, it is true in virtue of the truth of some set of statements of the uncontroversial class. (Dummett calls this 'reduc*tiv*ism' as opposed to 'reduc*tion*ism'.[13])

These issues are very often confused by casting the matter epistemologically—as an issue about whether the truth transcends our 'recognitional capacities'. This is a sloppy way of casting the issue, which is about whether some sort of fact transcends another sort of fact, which may or may not be more epistemologically problematic than the disputed sort of fact. The issue is not essentially about whether the truth in a certain area transcends our epistemic capacities. This is only relevant if we assume that we only have unproblematic access to the uncontroversial facts. But what is held problematic in the context of one debate may be unproblematic in the context of another. For example, when discussing the reality of other minds, we assume the reality of behavior. But the existence of behavior is as problematic as the existence of anything physical when we are discussing the reality of the external world. We should not cast the issue epistemologically unless we actually *like* confusion!

Dispositional theories might seem to be a third alternative besides realism and reductionism: objects are dispositions to cause sense-experiences; mental states are dispositions to cause behavior. But such dispositional theories are empty in themselves. We need to know in virtue of what the dispositions hold. Only the answer to *that* question gives content to the theory. When that question is answered, the dispositional theory always turns out to be either realism or reductionism in disguise. Neo-Wittgensteinian 'criterial' theories tended to fudge the issue, of course, largely because they operated with a stupendously uncritical notion of a criterion. They did not succeed in providing an alternative to realism and reductionism.

The choice between realism and reductionism about the external world, the past, and other minds is different in important ways from the choice between realism and projectivism over morality or causality. The issue is not one about cognitive and non-cognitive states; it is about the scope of our cognitive states. In one case realism contrasts with non-cognitivist projectivism, in the other with reductionist cognitivism.

To recap: the realist believes that the controversial facts transcend the uncontroversial facts and that they stand in causal relation with them. The reductionist denies this. And the disagreement about our thought is that the realist thinks that we represent the controversial facts as transcending the un-controversial facts and as standing in causal relation with them. The reductionist denies this. This is important for our background issue. What it means is that we seem to be able to rehabilitate Blackburn's appeal to explanation. The thought that only what is real can have causal oomph has more weight here than it had when we were dealing with cases such as morality. A reductionist cannot emulate the realist's causal explanations. And if the reductionist cannot do that, reductionism cannot explain the way we conceive of controversial facts as explaining our beliefs about them, via the uncontroversial facts. Only a realist can do that. We now have what we need: only a realist about the external world can think of judgments about the external world as being caused, in a certain way, by the external world: the external world causes sense-experiences, and the sense-experiences cause our judgments about the external world. This is something which realism asserts and the non-realist denies. We have a way of saying what the difference between them amounts to. We do not need to go as far as to suggest that explanatory considerations give us a good *argument for realism* about the external world—only that they give content to the issue. We have not established realism, but we do seem to have established anti-quietism or loudism. The non-realist cannot say everything that the realist says. So the existence of a genuine debate is not in doubt. The same goes for the past and other minds. Quietism has come to grief in these cases. We can rest assured that these debates have content.

Now, as Blackburn notes, in the cases of the external world, the past, and other minds, our everyday employment of the controversial concepts involves a commitment to certain causal explanations. It is not just that some clever theorist can come along and give a causal explanation of our ways of thought from some external perspective. Rather, we conceive of ourselves as causally responsive to the external world via our sensory experiences; we conceive of ourselves as causally responsive to the past via memory and traces; and we conceive of ourselves as causally responsive to other minds via other behavior. Having the very concept of perception and memory, for example, involves the knowledge that the external world causes our sense experiences and that past events cause present memories. If this is right, it explains that fact that reductionist views quickly begin to look like 'eliminativist' views. For if we hold a reductionist view, we have abandoned the causal explanations which are embedded in ordinary thought. If F facts do not transcend G facts, then there cannot be causal relations between the two. Only if one fact transcends another can the two stand in causal relation. A reductionist rejects such causal relations; but such causal relations are built into our thought. The reductionist might *start off* wanting to say that F facts are reducible to G facts; but that means that F facts do not cause G facts. Since we fail to have a conception of F facts unless we conceive of them as causing G facts, it cannot be F facts which are reducible to G facts. Reductionism undermines itself. Ordinary thought about the external world, the past and other minds, is implicitly laden with a causal theory about the genesis of our thought. Only realism can admit these explanations. It follows that ordinary thought is realistic. If a commitment to these causal relations is built into ordinary thought about the external world, past, and other minds, then reductionism fails to capture ordinary thought. Opposition to realism must, therefore, be eliminativist, that is, it must embrace an error theory about ordinary thought. The choice is rather stark: realism or eliminativism.

We could imagine the reductionist trying, as a last resort, to take on an added projectivistic element. (Perhaps this is what the neo-Wittgensteinian criterial theorists were aiming at all along.) This more sophisticated reductionist option might be better called 'constructivism' than 'projectivism', since the idea would be that the external world is *constructed out of* my sense-experiences; the past is *constructed out of* memories and traces; other minds are *constructed out of* bodily behavior. We erect a new reality from meager constituents. And having erected a new reality, we could think of it as having independent causal standing. It could thus be thought of as causing the uncontroversial facts and as indirectly causing our beliefs about the controversial 'facts'. If quasi-realism has a future in these cases, such causal stories must be captured along with the claim that there exists a range of controversial facts. In his 1980 essay, Blackburn seems to leave it open that quasi-realism in these cases might achieve this. And given what I have said about the cases of morality and causality, I ought to be sympathetic. But I am not. The objection is a 'transcendental' one: that we cannot *conceive* of the uncontroversial facts except in terms of the controversial facts. Sense experience is not sense experience unless it represents the external world. Memories are not memories unless they represent the past. Contrast moral projectivism: we *can* conceive of the natural entirely without moral categories.[14] The transcendental point means that we cannot *construct* the external world out of sense experience; for, in a sense, the external world is *already present in* sense experience, in that it is the essence of sense experience that it represents the external world. And we cannot *manufacture* the past out of memories; for in a sense they *already contain* the past, in that it is the essence of memories that they represent the past. You cannot construct what you already have, just as you cannot get what you have already got. Hence, constructivism is not an option in the cases of the external world and the past. The other mind case looks different, since we *can* conceive of behavior in entirely non-mentalistic terms; but let us not worry about other minds for a moment. In the cases of the external world and the past, at least, reductionism cannot quasi-realistically manufacture the idea of an external world which transcends sense-experience or the idea of a past which transcends memory. And if so, reductionism in these areas cannot acquire the apparently realistic causal explanations. So those causal explanations succeed in giving content to the realism issue. In these cases, loudism is safe.

10. LEAPING SIDEWAYS

Let us return to morality and causality. Quietist quasi-realism seemed to do rather well here; even explanation failed to give content to the realism issue. By contrast, explanation did succeed in giving us a reply to quietism in the cases of the external world and the past. Are we then forced to say that while the debates over the external world and the past have content, those over morality and causality have none?

I suggest that we argue as follows. First note that wherever we have a debate about whether some disputed sort of property should be construed realistically or non-realistically, we distinguish the disputed properties from another sort of property which for the purpose of the debate is considered uncontroversial. Both realist and non-realist *agree* that there are facts of the *un*controversial sort. What is at issue is whether there is another layer of controversial fact in addition. For the projectivist, the real layer of uncontroversial fact is that upon which reactions are projected, while for the reductionist the real layer of uncontroversial fact is that to which the disputed reality is reduced. Moral realists and projectivists agree that there are natural facts about what people want, feel, and do; it is assumed by both sides that realism is the correct theory about *these* natural facts. Causal realists and projectivists agree that the world contains a succession of events; it is assumed by both sides that realism is the correct theory about *these* facts. Realists and reductionists about the past both believe in the existence of memories and traces. Realists and reductionists about other minds both believe in the existence of other behavior. In all these cases, when both sides assume realism about the *un*controversial facts, anti-quietism is assumed *here*.

This allows us to make sense of a local issue. We can 'leap sideways'. Even if quasi-realism is entirely successful within, say, moral philosophy, we can still fall back on saying that it is the notion of fact which is applicable in the uncontroversial area which is the one which the realist asserts and the non-realist denies of the controversial area. When the moral realist says 'There are moral facts', this is intended as saying that there are moral facts *in the sense in which* even according to a projectivist, there are the natural facts upon which we project our attitudes. So when the projectivist utters the words 'There are moral facts' in order to express enthusiasm for moralizing, this is not meant in the same sense as when the projectivist asserts that there are natural facts. But *that* is the sense in which the realist is asserting that there are moral facts. Similarly, the causal realist says that there are causal facts, in the sense in which, according to a causal projectivist, there is the succession of events upon which we project our expectations. Again, in the other sort of case, the realist about the past can say that the past exists as something independent of memories and traces, in the sense in which even the reductionist admits that memories and traces exist. Yet again, the disagreement between realism and reductionism about other minds can be characterized in terms of whether there are facts about other minds which transcend behavior, in the sense in which both agree that there are facts about behavior. In general, the disagreement between realism and non-realism can be characterized in terms of whether there are facts of the controversial sort, in the sense in which both agree that there are facts of the uncontroversial sort. Hence, realism and non-realism can agree about what they disagree about.

This sideways leap solves another problem—one which I have not so far raised. After having attempted to throw doubt on the sufficiency of (RR) for realism, Blackburn rightly goes on to doubt its necessity:

> taking [RR] as even a necessary commitment of a realist has one unattractive consequence. This is that states of affairs are only allowed if they play a part in causing opinion. Now it seems at least possible that one would wish to be a realist about mathematics yet deny that mathematical reality is a cause of anything. (p. 368)

The example of mathematical Platonism seems to raise a serious difficulty for the explanatory idea. The trouble is that (RR) begs serious epistemological questions. It may *turn out* to be true that a non-spatial, non-temporal, acausal realm of abstract objects is irredeemably queer, and *perhaps* we could have no epistemic access to such a realm since our epistemic faculties always involve causal interaction with what is known. But this could never be *trivial and obvious*. These are substantive and controversial theses which certainly do not seem to be *definitive* of realism. What we need, once again, is our sideways leap. When the mathematical realist says that there are mathematical facts (mathematical objects standing in mathematical relations), this is intended as the view that such facts exist in the sense in which both realists and nominalists are committed to the existence of physical facts. This gives content to the debate over mathematical facts without a direct appeal to explanation. It is the notion of fact which is applicable to the physical world which is the one which the mathematical realist asserts and the nominalist denies of mathematical facts.

So quietism is no threat: explanation deals with the external world and the past; and the sideways leap secures morality, causality, other minds, and even mathematics. The sideways leap gives us a way of getting over the quietist hurdle.

11. GLOBAL QUIETISM?

This is not quite the end of the matter. Let us distinguish 'local' and 'global' quietism. 'Local quietism' is the conclusion we reach in some area if it turns out that quasi-realism can capture everything which the realist in that area wants to say. As we have just seen, where explanation does not work, we can defeat local quietism by falling back on saying that it is the notion of fact which we take to be applicable in some other area which is the one which the realist asserts and the non-realist denies of the local sort of facts. For example, in morality, this uncontroversial realm of fact is the natural world of physical and psychological states of affairs. It is assumed by both sides that realism is the correct theory about the natural facts. We rely on a robust sense of fact for the natural in order to give sense to the debate about morality. But this strategy assumes that the debate about the existence of natural facts has content, and thus that anti-quietism is the correct attitude to the realism/nonrealism debate about natural facts. The debate about morality is safe so long as the debate about natural facts makes sense. Contraposing, however, if the debate about the natural facts evaporates, then so does the debate about morality.

'Global quietism' would be the conclusion that we reach if in *every* area we might choose, quietism turns out to be correct. As I have argued, local quietism is no threat so long as there is some area outside the area under consideration where quietism is incorrect. But perhaps there is no such area. Quietism must go global to survive. For if there is any area where realism is coherent, the local realist or non-realist can point to that area as an exemplar of the notion of fact or state of affairs which is intended in the disputed local area. Global quietism remains hovering in the background as a threat to the meaningfulness of local realism debates.

However, we saw that the explanatory idea *did* succeed in giving a reply to quietism in the case of the external world and the past. Surely we have an unshakably robust sense of reality of the external spatio-temporal physical world and of the reality of the past. Mount Everest is as real as can be. So was the Second World War. We conceive of ourselves as a *proper part* of a wider spatio-temporal world, causally interacting with it. (We may be wrong, but this is how we conceive of ourselves.) If quietism is not an option in the cases of the external world and the past, then neither is global quietism an option. Given that local quietism rests on global quietism, local quietism is no longer an option in areas like the philosophy of morality and causation. Moral and causal realists can turn to the realist about the external world or the past and say "I want to be a realist just like you."

CONCLUSION

Quasi-realism may live to fight another day under the banner of projectivism about morality, causality, or whatever. But that would be another matter, and it would assume that both realism and projectivism were coherent positions. The refutation of *quietist* quasi-realism leaves *criterial* quasi-realism in the field. Projectivism, like realism, only becomes a live option after we have turned our back on quietism. With quietism vanquished, we can then engage in the debate between realism and projectivism with confidence in its genuineness.

We need not do metaphysics with the guilty Wittgensteinian feeling that what we are discussing has no substance. We need not be constantly looking over our shoulder in case the quietist is lurking. Let us gather confidence and be metaphysically noisy. Metaphysics is full of sound and fury, signifying plenty.[15]

Notes

1. Blackburn discusses quasi-realism in many places. One fairly extensive discussion is in his book *Spreading the Word* (Oxford, 1984). For reasons which will become apparent, I shall mostly discuss his essay "Truth, Realism, and the Regulation of Theory." This essay can be found in *Midwest Studies in Philosophy, Vol. 5, Studies in Epistemology* (Minneapolis, 1980).

2. See chapter 1 of John Mackie, *Ethics: Inventing Right and Wrong* (Harmonsworth, 1977).

3. See pp. 354–55 of "Truth, Realism, and the Regulation of Theory." Ramsey's 'redundancy theory' is supposed to be the model here; but see Brian Loar's "Ramsey's Theory of Belief and Truth" for a very different view of what Ramsey was up to. Loar's essay can be found in *Prospects for Pragmatism*, edited by D. H. Mellor (Cambridge, 1980).

4. See, for example, section 6.6 of *Spreading the Word*.

5. It would not be quite correct to say that if this sort of quasi-realism is successful, there is no debate. There is still disagreement—only it is not a metaphysical one. A disagreement over 'There are comic facts' might express a clash of senses of humor.

6. Quietism would be the *philosophical* truth, not the *metaphysical* truth; if quietism is correct, there are no metaphysical truths.

7. Simon Blackburn, "Rule-following and Moral Realism," in *Wittgenstein: To Follow a Rule*, edited by S. Holtzman and C. Leich (London, 1981), 164–65.

8. Ibid., 185–86.

9. Blackburn, *Spreading the Word*, 211.

10. Crispin Wright, review of *Spreading the Word*, Mind (1985): 318–19.

11. Blackburn, *Spreading the Word*, 257.

12. I do not think that it is a serious objection to causal projectivism that it appeals to a causal explanation of our expectations. We can bracket off what we say about those causal explanations. The general theory of causation can apply to those explanations of our expectations along with more usual cases of causal explanation.

13. See Michael Dummett, "Realism," *Synthese* (1982).

14. The greatest difficulty for a causal projectivist is that a similar transcendental point might hold in our causal thought. Some philosophers argue that we cannot conceive of an object or event except in terms of its causal powers. If so, the projectivist's allegedly acausal succession of events onto which our expectations are projected is chimerical.

15. I am very grateful to Roger Teichmann for helpful comments.

Authorship and Authenticity:
Kierkegaard and Wittgenstein

D. Z. PHILLIPS

"In this age, and indeed for many ages past, people have quite lost sight of the fact that authorship ought to be a serious calling implying an appropriate mode of personal existence."[1] So wrote Kierkegaard in his *The Point of View for My Work as an Author*. He accused metaphysicians of losing sight of this serious calling. There is a comic pretentiousness in the disparity between their speculative systems and the actualities of human existence. Kierkegaard said that they built castles in the air, dwellings no one lives in, and created a fantastic language for fantastic beings. Wittgenstein recognized that the problems which lead to metaphysical systems are deep problems. Nevertheless, he said that language in such systems is idle language which has gone on holiday. His aim was to bring words back from their metaphysical to their ordinary use; to bring us back from castles in the air to rough ground. Wittgenstein insisted that what is ragged should be left ragged.

Kierkegaard and Wittgenstein oppose philosophy's foundationalist pretensions, its claim to possess a rational measure by which all our practices must be assessed. No such rationale exists, and no theses concerning it can be 'said'. What philosophy provides is an elucidative 'showing' of what our practices come to, in face of our tendencies to be confused about them. Foundationalism's direct method of demonstration is replaced by an indirect method of perspicuous representation.

But how can there be a serious philosophical authorship after the demise of foundationalism? What style can philosophy have? In their struggles with this issue, both writers adopted striking literary devices. Kierkegaard wrote a number of pseudonymous works, claiming that the perspectives elucidated in them were not his, but those of the pseudonymous authors. Wittgenstein presented his work in numbered paragraphs, in which we meet different voices he argues with and voices expressing different perspectives. His early readers found this difficult to grasp and many critics concluded that Wittgenstein provides us with no more than, what he himself called disparagingly, an album of unconnected remarks.[2] Both authors endeavor to teach us conceptual differences, without claiming that these differences form a systematic unity. But, it has been asked, how can such endeavors constitute a serious philosophical authorship? If Kierkegaard, in his pseudonymous works, shows us a variety of perspectives, what is his *own* relation to them? If Wittgenstein introduces us to a variety of voices, how can he have *a voice of his own*? No matter how confused he might be, the foundationalist has a noble aim: he wants to be our guide in helping us to distinguish between the rational and the irrational. Since Kierkegaard and Wittgenstein forsake this task, how can there be a philosophical voice which is no voice in particular?

Once the tasks of foundationalism are forsaken, does not philosophical enquiry become no more than a form of aestheticism, a parody of or an ironic play with real voices? In fact, this possibility worried Kierkegaard in his student dissertation, *The Concept of Irony*, in which he suggests that there is a necessary tension between Socrates' elucidations of different possibilities and the actual life Socrates has to live, a tension which involves Socrates in irony:

> The ironist stands proudly withdrawn into himself; he lets mankind pass before him, as did Adam the animals, and finds no companionship for himself. By this he constantly comes into conflict with the actuality to which he belongs.... For him life is a drama, and what engrosses him is the ingenious unfolding of that drama. He is himself a spectator even when observing some act.... He is inspired by the virtues of self-sacrifice as a spectator is inspired by them in a theatre; he is a severe critic who well knows when such virtues become insipid and false.[3]

In rejecting every definition of piety and justice put to him, by suggesting further possibilities and never coming to rest in a definition of his own, there is a danger of Socrates' life becoming one of 'infinite negativity'. Kierkegaard thought that because, in his view, Socrates "lives hypothetically and subjunctively, his life finally loses all continuity. With this he sinks completely into mood. His life becomes *sheer mood*."[4]

Josiah Thompson has argued that Kierkegaard succumbs to this danger in his own work. In depicting aesthetic, ethical, and religious perspectives in his pseudonymous works, Kierkegaard is simply playing with possibilities. This form of play developed early in him. One day, Kierkegaard's father returned home too late to take his young son for a promised walk. They imagined going on the walk instead: acting out the scenes they might have witnessed and the people they might have met. Kierkegaard noted, later, that too much of his childhood was lived in the imagination. Yet, Thompson argues, the child was developing an appetite for the imaginary which would lead him to philosophy: "Slowly, inevitably, a singular thought has taken root in the young boy's mind. It is not necessary to live in the world. On the contrary, the world— its resistance, its burdens, its conflicting demands—can be transformed. One need only dream. Narcissus has found his solitary pool, and Kierkegaard his future: he will be a dreamer."[5]

Thompson reminds us that Kierkegaard succumbed to this aestheticism in his life. His nephew related an incident in which Kierkegaard, hearing a poorhouse inmate say she would be happy if someone gave her some money, approached her, gave her with a flourishing gesture the exact amount she had asked for, and disappeared without saying a word. Later, in philosophical tranquillity, he enjoyed thinking of possible ways in which the old woman might have thought of the incident. The old woman simply occasions a mood. According to Thompson, so do the pseudonymous works. They are "Nonparticipants in life, they are its critics and spectators."[6] The fact that Kierkegaard is their single author does not imply any singlemindedness in him. On the contrary, the pseudonyms testify to the activity of a playful aesthete, withdrawn from the actualities of life, which is all philosophy can be once its metaphysical pretensions have been put aside. Thompson concludes that in the pseudonymous works, "there is an underlying black humour. For finally the joke is on the reader, and the smarter he is, the sooner he realises it. But to see through all the pseudonyms, to recognise that the vision of any one of them is not to be preferred to that of any other, is finally to join Kierkegaard in his cloister. It is to share with him that peculiarly modern laceration—'I must believe, but I can't believe'—which since his time has become even more painful."[7] Looking at the range of Kierkegaard's pseudonymous works, Thompson says: "It is as if his life had been refracted by a powerful prism into a multitude of images, each of which retained some mark of the original."[8] Kierkegaard shares the fate he ascribed to Socrates in his doctoral dissertation. Is this Wittgenstein's fate, too? In Wittgenstein's philosophizings about religion, R. F. Holland finds that modern laceration in him—'I must believe, but I can't believe'—which creates tensions for his authorship. On the one hand, Wittgenstein says, "I cannot kneel to pray, for it is as though my knees were stiff. I am afraid of dissolution (of my own dissolution), if I were to become soft."[9] But, on another occasion, he says, "I am not a religious person, but I cannot help seeing every problem from a religious point of view."[10] In these remarks, Holland argues, we have a tension between Wittgenstein's philosophical investigations and the actuality to which he belongs; the same tension that worried Kierkegaard in his doctoral dissertation. Wittgenstein seems to give an independent sense to "seeing the world (or seeing life, seeing one's work) from a religious point of view and being a religious person."[11] Holland has difficulty in seeing how this is possible: "We are presented with the suggestion that a person's point of view can be religious although he himself is not. But how can a point of view be made religious except by a religion? And must not the religion enter the viewpoint through the mind of the person who is taking this view?"[12] The danger is that the philosophical point of view which is called 'religious' is no more than *pathetisch* religion. Expounding the notion of the *pathetisch*, Holland says he "might speak controversially of Mahler's *pathetisch* pantheism, and ... might also use the term or the English word 'sentimental', in describing the man who muttered words such as 'Gott', 'Himmel' and 'Danke' when looking over the mountains from his chalet at Terchtesgarten in 1939."[13] If this were our final verdict, Wittgenstein's investigations would make no more contact with religion than Kierkegaard's pseudonyms have contact, according to Thompson, with the subjects they purport to engage with.

Can it really be said, however, that Kierkegaard and Wittgenstein lack integrity as philosophical authors because they reduce philosophical enquiry to a form of aestheticism? Do they, like Kierkegaard and his father on their imaginary walk, doff their hats at the various possibilities in human life without engaging with any of them? Thompson's attempt to depict Kierkegaard as a playful aesthete based on biographical evidence is manifestly unreliable. For example, in his use of Kierkegaard's treatment of the woman from the poorhouse, he omits to say that Kierkegaard was severely critical of his own conduct. In the second volume of *Either/Or*, he attributes the incident to the aesthete and subjects it to moral censure: "So what you wanted was to play the part of fate; what you really enjoyed were the multifarious reflections which could be spun from this."[14] The dangers of aestheticism in the realm of the intellect are clearly recognized: "One is struck by seeing a clown whose joints are so limber that all necessity for maintaining the human gait and posture are done away. Such are you in an intellectual sense, you can just as well stand on your head as on your feet, everything is possible for you, and by this possibility you can astonish others and yourself; but it is unwholesome, and for the sake of your own tranquillity I beg you to see to it that what is your advantage, does not end by being a curse. A man who has a conviction cannot turn topsy-turvy upon himself and all things. I warn you, therefore, not against the world but against yourself, and I warn the world against you."[15] The problem for Thompson is obvious: how can the author of this blistering attack on aestheticism be called an aesthete?

R. F. Holland says that "it *is* possible for a charge of sentimentality to be thoughtfully mounted against any philosopher who camps under the portico of historical religion instead of going inside,"[16] but he says also that Wittgenstein cannot be found guilty of it. The aesthete goes as he pleases where religion is concerned, but, Holland argues, this cannot be said of Wittgenstein: Wittgenstein "takes up a position that is actually very austere, like an unfurnished room by comparison with what is available in the historical religions. I would also say that if someone is prone to sentimentality, then sentimental he is going to be, when he gets the chance. There is no sign of Wittgenstein's being that way inclined and plenty of evidence in the other direction."[17]

Since it can be shown that Kierkegaard's and Wittgenstein's attacks on metaphysical systems do not involve reducing philosophy to a form of aestheticism, it may be thought that we can conclude, without more ado, that both were concerned with the struggle for clarity, the working through to grammatical distinctions we are tempted to confuse or ignore. The only difference between them, it may be said, is that Kierkegaard was concerned with combating confusions about Christianity, whereas Wittgenstein combated confusions in a wide range of contexts. I shall now examine this view at some length.

Kierkegaard wanted to dispute what he called "the monstrous illusion," namely, the widespread conviction in the Denmark of his day that one could be a Christian simply by being a citizen. People who embraced aesthetic or ethical perspectives in their lives thought they were Christians. Kierkegaard did not think they could be disabused of this fact by any direct method. He writes: "there is a difference between writing on a blank sheet of paper and bringing to light by the application of a caustic fluid a text which is hidden under another text."[18] The pseudonymous works were meant to act as such a fluid by giving perspicuous representations of aesthetic and ethical perspectives. Kierkegaard says: "if real success is to attend the effort to bring a man to a definite position, one must first of all take pains to find HIM where he is and begin there. . . . In order to help another effectively I must understand more than he—yet first of all surely I must understand what he understands. If I do not know that, my greater understanding will be of no help to him."[19] Contrary to Thompson's suggestion, Kierkegaard's pseudonymous works are not exercises in aesthetic self-indulgence. Rather, they call for a disinterested reflectiveness in the elucidation of different perspectives. E. D. Klemke comments:

> One of the most impressive features of Kierkegaard's writings is the remarkable philosophical detachment with which he wrote. A high degree of disinterestedness pervades his writings and displays the objectivity with which he could practice even on matters which have a highly subjective and personal concern.[20]

Kierkegaard himself testifies: "So in the pseudonymous works there is not a single word which is mine. I have no opinion about them except as a third person, no knowledge of their meaning except, as a reader, not the remotest private relation to them."[21] He does not look for a philosophical underpinning for his own Christian beliefs. On the contrary, Kierkegaard says "One single word of mine uttered personally in my own name would be an instance of presumptuous self-forgetfulness, and dialectically viewed would ensure with one word the guilt of annihilating the pseudonyms."[22] Of course, Kierkegaard's hope was that when aesthetic and ethical perspectives were seen for what they are, those who confused them with Christianity would realize the error of their ways and turn to Christianity. But even if this did not happen, and they preferred to stay where they were, at least the monstrous illusion would have been dispelled: "Therefore it is possible for misunderstanding to be removed and become agreement and understanding, but it is possible also for it to be removed and to become real disagreement."[23] It follows that clarity is in "every man's interest, whether he be a Christian or not, whether his intention is to accept Christianity or reject it."[24]

This search for clarity is found in Wittgenstein, too. In his work we find at least five different contexts in which he discusses the relation of philosophy to religion. Having discussed them elsewhere, I shall do no more than note them here.[25] First, Wittgenstein criticizes philosophers who argue that all forms of religious belief are meaningless. Second, he criticizes confused grammatical accounts of religious belief. Third, he discusses the distinction between religion and superstition. Fourth, he discusses reactions to different forms of religion, emphasizing that which are called 'higher' or 'lower' forms of religion must be a personal matter. Fifth, he notes that we have to be pragmatic in our reactions to religion. Sometimes, there may be little to say about a phenomenon claimed to be religiously significant. (He saw a blinding flash and that was that, except that he keeps talking about it!) When one of Wittgenstein's pupils wrote to tell him that he had become a Roman Catholic, Wittgenstein replied, "When I hear someone has bought himself equipment for tight-rope walking, I'll be impressed when I see what he does with it." In all five contexts, Wittgenstein is bringing out the grammar of our practices. In order to do so, what we need is not more information, but clarity concerning what lies before us. Holland, on the other hand, is in danger of succumbing to *pathetisch* philosophy when he endorses A. E. Taylor's view that, in religion, there is a "never wholly removable misfit between the real and the categories in which we try to confine it."[26] We are reminded of Locke's claim that our faculties are inherently inadequate to grasp reality, and Berkeley's apt reply, "We first throw up a dust and then complain we cannot see."

In this struggle for clarity, Wittgenstein urged his students, 'Go the bloody hard way', but Holland wonders whether it is hard enough. He poses this question because, when A. E. Taylor gives the same advice, it involves doing something Wittgenstein does not do: "When Taylor gives the advice the sense of it is:—Don't let the difficulties bring you to a halt. Commit yourself to a traditional form of worship, and do not be content with some wishy-washy kind of 'philosophical religion'."[27] A historical religion, Holland reminds us, presents us "with *this* founder, *these* scriptures, *these* beliefs" and he says, "I am inclined to go along with the suggestion that to take all that away is to strip religion of its body and turn it into a pale sort of ghost. Taylor speaks of 'the thin and sentimental devotions of eighteenth century English Deism'."[28] But what of Wittgenstein? Holland replies: "Wittgenstein of course said that he was not religious. Taylor, however, in agreeing, would have added that looking at things ... in the way Wittgenstein did was just one form among others of that dilute thing, philosophic religion, which is a surrogate for genuine religion."[29]

It is true that Wittgenstein did not embrace any historical religion but, as Holland admits, the accounts he gives of religion are not reductive. There is certainly no question of Wittgenstein constructing a deistic philosophic religion. One of the main objects of his attack was the deistic assumptions which still pervade twentieth-century philosophy of religion. Kierkegaard would have enjoyed the irony in the claim by contemporary purveyors of philosophic religion, still a recognizably English mode of philosophizing, that they have gone the hard, systematic way in philosophy. Wittgenstein thinks that kind of philosophy is as wishy-washy as the devoutness Taylor saw Deism generate.

At times, Holland suggests that the obedience to authority which religion calls for "is a scandalum to the philosophic mind."[30] At the outset of his essay, he argues as though there is a *necessary* tension between philosophy and religion: "Philosophy consists in the struggle for clarity. In religion there is no virtue in arriving at that. What is wanted is charity, not clarity. I would go as far as to suggest that clarity is a hindrance to the kind of spirituality expressed in religious devotion. In any case it is not available there: you can only see through a glass darkly, and even then your account of what you see is subject to unexplained alteration at the hand of authority. The meek acceptance of this is *docility*—one of the loveliest words in religious language; but in the vocabulary of philosophy it is suitable only for animals."[31] The difficulty is in knowing how seriously these remarks are intended, since later in his essay, he endorses the following very different comments by Taylor: "In a critical age, like our own, the 'option' for Christianity, or any other historical religion, must bring a perpetual tension into one's intellectual life from which acquiescence in a 'religion within the limits of reason' would leave us free. . . . We could get rid of the tension equally readily by blind acquiescence in tradition and authority, or by a cheap and easy rejection of both."[32] As we have seen, Wittgenstein does not construct a philosophic religion, but neither do we find in him, as Holland would agree, blind acquiescence to or cheap and easy rejection of religion. In fact, the intellectual effort involved in paying attention to particular cases captures the spirit of Wittgenstein's attitude to religion, as exemplified in the five different contexts in which he discusses the relation of philosophy to religion.

We have been emphasizing what philosophical enquiry became for Kierkegaard and Wittgenstein. They taught us conceptual differences, elucidated a heterogeneity of perspectives, which cannot be reduced to the unity of any metaphysical system. But misleading conclusions have been drawn from their philosophical endeavors, even by those sympathetic to them. It has been said that according to Kierkegaard and Wittgenstein, all perspectives other than one's own must be regarded as alternatives; moral criticism of others is impossible; all perspectives can be given equal plausibility. Anyone who advances such conclusions, it is said, surrenders any claim to serious philosophical authorship. But do these three conclusions follow from Kierkegaard's and Wittgenstein's methods?

First, E. D. Klemke claims that the purpose of Kierkegaard's literary style of presentation in the pseudonymous works "is to show that to a disinterested and cognizing subject there are always genuine ethical *alternatives*. Reflection does not reduce the multiplicity to a unity. . . . A scientific or philosophical ethics—in the sense of a discipline which can remove ultimate differences concerning the good, etc.—is hence a chimera."[33] Klemke's conclusion is correct, but it does not entail regarding all perspectives as alternatives. People differ morally, not simply in the choices they make given the same alternatives, but in what they are prepared to count as alternatives. To say that all moral perspectives other than one's own *must* be seen as alternatives is already to impose a definite attitude towards them which is but one possible attitude among others.[34] Nothing in Kierkegaard's or Wittgenstein's methods need lead to such an imposition.

Second, Klemke thinks that, according to Kierkegaard, "There is no immediate ethical relationship between one individual and another. Therefore, any individual can question only himself ethically. None can question another. . . . Therefore, the attempt to find inter-subjectively valid ethical judgements ('One ought to do . . .') is futile. There are, and can be, no such judgements."[35] Wittgenstein's insistence that in ethical matters he has to speak for himself has been thought to lead to the same conclusions. But the absence of a science of ethics does not imply that people do not reflect on moral matters.[36] There is a difference between reflective and unreflective criticism, the former often being one of the marks of moral responsibility.[37] Moral differences do not rule out the possibility of criticism of others. Kierkegaard and Wittgenstein are simply calling attention to the moral form such criticism takes.

Third, Klemke thinks that Kierkegaard is saying: "*All* of the various modes of existence, that is, all of the alternative answers to the questions 'What is the good?', 'What ought I to do?', etc. can be given equal plausibility to the genuinely reflective man."[38] This suggestion is contradictory, since the judgment of 'equal plausibility' implies the very notion of a common rationality Kierkegaard and Wittgenstein are attacking. So far from being the only judgment open to the genuinely reflective, such a person would recognize its vacuity.

Neither Kierkegaard nor Wittgenstein, then, hold the three views attributed to them. But neither need they embrace the only mode of judgment many think is open to them once a science of ethics is rejected. It is the mode of judgment Klemke ascribes to Kierkegaard. Speaking of moral judgment, he says: "the condition for such certitude (as distinct from rational and objective certainty) is passionate inwardness, not reflection. The problem is, therefore, 'resolved' by an existential choice, a leap."[39] To argue in this way, however, suggests that the possibility of reflection and objectivity *does* depend on a science of ethics. Further, by placing 'the choosing self' outside all possible relations, movements, and institutions, the notion of such a self and its choice or leap become as metaphysically suspect as the science of ethics they were meant to replace.

The essential burden of Kierkegaard's and Wittgenstein's remarks need not involve these difficulties. Think of the ways in which various things may absorb us.[40] This does not involve a choice externally related to what is embraced any more than we have an external relation between willing and acting. In criticizing the notion of a science of ethics, Kierkegaard and Wittgenstein clear a conceptual space in which our allegiances to various values can be themselves. They show that these allegiances cannot be reduced to a unity and combat confusions concerning them. Wittgenstein says in *Culture and Value*, "My ideal is a certain coolness. A temple providing a setting for the passions without meddling with them."[41]

Having noted these various misunderstandings concerning Kierkegaard's and Wittgenstein's philosophical methods, are we now able to endorse the previous suggestion that nothing separates them? O. K. Bouwsma is correct in noting an analogy between what he calls "the logical aspects" of their investigations: "There is illusion in both cases. The task in both cases is conceived as that of dispelling illusions. The illusion is in both cases one of misunderstanding certain languages.... But those who seek to understand ordinary language and those who seek to understand the Scriptures run into confusion due to mistaken expectations concerning what the language must mean."[42] Bouwsma says that the indirect method by which such confusions are unravelled is what Socrates, Kierkegaard, and Wittgenstein have in common:

> the way to dispel an illusion is not by presenting the subject in a direct way—one must change the person who is under the illusion. No one is going to understand what it means to become a Christian until he has first understood what such a man is before he becomes a Christian. Those young friends of Socrates also had to come to understand something about themselves before they could join Socrates in asking his questions. All of us who learn from Wittgenstein had to come to understand something about ourselves, about our confusions, before we could return to where we were when as children we understood. Philosophy is generally an ailment which children don't have. There is no commonsense answer to a philosophical problem—hence the long way round.[43]

The only difference between Kierkegaard and Wittgenstein, it may be thought, is that "Wittgenstein's interest is more general because he is interested in all philosophical confusion, and not simply in confusions that arise in connection with Christianity."[44]

Yet, as Bouwsma recognizes, it would be misleading to be content with this conclusion. This is because it gives insufficient weight to the fact that "Kierkegaard introduces the distinctions he needs for his special purposes" whereas "Wittgenstein introduces those that anyone may need in clearing up confusion."[45] As we have seen, Kierkegaard's special purposes concerned his hope of freeing people from 'the monstrous illusion'; from confusions concerning what it means to become a Christian. This aim was his main priority. To be sure, philosophical clarifications are provided in the course of pursuing it, but these, for Kierkegaard, are a secondary consideration. From the outset he saw himself as a religious writer in Christendom, and he speaks of his *tactics* in his pseudonymous works. He insists that anyone who does not appreciate these tactics misunderstands the whole corpus of his work: "Supposing that ... a reader understands perfectly and appraises critically the individual aesthetic productions, he will nevertheless totally misunderstand me, inasmuch as he does not understand the religious totality in my whole work as an author. Suppose, then, that another understands my works in the totality of their religious reference, but does not understand a single one of the aesthetic productions contained in them—I would say that this lack of understanding is not an essential lack."[46] Bouwsma brings out well how Kierkegaard's religious priorities affect the task he took himself to be confronted with; a task importantly different from Wittgenstein's: "In the work of Wittgenstein there is ordinary language we understand. That ordinary language is related to words or expressions that give us trouble. In ordinary language we discover the corrective of the language which expresses the confusion. In the work of Kierkegaard there corresponds to ordinary language in Wittgenstein the language of Scriptures, which Kierkegaard understands. Without this latter assumption Kierkegaard cannot be effective. And this is not how it is in Wittgenstein. There, ordinary language is taken to be language which we all understand. Here, there is agreement. But Kierkegaard's task is in that way more formidable. He has first to teach us how to understand the language of Scripture."[47] But what form does the teaching take? As Bouwsma says, "The question is as to how much of what Kierkegaard describes as the illusion is to be described as grammatical."[48] What needs to be emphasized is that Kierkegaard is not simply clearing up grammatical confusions but, in depicting aesthetic, ethical, and religious perspectives, challenging people about the meaning of their own lives. Bouwsma is right in saying that Kierkegaard "was not ... merely presenting possibilities. There is more. He was more interested in filling our hearts with something like terror. You are at stake. What is to become of you?"[49] Kierkegaard did this in relation to clearing up 'the monstrous illusion'. I think it would be problematic to argue that Kierkegaard thought, in a wider context, that philosophical reflection, if carried out with integrity, should lead one to see Christianity as the only adequate positive answer to the question of the meaning of life.[50]

Holland seems to find tensions in Wittgenstein's authorship because he thinks that Wittgenstein, too, aspires to a religious point of view. When Wittgenstein says that he cannot help seeing every problem from a religious point of view, Holland assumes that he must be expressing some form of religious belief. Naturally, he then wonders which form of religion it is. He agrees with Taylor that "A man who is religious without having any religion in particular is hard to come by for the same reason that it would be hard to find a man who is a good citizen, but a citizen of no city in particular."[51] But did not Wittgenstein say, "The philosopher is not a citizen of any community of ideas, that is what makes him a philosopher"?[52] On Holland's view, what could this mean?

Among dictionary definitions of 'religious' we have: 'strict', 'rigid', 'scrupulous', and 'conscientious'. Rush Rhees suggested to me that it is dangerous to say more of Wittgenstein's remark: he applied himself to philosophy religiously, that is all. It would be absurd to ask in which historical religion this application takes place! Holland seems to appreciate this sense of 'religious application' when he says of Wittgenstein: "The fact that the problems were there had the same sort of significance for him as the fact that good and evil are there. This is how it was that the sphere of his work and the sphere of the ethical were both seen by Wittgenstein from a religious point of view. And one of the consequences of the two being connected in this way was, I think, that his work demanded of him what a religious vocation would have demanded."⁵³ But then, Holland turns the philosophical vocation into a religion: "His work, I suggested, was like a religious vocation in what it demanded of him. If that was right, we have in effect arrived at the following result already—Wittgenstein cannot pray lest he become soft. And he cannot become soft because his religiously given, or as we might also venture to say, his divinely appointed vocation, will not allow it. In short, God does not want him to worship."⁵⁴ But no such result follows from saying that Wittgenstein applied himself to philosophy religiously. The problems he wrestled with were conceptual, not personal. Thus it is a mistake to suggest, as Bouwsma does, that a philosophical clarification of the language of Scripture is deficient if one does not respond to it religiously as Kierkegaard did: "We get, accordingly, a grammatical elaboration of the language when what is required is obedience and surrender. The elaboration is cheap in that one can indulge in that and enjoy at the same time one's intellectual respectability."⁵⁵ But the grammatical elucidation may take the form of clarifying that the language of Scripture makes demands of its readers. This is not itself a form of religious surrender, but why should it be? Philosophy is concerned with clarity, not religious confessions. No doubt, if clarity does not lead to confession that is an offence in the eyes of Christianity. But it does not follow that Christianity is an offense to philosophy,⁵⁶ or that grammatical clarifications are cheap.

Wittgenstein's problems have their roots not in his personal life, but in tendencies of thought to which anyone can be susceptible, since they arise from the language we share. This remains so even if we agree with Holland's further claim that religion influenced the way in which Wittgenstein saw philosophical problems: "the ethical and . . . the Supernatural, entered into the conditions of their existence. In other words, the wonder was that these great problems—concerning the foundations of knowledge, and the relation between thinking and reality, and what it is to say something—should be there at all."⁵⁷ If this wonder is the result of religious influence, we may ask whether someone could see philosophical problems as Wittgenstein did, without having in him the possibility, at least, of religious belief.⁵⁸ On the other hand, we must remember that this religious influence is consistent with Wittgenstein's saying, "I am not a religious man."

Given that Kierkegaard's aims differ from Wittgenstein's, why not bring our deliberations to a close by saying that while Kierkegaard fully appreciated the clarificatory role of philosophy, he turned from it quite consciously to pursue his religious purposes?⁵⁹ After all, does he not say, "All honour to learning and scholarship, all praise to the man who can control the material detail, organising it with the authority of genuine insight, with the reliability that comes from acquaintance with the original sources"?⁶⁰ But this conclusion is too simple. Kierkegaard's comments refer to scholarship in general. We need to pay attention to what he says about philosophy in particular. When we do so, we find that Kierkegaard ignores the aspects of authenticity in philosophical authorship which one finds in Wittgenstein. Kierkegaard says: "I can very well call

Socrates my teacher—whereas I have only believed, and only believe in One, the Lord Jesus Christ."[61] Why did Kierkegaard turn from Socrates to Christ? Partly, because he saw that philosophy as such cannot determine the meaning of life. Socrates' achievement was to recognize this. Kierkegaard reveals the comic aspect of trying to attach one's eternal happiness to philosophy: "The comical appears only when the subject with an infinite passionate interest tries to attach his eternal happiness to philosophical speculation. But the speculative philosopher does not pose the problem of which we speak; for precisely as a speculative philosopher he becomes too objective to concern himself about an eternal happiness."[62] Thus Kierkegaard revises his early criticisms of Socrates. He no longer accuses him of infinite negativity. On the contrary, he regards the famous Socratic ignorance concerning the nature of the good life as the highest attainment of paganism: "Humanly speaking, that was surely a magnanimous undertaking."[63] But, where the meaning of one's life is concerned, one cannot remain with these negative conclusions. Hence, Kierkegaard continues: "But Christianity is a power far too great to be willing as a matter of course to make use of a man's magnanimous resolution . . . wherefore Christianity or Governance took the liberty of so arranging my subsequent life that there could be no misunderstanding (as indeed there was not from the beginning) as to whether it was I that stood in need of Christianity or Christianity that stood in need of me."[64]

Kierkegaard, as I noted at the outset, wants authorship to be a serious calling. He protests against the assumption "that one need not enquire about the communicator, but only about the communication," and insists that we should see whether an "author's personal existence comports with his communication."[65] Kierkegaard writes in his Journals: "I surely do not deny that I still recognise an *imperative of understanding* and that through it one can work upon man, *but it must be taken up into my life*, and that is what I now recognise as the most important thing."[66] But because the imperative of understanding cannot determine the meaning of life in some theoretical way, Kierkegaard assumes that it can only be taken up into one's personal life if it serves some other purpose. In his case, that purpose was the aim of bringing people to Christianity. Kierkegaard does not give sufficient attention to ways in which philosophical imperatives *as such* can be taken up into a person's life and, as a result, neglects important aspects of authentic authorship in philosophy.

The same neglect, it seems to me, is found in Holland's treatment of Wittgenstein. As we have seen, he sees Wittgenstein's struggle for clarity as an expression of his wonder at the world; a wonder which is shown in his endeavors to show us language as a city with no main road. This involved Wittgenstein in elucidations of perspectives he did not embrace personally. Holland says: "As a matter of fact, there is a kind of insight that enables a few gifted people who have it, not only to feel the full force of spiritual possibilities which they do not occupy, but even to be better perceivers of what is involved than the occupants themselves; and Wittgenstein probably had that insight."[67]

But Holland has difficulty in seeing how the struggle for such insight could be connected with one's personal problems. He says: "the idea of somebody's arriving at a view of *his own problems* by that route is preposterous."[68] Similarly, Kierkegaard says, "The person of an abstract thinker is irrelevant to his thought."[69] But what of non-abstract, non-metaphysical thinkers, such as Socrates and Wittgenstein? Kierkegaard's view is that in relation to the philosophical work of such thinkers, questions concerning their personal lives simply do not arise. According to him, that is what such thinkers have come to realize. Bouwsma concurs with this judgment: "whereas Kierkegaard's interest lies in saving Christianity for the world or to make sure that Christianity is understood, Wittgenstein is interested in saving intelligence—which means us—from the corruption that comes as natural to us. Purity of heart would be incidental to this."[70] Wittgenstein would not agree. To accept Kierkegaard's, Bouwsma's, and Holland's conclusions would be to miss an important aspect of what is involved in philosophical authorship for Wittgenstein. No doubt Holland and Bouwsma want to remind us that the source of Wittgenstein's philosophical problems is not personal. They arise from a wonder at the world. Quite so, but *the struggle with these problems is personal.* In fact, the struggle for clarity has analogies with a moral struggle. It is in this context, it seems to me, that Wittgenstein's concern with style is deeper than Kierkegaard's.

In 1937, Wittgenstein wrote: "What one writes about oneself cannot be more truthful than one is."[71] According to Rush Rhees,[72] Wittgenstein said, later, that self-deception must have a harmful effect on one's style, and that a person's state of soul could hide these deficiencies from him. He thought something akin to this had happened in Mahler's music. Holland spoke of Mahler's *pathetisch* pantheism. Wittgenstein wrote in 1948: "If it is true that Mahler's music is worthless, as I believe to be the case, then the question is what I think he ought to have done with his talent. For quite obviously it took a *set of very rare talents* to produce this bad music. Should he, say, have written his symphonies and burnt them? Or should he have done violence to himself and not written them? Should he have written them and realised that they were worthless?"[73] But how could Mahler recognize this? Wittgenstein writes: "I can see it, because I can compare his music with what the great composers wrote. But *he* could not."[74] Self-deception is likely to get in the way: "If nobody you admire is like you, then presumably you believe in your own value only because you are *you*. Even someone who is struggling against vanity will, if his struggle is not entirely successful, still deceive himself about the value of his own work."[75] Rhees said that Wittgenstein's own struggle to overcome the tendency to lie to himself about his own self-deception, drove him, at times, near to madness. Here, there is little distinction between Wittgenstein's philosophical struggle with the issue and his personal struggle with it in his work, hence the remark: "how can I be a logician if I'm not yet a human being?"[76]

Rush Rhees was with Wittgenstein on one occasion when he was thinking of sending to the publishers, as soon as possible, a draft of *Philosophical Investigations* which he had almost finished. He was very gloomy about it all.

Rush Rhees said to him, "You must know that it's head and shoulders above most of what is produced." Wittgenstein replied, "There's talent enough in it," but kept walking around the room, scowling. Contrast this with Kierkegaard's confident assertion that, from the outset, he knew he was a religious writer, and that, through the disinterested elucidations of his pseudonymous works, he was hoping to awaken others to an understanding which he possessed, but which they lacked. I shall not comment further on Kierkegaard's tactics as a religious writer in Christendom. What I do want to say is that, in Wittgenstein's case, we have a man greatly concerned with the style of his writing; absorbed, one might say, with how one can be an authentic philosophical author.

Notes

1. Søren Kierkegaard, *The Point of View for My Work as an Author*, translated by Walter Lowrie (Oxford, 1939), 44.

2. See his preface to *Philosophical Investigations*. Wittgenstein could not have been more wrong about his achievement.

3. Søren Kierkegaard, *The Concept of Irony*, translated with an introduction by Lee M. Capel (London, 1966), 300–302.

4. Ibid.

5. Josiah Thompson, *Kierkegaard* (London, 1974), 40.

6. Ibid.

7. Ibid., 147.

8. Ibid., 139

9. Wittgenstein, *Culture and Value*, edited by G. H. von Wright, translated by Peter Winch (Oxford, 1977), 56.

10. *Ludwig Wittgenstein: Personal Recollections*, edited by Rush Rhees (Oxford, 1981), 94.

11. R. F. Holland, "Not Bending the Knee," *Philosophical Investigations* (Jan. 1990): 20.

12. Ibid. However, I am not concerned with whether Wittgenstein was, in fact, a religious person. It would not affect the conclusions of my essay if it could be shown that he was.

13. Holland, "Not Bending the Knee," 21.

14. Søren Kierkegaard, *Either/Or*, vol. 2, translated by Walter Lowrie (Oxford, 1946), 11.

15. Ibid., 14.

16. Holland, "Not Bending the Knee," 27–28.

17. Ibid.

18. Kierkegaard, *Point of View*, 40.

19. Ibid., 27

20. E. D. Klemke, *Studies in the Philosophy of Kierkegaard* (The Hague, 1976), 10–11.

21. Søren Kierkegaard, *Concluding Unscientific Postscript*, translated by David F. Swenson (Princeton, 1944) (p. 551, unpaginated).

22. Ibid.

23. Kierkegaard, *That Individual* in *Point of View*, 123.

24. Kierkegaard, *My Position as a Religious Writer in Christendom and My Tactics* in *Point of View*, 159.

25. See "Religion in Wittgenstein's Mirror," in *Wittgenstein: Centenary Essays*, edited by A. Phillips Griffiths (Cambridge, 1991).

26. Holland, "Not Bending the Knee," 27.

27. Ibid., 25.

28. Ibid., 27.

29. Ibid., 25–26.

30. Ibid., 27.

31. Ibid., 18–19.

32. Ibid., 25.

33. Klemke, "Some Misinterpretations of Kierkegaard," in *Studies in the Philosophy of Kierkegaard*, 28.

34. Cf. "What Can We Expect from Ethics?" *Proceedings of the Aristotelian Society*, supplementary volume (1989), where I argue against Bernard Williams's claim that critical reflection on ethical diversity entails viewing different moral perspectives as options or alternatives.

35. Klemke, "Some Misinterpretations of Kierkegaard," 34.

36. This is not denied by my claim in "What Can We Expect from Ethics?" that intellectual reflection does not determine *the form* of the good life.

37. See Rush Rhees's papers on ethics in *Without Answers* (London, 1969).

38. Klemke, "Some Misinterpretations of Kierkegaard," 28–29.

39. Ibid.

40. I owe this suggestion to Peter Winch's "Moral Integrity" in *Ethics and Action* (London, 1972).

41. *Culture and Value*, 2.

42. O. K. Bouwsma, "Notes on Kierkegaard's 'The Monstrous Illusion'," in *Without Proof or Evidence, Essays of O. K. Bouwsma*, edited by J. L. Croft and Ronald E. Hustwit (Lincoln, Neb., 1984), 85.

43. Ibid. 79.

44. O. K. Bouwsma, "A New Sensibility," in *Towards a New Sensibility: Essays of O. K. Bouwsma*, edited and translated by J. L. Croft and Ronald E. Hustwit (Lincoln, Neb., 1982), 4.

45. Ibid.

46. Kierkegaard, *Point of View*, 6.

47. Bouwsma, "Notes on Kierkegaard's 'The Monstrous Illusion'," 85. This is too sweeping a claim. For example, it ignores Wittgenstein's discussion of conceptual indeterminacy and of how some people may be complete enigmas to others.

48. Bouwsma, "Notes on Kierkegaard's 'The Monstrous Illusion'," 83.

49. Ibid., 74.

50. Michael Weston seemed to urge a consideration of this wider view in a discussion of the second version of my paper at a seminar at the University of Essex.

51. Holland, "Not Bending the Knee," 25.

52. Wittgenstein, *Zettel*, translated by G. E. M. Anscombe (Oxford, 1967), 455.

53. Holland, "Not Bending the Knee," 23.

54. Ibid., 24.

55. Bouwsma, "Notes on Kierkegaard's 'The Monstrous Illusion'," 77.

56. For a further discussion of the distinction, see my critical notice of C. Stephen Evans, *Kierkegaard's Fragments and Postscript* and H. A. Nielsen, *Where the Passion Is: A Reading of Kierkegaard's Philosophical Fragments* in *Philosophical Investigations* 9, no. 1 (Jan. 1986).

57. Holland, "Not Bending the Knee," 22.

58. I owe this consideration to my colleague, R. W. Beardsmore.

59. This suggestion was put to me by my colleague, H. O. Mounce, in a discussion of the first version of this essay at the Philosophical Society at University of Swansea.

60. Kierkegaard, *Concluding Unscientific Postscript*, 15.

61. Kierkegaard, *Point of View*, 41.

62. Kierkegaard, *Concluding Unscientific Postscript*, 54.

63. Ibid., 97.

64. Ibid.

65. Kierkegaard, *Point of View*, 45.

66. Søren Kierkegaard, *Journals*, edited and translated by Alexander Dru (Oxford, 1951), 15.

67. Holland, "Not Bending the Knee," 20.

68. Ibid.

69. Kierkegaard, *Concluding Unscientific Postscript*, 319.

70. Bousma, "A New Sensibility," 4.

71. *Culture and Value* (Rush Rhees's translation). Peter Winch's published translation reads: "You cannot write anything about yourself that is more truthful than you yourself are."

72. The comments on Wittgenstein which follow I owe to seminars on *Culture and Value* by Rush Rhees at the University College of Swansea in 1979.

73. *Culture and Value*.

74. Ibid.

75. Ibid.

76. See Wittgenstein, *Letters to Russell, Keynes and Moore*, edited by G. H. von Wright, assisted by B. F. McGuinness (Oxford, 1974), 57–58.

Wittgenstein and Infinite Linguistic Competence

IAN NILES

M any philosophers and linguists have been struck by the ability of competent speakers to understand an infinite number of sentences (hereafter referred to as infinite linguistic competence), and they have claimed that the only explanation for this ability is that competent speakers have an internal representation of linguistic rules. In this essay, I will argue that this claim is open to question and that its truth can be decided only when there is agreement about the nature of linguistic understanding. There are, broadly speaking, two views about what understanding an expression of language amounts to. On the one hand, we find the very appealing traditional view, which has been embraced by prominent figures throughout the history of philosophy. According to this view, understanding an expression of language is a matter of pairing it with a mental or abstract entity. If the traditional view of understanding turns out to be correct, then the claim that infinite linguistic competence can be explained only by postulating internally represented linguistic rules can stand. The other perspective on linguistic understanding is Wittgenstein's. This philosopher has compelling reasons for thinking that the traditional view is radically incorrect, and he has his own, largely neglected, picture of what linguistic understanding amounts to. If Wittgenstein is right, then the claim regarding infinite linguistic competence will have to be rejected, and a revision of theoretical linguistics may be required.

Before we examine the purported justification for the claim that infinite linguistic competence can be explained only by postulating internally represented linguistic rules, it will be useful to provide some evidence that this claim has commanded widespread assent among linguists and philosophers. Consider Dummett, for example. In his essay "Can Analytical Philosophy Be Systematic, and Ought it to Be?" he writes,

The fact that anyone who has a mastery of any given language is able to understand an infinity of sentences of that language—an infinity that is, of course, principally composed of sentences he has never heard before— ... can hardly be explained otherwise than by supposing that each speaker has an implicit grasp of a number of general principles governing the use in sentences of words of the language.[1]

In their work *Language and Reality*, the philosophers Devitt and Sterelny make it clear that they are of the same opinion.

People have the capacity to produce and understand any of an indefinite number of sentences; their capacity is "productive".... It is plausible to think that this is to be explained by their internalizing *something like* the grammar linguists are discovering.[2]

Although he is concerned exclusively with semantic rules and does not explicitly invoke the notion of mental representation, Davidson attributes the same general claim to the majority of philosophers of language in his essay "Truth and Meaning":

It is conceded by most philosophers of language, and recently by some linguists, that a satisfactory theory of meaning must give an account of how the meanings of sentences depend upon the meanings of words. Unless such an account could be supplied for a particular language, it is argued, there would be no explaining the fact that we can learn the language: no explaining the fact that, on mastering a finite vocabulary and a finitely stated set of rules, we are prepared to produce and to understand any of a potential infinitude of sentences.[3]

For a final example, consider Chomsky. In his work *Language and Mind*, he asserts that the ability to understand an indefinite number of sentences and to understand novel sentences is largely what characterizes human language.[4] He then implies that the explanation of this fact is that there is "a system of rules that assigns sound and meaning in a definite way for an infinite class of possible sentences."[5]

At this point let me outline the structure of my argument in this essay. In the first section, I will construct an intuitively appealing chain of reasoning for the claim that infinite linguistic competence can be explained only by postulating an internally represented set of linguistic rules (a feat which has never before been accomplished). I will then show that this argument is unacceptable as it stands and must be either modified or rejected. In the next section, I will offer two revisions of this line of reasoning. The first, it will be seen, does not accomplish everything that is required. As for the second, I will demonstrate that it presupposes the traditional view of understanding, viz. that understanding is a matter of associating expressions of language with mental or abstract entities. In the following section, I will show that this view is intuitively attractive, explanatorily powerful, and possesses imposing historical roots. I will devote the final section to outlining Wittgenstein's views on understanding and arguing that they represent a formidable, albeit largely ignored, challenge to the traditional view of understanding. The upshot of this is, as I stated in the opening paragraph, that the claim regarding infinite linguistic competence is debatable and that the debate can be settled only when there is agreement among Wittgensteinians and proponents of the traditional view about the nature of linguistic understanding.

THE INFINITE COMPETENCE ARGUMENT (ICA)

Very little has been offered in the way of support for the claim that infinite linguistic competence can be explained only by positing internally represented linguistic rules. In fact, the only justification found in the literature, as far as I am aware, occurs in the passage from Davidson quoted earlier.[6] There Davidson writes that without a compositional semantics there would be, according to most philosophers of language,

> no explaining the fact that, on mastering a finite vocabulary and a finitely stated set of rules, we are prepared to produce and to understand any of a potential infinitude of sentences.[7]

The idea here seems to be, roughly speaking, that the enormous gulf between the finite mind and the infinite number of sentences that a competent speaker can understand can be bridged only by postulating internally represented linguistic rules. In other words, such rules afford the only means of ensuring that the mind is not "filled" with too much linguistic stuff. This intuitively appealing picture can be fleshed out into the following argument: since human minds are finite and since a competent speaker can understand an infinite number of sentences, there must be some finite mechanism within the mind of the competent speaker which is capable of generating in some way this infinity. Now, it seems that the only possible candidate for such a mechanism is a finite set of recursive rules. These rules must be recursive, because they are to be capable of generating an infinite number of sentences, and they must be finite in number, because they have to "fit" into the finite mind. If this is right, then infinite linguistic competence can be explained only by positing an internally represented, finite set of recursive rules. In what follows, I will refer to this line of reasoning as the infinite competence argument, or ICA for short.

Although this argument is tempting, it is much more problematic than it appears at first sight. To demonstrate this, I will construct an analogue of ICA. To begin, consider a child's plastic dart gun, of the sort that can be bought at a dime store. In some sense, guns of this kind can fire an infinite number of shots. For each time I fire the gun, it makes a different shot. Whenever I load the gun, aim it, and pull the trigger, the projected dart has a different trajectory and a different final resting place. For example, when I fire the gun this time, the dart bounces off the t.v. screen and hits the cat; when I shoot the gun the next time, the dart hits the wall and eventually comes to rest on top of the clock radio; when I fire the gun on the following occasion, the dart slightly grazes my copy of the *Critique of Pure Reason* before colliding with the left edge of my window fan; etc. Now it is also clear that in another sense the plastic dart gun cannot fire an infinite number of shots. One of the components of the gun will cease to function (e.g., the spring will wear out or the trigger will snap off) or the whole gun will simply come apart after the gun has made a finite number of shots. Thus, the dart gun can never actually make the infinite number of shots that it is, in the first sense, capable of making. This being so, the dart gun is not capable, in another sense, of making an infinite number of shots.

Now compare dart guns with competent speakers of a natural language. The capacity of the former to fire an infinite number of shots is, I claim, exactly parallel to the ability of the latter to understand an infinite number of sentences. In one sense, a competent speaker of a natural language clearly can understand an infinite number of sentences. There are an infinite number of sentences such that, if any one of these sentences were presented to the competent speaker under the appropriate conditions, the sentence would be understood by the speaker.[8] In a perfectly parallel sense, a dart gun can fire an infinite number of shots. For there are an infinite number of shots such that, if the dart gun were placed under the appropriate conditions, the dart gun would make any one of these shots. Now, in some sense, a competent speaker cannot understand an infinite number of sentences. Competent speakers, at least human competent speakers, will only come across a finite number of sentences in their lifetimes. Such speakers will die before they actually understand the infinite number of sentences that they are, in the first sense, able to understand. Now, this is precisely the sense in which a dart gun cannot fire an infinite number of shots: such a gun will inevitably break or wear out before it actually makes all of the shots that it is, in the first sense, capable of making. The conclusion of all of this is that the respective infinite abilities of competent speakers and functional dart guns are perfectly parallel to one another.[9]

We can now construct the following argument about dart guns which has the same form as ICA. Since dart guns are finite and since the number of shots which a dart gun is capable of making is infinite, there must be some finite mechanism within the dart gun which is capable of generating in some way this infinity. Now, it seems that the only possible candidate for such a mechanism is a finite set of recursive rules represented in the dart gun. These rules must be recursive, because they are to be capable of generating an infinite number of shots, and they must be finite in number, because they have to "fit" into the dart gun. Therefore, the capacity of the dart gun to fire an infinite number of shots can be explained only by supposing that there is a finite set of recursive rules represented within the dart gun.

Let us now examine the relation between the assumptions and the conclusion of this line of reasoning. These assumptions do not seem to necessitate this conclusion in the same way that the premises of ICA compel our assent to its conclusion. In the case of ICA, the juxtaposition of the fact that a competent speaker can understand an infinite number of sentences with the fact that the human mind is finite produces a cognitive cramp which, one feels, can be alleviated only by postulating internally represented linguistic rules. However, with respect to the parallel argument, there is no corresponding cognitive cramp. The gap between the capacity of the plastic dart gun to fire an infinite number of shots and the physical finitude of the gun itself is, perhaps, a marginally interesting phenomenon, but it is hardly the sort of thing that causes intellectual discomfiture, nor does it strike us as a chasm that must be spanned with an explanation of some kind. Furthermore, whatever feelings are aroused by the assumptions of the parallel argument, they do not inspire thoughts of recursive rules and the gun's representing these rules. In fact, the conclusion of the parallel argument does not even seem meaningful. The very idea of a dart gun "representing" a finite set of recursive rules appears ludicrous. A dart gun, unlike the human mind, just is not the sort of thing that can represent rules. For these reasons, it is tempting to claim that the conclusion of the parallel argument is not entailed by its premises and, hence, that this argument is invalid. If this is right, it has severe repercussions for ICA. Since this argument and its analogue have the same form, the two arguments stand or fall together. Therefore, if the parallel argument is invalid, ICA too must be invalid.

This line of reasoning is very appealing, but perhaps it goes too quickly. Perhaps, implausible as it may seem, the assumptions of the parallel argument do imply that a dart gun in some sense represents a finite set of recursive rules. Let us suppose then, at least for the sake of discussion, that both ICA and the parallel argument are valid. The problem then becomes: how are we to interpret the conclusion of the latter argument, viz. that the capacity of a dart gun to fire an infinite number of shots can be explained only by supposing that there is a finite set of recursive rules represented within the dart gun? In particular, what could the rules mentioned here be and in what sense could the dart gun represent these rules? Assuming that it makes sense to speak of the dart gun representing rules, the only possible candidates for the rules involved would be, it seems, either physical laws relevant to the behavior of the dart gun and the environment in which it is employed or a set of diagrams revealing the structure and inner workings of the gun, i.e., blueprints of the gun. As for the notion of representation appealed to, the gun does not represent diagrams of its structure and workings in the same way that it represents physical laws which are applicable to it. Blueprints are represented by the gun in the sense that they are physically encoded in the gun. Physical laws, on the other hand, are represented by the gun in a much weaker sense. For to say that the dart gun represents such laws could only mean that the latter play a part in explanations and/or predictions of the functioning of the dart gun (under certain conditions). If this is right, then the conclusion of the parallel argument must be given a very weak interpretation. It means merely that the capacity of the dart gun to fire an infinite number of shots can be explained only if blueprints are encoded in the gun or physical laws of such and such a sort play a part in explanations and/or predictions of the functioning of the dart gun (under certain conditions).

This interpretation of the parallel argument's conclusion shows that ICA's conclusion must be given a similarly pithless reading. If the conclusion of the parallel argument is true only under the interpretation just discussed, then the premises of this argument entail at most that the conclusion is true in this sense. Therefore, since this argument has the same form as ICA, the assumptions of ICA, in turn, entail at most that the conclusion of ICA is true in a sense analogous to the very weak interpretation of the parallel argument's conclusion.

The problem is to determine what such an interpretation of ICA's conclusion would look like. Recall that ICA's conclusion runs as follows: infinite linguistic competence can be explained only by positing an internally represented, finite set of recursive rules. What we need to do, then, is to determine what these rules could be and in what sense they would be internally represented under this interpretation. Unfortunately, this is a very difficult task. Consider first the question of what the rules referred to in ICA's conclusion would be under this interpretation. Perhaps the most plausible answer is that they would simply be physical laws, neurophysiological laws, or neural diagrams. For these seem to be the closest counterparts of the rules in the innocuous interpretation of the parallel argument's conclusion, viz. physical laws governing the functioning of dart guns and blueprints of such guns. Now, in what sense could physical laws, neurophysical laws or neural diagrams be internally represented? As was the case with the parallel argument's conclusion, there are two different answers here. If the rules are neural diagrams, then they are represented in the sense that they are physically encoded in the brain. If the rules are physical or neurophysical laws, then to say that these rules are internally represented could mean merely that they have explanatory and/or predictive power with respect to the linguistic behavior of the speaker in question. Thus, the reading of ICA's conclusion corresponding to the very weak interpretation of the parallel argument's conclusion is as follows: infinite linguistic competence can be explained only if neural diagrams are encoded in the brain or physical or neurophysical laws play a part in explaining and/or predicting the linguistic behavior of the speaker in question.

Clearly this interpretation will not suit the philosophers and linguists who claim that infinite linguistic competence can be explained only by postulating internally represented linguistic rules. For physical laws, neurophysiological laws, and neural diagrams are not the sort of rules that the people who espouse this claim have in their sights. The rules these people are after are, for example, those that make up generative grammars of natural languages. Thus, if ICA's conclusion is given the interpretation of the preceding paragraph, then this conclusion does not have the significance that it is intended to have by the philosophers and linguists who embrace it.

These philosophers and linguists will no doubt try to argue that the interpretation of ICA's conclusion considered above is not the analogue of the very weak interpretation of the parallel arguments conclusion. They will want to hold that the true analogue of the latter interpretation refers to rules of the generative grammar variety. Although there may be some good reasons to hold this, the central point here is simply that it is not clear what the true analogue is. On the one hand, there are no decisive arguments that the rules in question are of the generative grammar variety. On the other hand, there is, as we have seen, some reason to think that the rules in question are physical laws, neurophysiological laws, or a neural diagram. We must conclude, then, that, at the very least, it is debatable which interpretation of ICA's conclusion follows from the assumptions of this argument.

At this point let me summarize what has been accomplished in this section. At the beginning I offered a seemingly plausible argument, ICA, for the claim that infinite linguistic competence can be explained only by positing internally represented linguistic rules. I then constructed a chain of reasoning having the same form as ICA and showed that it is either invalid or its assumptions imply only an innocuous interpretation of its conclusion. I then drew the inference that either ICA, too, is invalid or its assumptions imply merely that its conclusion is true in a sense corresponding to the innocuous interpretation of the parallel argument's conclusion. Finally, I showed that there are grounds for thinking that this reading of ICA's conclusion is one that would not satisfy the people who claim that infinite linguistic competence can be explained only by positing internally represented linguistic rules. Of course, these grounds are not decisive, but they demonstrate at least that ICA is a very problematic chain of reasoning. The upshot of all of this is that ICA is not, as it stands, a satisfactory argument for its conclusion.

TWO NEW ARGUMENTS

The task before us now is, quite predictably, to construct such an argument. It seems that we have two alternatives: we can either try to repair ICA or we can start over from scratch. The latter option is unattractive, since it is very difficult to imagine a line of reasoning which does not incorporate the intuition behind ICA. This intuition is, it will be recalled, that there would be too much stuff in the mind of the competent speaker if there were no internally represented linguistic rules. In other words, there is an enormous gap between the infinite linguistic competence of a competent speaker and the finitude of a competent speaker's mind, and the only means of bridging that gap seems to be a mental representation of a finite set of linguistic rules. Since there seems to be no alternative to the basic strategy behind ICA, let us try to fix this argument. We need to revise ICA in such a way that it will no longer be susceptible to anything like the argument involving the dart gun and in such a way that it becomes clear why the infinite-finite gap is so problematic in this case and not in cases like the one involving the dart gun.

Suppose that a competent speaker can understand a sentence only if he has a mental representation of the sentence. This supposition, in conjunction with the framework of ICA, can be used to generate the conclusion that infinite linguistic competence can be explained only by positing internally represented linguistic rules. First of all, this supposition and the fact that a competent speaker is able to understand an infinite number of sentences jointly imply that a competent speaker mentally represents an infinite number of sentences. This latter state of affairs would be possible, it seems, only if one of two alternatives were realized. Either every competent speaker has an internal representation of a finite set of recursive, linguistic rules which generate all of the sentences which the speaker can understand or there is within the mind of the competent speaker a list enumerating every one of the infinite number of sentences which the speaker can understand. Since the human mind is finite and, thus, cannot accommodate an infinite list of any sort, the second alternative is ruled out. Therefore, infinite linguistic competence can be explained only if every competent speaker has an internal representation of a finite set of recursive, linguistic rules. In what follows, I will refer to this line of reasoning as ICA-SYN (where "SYN" stands for "syntax").

There are several things to point out about this argument. First of all, the dart gun analogy, which constituted a potent objection to ICA, has no point of contact with ICA-SYN for the latter argument depends upon the assumption that one can understand a sentence only if one has a mental representation of that sentence, and no analogue of this assumption is true of dart guns. Second, ICA-SYN, unlike the argument which I will soon discuss, does not contain premises which are clearly inconsistent with compelling and neglected Wittgensteinian views about language and the mind.[10] The final thing to notice about ICA-SYN is that, for many theorizers about language, it is not in itself sufficient. The rules referred to in this argument have to do solely with generating sentences of the given language. They do not concern meaning-assignments or, speaking more generally, interpretations of sentences. Therefore, ICA-SYN demonstrates at most that competent speakers have an internal representation of *syntactic* rules. The question of whether such speakers have an internal representation of *semantic* rules is left completely untouched by this argument. However, we need to show that infinite linguistic competence can be explained only by supposing that competent speakers have an internal representation of semantic rules. For the linguistic rules that are alleged to be internally represented by competent speakers are presumably something very much like a generative grammar, and, according to most linguists and philosophers, a generative grammar contains, as an essential component, semantic rules. Furthermore, according to the passage from Davidson quoted above, many philosophers and linguists believe that infinite linguistic competence can be explained only by postulating a compositional semantics.

How can we construct an argument for the claim that infinite linguistic competence can be explained only if competent speakers have an internal representation of semantic rules? Once again, we must, lacking any alternative, apply the basic strategy behind ICA and ICA-SYN. That is, we must show that the mind would "contain" too many objects of a certain sort if it did not also represent semantic rules for the language in question. The problem is to figure out what sort of objects they would be. We know that they are not mental representations of sentences. For, as was seen above, *syntactic* rules are sufficient to keep the mind from overflowing with such representations. But what could the objects in question be if not mental representations of sentences? The answer, it seems, is meaning objects, that is, mental or abstract entities which constitute the meanings of the linguistic expressions with which they are associated.

If we suppose that there are such entities and that understanding a linguistic expression is a matter of associating it with its corresponding meaning object(s),[11] we can then argue as follows (on analogy with ICA-SYN). Since a competent speaker is capable of understanding an infinite number of sentences, it follows from our supposition that such a speaker is capable of associating an infinite number of meaning objects with an infinite number of sentences. Now, there are, it seems, only two ways in which this could be done.[12] The first possibility is that the mind represents a finite set of primitive meaning objects and a finite set of recursive rules which (i) generate more complex meaning structures[13] out of less complex meaning structures and (ii) indicate which meaning structures are paired with which linguistic expressions. This first alternative says, in other words, that a competent speaker has an internal representation of a compositional semantics. The second alternative is that every competent speaker has an internal representation of an infinite number of ordered pairs whose first elements are meaning structures and whose second elements are expressions of the language in question. Since the human mind is finite, this second alternative is not possible. Therefore, the first alternative holds, i.e., every competent speaker has an internal representation of a compositional semantics. In what follows, I will refer to this line of reasoning as ICA-SEM (where "SEM" stands for "semantics").

There are two important things to notice about this argument. First of all, its initial assumptions, viz. that the meaning of a linguistic item is an abstract or mental entity and that understanding a linguistic item is a state or process which consists of associating the linguistic item with (one of) its meaning(s), are very weighty claims about the nature of linguistic understanding. In what follows, I will jointly refer to these two assumptions as the traditional view of understanding, or TVU for short. The second thing to notice about ICA-SEM is that it too, like ICA-SYN, is immune to the dart gun analogy, simply because no analogue of TVU is true of plastic dart guns.

In the next section I will discuss TVU in detail and show that for several different reasons it is a seemingly undeniable view. In the following section, I will demonstrate that Wittgenstein had compelling reasons for thinking that TVU is radically incorrect, and I will outline his own picture of what linguistic understanding amounts to. Both these reasons and this picture have not been given due consideration by linguists and contemporary philosophers of language. Thus, the only apparent line of reasoning for the claim that infinite linguistic competence can be explained only by positing internally represented semantic rules assumes that a very plausible and largely ignored view of linguistic understanding is false. The upshot of this is that this claim is open to question and that its truth can be determined only after it is decided which picture of linguistic understanding, Wittgenstein's or TVU, is correct.

THE TRADITIONAL VIEW OF UNDERSTANDING

TVU has much to recommend itself. For one thing, it is implied by the following extremely attractive philosophical argument. We are inclined to think that understanding must be a state or process of some sort. Given that reductive behaviorism is no longer a tenable philosophical position, this state or process cannot be behavioral in nature. It seems, then, that it must be a state or process of the mind or brain. Furthermore, one would be hard-pressed to deny that understanding a linguistic expression is a matter of knowing the expression's meaning. Therefore, understanding a linguistic expression must be a mental state or process which involves knowing the meaning of the linguistic expression.

Supposing that this conclusion is true, what are the meanings of linguistic expressions? One is almost irresistibly attracted to the view that they must be a particular kind of object. The question, then, is what kind of object they are. Since the state or process of understanding a linguistic expression, when it occurs, must happen either instantaneously or over a very short period of time, meaning entities must be readily accessible to the mind. For this reason, such entities could not be physical objects. For a physical object corresponding to a particular word is often not available to one who understands the word. The only possibility is, it seems, that meanings are either mental or abstract objects, since these are the only kind of thing with which one could be in immediate contact regardless of time and circumstance. We have now reached the first component of TVU, viz. that the meaning of a linguistic expression is an abstract or mental entity.

Now, what about the second component? Given that understanding a linguistic expression is a mental state or process that involves knowing the expression's meaning, we need to determine what this "knowing" amounts to. Of course, it is difficult to say anything very specific, but, since it has just been shown that meanings must be abstract or mental entities, it seems that this "knowing" must consist of an association between the mind and such an entity. Thus, understanding a linguistic expression is a mental state or process which consists of grasping the meaning of the expression. We have now succeeded in deriving both components of TVU from seemingly undeniable principles concerning understanding and meaning.

Aside from being the conclusion of an extremely attractive argument, TVU is also an explanatorily powerful theory in the philosophy of language and the mind. It can be used to generate skeletal accounts of what thought amounts to, of how a speaker is able to mean something by a linguistic item, and of how communication and reference are possible. If the meaning of a linguistic item is a mental or abstract entity, then it is very plausible to suppose that thinking is a matter of manipulating these entities in some way with or without their corresponding linguistic items. An account of how X can mean Y by Z is got by applying TVU's account of linguistic understanding in reverse. If understanding is a matter of "linking" a linguistic item with an abstract or mental entity, then someone means something by a given word, it is plausible to suggest, by "linking" an abstract or mental entity with a word. In the case of understanding, one moves from the linguistic item to the meaning object; in the case of meaning, one proceeds from the meaning object to the linguistic item. TVU also leads to an account of how communication is possible. It seems, intuitively, that communication is successful only because communicants have the same relevant stuff in mind. For example, Tom is able to carry out the order that Jane gives him and the man on the side of the road responds by giving directions when I ask him where the local Burger King is located, only because the parties in these communicative exchanges share, to a certain extent, the same cognitive content. Now, what is this cognitive content and how are communicants able to share it? TVU has an answer that is made to order. The meaning objects of TVU are cognitive content, and communicants are able to share this content because they are able to grasp the same abstract entity or sufficiently similar mental entities. Finally, TVU can be used to frame a persuasive, albeit controversial, picture of how reference is possible. Language "hooks up" with the world, according to this picture, because the meaning objects of TVU are intensions and intensions determine extensions.

Since TVU is, for all of the reasons indicated, an extremely seductive account of linguistic understanding, it is not surprising that it has been espoused by prominent figures in the history of philosophy. For example, as Baker and Hacker point out in their work *Wittgenstein: Meaning and Understanding*, Plato and Frege embraced both components of what I am labeling TVU.[14] According to these two philosophers, the meaning of a word is an abstract entity; for Plato it is a form, and for Frege it is a *Sinn*. Furthermore, for both Plato and Frege, understanding is a matter of grasping the appropriate abstract entity. A more contemporary example of TVU is the traditional doctrine of meaning that Putnam attributes to Carnap and his followers, among others, in his essay "The Meaning of 'Meaning'." According to this doctrine, "knowing the meaning of a term is just a matter of being in a certain psychological state."[15] Moreover, meanings are abstract or mental entities on this doctrine.[16] Although TVU has been adopted or discussed by other eminent philosophers (e.g., Locke), it will not be possible to trace further in this essay the historical roots and contemporary expressions of TVU.

WITTGENSTEIN'S RESPONSE

For all of the reasons I have adduced (and probably others as well), TVU is an imposing and seemingly undeniable picture of what linguistic understanding amounts to. Wittgenstein, however, believes that it is radically incorrect. In this section, I will sketch some of the reasons Wittgenstein has for believing this, and I will outline Wittgenstein's picture of linguistic understanding. My purpose here will not be to provide a comprehensive exegesis of Wittgenstein's views on understanding and meaning; there already exist good exegeses of this sort.[17] I will simply argue here that some of Wittgenstein's thoughts on these matters are sufficiently compelling to render TVU questionable.

Let us begin by considering the first component of TVU, viz. that meanings are abstract or mental entities. Wittgenstein would reject this proposition, because, as he makes clear in *The Blue and Brown Books*, he does not believe meanings are entities of any kind:

> The mistake we are liable to make could be expressed thus: We are looking for the use [read: meaning] of a sign, but we look for it as though it were an object co-existing with the sign.[18]

Wittgenstein argues in the *Philosophical Investigations* that the meanings of words are not objects, because no object can do everything that is required of the meaning of a word. Suppose that meanings are abstract or mental entities, and consider the question of what kind of abstract or mental entities they could be. One is inclined to say that they are symbols of some sort. But of what sort? The only possibilities are, it seems, images (e.g., in the imagination or in platonic space) or linguistic expressions (e.g., of mentalese or of a natural language).

Neither an image nor a linguistic expression can be the meaning of a word, according to Wittgenstein, because neither of these can determine the application of a word to which it corresponds. Wittgenstein writes,

> What is essential is to see that the same thing can come before our minds when we hear the word and the application still be different. Has it the *same* meaning both times? I think we shall say not.[19]

Both images and linguistic expressions are interpretations, and "any interpretation still hangs in the air along with what it interprets, and cannot give it any support. Interpretations by themselves do not determine meaning."[20] All of this will become clearer if we consider in some detail the view that meanings are images. Suppose, for example, that the meaning of the word "cube" is a picture of a cube. Wittgenstein deals with this example as follows,

> Well, suppose that a picture does come before your mind when you hear the word "cube", say the drawing of a cube. In what sense can this picture fit or fail to fit a use of the word "cube"?—Perhaps you say: It's quite simple;—if that picture occurs to me and I point to a triangular prism for instance, and say it is a cube, then this use of the word doesn't fit the picture.'—But doesn't it fit? I have purposely so chosen the example that it is quite easy to imagine a *method of projection* according to which the picture does fit after all.[21]

Wittgenstein's point here is that there are a number of different and equally legitimate ways of applying the picture of the cube. For there is nothing in the picture which tells me that I must apply the word "cube" only to those things which resemble the picture in certain respects.[22] Since a picture does not determine the application of a word to which it corresponds, it cannot be the meaning of a word. For the same reason, the meaning of a word cannot be a linguistic expression. Actually, the latter view is burdened with even more severe problems. For, unlike a picture, a linguistic expression does not even suggest an application of the corresponding word. As is well known, the relation between a linguistic expression and its corresponding meaning is, excepting onomatopoetic words, perfectly arbitrary.[23]

Now consider the second component of TVU, viz. that understanding is a mental state or process which consists of associating a linguistic item with its meaning. Wittgenstein would object to this claim, because understanding is not, according to him, a mental state or process. He writes,

> In the sense in which there are processes (including mental processes) which are characteristic of understanding, understanding is not a mental process.[24]

> "Understanding a word": a state. But a *mental* state?—Depression, excitement, pain, are called mental states.[25]

Wittgenstein argues that understanding is not a mental state or process in two distinct ways.

First, he compares the use of the word "understanding" with the use of the terms "depression," "excitement," and "pain."[26] Clearly, it is completely meaningful to speak of being in a continuous state of depression, excitement, or pain, just as it makes perfect sense to say that one was in a state of depression, excitement, or pain which was interrupted at some point in time. However, according to Wittgenstein, it is senseless to say that one has continuously understood a word over some span of time. Furthermore, we cannot, according to Wittgenstein, speak of an interruption in our understanding of a word in the same way we speak of an interruption in a state of depression, excitement, or pain. It is meaningful to say, with more or less precision, that a state of depression, excitement, or pain ended at a given time, but it is not clear how we are to interpret the same thing said of one's understanding of a word. For example, one can say "My pain ended at 10:32 tonight" and "I recovered from my state of excitement this afternoon," but what are we to make of "My understanding of the word 'ubiquitous' ended at 10:32 tonight" or "My understanding of this word ended sometime this afternoon"? For these reasons, "understanding" does not seem to be used in the same way as "depression," "excitement," and "pain." Since the latter are commonly taken to be paradigmatic examples of terms expressing mental states, the conclusion of this "grammatical investigation" is that understanding is not a mental state.

Wittgenstein also tries to persuade us that understanding a word is not a mental state or process by comparing it with the activity of reading and arguing that the latter is not a state or process of this sort.[27] The reason for this comparison is, perhaps, that we are even more inclined to say of reading than of understanding that it is a particular cognitive state or process. Thus, if Wittgenstein can persuade us that reading is neither of these, we will have all the more reason to think the same is true of understanding. Wittgenstein first claims that reading cannot be a *conscious* mental state or process. For one thing, there is not a particular, introspectible state or process which is common to all cases of reading.[28] For another thing, what is going through the consciousness of someone who is actually reading may be identical to what is going through the consciousness of someone who is only pretending to read.[29] Someone who is convinced that reading is not a conscious mental state or process will probably retreat to the claim that this activity must be a state or process of either the brain or the unconscious mind (whatever exactly this latter might amount to). The problem with this move, according to Wittgenstein, is that the state or process in question then becomes a "hypothesis" or "model,"[30] since we no longer have direct evidence for it. Furthermore, we must now ask: what empirical grounds do we have for postulating this "model"? The answer seems to be that there is little or no evidence of the required sort.[31]

It should be clear at this point that Wittgenstein has cogent objections to both components of TVU, but perhaps these objections are not sufficiently weighty to make one think twice about embracing TVU. After all, one can argue as follows. Perhaps, as Wittgenstein claims, we have no idea what sort of object meanings are, nor what kind of mental state or process understanding is. Nevertheless, we all have to agree that the meaning of a word is some sort of object and that understanding is some kind of state or process. For clearly the words "meaning" and "understanding" have sense, and, since they have sense, they must denote or express *something*. Now, what could "meaning" refer to other than objects of a certain type and what could "understanding" express but a particular state or process? If this is right, then we can proceed directly to the conclusion that TVU is true. For the two crucial assumptions of the argument for TVU at the beginning of the previous section are that the meaning of a word is an object and that understanding is a state or process. The only other supposition of note in this argument is that understanding a word is a matter of knowing what the word means, and no philosopher, Wittgenstein included, could raise any objections to this.

Although this line of reasoning seems, on the face of it, to be quite convincing, it cannot be used against Wittgenstein. The reason is simply that it begs the question against him. He would claim that we are inclined toward the views that understanding is a state or process and that meanings are objects because we have in mind a certain, very general philosophical picture of language. According to this picture, every word denotes a thing or kind of thing in the world.[32] These things and kinds of thing may be of the garden variety (e.g., physical objects, states, or processes) or they may have a somewhat shadowy character (e.g., properties, abstract entities, or conceptual entities). This picture has an extraordinary intuitive appeal and is the foundation of most conceptions of language that have been embraced throughout the history of philosophy. It is the foundation of *most* conceptions of language, but not all of them. In the *Philosophical Investigations*, Wittgenstein devotes a good deal of space to arguing that this model is not true of many elements of language. Now, presumably one would embrace the claims that understanding is a state or process and that meanings are objects of some sort only if one also accepted this model. It is very difficult to see how one could be led to these views without having in mind the picture of words picking out things and kinds in the world. For this reason, the model is essentially a suppressed premise of the argument of the preceding paragraph. Therefore, since Wittgenstein rejected this model, the argument begs the question against him and is of no use in opposing his views about understanding and meaning.

The question that naturally arises at this point is: What could understanding be if it is not a state or process and what could meanings be if they are not a sort of object? According to Wittgenstein, understanding and meaning are family-resemblance concepts.[33] Such concepts differ markedly from the paradigm that most philosophers accept. According to this paradigm, the things to which a concept can be truthfully applied have a common property or set of properties in virtue of which they are instances of the concept. As for family-resemblance concepts, on the other hand, there is no property or set of properties which all instances of such a concept have and in virtue of which they are instances of the concept. Among the instances of a family-resemblance concept, there is instead, "a complicated network of similarities overlapping and criss-crossing: sometimes overall similarities, sometimes similarities of detail."[34] Such concepts get their name from the fact that members of a family are related to one another in this manner: "the various resemblances between members of a family: build, features, colour of eyes, gait, temperament, etc. etc. overlap and criss-cross in the same way."[35] Since meaning and understanding are family-resemblance concepts, there is no one kind of thing to which each refers, and yet these words still have meaning.

CONCLUSION

I have now accomplished what I set out to do at the end of the section on ICA-SYN and ICA-SEM. I have shown, in the section devoted to TVU, that this view of understanding is intuitively attractive, explanatorily powerful and has been embraced by prominent figures in the history of philosophy. In the previous section, I outlined Wittgenstein's persuasive objections to TVU, objections which have not been taken seriously, let alone refuted, by the contemporary philosophical community, and I sketched his own plausible picture of what understanding amounts to. For these reasons, it is far from clear which view, Wittgenstein's or TVU, provides a correct account of linguistic understanding. Since TVU is a premise of ICA-SEM and since ICA-SEM is apparently the only plausible argument for the claim that infinite linguistic competence can be explained only by postulating internally represented semantic rules, we must conclude that this claim is debatable and that settling the debate hinges upon answering the question of what linguistic understanding amounts to. In other words, the upshot is that it is not clear whether this claim is true or false, and the dispute over its truth can be settled only when there is prior agreement among Wittgensteinians and adherents of TVU about the nature of linguistic understanding.[36] If TVU turns out to be correct, then ICA-SEM and the claim can stand. However, if Wittgenstein is right, then ICA-SEM and the claim will have to be rejected.

Wittgenstein's opponents might concede at this point that ICA-SEM does indeed beg the question against compelling philosophical views about understanding, but argue in the following way that this ought not to prevent us from embracing the claim in question. On the one hand, it is clear that internally represented semantic rules are part of a putative explanation of infinite linguistic competence. Competent speakers are able to understand an infinite number of sentences, on this explanation, because (i) they have a representation of a finite set of recursive, syntactic rules which generate all of these sentences, (ii) they have a representation of a finite set of recursive, semantic rules which generate all of the meaning structures corresponding to these sentences, and (iii) understanding is a matter of pairing a sentence with an appropriate meaning structure. On the other hand, it is not apparent whether and how Wittgenstein's views can provide us with an account of infinite linguistic competence. Therefore, in the absence of any such Wittgensteinian account, we must conclude that infinite linguistic competence can be explained only by postulating an internal representation of semantic rules. In other words, we are compelled to accept the conclusion of ICA-SEM by an inference to the best explanation.

Although I am not sure how Wittgenstein would account for infinite linguistic competence,[37] it is important to keep things in proper perspective. Our examination of Wittgenstein's views about understanding and meaning has in effect shown that TVU does not, on these views, explain infinite linguistic competence. For, according to Wittgenstein, TVU is a radical misconstrual of what linguistic understanding amounts to. Since TVU does not, on Wittgenstein's picture of understanding, explain infinite linguistic competence and since it is not clear which model of understanding is correct, Wittgenstein and his opponents are presently on the same footing. There is work to be done on both sides before either can claim to have an account of infinite linguistic competence.

Of course the argument in the paragraph before last is not the only counterattack available to Wittgenstein's opponents. They could also argue that this philosopher's picture of understanding cannot explain how communication is possible nor how language "hooks up" with the world, whereas TVU can, as we saw in the section devoted to this view, provide a skeletal account of the mechanisms of reference and of the sharing of cognitive content. A convincing response to this criticism is, I believe, available to Wittgenstein, but, unfortunately, I will not have space to sketch it here. Fortunately, it is not necessary for my purposes that this be done. I am not arguing that Wittgenstein is right and that TVU is wrong. My aim in this essay is simply to show that it is not clear which view of understanding is correct and, hence, that the claim that infinite linguistic competence can be explained only by postulating an internal representation of semantic rules is, for the time being, up in the air.

To wrap things up, I would like briefly to indicate some of the short-comings and implications of this essay. One obvious deficiency is that I have considered only one strategy of argumentation for the conclusion of ICA-SEM. The reason for this is that I do not know of and cannot even imagine a plausible line of reasoning for this claim which is substantially different from ICA-SEM. Because of this defect, someone could conceivably respond to what I have done in this essay by constructing an argument whose centerpiece is not an attempt to bridge the gap between the finitude of the mind and the infinitude of meaning objects by postulating an internal representation of semantic rules. Another shortcoming is that I have not adequately dealt with ICA-SYN. It remains to be seen whether any Wittgensteinian objections to this line of reasoning can be formulated which would be sufficiently impressive to render it problematic.

Aside from these two deficiencies, there are some interesting implications of what I have tried to do in this essay. First of all, the conclusions I have reached may pave the way for a new theory of linguistic competence. If understanding turns out to accord with something resembling Wittgenstein's views, then Wittgenstein's opponents will, in the absence of a replacement for ICA-SEM, have to abandon the claim that infinite linguistic competence can be explained only by postulating internally represented semantic rules. In this case, Wittgenstein's opponents would be compelled either to jettison the notion of internally represented semantic rules or to bring forward evidence other than infinite linguistic competence for the internal representation of such rules. If the former course were followed, then all accounts of linguistic competence that depend upon postulating internally represented semantic rules would also go out the window. This would be quite a significant state of affairs, since such accounts are far and away the explanations of linguistic competence with the most currency. Thus, if Wittgenstein's picture of understanding is correct, it is possible that we will need a radically new explanation of our ability to use language. Secondly, what I have done here undermines some of the evidence for the existence of semantic rules. For the claim that infinite linguistic competence can be explained only by postulating internally represented semantic rules is a reason not just for thinking that semantic rules are internally represented but also for believing that such rules exist in any sense. Thus, if this claim has to be abandoned, it may turn out that the whole notion of semantic rules will need to be stricken from linguistics and philosophy. At least, if we are forced to dispose of this claim, we will need to reevaluate the remaining evidence for such rules. Finally, and more generally, what I have done in this essay suggests the need (i) to make clear and explicit the justification for the various components of theoretical linguistics and (ii) to examine more closely from a Wittgensteinian perspective the justification for these components. It is an exciting, although perhaps remote, possibility that much of theoretical linguistics presupposes philosophical views of language and the mind that are inconsistent with persuasive and neglected elements of Wittgenstein's thought. If this possibility turns out to be an actuality, then a thorough revision of much of theoretical linguistics may be required.

Notes

I would like to thank first and foremost Alan Nelson. Without his encouragement and suggestions, this essay never would have evolved beyond a criticism of an argument by Dummett. I would also like to thank the participants of the 1990 Discipuli at the University of Southern California, where a remote ancestor of this essay was read. In particular, I extend my gratitude to Mark Perlman who replied to my essay at this event. Finally, I want to thank Penelope Maddy, who provided helpful comments and criticisms on several drafts of the present essay.

1. Dummett (1987), 206.
2. Devitt and Sterelny (1987), 146.
3. Davidson (1984), 17.
4. It should be noted that there are several different formulations of the competent speaker's ability. Some philosophers and linguists emphasize the fact that a competent speaker can understand an indefinite number of sentences; others point out that a competent speaker can understand sentences which he has never before encountered in his life, i.e., *novel* sentences. In this essay, the particular formulation of the ability in question is not important, and my arguments will go through regardless of which one is employed. For convenience, I will consistently use the "infinite number of sentences" formulation.
5. Chomsky (1972), 103.
6. Actually, Dummett argues, in "Can Analytical Philosophy Be Systematic, and Ought it to Be?" that infinite linguistic competence can be explained only if a "complete theory of meaning" is possible. Unfortunately, this argument is of no use here. For one of the premises of the argument is that infinite linguistic competence can be explained only if each speaker of a language "has an implicit grasp of a number of general principles governing the use in sentences of words of the language" (1987, 206). Thus, Dummett's argument assumes just what we are interested in constructing an argument for, viz. that infinite linguistic competence can be explained only by positing internally represented linguistic rules.
7. Davidson, (1984), 17.
8. It should be kept in mind that the infinity of sentences that a competent speaker can understand is not equivalent to the infinity of well-formed sentences of the language in question. For, as has been repeatedly acknowledged, there are well-formed sentences which are too long or too complicated to be understood by any speaker.
9. Someone might object that the infinite ability of the competent speaker and the infinite capacity of the dart gun are not parallel to one another, because the former is "internal" while the latter is "external." In other words, the competent speaker is in and of herself able to understand an infinite number of sentences, whereas a dart gun can fire an infinite number of shots only if and only as long as there is someone or something there to shoot it. There are several problems with this objection. First, it is not clear that the competent speaker's ability is "internal." For the competent speaker can understand an infinite number of sentences only if and only as long as certain conditions are satisfied, e.g. she is not starving, sleeping or drugged; there is a sufficient supply of oxygen; atmospheric pressure is normal, etc. The objector could respond to this by arguing that the non-fulfillment of such conditions merely prevents the exercise of the ability and does not destroy it and, hence, that the ability itself is not dependent upon the satisfaction of such conditions. But, if this response is plausible, one could argue, in the same way, that the absence of someone or something to fire the dart gun merely prevents the exercise of its capacity to fire an infinite number of shots and, hence, that the capacity of the dart gun is also not dependent upon

external factors. In any case, the burden of proof lies with the objector to show that the ability of the competent speaker is "internal" in a sense in which the capacity of the dart gun is not. Until this is done, we must assume that the former ability is parallel to the latter capacity.

10. Of course, Wittgenstein would not like ICA-SYN because it implies that natural language is a calculus of some sort, and Wittgenstein, as is well known, denied this (see, for example, *The Blue and Brown Books*, 25). However, Wittgenstein's denial, in itself, hardly constitutes a reason to reassess ICA-SYN. On the other hand, it may be that with a lot of work one could develop a potent Wittgensteinian objection to the notion of mental representation appealed to in this argument.

11. The parenthesed plural here is to allow for the fact that some linguistic items are ambiguous and, hence, would be associated with more than one meaning object.

12. We are assuming here that, if meaning objects are abstract entities, they are correlated with mental entities of some sort. If we do not make this assumption, we cannot argue across the board for internally represented semantic rules. Since abstract entities are not in the head, an infinite number of these alone would not overburden the finite capacity of the mind. An infinite number of such entities would supersaturate the latter only via analogous objects in the mind or brain.

13. As should be clear from the context, a meaning structure is either a meaning object or a complex consisting of meaning objects and, perhaps, other elements as well.

14. Baker and Hacker (1983b), 351–57.

15. Putnam (1975), 219.

16. Ibid., 218.

17. Three examples are Baker and Hacker's *Wittgenstein: Meaning and Understanding* and *An Analytical Commentary on Wittgenstein's Philosophical Investigations*, and Colin McGinn's *Wittgenstein on Meaning*. My interpretation and discussion of Wittgenstein in the present section has been heavily influenced by these three works.

18. Wittgenstein (1960), 5.

19. Wittgenstein (1958), sect. 140. In accordance with usual practice, most references to the *Philosophical Investigations* will be by section rather than page number.

20. Ibid., sect. 198.

21. Ibid., sect. 139.

22. Actually, the problem is even worse, since I could easily interpret the picture of a cube to be that of a wire frame, a box or a solid angle (see *Philosophical Investigations*, p. 193), and, to each of these interpretations, there corresponds a number of different applications.

23. Wittgenstein (1960), 34–35. One could protest that mentalese is here being conflated with natural language. The crucial difference between expressions of mentalese and expressions of natural language is, so one might argue, that the former, but not the latter, determine the meanings that are correlated with them. The problem with this objection is that it is not clear how a linguistic expression of any sort could determine its meaning. For one thing, no linguistic expression that we encounter in the world, whether it be of a natural language, a formal language or a pictorial language, for example, wears its meaning on its sleeve. Thus, the objection can be accepted only once there is an explanation of the crucial difference between ordinary linguistic expressions and expressions of mentalese which enables the latter to determine their respective meanings.

24. Wittgenstein (1958), sect. 154.

25. Ibid., p. 59.

26. My discussion here is essentially an exegesis of the paragraph at the bottom of p. 59 of the *Philosophical Investigations*.

27. This comparison occurs in sections 156–78 of the *Philosophical Investigations*. Unfortunately, I do not have space to reconstruct all of the subtle and ingenious lines which Wittgenstein deploys to convince us that reading and, hence, understanding are not mental states or processes. I will merely sketch in broad strokes the structure of the argument

there. Although it would be helpful to examine Wittgenstein's reasoning in detail, this is not necessary for my purposes. As I mentioned earlier, my aim in this section is just to show that Wittgenstein has a compelling response to TVU which has not been adequately dealt with.

28. Ibid., sect. 171.

29. Ibid., sect. 156.

30. Ibid.

31. Ibid., sect. 158. See also section 149, where Wittgenstein appears to make the same point.

32. Ibid., sect. 1.

33. It is clear from the following passage that Wittgenstein takes understanding to be a family-resemblance concept: "The criteria which we accept for 'fitting', 'being able to', 'understanding', are much more complicated than might appear at first sight. That is, the game with these words, their employment in the linguistic intercourse that is carried on by their means, is more involved—the role of these words in our language other—than we are tempted to think" (*Philosophical Investigations*, sect. 182). As for meaning, the closest thing to a declaration that it is a family-resemblance concept is Wittgenstein's implicit denial that this concept can be given conditions which are jointly sufficient and individually necessary for its application: "For a *large* class of cases—though not for all—in which we employ the word "meaning" it can be defined thus: the meaning of a word is its use in the language (*Philosophical Investigations*, sect. 43).

34. Ibid., sect. 66.

35. Ibid., sect. 67.

36. In fact, if this is right, it means that the traditional order of investigation in the philosophy of language is inverted in this case. According to the traditional order, one assumes that understanding works along certain lines, i.e., that it accords with TVU, and then one tries to come up with an account of how language functions. According to my conclusion, however, one ought, in this case, first to get clear about the nature of understanding and then proceed to an investigation of the functioning of language.

37. There are several interesting directions in which a Wittgensteinian explanation of infinite linguistic competence could proceed. For example, one could argue, on the basis of analogies like the one involving the dart gun, that infinite linguistic competence is not a philosophical problem. One could also try to deal with infinite linguistic competence by bringing Wittgenstein's philosophy of mathematics to bear. For a problem analogous to the explanation of infinite linguistic competence exists in connection with Wittgenstein's views about the expansion of irrational numbers. This problem arises in the following way. There are people who have the ability to expand a given irrational number to an arbitrary decimal place. Thus, these people have infinite (or indefinite) decimal expansion competence. Now, Wittgenstein appears to be committed to the view that the explanation of such competence is not to be found in postulating internal representations of mathematical rules, e.g., algorithms (see, for example, Wittgenstein [1978], 266–67). Thus, Wittgenstein must provide an alternative account of infinite decimal expansion competence. Such an account, if it exists or can be developed, could then be applied in the obvious way to the problem of explaining infinite linguistic competence.

References

Baker, G. P., and P. M. S. Hacker. 1983a. *An Analytical Commentary on Wittgenstein's Philosophical Investigations*. Oxford.

———. *Wittgenstein: Meaning and Understanding*. 1983b. Oxford.

Chomsky, Noam. 1972. *Language and Mind*. Enlarged ed. New York.

Davidson, Donald. 1984. "Truth and Meaning." *Synthese* 17 (1967): 304–23. Reprinted in D. Davidson, *Inquiries into Truth and Interpretation*. Oxford, 1984.

Devitt, Michael, and Kim Sterelny. 1987. *Language and Reality*. Oxford.

Dummett, Michael. 1987. "Can Analytical Philosophy Be Systematic, and Ought it to Be?" *Hegel-Studien* supplement 19 (1977): 305–27. Reprinted in *After Philosophy: End or Transformation*, edited by K. Baynes, J. Bohman, and T. McCarthy. Cambridge, Mass., 1987.

McGinn, Colin. 1984. *Wittgenstein on Meaning*. New York.

Putnam, Hilary. 1975. "The Meaning of 'Meaning'." in *Language Mind and Knowledge*, edited by K. Gunderson, Minnesota Studies in the Philosophy of Science, VII. Minneapolis. Reprinted in H. Putnam, *Mind, Language and Reality*. Cambridge, 1975.

Wittgenstein, Ludwig. 1958. *Philosophical Investigations*. Third ed. Translated by G. E. M. Anscombe. New York.

———. 1960. *The Blue and Brown Books*. Second ed. New York.

———. 1978. *Remarks on the Foundations of Mathematics*. Edited by G. H. von Wright, R. Rhees, and G. E. M. Anscombe. Translated by G. E. M. Anscombe. Revised ed. Cambridge, Mass.

The Anti-Realist's Master Argument

ANTHONY BRUECKNER

One central claim of the anti-realist theorist of meaning is that the notion of a sentence's truth-conditions plays no important role in the theory of meaning. The familiar but ill-understood argument is that a theory of meaning must be a theory of linguistic understanding and that a speaker's understanding of a sentence does not always consist in his grasping of the sentence's truth-conditions. Michael Dummett, the most influential and distinguished champion of the argument, sees its main ideas as flowing from the later Wittgenstein's views about what knowledge of language consists in. Once a generalized truth-conditional theory of meaning is discredited by the Wittgensteinian argument, one might try to draw metaphysical or epistemological conclusions of an anti-realist nature, reasoning that the argument establishes that some sentences (those *not* understood by means of grasping truth-conditions) do not *have* truth-conditions, or at least do not have truth-conditions which in some sense outstrip our powers of verification or recognition. In this essay, I will critically discuss the argument to show that linguistic understanding does not in general consist in grasping of truth-conditions. I call this the anti-realist's *master argument*, and I believe that it is the cornerstone of the semantical anti-realist's position.[1] If one accepts the view that a theory of meaning must be a theory of understanding, then the success of the master argument spells the demise of the truth-conditional theory of meaning. I shall claim that the master argument is too problematic to bear the anti-realist's semantical burden and *a fortiori* too problematic to establish any metaphysical or epistemological results.

Let us begin by considering the question: 'What does linguistic understanding—knowledge of meaning—consist in?' Suppose it is said that knowledge of meaning is knowledge of truth-conditions, so that to understand a sentence is to grasp its truth-conditions. Then we want to ask what form this knowledge takes. It cannot reasonably be maintained that in all cases this knowledge takes a discursive, verbalizable form. To see this, note first that for some sentences in a speaker's language, there will be a corresponding reductive class of sentences. That is, for each sentence in a given 'reducible' class, there will be some (possibly quite complex) logically equivalent sentence from a distinct, reductive class whose members, in Dummett's phrase, *render true* the reducible sentences.[2] In the case of sentences for which there *is* a reductive class, the speaker will be able to state non-trivial truth-conditions. But there will be some sentences in the language which, in Dummett's phrase, are *barely true*. These are sentences such that the best a competent speaker can do is to state disquotational truth-conditions for them, since for these sentences there is no corresponding reductive class. Knowledge of the meaning of barely true sentences does not consist in the ability to state their trivial Tarskian truth-conditions. Rather, knowledge of their meaning must consist in some sort of recognitional capacity. And if knowledge of meaning is knowledge of— grasping of—truth-conditions, then the recognitional capacity associated with a speaker's use of a barely true sentence will be a capacity for recognizing truth-conditions, a capacity for recognizing when a sentence's truth-conditions are satisfied and when its truth-conditions are not satisfied. Further, for reasons having to do with learning, communication, and the attribution of mental states generally, this recognitional capacity must be manifestable in the speaker's use of such a sentence.[3] "This amounts," says Dummett, "to an interpretation of one component in Wittgenstein's slogan 'Meaning is use'."[4]

Let us suppose, contra the phenomenalist, that 'Here is a tree' is a barely true sentence. In this case, it will be quite plausible to hold that a speaker who understands the sentence has a manifestable recognitional capacity for the sentence's truth-conditions. In this case, it will be quite reasonable to say that the speaker's understanding of the sentence—his knowledge of its meaning— consists in his knowledge of, or grasping of, its truth-conditions. This is because the latter knowledge, in turn, can quite reasonably be said to consist in a manifestable recognitional capacity for the sentence's truth conditions. When visibly confronted with a tree, the speaker audibly utters the sentence 'Here is a tree'. On the other hand, for some barely true sentences which a speaker understands (i.e., for some sentences which have no corresponding reductive class), it will not be at all plausible to hold that the speaker has a manifestable recognitional capacity for the sentences' truth-conditions. These are the so-called *verification-transcendent* (or *recognition-transcendent*) sentences. They can be specified in a list-like manner by means of the familiar anti-realist litany: sentences about the distant past, sentences involving quantification over an infinite domain, unrestricted spatial or temporal generalizations, subjunctives, sentences about other human (or animal) minds. These are, quite roughly speaking, sentences such that if they have truth conditions of the standardly conceived sort, then these conditions may well hold (not hold) even though speakers are unable to recognize that they hold (do not hold). Setting aside for the moment the question of how to precisely characterize them, there are, then, sentences—call them *problematic* sentences—which, according to the anti-realist, have the following features: (1) They are meaningful and are understood by speakers of the language, (2) they are barely true (in the negative sense that they lack non-trivial truth-conditions), and (3) speakers do not have a manifestable recognitional capacity for their truth-conditions.

Knowledge of the meaning of problematic sentences cannot be said to consist in knowledge of their truth-conditions. This could be said only if the sentences were not barely true (contra (2)), or else speakers had manifestable recognitional capacities for their truth-conditions (contra (3)). Under the first alternative, there would be, on the truth-conditional theory, something for a speaker's understanding of the problematic sentences to consist in, viz. the speaker's ability to state non-trivial truth-conditions. Under the second alternative, there would also be, on the truth-conditional theory, something for a speaker's understanding to consist in, viz. his manifestable recognitional capacity for truth-conditions. But as it stands, there is nothing, on the truth-conditional theory, for a speaker's understanding to consist in. Hence the truth-conditional theory is unable to account for a speaker's understanding of problematic sentences. Hence the truth-conditional theory is inadequate: it is not the case that knowledge of meaning—linguistic understanding—consists, in general, in knowledge of truth-conditions. As Wittgenstein came to do, says Dummett, the anti-realist will "substitute the notion of the justification of an assertion for that of truth as the central notion of the theory of meaning."[5]

This is the master argument. The first thing to note is that the argument, often held to be somehow verificationistic, actually runs counter to classical verificationism in an important respect. Problematic sentences are *not* held to be meaningless on account of their certification-transcendent status. Indeed, it is critical to the argument that problematic sentences are meaning*ful*. It is held that speakers *understand* problematic sentences—know what they *mean*—and the crux of the argument is the contention that since speakers cannot be said to have a manifestable recognitional capacity for their truth-conditions, their understanding of the sentences cannot consist in knowledge of truth-conditions. The fact that the master argument requires the assumption that speakers understand problematic sentences will help us appreciate the difficulties which beset the argument.

Since problematic sentences are barely true (in that they lack non-trivial truth-conditions), a speaker's understanding of such a sentence must, according to the master argument, consist in some manifestable recognitional capacity or other. Now consider meaningful sentences which are barely true and *not* problematic, e.g., 'Here is a tree'. Call such sentences *unproblematic* sentences. A speaker's understanding of such a sentence consists in a manifestable recognitional capacity which *can* be said to be a recognitional capacity for truth-conditions. But what is the key difference between a speaker's recognitional capacity for the unproblematic 'Here is a tree' and his recognitional capacity for the problematic 'There were 17 pigeons in Trafalgar Square at midnight, January 1, 1900'? One capacity, according to the master argument, *can* be said to be a recognitional capacity for truth-conditions (the speaker *can* be said to know, or grasp, truth-conditions), while the other capacity can*not* be said to be a recognitional capacity for truth-conditions (the speaker can*not* be said to know, or grasp, truth-conditions). But what is the relevant difference between the two capacities?

It is obvious that the relevant difference is not that, in one case, the speaker knows that the unproblematic sentence's truth-conditions are satisfied, whereas in the other case, the speaker does not know whether or not the problematic sentence's truth-conditions are satisfied. Though the speaker may well have such knowledge in the former case, it is obvious that a speaker can have knowledge of, or a grasp of, a sentence's truth-conditions (thereby understanding the sentence) without knowing whether or not the sentence is true. At least, this can be taken to be obvious until the anti-realist's master argument has somehow discredited the notion of knowledge of truth-conditions, since it is constitutive of the latter notion that knowledge of truth-*conditions* does not require knowledge of truth-*value*.

Clearly, when knowledge of truth-conditions is said to be a recognitional *capacity* of some sort, it is not required that the possessor of such a capacity have *exercised* the capacity and thereby determined whether or not a given sentence's truth-conditions are satisfied. Thus, it might be held that one who understands an unproblematic sentence has a capacity for determining whether or not the sentence's truth-conditions are satisfied, even though he may well not have actually made such a determination. As it stands, though, this is a stronger requirement than that which is laid down by the anti-realist proponents of the master argument. It is held that for contingent sentences (apart from some sentences, perhaps, concerning one's current sense-experience), no amount of evidence will entail that the sentence's truth-conditions are satisfied. There is no such thing as conclusive verification even for unproblematic contingent sentences like 'Here is a tree'.[6] For such unproblematic sentences, then, it might be thought that a speaker's knowledge of truth-conditions consists in his capacity for recognizing evidence which confirms that the sentence's truth-conditions are satisfied or which disconfirms this. Knowledge of truth-conditions would not be said to consist in a manifestable capacity for recognizing that the sentence's truth-conditions are satisfied (not satisfied) but rather in a capacity for recognizing that such and such is good evidence that the truth-conditions are satisfied (not satisfied). Some such account seems to be required once it is agreed that conclusive verification is not available for contingent sentences.

However, a speaker's understanding of a *problematic* sentence would presumably consist in such an evidential recognitional capacity, a capacity for recognizing evidence which would justify assertion or denial of the sentence.[7] I understand Goldbach's conjecture (a paradigmatic problematic sentence), and my understanding presumably consists in my capacity for recognizing a proof (disproof) of the conjecture if one were presented to me. Similarly, my understanding of the past-tense sentence about the pigeons presumably consists in my capacity for recognizing historical evidence about pigeons in Trafalgar Square if such were presented to me. But if for unproblematic sentences, knowledge of their truth-conditions consists in the sort of evidential recognitional capacity under discussion, so should knowledge of truth conditions consist in a such capacity in the case of problematic sentences. This would block the master argument, though, since the argument's crucial claim is that a speaker *lacks* knowledge of truth-conditions in the case of problematic sentences. The problem for the anti-realist is this: the master argument depends upon the assumption that a speaker understands problematic sentences, yet the argument also requires that the recognitional capacity which is identified with this understanding must somehow be distinguished from the sort of recognitional capacity a speaker has in the case of unproblematic sentences. Some distinction must be made, since the recognitional capacity a speaker has in the case of unproblematic sentences is what his *knowledge of truth-conditions* for such sentences consists in.

At this point, the anti-realist will attempt to draw the required distinction by reference to the notion of an *effective procedure*, a mathematical notion which the anti-realist will apply in the realm of contingent, as well as necessary, sentences. We have seen that it cannot be said that a speaker who understands even an unproblematic sentence has an effective procedure for determining the sentence's truth-value, given the unavailability of conclusive verification. Even such sentences are not effectively *decidable*. Yet in the case of unproblematic sentences like 'Here is a tree' and 'There is a clock in the basement', a speaker who understands the sentence does have an effective procedure for gaining confirming or disconfirming evidence, evidence which would justify assertion or denial of the sentence. By contrast, a speaker does not have such a procedure either in the case of Goldbach's conjecture and the case of the past-tense sentence about pigeons. A speaker might well be presented with a proof of the conjecture some time in the future, and he might well stumble upon some evidence concerning the past pigeon population of Trafalgar Square, but he has no effective procedure for arriving at a proof and no effective procedure for gathering evidence about long-dead pigeons. Thus a speaker may lack an effective procedure for acquiring evidence regarding a sentence even though it is logically and physically possible that he should acquire such evidence. So we can now see that even though a speaker who understands a problematic sentence and an unproblematic sentence has in each case an evidential recognitional capacity (otherwise he could not be said to understand the sentences): in one case he has an effective procedure for getting confirming (disconfirming) evidence which he will recognize as such, while in the other case he lacks such a procedure (though he would recognize evidence were he to receive it).

The problem with this way of distinguishing among a speaker's recognitional capacities is that the (rather vague) distinction between having an effective procedure for acquiring confirming (disconfirming) evidence and lacking such a procedure is not obviously the same as the distinction between having knowledge of truth-conditions and lacking such knowledge. The realist opponent of the master argument will grant the distinction among a speaker's recognitional capacities: some capacities are allied with an effective procedure for acquiring the recognizable evidence and some are not. But the realist will maintain that this distinction concerns the ability to *acquire*, rather than to recognize, evidence, and he will deny that such a practical distinction has any relevance to the cognitive question of whether or not a speaker grasps a sentence's truth-conditions. With regard to the ability to *recognize* evidence for the satisfaction of truth-conditions, there need be no difference between a speaker's understanding of a problematic sentence and his understanding of an unproblematic one. That which is supposed to make the difference between grasping truth-conditions and not grasping truth-conditions is the availability of evidence in one case and the unavailability of evidence in the other case. But this will not seem to the realist to be a cognitively relevant difference, and it will seem arbitrary, in particular, to describe this difference as the difference between grasping and not grasping truth-conditions.

Of course, a central contention of the semantical anti-realist is that in the case of sentences that are barely true, there is nothing for knowledge of truth-conditions to *be* other than a sort of practical ability: a recognitional capacity manifestable in linguistic behavior. Hence practical differences might well amount to cognitive differences. Yet this remark is of no use to the anti-realist. His task was to show how a recognitional capacity for an unproblematic sentence could be construed as a grasping of truth-conditions in a way that a recognitional capacity for a problematic sentence could not be so construed. Each capacity, though, must be *equally* manifestable in use. So nothing following from the practical requirement of manifestability will serve to *distinguish* the two kinds of capacity on a manner useful to the master argument.

In fact, the manifestability requirement seems to raise problems for the master argument. In the case of problematic sentences, a speaker has no effective procedure for getting himself into a position in which he can manifest his recognition that such and such evidence is confirming (disconfirming) evidence for the sentence. So it looks as if it cannot be said that the speaker's understanding of a problematic sentence consists in an effectively manifestable recognitional capacity for evidence. Hence the manifestability requirement actually distinguishes recognitional capacities (effectively manifestable for unproblematic sentences, not effectively manifestable for problematic sentences) in a manner which is injurious to the master argument.[8]

At this juncture, the anti-realist defender of that argument might say that he was only granting *arguendo* that for some sentences (unproblematic ones), understanding consists in grasping truth-conditions. His real view, he might continue, is that in *no* case does understanding consist in grasping truth conditions. So a speaker's understanding of 'Here is a tree' no more consists in his grasping of its truth-conditions than does his understanding of the past-tense sentence about pigeons. This move, however, is problematic. The original difficulty for the anti-realist was to find a way of distinguishing a speaker's understanding of the sentence about pigeons from his understanding of 'Here is a tree' in such a way that it could be seen by contrast that the former understanding cannot be a grasping of truth-conditions, whereas the latter understanding is a grasping of truth-conditions. But now the difficulty is to explain why a speaker's understanding can *in neither case* be a grasping of truth-conditions. Obviously, the anti-realist cannot appeal to the implausibility of the truth-conditional theory of meaning, since this is what the master argument is aimed at establishing. Suppose that the anti-realist claims that in both cases, the unavailability of conclusive verification is what explains the impropriety of holding understanding to be knowing truth conditions. Since a speaker can in neither case have evidence which entails that the sentence in question is true, it follows that he can in neither case be seen to utter the sentence *in response to his recognition that its truth-conditions are satisfied.* That is, the speaker can in neither case manifest a recognitional capacity for truth-conditions.

This move is subject to an objection which is similar to one raised above. It was objected that the anti-realist takes an epistemological distinction which everyone will grant—the distinction between (i) having an evidential recognitional capacity allied with an effective method for acquiring the relevant evidence, and (ii) having such a capacity while lacking such a method—and then unjustifiably redescribes it as the distinction between grasping truth-conditions and not grasping truth-conditions. Now the anti-realist takes an epistemological phenomena which both sides of the dispute will grant—the unavailability of conclusive verification for contingent sentences—and then unjustifiably redescribes it as the non-existence (for such sentences) of a recognitional grasp of truth-conditions. Such a redescription would in fact be quite ironic, since a semantical realist who is prone to epistemological skepticism would hold that given the unavailability of conclusive verification, there is a serious problem about knowing whether or not the truth-conditions for contingent sentences are ever satisfied even when the best possible evidence is in. Where the realist sees grasping of truth-conditions together with inability to know whether they are satisfied, the anti-realist sees gaping absence of such grasping.[9] Finally, the move under consideration cannot accommodate the anti-realist's desire to maintain that in understanding a necessary sentence for which a speaker possesses a proof, the speaker is not grasping truth-conditions. This desire cannot be accommodated if unavailability of entailing evidence for a sentence is what shows that an understanding of the sentence cannot consist in a grasping of its truth-conditions.

At this point, the semantical dispute between the realist and the anti-realist might begin to seem rather murky. If it is now quite unclear whether the anti-realist has shown that linguistic understanding must consist in something other than grasping truth-conditions, this may be due to the *realist's* having failed to clarify the controversial notion of *grasping truth-conditions.* There may well be Wittgensteinian problems with a realist claim that a speaker's grasping of a sentence's truth-conditions *explains* his linguistic behavior.[10] But problems about the internalization of a rule which can somehow guide or determine linguistic behavior will arise, if they arise at all, for *any* explanation of linguistic behavior in terms of posited cognitive states of the speaker, regardless of whether the state is held to be a grasping of truth-conditions. At any rate, the realist can at least say the following without committing himself to any dubious explanatory claims. Problematic sentences, he will say, are rendered true or false by recognition-transcendent truth-conditions. A speaker lacks an effective procedure for acquiring evidence concerning the satisfaction of these truth-conditions. But in knowing the meaning of problematic sentences, one thing the speaker knows is that he is in the foregoing unhappy evidential situation with respect to the facts which render the sentences true or false. He knows this in virtue of knowing what counts as evidence for the satisfaction of such sentences' truth-conditions.[11]

Now one way of gauging the damage suffered by the master argument as a result of the problems raised herein is to see whether the argument, in the face of these problems, can controvert the above realist claims about the existence of recognition-transcendent truth-conditions by establishing metaphysical or epistemological theses of an anti-realist nature. Can the considerations embodied in the master argument help discredit the notion of a recognition-transcendent truth-condition in some *direct* way, in some way which does not depend on first discrediting the admittedly murky notion of *grasping* such truth conditions?

As I said at the outset, if the master argument could succeed in showing that understanding a problematic sentence does not consist in grasping its allegedly recognition-transcendent truth-conditions, it would be tempting to go on to conclude that the sentence does not have such truth-conditions. If this conclusion is warranted, then it seems to yield substantial metaphysical and epistemological results. If, say, a sentence about the distant past does not have recognition-transcendent truth-conditions, then there is no recognition-transcendent fact about the past which renders the sentence true or renders it false. If, say, a sentence about another's mental state does not have recognition-transcendent truth-conditions, then there is no epistemological problem of knowing whether or not a recognition-transcendent mental fact exists beyond one's powers of verification. However, given the apparent inability of the master argument to show that understanding a problematic sentence must consist in something other than grasping recognition-transcendent truth-conditions, we need to see whether there is some more direct route to such metaphysical and epistemological results.[12]

Let us ask whether the master argument could possibly establish in some direct way the above metaphysical result about the reality of the past. No such result seems to follow from the mere fact that even though we have an effective procedure for acquiring evidence concerning some present-tense sentences, there are some past-tense sentences for which we lack such a procedure. The existence of this epistemological distinction might be relevant to the nature of a speaker's understanding of a sentence (though we have seen above that this is dubious). But the existence of the distinction hardly seems relevant to the metaphysical question of whether a certain fact about the past renders a problematic sentence true. Similar remarks apply to the question of whether a certain mental fact lying beyond our ken renders a problematic mentalistic sentence true in such a way as to preclude our *ever knowing* it to be true.

A classical verificationist nevertheless might argue in response that whether a sentence is meaningful is a function of the obtainability of evidence regarding it. Therefore, he might continue, whether there exists a fact purportedly described by a sentence is a function of the obtainability of evidence regarding the sentence. But we have already noted how the anti-realist position differs in this regard from that of the classical verificationist. There are two further reasons against making such a verificationist appeal. First the classical verificationists never held that a sentence lacks meaning if there is no effective procedure for gaining evidence for or against it. Sophisticated verificationists such as Ayer and Schlick held instead that a sentence lacks meaning if it is *logically impossible* that speakers should acquire evidence for or against it.[13] Second, it will obviously not speak well for the master argument if it must be *supplemented* by some substantial verification principle.

Things go no better for the anti-realist proponent of the master argument if he concentrates on the unavailability of conclusive verification for contingent sentences. This epistemological fact has no obvious bearing on metaphysical questions unless it is bolstered by some substantial verification principle. Further, an epistemological fact which a realist might see as *engendering* skeptical problems obviously cannot be called upon to *solve* such problems., e.g., the problems of other minds.

The anti-realist proponent of the master argument fixes upon certain epistemological facts about a speaker's use of language. But these facts (absence of an effective procedure for acquiring evidence, unavailability of conclusive verification) do not obviously yield the desired anti-realist semantical results and obviously do not yield the desired anti-realist metaphysical and epistemological results.

Notes

1. See especially Michael Dummett's "What Is a Theory of Meaning? (II)," in *Truth and Meaning*, edited by G. Evans and J. McDowell (Oxford, 1976), Crispin Wright's "Truth Conditions and Criteria (II)," in *Proceedings of the Aristotelian Society*, Supplementary Volume 50 (1976), and his introduction to *Realism, Meaning and Truth* (Oxford, 1987).

2. See Dummett's "Realism," in *Synthese* 52 (1982). According to what Dummett calls a *reductive* (as opposed to a translational *reductionist*) thesis for a class of sentences, a reducing sentence may be, or have as a constituent, an infinite disjunction or conjunction. Hence there need be no equivalence in meaning between sentences of the reducible class and those of the reductive class. A reductive theses is a kind of supervenience thesis and does not by itself entail anti-realism with respect to the reducible class, on Dummett's view.

3. The role of the requirement of manifestability in the argument is unclear, as will emerge in the following discussion. For a useful discussion of how claims about learning and communication figure in the anti-realist's position, see Edward Craig's "Meaning, Privacy and Use," in *Mind* 91 (1982). For a useful discussion of how anti-realists conceive the attribution of mental states, see Wright's tribe-chess analogy in "Truth Conditions and Criteria (II)." For objections that the requirement of manifestability somehow renders the argument question-begging, see Kenneth Winkler's "Skepticism and Anti-Realism," in *Mind* 94 (1985) and Michael Devitt's "Dummett's Anti-Realism," in *Journal of Philosophy* 80 (1983).

4. Michael Dummett, *The Logical Basis of Metaphysics* (Cambridge, Mass., 1991), 341.

5. Ibid., 314.

6. See, e.g., the Preface to Dummett's *Truth and Other Enigmas* (Cambridge, Mass., 1978).

7. For the sake of simplicity, I do not distinguish here between confirming evidence for a sentence and evidence which would justify assertion of the sentence. It might be held that the former sort of evidence can be weaker than the latter. If this is correct, then presumably a speaker who understands a sentence will be capable of recognizing both kinds of evidence for what they are.

8. A remark of Neil Tennant's might seem to contain the seeds of a reply to this objection. In "Is This a Proof I See Before Me?" (*Analysis* 41.3 [1981]), he says:

> We have no right to insist that grasp of meaning be confirmed sentence by sentence. . . . The intuitionist has compositional capacities like those of the classicist. He can understand individual words and operators and grasp sentential pedigree. And this allows him to grasp the meaning of new sentences, including Goldbach's conjecture. Moreover, the "basic grasps" involved can be ascertained by investigating his general ability to infer conclusions, reduce proofs to canonical proofs, find proofs of simple theorems, etc. etc.

If the anti-realist tries to extend this sort of view to the case of sentences about the past, then even if he succeeds, he is left with the problem of somehow using the requirement of effective manifestability to *distinguish* between a recognitional capacity for a problematic sentence and a recognitional capacity for an unproblematic sentence. (It is worth noting that Tennant's suggestion might afford the anti-realist a way of accounting for a speaker's understanding of a provably undecidable sentence, whereas the 'sentence by sentence' account could not do this in any obvious way.)

9. I am not endorsing the claim that the unavailability of conclusive verification for contingent sentences would be *sufficient* to engender Cartesian skeptical problems, though it would be necessary. That is, one might argue against the skeptic that one can be justified in believing a sentence for which one lacks conclusive verification.

10. See Winkler's "Skepticism and Anti-Realism" for some elaboration of this point.

11. See Winkler's "Skepticism and Anti-Realism" for the suggestion that an anti-realist could comfortably accept these claims so long as an explanatory, 'theoretical' realism is rejected. This view seems to me to misrepresent the anti-realist, in that it focuses his concerns on the Wittgensteinian sort of problem briefly mentioned in the text. As I implied in the text, this sort of problem would, on the face of it, equally afflict a claim that a speaker has internalized a rule about assertibility-conditions.

12. Note that even if the argument had succeeded in establishing that understanding a problematic sentence does not consist in grasping its allegedly recognition-transcendent truth-conditions, it would not obviously follow that the sentence lacks such truth-conditions. Suppose that one holds that only samples of liquid with a certain chemical structure fall in the extension of the term 'water'. Then one might consistently hold that a speaker has a competent understanding of 'Water is wet', that this understanding does not consist in his grasping of the sentence's micro-structure-sensitive truth-conditions, and that the sentence nevertheless *has* such recognition-transcendent (for the inexpert speaker) truth-conditions. One might hold that the sentence is true (as uttered by him) only if the referent of its constituent term 'water' is a liquid with a certain chemical structure, even if he has no way of recognizing the liquid's structure. See, for example, Hilary Putnam's "The Meaning of 'Meaning'," in *Mind, Language and Reality* (New York, 1975). For a similar objection stemming from the causal theory of names, see Michael Devitt's "Dummett's Anti-Realism."

13. See, for example, Ayer's introduction to the second edition of *Language, Truth and Logic* (New York, 1946).

Thought and Language in the Tractatus

DONNA M. SUMMERFIELD

How is it possible for signs to point in any way at all? The apparently obvious fact that we represent the world in thought and language is puzzling because it is difficult to see how to avoid a threatened regress of interpretations. Ordinary linguistic signs can be interpreted in various ways. Linguistic signs, after all, are arbitrary. Once we notice this, we feel the need to find something that will single out just one of the possible alternative interpretations in order for signs to succeed in pointing to something beyond themselves; we feel that if a sign fails to point determinately, it fails to point to anything at all. But how is this singling out to be accomplished? If that to which we appeal in the attempt to determine the interpretation of one sign is itself a sign that can be interpreted in various possible ways, we risk launching an infinite regress of interpretations.

Of those commentators who recognize that Wittgenstein addressed this puzzle in the *Tractatus*, some have supposed that, according to the *Tractatus*, propositional signs, as *used* by us, have the features required to stop the regress (Rhees 1970; Mounce 1981; Winch 1987). There is on this view no need for any level of representation beyond that of natural language. I argue, on the contrary, that the *Tractatus* assumes that, in order to stop the regress of interpretations, there must be some representations, in some way within our grasp, that need no interpretation. I believe that the *Tractatus* assumes there are such ideal representations, underlying written and spoken signs, that there is, in effect, a "language of thought." Such a language, as it stands, obeys the rules of logical syntax; it is by translating perceptible signs into a language of thought that we are able to interpret the ambiguous signs of natural languages and thereby understand the determinate sense intended by a speaker. In fact, if we did not have a language of thought, we would not be able to learn the meanings of natural language expressions, say the expressions of English, since learning

English presupposes the ability to interpret the expressions of English, and that in turn presupposes possession of a language in which to formulate and test hypotheses about what the correct interpretation is.

Several other commentators have likewise suggested that thoughts play an important role in the Tractarian account of linguistic meaning (Favrholdt 1964; Miller 1980; Kannisto 1986; Malcolm 1986; McDonough 1986). However, in my view, these commentators have tended to err by supposing not only that thoughts have *original* intentionality, but also that they have *intrinsic* intentionality. Contemporary philosophers of psychology insist on a distinction between *original* and *intrinsic* intentionality apparently ignored by commentators of Wittgenstein. If a state or event has original intentionality, its capacity to represent something other than itself cannot be explained by appeal to the *intentionality* of any other states or events (its "aboutness" is "first" or "original"), but its capacity to represent may nevertheless require explanation. If a state or event has *intrinsic* intentionality, its capacity to represent something other than itself cannot and need not be explained by appeal to anything other than itself.[1]

In my view, the *Tractatus* contains two arguments for the view that thoughts (that is, psychical facts, sentences in the language of thought) have original intentionality. However, thoughts, as conceived in the *Tractatus*, do not have intrinsic intentionality, because Wittgenstein asks for and offers us an explanation of that in virtue of which thoughts (and every other representation) represent: a fact represents something other than itself only in virtue of being a logical picture of a possible situation. In short, in my view Wittgenstein offers in the *Tractatus* what is intended to be an extremely general explanation of how intentionality is possible. Moreover, in my view of the *Tractatus*, the intentionality of thought, though not derivative from the intentionality of natural language, is explained by appeal to linguistic features (e.g., logical syntax). Thus, despite first appearances, my interpretation of the *Tractatus* is perhaps closer to the interpretation offered by commentators such as Rhees, Mounce, and Winch than it is to the interpretation offered by commentators such as Favrholdt, Malcolm, and McDonough.

At the same time, my interpretation of the *Tractatus* brings it much closer to positions held by contemporary philosophers of psychology than do either of the competing interpretations. Since publication of *The Language of Thought* (Fodor 1975), Jerry Fodor has been recognized as a leading defender of the view that we should explain linguistic representation by appeal to mental representation: the intentionality of language is explained by appeal to the intentionality of thought; the regress of interpretations is stopped because there are thoughts that need no interpretation in order to represent. However, in Fodor's view, thoughts themselves are simply sentences in a language of thought; they do not have *intrinsic* intentionality. Thus, in more recent writings (Fodor 1987; 1990a; 1990b), Fodor has attempted to explain the intentionality of the mental.[2] Commentators on Wittgenstein who stress the importance of thoughts in the *Tractatus* have noticed a parallel with Fodor's language of thought hypothesis, but they have tended to ignore the distinction between original and intrinsic intentionality when interpreting Fodor as much as when interpreting Wittgenstein (Malcolm 1986; McDonough 1986). Thus, they have interpreted Fodor's position, as well as Wittgenstein's, in a way that makes it seem far less sophisticated than it really is. Commentators on Wittgenstein who stress the importance of language in the *Tractatus* have tended to downplay the role of a language of thought in the *Tractatus*. Thus, they have not noticed the important parallels with contemporary work in the philosophy of mind and cognitive psychology.[3]

I shall argue for the proposed interpretation of the *Tractatus* in the following way. In the first two sections, I offer a reading of key passages according to which there are two main arguments in the *Tractatus* for a language of thought: (1) an argument from the possibility of now grasping determinate sense and thus stopping the regress of interpretations; (2) an argument from language learning. In section three, I reject a common reading of the *Tractatus* according to which something mental (e.g., a language of thought) is required to set up a connection between names and mind-independent objects. Section IV responds to two important objections to attributing a language of thought to the *Tractatus*.

I

Wittgenstein's claims about the possibility of simple signs and the subsistence of simple things are not conclusions arrived at on the basis of an examination of language or the world; nor are they linguistic or metaphysical assumptions used as premises in the argument of the *Tractatus*; rather, they are conclusions of a transcendental argument intended to uncover necessary and sufficient conditions for the possibility of determinate representation. The argument of the *Tractatus* begins in the middle of the actual *Tractatus*, not with the seemingly metaphysical pronouncements of the 1's and 2's, but with the attempt to understand how representation is possible (see 4.015, 4.016).

At 3.23, Wittgenstein writes "The requirement that simple signs be possible is the requirement that sense be determinate." At 2.02–2.023 he argues that, if there were no simple objects, it would be "impossible to form a picture of the world (true or false)." Thus, simple signs and simple objects alike are necessary preconditions of the possibility of determinate sense. Likewise, Wittgenstein insists that, if determinate sense is to be possible, the logical rules governing signs must be settled in advance. For example, 3.23 (quoted above) echoes a requirement stated in the *Notebooks 1914–1916*: "The demand for simple things *is* the demand for definiteness of sense" (p. 63). On the next page of the *Notebooks*, he writes: "We might demand definiteness in this way too: if a proposition is to make sense then the syntactical employment of each of its parts must be settled in advance.—It is, e.g., not possible *only subsequently to come upon* the fact that a proposition follows from it. But, e.g., what propositions follow from a proposition must be completely settled before that proposition can have a sense!" This requirement shows up again in the *Prototractatus*: "The requirement of determinateness could also be formulated in the following way: if a proposition is to have sense, the syntactical employment of each of its parts must have been established in advance. For example,[4] it cannot occur to one only subsequently that a certain proposition follows from it. Before a proposition can have a sense, it must be completely settled what propositions follow from it (*PT* 3.20103)." Thus, the possibility of simple signs, simple objects, and the logical rules that govern the elements of propositions are clearly viewed by Wittgenstein as both linked and necessary preconditions of the possibility of determinate representation.

Wittgenstein presents the concepts of fact, state of affairs, object, substance, and world at 1–2.063. At 2. 1, Wittgenstein introduces the concept of a picture, and he discusses this concept and the relation of pictures to reality from 2.1–2.225. Next Wittgenstein introduces the concept of thought (3: "A logical picture of facts is a thought") and the notion of what is thinkable (3–3.05). Finally, at 3.1, Wittgenstein speaks for the first time of propositions: "In a proposition a thought finds an expression that can be perceived by the senses." If we read the *Tractatus* as offering a transcendental argument, beginning in the 3's and 4's and working out towards the 1's and 2's, it is natural to suppose that thoughts are in some way presented as preconditions of the possibility of propositional signs with determinate sense.

Suppose Wittgenstein does think that thoughts are preconditions of the possibility of propositional signs with determinate sense. How would the argument go? As things are, the propositional signs (of natural languages) require interpretation. After all, written and spoken signs, "the part of the symbol perceptible by the senses" (3.32), are arbitrary (3.322); thus, "in the language of everyday life it very often happens that the same word signifies in two different ways—and therefore belongs to two different symbols" (3.323). Such signs need to be interpreted. To determine the correct interpretation of natural language expressions, one must look at more than the perceptible representation: "In order to recognize the symbol in the sign we must consider the significant use" (3.326); "The sign determines a logical form only together with its logical syntactic application" (3.327). Once we have gathered such information, we will be in a position to give the correct interpretation. To interpret a sign is to translate it; it is to provide another representation whose interpretation is not in question. But if all representations consist of signs that require interpretation, the regress looms. What will stop the regress?

Fortunately, according to Wittgenstein in the *Tractatus*, not all representations must consist of signs that require interpretation. At 3.325, Wittgenstein speaks of the possibility of using a symbolism "which obeys the rules of *logical* grammar—of logical syntax." In such a language, we would not apply "the same sign in different symbols" and we would not apply "signs in the same way which signify in different ways." In such a language, we would be able to read off the rules of logic from ordinary, non-logical propositions (6.122; see also *NB*, p. 107). Such a language presumably would consist of elementary propositions, consisting of names that stand proxy for simple objects, since "the requirement that simple signs be possible is the requirement that sense be determinate" (3.23). Thus, it seems clear that Wittgenstein assumes at least that it is *possible* for there to be a language whose terms are not ambiguous, a language whose terms require no interpretation.

And yet, the mere *possibility* of such a language does nothing to explain how the signs of our ordinary language succeed in pointing determinately. However, Wittgenstein indicates that he is not speaking merely of an *ideal* language, in the sense in which we could construct an artificial language, unconnected with our everyday language, that would obey the rules of logical syntax. To the contrary, Wittgenstein insists that "all the propositions of our colloquial language are actually, just as they are, logically completely in order" (5.5563). And at 5.5562, Wittgenstein writes: "If we know on purely logical grounds that there must be elementary propositions, then everyone who understands propositions in their unanalysed form must know it." Thus, Wittgenstein does not envisage the construction of an *ideal* language; in some sense, he wants to uncover what is already available to us, underlying or present in the everyday language we speak.

How could that be? Does Wittgenstein suppose that natural languages, e.g., German and English, as they stand, obey the rules of logical syntax and thereby have the features required to stop a regress of interpretations? Clearly, as indicated above, Wittgenstein does not suppose that the *signs* of natural languages obey logical rules, since the same signs are often used as different symbols, and so forth. Nevertheless, some have supposed that, according to Wittgenstein in the *Tractatus*, propositional signs, as *used* by us, have the features required to stop the regress (Rhees 1970; Mounce 1981; Winch 1987). Propositional signs require no interpretation simply because propositional signs, as used by us, have a determinate sense. As evidence for this reading, commentators appeal to 3.326–3.328:

> In order to recognize the symbol in the sign we must consider the significant use.

> The sign determines a logical form only together with its logical syntactic application.

> If a sign is *not necessary* then it is meaningless. That is the meaning of Occam's razor.
>   (If everything in the symbolism works as though a sign had meaning, then it has meaning.)

On this view, it is the use of a propositional sign within the language that gives it determinate sense.

Is this sufficient? Let us grant, at least for the purposes of argument, that the Wittgenstein *Tractatus* would suppose that the way a propositional sign is used within a language is sufficient to determine its sense. Let us grant that, according to the *Tractatus*, a sign's functional role within a language is sufficient to account for its intentionality. Let us suppose, further, that by looking at the way in which a sign is applied, we gain evidence as to what its determinate sense is; we gain evidence as to what symbol it is used to express. Presumably, in completely analyzed propositions, the propositions would be expressed in a such a way that all ambiguity would be eliminated.

But how am I now able to grasp that determinate sense and thus to understand what is being said? In *Zettel*, the later Wittgenstein writes: "How can I understand a proposition *now*, if it is for analysis to shew *what* I really understand?—Here there sneaks in the idea of understanding as a special mental process" (Z 455). This passage raises the possibility that something like a language of thought is called upon to explain how I can now grasp a determinate sense which is not fully expressed in ordinary language as it is.

Though no passage from Wittgenstein's later writings can by itself settle any interpretation of the *Tractatus*, there are passages in the *Tractatus* that, especially when compared with similar passages in the *Notebooks* and in the *Prototractatus*, suggest the view that there is a language of thought whose "sentences" consist of elements that are simple and governed by logical laws in a way that the unanalyzed sentences of natural languages are not.

At 4.002, Wittgenstein speaks of the "silent adjustments" (*die stillschweigenden Abmachungen*, translated as "tacit conventions" by Pears and McGuinness) needed to understand colloquial language. A similar sentence in the *Notebooks* 22.6.15, p. 70, is followed immediately with the claim that "there is enormously much added in thought to each proposition and not said." This *Notebooks* passage is preceded by:

> It is then also clear to the *uncaptive* mind that the sense of the proposition "The watch is lying on the table" is more complicated than the proposition (Satz) itself.

And it is followed by:

> I only want to justify the vagueness of ordinary sentences, for it *can* be justified.

> It is clear that I *know* what I *mean* by the vague proposition. . . .

These passages indicate that, at the time he wrote the *Notebooks*, Wittgenstein thought that what is not fully expressed in an ordinary sentence is filled out in thought. That he did not change his mind on this point by the time he wrote the *Tractatus* is suggested by 4.002 and its similarity to the *Notebooks* passages.

Where Wittgenstein apparently does change his mind, the change favors my interpretation. At 3.2, Wittgenstein describes the results of analysis in a way that plausibly can be interpreted as suggesting a language of thought whose elements are simple: in a completely analyzed proposition, "a thought can be expressed in such a way that elements of the propositional sign correspond to the objects of the thought."

In this passage, "objects of the thought" appears to be ambiguous. Does Wittgenstein intend to say that in a completely analyzed proposition the elements of the propositional sign correspond to thought-elements (i.e., psychical constituents) or to elements of reality? If the former, then Wittgenstein clearly believes that there are thoughts corresponding to, and separate from, propositional signs. Moreover, the goal of the analysis of propositions will be to see to it that the elements of the propositional sign correspond to the elements of thoughts. The text does not say directly which Wittgenstein intends, but Anthony Kenny notes that the Tractarian passage differs significantly from the corresponding passage in the *Prototractatus*: "In a propositional sign the simple signs correspond to the objects of reality" (*PT*, 3.14; Kenny 1984, 143–44). Why would Wittgenstein have made this change unless he wanted to convey that the elements of propositional signs correspond to thought-elements?[5] I suggest that the most plausible answer is that he would not have.

Let me summarize the argument for a language of thought from the need for now grasping the determinate sense of unanalyzed propositional signs: (1) As things are, the propositional signs (of natural languages) are ambiguous and so require interpretation. (2) A language whose signs need no interpretation is possible. (3) Moreover, a language whose signs need no interpretation is (in some sense) actual. (4) Even if language, as used by us, is sufficient to determine the correct interpretation of propositional signs, it is not sufficient to explain how I am now able to grasp determinate sense. (5) We can explain how this is possible only if there is a language of thought, a language whose elements *now* are simple signs that "obey the rules of *logical* grammar—of logical syntax." (6) Therefore, there is a language of thought.

Consider premise 5: How would the existence of a language of thought resolve the difficulty? In my view, when Wittgenstein says that "the method of projection is the thinking of the sense of the proposition" (3.11), he is speaking of a translation of the propositional sign into a "language of thought," a language whose elements, unlike ordinary, unanalyzed linguistic signs, already obey the laws of logic. By translating unanalyzed propositional signs into a language of thought, I am now able to grasp determinate sense.

The claim that the *Tractatus* presupposes that there is a language of thought is strengthened if we notice the marked asymmetry with which Wittgenstein treats pictures and thoughts on the one hand, and propositions and propositional signs, on the other. For example, pictures and thoughts are facts, whereas propositional signs, not propositions, are facts. Although he says directly that a picture is a fact (2.141), and implies that thoughts are facts (2.141, 3), he nowhere says directly that a proposition is a fact;[6] instead, he insists that a propositional sign is a fact (3.14).

Moreover, Wittgenstein speaks as though pictures and thoughts, qua facts, already include their representational relationships to the world in a way that propositional signs, qua facts, do not. First, Wittgenstein speaks as though a picture is a fact that requires no interpretation, translation, or projection onto the world. After introducing the concept of a picture at *Tractatus* 2.1, at 2.14 he says that a picture consists of elements "related to one another in a determinate way." A picture is thus a fact (2.141), and it is "the fact that the elements of a picture are related to one another in a determinate way" that "represents that things are related to one another in the same way" (2.15). Wittgenstein does not say that the fact that the elements of a picture are related to one another in a determinate way, together with a method of projection, represents that things are related to one another in the same way. Nevertheless, he writes at 2.1513 that a picture, "conceived in this way" (i.e., presumably, conceived as described from 2.1–2.1513), "also includes the pictorial relationship, which makes it into a picture." This pictorial relationship "consists of the correlations of the picture's elements with things" (2.1514). These correlations are the "feelers of the picture's elements, with which the picture touches reality" (2.1515) and this connection of a picture with reality is supposed to be direct (2.1511).

Correspondingly, Wittgenstein speaks of a thought as a "logical picture of the facts," and thus, given 2.141, as a fact. A fact is a definite configuration of objects (see 2, 2.01, 2.14, 2.141). Without any hint that anything needs to be done to project a thought or its objects onto the world, he says, at 3.02, that "The thought contains the possibility of the state of affairs which it thinks."

By contrast, Wittgenstein speaks of a propositional sign as a fact (3.14) that we use "as a projection of the possible state of affairs." Wittgenstein does not say that the propositional sign contains the possibility of a state of affairs. Instead, he says that "the possibility of what is projected" belongs to the proposition, not to the propositional sign (3.13). In short, pictures and thoughts, qua facts, appear to contain or to guarantee the possibility of a situation in a way that ordinary propositional signs, qua facts, do not.

At this point, we need to ask: What does Wittgenstein mean by 'thought' (Gedanke) in the cited passages? There are (at least) two possibilities. It is common to use the term 'thought' in two different ways: to pick out what is thought, the content, or to pick out a particular thought, that is, a particular mental state or event. We speak of the thought expressed in a particular sentence, and also of having a thought go through our minds at a particular time. In the former use, 'thought' is roughly equivalent to 'proposition', and the same thought can be expressed in written signs, spoken signs, or in a particular mental fact or event. In the latter use, 'thought' is not equivalent to 'proposition', it is a particular mental token, not a type. Thus, by 'Gedanke' in the *Tractatus*, Wittgenstein may mean, roughly, 'proposition', that is, what can be expressed by written signs, spoken signs, or thought signs, or he may mean 'psychical fact', that is, a particular mental fact, consisting of elements in a determinate configuration.

Many commentators insist that Wittgenstein, at least in the 3's, uses 'Gedanke' in the former sense, as something akin to a Platonic abstractum which can be expressed both in perceptible episodes of speech or writing and in inner episodes of thinking.[7] One reason commonly given for this interpretation is that Wittgenstein was influenced by Frege, and Frege used 'Gedanke' in this sense, insisting that thoughts should be distinguished from anything falling within the scope of psychology. Some commentators even go so far as to claim that, in the *Tractatus*, Wittgenstein always uses 'Gedanke' in the Fregean sense (Griffin 1964, 120–21).

It is important to decide this interpretive issue, since, if Wittgenstein always or usually means by 'Gedanke' simply the content of representations, no use of 'Gedanke' in the *Tractatus* will give us any reason to attribute to the *Tractatus* an argument for a language of thought (i.e., a language whose "sentences," unlike the sentences of ordinary language, are now governed by the laws of logical syntax). For example, "the objects of the thought" at 3.2 will not be ambiguous in the way indicated above. Moreover, the fact that Wittgenstein, without any hint that anything needs to be done to project a thought onto the world, says at 3.02 that "the thought contains the possibility of the state of affairs which it thinks" will hardly be surprising. He will be saying only that what is represented (the representational content of any linguistic or mental representation) contains its own possibility.

However, if this Fregean interpretation of 'Gedanke' is correct, it is surprising that Wittgenstein seems to imply that thoughts are facts, that is, determinate configurations of objects, whereas propositional signs, not propositions, are facts. On the Fregean interpretation, if propositions are not facts, neither should thoughts be, since 'thought' is roughly equivalent to 'proposition'.

Moreover, the Fregean interpretation conflicts sharply with Wittgenstein's own report to Russell about the meaning of 'Gedanke' in the *Tractatus*:

> ... "But a Gedanke is a Tatsache: what are its constituents and components, and what is their relation to those of the pictured Tatsache?" I don't know *what* the constituents of a thought are but I know *that* it must have such constituents which correspond to the words of Language. Again the kind of relation of the constituents of the thought and of the pictured fact is irrelevant. It would be a matter of psychology to find out (*NB*, p. 129).

> "Does a Gedanke consist of words?" No! But of psychical constituents that have the same sort of relation to reality as words. What those constituents are I don't know (*NB*, p. 130).[8]

Since in this letter Wittgenstein is trying to answer Russell's questions about the *Tractatus*, the Fregean interpretation of 'Gedanke' in the *Tractatus* requires us to believe that Wittgenstein either did not know or forgot what he meant by 'Gedanke'.[9] At the very least, this passage from the *Notebooks* shifts the burden of proof to those who would give the Fregean interpretation.

Some would respond that it is quite easy to accept the burden of proof, since Wittgenstein echoes Frege's vehement anti-psychologism at 4.1121:

> Psychology is no nearer related to philosophy, than is any other natural science.
> The theory of knowledge is the philosophy of psychology.

Does not my study of sign-language correspond to the study of thought processes which philosophers held to be so essential to the philosophy of logic? Only they got entangled for the most part in unessential psychological investigations, and there is an analogous danger for my method.

However, this passage does not settle the issue of what Wittgenstein means by 'thoughts', since it is perfectly consistent with my view of the relationship of thoughts to language in the *Tractatus*. Although I have argued that a language of thought is presupposed by the *Tractatus*, in my view it is only the logical features of psychical facts that are relevant to their representational power; if thoughts have any other features,[10] they are not features in virtue of which thoughts represent something other than themselves. A similar claim is frequently made by contemporary defenders of the computational theory of the mind: brain matter is irrelevant, since it is only the formal features of brain-states in virtue of which they represent; anything that instantiated the right program would serve equally well; nevertheless, it is crucial that there be something that instantiates the right program. As this parallel shows, we cannot conclude that Wittgenstein considers the question of whether there are psychical facts to be irrelevant. Wittgenstein may still insist, as he seems to do in his response to Russell's question about Gedanke, that there must be psychical facts with the right logical features.

Moreover, the natural answer to Wittgenstein's question, "Does not my study of sign-language correspond to the study of thought processes which philosophers held to be so essential to the philosophy of logic?" is "Yes, it does." Of course, Wittgenstein emphasizes the analysis of language in a way that the philosophers he speaks of did not, but that is equally compatible with my view. Thoughts, that is, psychical facts composed of simple elements that obey the rules of logical grammar/syntax, may be preconditions for grasping determinate sense in the unanalyzed expressions of ordinary languages, even though we must investigate the structure of ordinary language expressions to discover the structure of the thoughts that underlie them.

II

In my view, there is a second argument in the *Tractatus* for a language of thought, in addition to the argument sketched above: without a language of thought, we would not be able to learn natural languages, even when they are completely analyzed. At 4.02, Wittgenstein refers back to 4.01, suggesting that we see that "the proposition is a picture of reality" (4.01) "from the fact that we understand the sense of the propositional sign, without having had it explained to us" (4.02). A proposition "*shows* its sense," by showing "how things stand, *if* it is true" (4.022). To grasp the sense of a proposition, we do not need to know whether it is true; we need only to understand its constituent parts (4.024). How do we come to understand those parts? 4.025 speaks of a process of translation, where what is translated is not whole propositions, but only constituent parts.

Note, however, that any process of translation from one language to another will presuppose that we know some language already. At 4.026, Wittgenstein points out that, although we use propositions to "explain ourselves," "the meanings of the simple signs (the words) must be explained to us, if we are to understand them." How is this explaining to be accomplished? Thus far, the only clue we have, from 4.025, is that the constituents of propositions (words) may be translated into another language. But how will that help?

The only answer we get from the *Tractatus* is to be found at 3.263:

> The meanings of primitive signs can be explained by elucidations. Elucidations are propositions which contain the primitive signs. They can, therefore, only be understood when the meanings of these signs are already known.

This passage has puzzled commentators, since it sounds, at first blush, as though Wittgenstein is saying that we can only grasp the meanings of primitive signs if we already know the meanings of these same primitive signs. But this appears to be viciously circular: If we already know what 'a' means, then we have no need to learn what 'a' means, and if we do not know what 'a' means, then no such "elucidation" will help.

I suggest that this passage is not viciously circular; instead, Wittgenstein appeals to a language that does not need to be learned (a language of thought) to explain how we learn the words of natural languages. On this interpretation, when Wittgenstein says that elucidations can "only be understood when the meanings of these signs are already known," he is not saying that we must already know what a particular sign of natural language (e.g., 'cow' means); rather, he is saying that we must already have a language in which we can formulate and test hypotheses about what the sign 'cow' means. To be able to do this, we will already have to have a language which is conceptually rich enough to refer to cows. Thus, in order for us to learn the signs of natural languages by means of elucidations, there must be a language whose elements do not need to be learned. A language of thought would be such a language.

This interpretation of 3.263 gains support from the fact that, at 4.025, just after Wittgenstein has mentioned our need to understand the constituent parts of a proposition, he speaks of a process of translation, and from the fact that it enables us to make sense of an otherwise extremely puzzling passage. Moreover, a comparison of 3.263 with Augustine's explanation of language-learning (*PI*, 1) and Wittgenstein's commentary on it makes the proposed interpretation even more plausible:

> "When they (my elders) named some object, and accordingly moved towards something, I saw this and I grasped that the thing was called by the sound they uttered when they meant to point it out. Their intention was shewn by their bodily movements, as it were the natural language of all peoples.... Thus, as I heard words repeatedly used in their proper places in various sentences, I gradually learnt to understand what objects

they signified; and after I had trained my mouth to form these signs, I used them to express my own desires." (*PI*, 1)

At *Philosphical Investigations* 32, Wittgenstein insists that Augustine's explanation of language-learning presupposes a language of thought: "Augustine describes the learning of human language as if the child came into a strange country and did not understand the language of the country . . . as if the child could already *think*, only not yet speak. And 'think' would here mean something like 'talk to itself'."

Like Augustine, Wittgenstein at 3.263 insists that the meaning of words is to be learned from their use within whole sentences. Like Augustine, Wittgenstein at 3.263 presupposes that the learner can already represent the meanings of the primitive signs to herself in some language. Like Augustine, I suggest, Wittgenstein at 3.263 describes the learning of language as presupposing a language of thought.[11]

Thus far, I have argued that the *Tractatus* contains two arguments for the existence of a language of thought. Such a language is needed: (1) to account for our present grasp of the determinate sense of ordinary, unanalyzed sentences; (2) to account for the possibility of language-learning. Note, however, that it is not a part of my argument that only psychical facts could have sense or that thoughts, in virtue of being psychical facts, have their intentionality intrinsically. In fact, I think, the Wittgenstein of the *Tractatus* (like contemporary proponents of a language of thought) would deny the thesis (associated with Brentano and Husserl) that intentionality is a primitive and irreducible mark of the mental.

Thoughts, as conceived in the *Tractatus*, do not have intrinsic intentionality, because Wittgenstein asks for and offers us an explanation of that in virtue of which thoughts (and every other representation) represent: A fact represents something other than itself only in virtue of being a logical picture of a possible situation. Any fact is a logical picture of a possible situation if and only if the following conditions are met: The elements of a representing fact share logical form with the elements of the represented situation, in the sense that they have the same logical possibilities for combining to form facts; thus, the elements of the former stand in for elements of the latter; the elements of the representing fact are actually combined in a determinate way, which shows how elements of the represented situation would be combined if it actually obtained, whether or not it does.[12]

Thoughts are themselves facts, that is, determinate configurations of objects. Unlike the sentences of unanalyzed natural languages such as English and German, thoughts, that is, sentences in the language of thought, are sentences that obey the rules of logical syntax. And yet, thoughts represent, not because that which is mental has intrinsic intentionality, but in the way that any facts represent something other than themselves, that is, in virtue of sharing logical form with what they represent. In short, in my view Wittgenstein offers in the *Tractatus* what is intended to be an extremely general explanation of how intentionality is possible. Moreover, as pointed out above, though the intentionality of thought does not derive from the intentionality of natural language, it is explained by appeal to linguistic features (e.g., logical syntax).

III

Thus far, I have been writing as though the regress of interpretations will be stopped, as though language will have a determinate sense, so long as its elements obey the rules of logical grammar/syntax. But this is controversial. Even if this is, as Wittgenstein clearly thinks, necessary, surely (so the argument goes) it is not sufficient. Apart from form, there is also the question of content. Apart from the question of the rules of combination of simple signs and the rules of correct inference, there is also the question of what particular objects names stand for. Logical syntax by itself does not determine semantics. Something must hook individual names onto individual objects.

In fact, the apparent need for something to hook language onto the world, something to link representations with what they represent, something to make a name stand for a particular object, has seemed to a number of commentators to provide the most compelling argument for giving primacy to thought in the *Tractatus*. Surely, so the argument goes, the *Tractatus* presupposes something mental to hook names onto objects; to accomplish this, there must be thoughts with irreducible and intrinsic intentionality whose elements simply do latch onto objects in reality.[13]

In my view, however, this is an argument for the primacy of thought that is not found anywhere in the *Tractatus*.[14] In my view, Wittgenstein in the *Tractatus* sees no need for language-world correlations because he thinks that correlations among representations suffice. To substantiate this claim would require exegesis that goes beyond the scope of this essay.[15] Here I will merely point to passages which challenge the alternative interpretation.

The question, again, is this: Given that logical form is *necessary* for representation to occur, according to Wittgenstein, is it *sufficient*? What gives thoughts their representational *content*? The simple elements of a thought purportedly share logical form with the simple objects for which they stand, but in virtue of what does a thought-element stand for a particular object? There are two obvious possibilities. On the one hand, one might maintain, as commentators often do, that a special connection must exist or be set up between objects in reality and elements of our representations. On the other hand, one might maintain that the logical rules according to which simple signs combine determine the referents of those elements. On the former view, syntax alone does not determine semantics. On the latter view, it does.

At 2.18, Wittgenstein insists that "what every picture, of whatever form, must have in common with reality in order to be able to represent it at all—rightly or falsely—is the logical form, that is, the form of reality." This passage says only that logical form is necessary, not that it is sufficient, but there is arguably no suggestion in the surrounding passages as to what else might be needed. As noted earlier, Wittgenstein explicitly links the demand for determinate sense, not only with the demands for the possibility of simple signs and the subsistence of simple objects, but also with the demand for syntactical rules governing the elements of representations, and he writes as though these demands all amount to much the same. At 3.144 and 3.3, Wittgenstein indicates that names, taken alone, do not point to anything other than themselves: names are to propositions as points are to arrows. Propositions, and only propositions, have sense, and so point; names stand in for objects, but only in the context of a proposition.

Moreover, the "method of projection" Wittgenstein speaks of at 3.11, our use of "the sensibly perceptible sign (sound or written sign, etc.) of the proposition as a projection of the possible state of affairs," arguably is not a matter of managing to hook names onto mind-independent objects; instead, it is a matter of grasping translation rules, rules of the kind Wittgenstein cites at 4.0141: "In the fact that there is a general rule by which the musician is able to read the symphony out of the score . . . herein lies the internal similarity between these things which at first sight seem to be entirely different. And the rule is the law of projection which projects the symphony into the language of the musical score. It is the rule of translation of this language into the language of the gramophone record."

That Wittgenstein denies the need for (or possibility of) language-world connections is further indicated at 5.526: Wittgenstein speaks of correlating names with objects, but the procedure he describes is one of connecting language with more language.[16] Though such passages by themselves are not conclusive, they present a challenge to the claim that the *Tractatus* calls upon the mind to forge a link between names and reality.

IV

The thesis that the *Tractatus* presupposes a language of thought seems, *prima facie*, to be incompatible with a cluster of remarks (2.182, 3, 3.5, 4) that appear to license the conclusion that thoughts are nothing but propositions with a sense. Consider the following passages:

Every picture is *at the same time* a logical one. (On the other hand, not every picture is, for example, a spatial one.) (2.182)

A logical picture of facts is a thought. (3)

A propositional sign, applied and thought out, is a thought. (3.5)

A thought is a proposition with a sense.[17] (4)

Notice first that it apparently follows from 2.182 and 3 that every picture is a thought. Moreover, at 3.5 and 4, Wittgenstein apparently identifies "applied and thought out" propositional signs with thoughts, and thoughts with "propositions with a sense." If all pictures are thoughts and all thoughts are propositions, then all pictures are propositions. This is counterintuitive: whereas Wittgenstein certainly believes that all propositions are pictures, there is little independent reason to attribute to him the belief that all pictures are propositions. Surely Wittgenstein would grant that the concept of a picture is more general than the concept of a proposition. More troubling from my perspective is the apparent implication that all thoughts are simply propositions with a sense. This appears to imply that thoughts must be expressed in propositional signs.[18]

I believe it is plausible to interpret Wittgenstein's apparent identifications at 2.182, 3, 3.5, and 4 in a way that is entirely consistent with my general thesis about the relation of thought and language in the *Tractatus*. My reading of the *Tractatus* suggests that spatial facts (e.g., a three-dimensional model of a car accident), psychical facts (e.g., the thought that two cars collided head-on), and propositional signs (e.g., 'Two cars collided head-on') are representations only in virtue of sharing logical form with what they represent. Wittgenstein identifies pictures and thoughts, not because spatial facts are literally psychical facts or vice versa, but because, qua representations of the same situation, spatial facts and psychical facts have the same logical form. Wittgenstein identifies propositions and thoughts, not because propositional signs are literally psychical facts or vice versa, but because, qua representations of the same situation, propositional signs and psychical facts have the same logical form.

One may object to a non-literal reading of Wittgenstein's identifications at 2.182, 3, 3.5, and 4. One may wonder whether mere identity of logical form is all that Wittgenstein intends. I believe *Tractatus* 4.014 makes it highly plausible to suppose that it is:

> A gramophone record, the musical idea, the written notes, and the sound-waves, all stand to one another in the same internal relation of depicting that holds between language and the world. They are all constructed according to a common logical pattern. (Like the two youths in the fairy-tale, their two horses, and their lilies. They are all in a certain sense one.)

It is absurd to suppose that a gramophone record, the musical idea, the written notes, and the sound-waves are literally identical, but Wittgenstein insists that "they are all in a certain sense one" in that "they are all constructed according to a common logical pattern." Analogously, I believe Wittgenstein would regard it as absurd to suggest that the following are literally identical: the physical model of a particular accident, the psychical fact that is the thought of the accident, and the propositional sign describing the accident. Nevertheless, they are "all in a certain sense one" in that they share logical form. This is precisely the kind of identification the later Wittgenstein attributes to the *Tractatus*:

> ... Thought, language, now appear to us as the unique correlate, picture, of the world. These concepts: proposition, language, thought, world, stand in line one behind the other, each equivalent to each.... Thought is

surrounded by a halo.—Its essence, logic, presents an order, in fact the a prior order of the world: that is, the order of *possibilities*, which must be common to both world and thought.... (*PI* 96–97)

I see in 2.182, 3, 3.5, and 4 no more need literally to identify physical and psychical facts, psychical facts and propositional signs, than there is literally to identify representations in general with the facts that make them correct when they are correct. If my interpretation of these passages is plausible, as I believe it is, then these passages cannot be used as a refutation of my claim that the *Tractatus* resupposes a language of thought.

There is another cluster of remarks in the *Tractatus* that has been taken by some to be a decisive refutation of the claim that the *Tractatus* presupposes a language of thought, namely, the remarks in the 5.54's about ascriptions of propositional attitude (e.g, "A believes that *p*," "A thinks *p*"). For example, Peter Winch uses these passages to argue that Norman Malcolm's view of the relationship of thought to language in the *Tractatus* simply cannot be right.

> There is another place in the *Tractatus* in which something important is said that is incompatible with the mentalistic interpretation of thought. I am thinking of the discussion of 'certain propositional forms of psychology, like "A thinks, that *p* is the case", or "A thinks *p*", etc.' which runs from 5.541 to 5.5423. Wittgenstein there objects to Russell's theory that in the situation described by such propositions the subject, A, stands in a certain relation to the proposition *p*. The relation in question is surely that which the interpretation of 3.11 that I am rejecting understands by thinking the sense of the proposition'. On this interpretation it is this thinking that actually gives the proposition its sense. But Wittgenstein's objection to Russell in 5.5422 is: 'The correct explanation of the form of the proposition "A makes the judgment *p*" must show that it is impossible for a judgment to be a piece of nonsense. (Russell's theory does not satisfy this requirement.)' So it is quite clear that Wittgenstein did not think that an act of thought could *confer* sense on an expression which otherwise would not possess it. On the contrary, he thought that any account of thought must be *based* on an account of what it is for an expression to have sense. (Winch 1987, 14–15)

The "mentalistic interpretation of thought" Winch intends to reject in this passage is the claim that in the *Tractatus* "a psychical state of affairs is needed in order to transmute a string of perceptible signs into a proposition" (Winch 1987, 13). According to Winch, someone who says that 3.11 ("The method of projection is the thinking of the sense of the proposition") explains the method of projection of a propositional sign in terms of thinking the sense must be subscribing to Russell's theory that in the situation described by attributions of propositional attitude, "the subject, A, stands in a certain relation to the proposition *p*." But at 5.5422 Wittgenstein rejects Russell's theory on the grounds that it fails to show that "it is impossible to judge a nonsense."

Winch concludes that "it is quite clear that Wittgenstein did not think that an act of thought could *confer* sense on an expression which otherwise would not possess it. On the contrary, he thought that any account of thought must be *based* on an account of what it is for an expression to have sense."

I have not claimed that "a psychical state of affairs is needed in order to transmute a string of perceptible signs into a proposition," if by that Winch means that no string of perceptible signs whatever could have sense without a corresponding thought.[19] I *have* argued, however, for attributing at least this much to the *Tractatus*: Given that natural languages, as they are, are not completely analyzed, a language of thought is required to enable us now to grasp determinate sense, and, given that natural languages, as they are, are learned, a language of thought is required to explain how that is possible. Though Winch's attack is not aimed directly at the view I defend, it is incumbent upon me to explain these passages in a way that is consistent with my view of the relationship of thought to language in the *Tractatus*.

Fortunately for my interpretation, Winch's conclusion simply does not follow from the *Tractatus* passage he cites. To see why, we need to understand both why Wittgenstein thinks his explanation of "A thinks *p*" (5.542) shows that a judgment cannot be nonsense and why he thinks Russell's does not. Wittgenstein repeats this demand in the *Notes on Logic*:

> When we say that A judges that, etc., then we have to mention a whole proposition which A judges. It will not do either to mention only its constituents, or its constituents and form but not in the proper order. This shows that a proposition itself must occur in the statement to the effect that it is judged. . . . Every right theory of judgment must make it impossible for me to judge that "this table penholders the book" (Russell's theory does not satisfy this requirement) (*NB*, p. 96(b)).

According to Russell's 'multiple theory of judgment', to which Wittgenstein refers here and in 5.5422, judgment involves a relation between a mind and the constituents of the proposition. So, for example, '*A* judges that Socrates is a man' involves a relation between *A*'s mind, Socrates, and manhood. Nothing in this view prevents *A* from judging that this table penholders the book, since there are no non-arbitrary restrictions either on the constituents that may combine to form propositions or on the ways in which the combined constituents must be ordered (Black 1964).

In my view, at 5.542, Wittgenstein is comparing sentences ascribing propositional attitudes to sentences about the meaning of words. The major point of the comparison is this: For there to be representations of any type, there must be articulate facts, consisting of elements combined in a determinate way. Just as for a propositional sign "p" to picture a situation, the propositional sign must be a fact, consisting of physical elements in a definite configuration, so too, for someone to think something or believe something (etc.), there must be a fact (i.e., a thought) consisting of psychical elements in a definite configuration.

Propositional attitudes involve mental representations, and all representations involve facts.

As the last part of 5.542 makes clear, one fact can represent another only because their objects are correlated—that is, the individual elements of the representing fact stand in for individual objects in the represented fact. If representations consisted of elements (names) standing for objects alone, however, no representation could be false: for the name to have meaning (Bedeutung), the object for which it stands would have to exist, and so there would be only two possibilities—i.e., the representation would be either true or meaningless. But if representations consist of names that are combined to form facts and can be combined in various ways to form other facts, the problem is solved. A representation is false if the objects for which the elements of the representation stand are not combined as the elements are combined in the representation.

A remark in the notes Wittgenstein dictated to Moore confirms my reading of 5.542 as a comparison (rather than an analysis) of sentences such as '*A* believes *p*' and ' "*p*" says *p*':

> The relation of "I believe p" to p can be compared to the relation of " 'p' says (besagt) p" to p: it is just as impossible that *I* should be as simple as that "p" should be. (*NB,* p. 118[2])

The quoted remark shows also that the major point of the passage is simply that the possibility of representation, whether it involves propositional signs that can be "perceived by the senses" (3. 1) or not, requires facts (objects in a definite configuration) rather than objects alone. Representation of whatever sort is possible only because there are facts whose elements stand for (or stand in for) objects.

How does Wittgenstein's analysis show that it is impossible to judge a nonsense? At least part of the point of requiring pictures to be *facts* is that, unlike sets of objects, in a fact the elements have a determinate relationship to one another. The fact that the cat is on the mat is different from the fact that the mat is on the cat, even though the constituents of each fact are the same. Unlike Russell's theory that judgment involves a relation between objects that can be ordered in any way, Wittgenstein's theory is that judgment involves *facts*, elements that are combined in a determinate way and therefore have a definite structure. Furthermore, facts have a certain form, which is the possibility of structure (i.e., the objects that constitute facts are capable of combining in some ways but not in others). (See 2.032, 2.033, 2.15.) In order for one fact to represent another, they must have logical form in common. Logical form guarantees that any structure possible for the elements of the representing fact will be possible for the elements of the represented fact. Making the judgment *p* involves representing *p*; therefore, "it is impossible for a judgment to be a piece of nonsense" (5.5422).

Given this interpretation, Wittgenstein's objection to Russell in the 5.54's is incompatible with the view that the mind is *simple*. The point of 5.542 was that mental representations must be facts, not mere objects. 'A' in 'A has the thought p' does not stand for an object; instead, it represents a fact (or bundle of facts) whose elements stand for objects. Now a soul or subject, Wittgenstein insists, must be simple, but what 'A' represents is a complex. Thus, "there is no such thing as the soul—the subject...." There is no simple object A; what we call 'A' is a set of psychical facts or mental representations. For Wittgenstein, A, the "human soul, with which psychology deals" (5.641 [c]) is what we might call the 'empirical ego', not a metaphysically simple object but a "train of mental states" (*BB*, p. 5).

However, given this interpretation, Wittgenstein's objection to Russell in the 5.54's is entirely compatible with my thesis about the relationship of thought and language in the *Tractatus*. It is clear from 5.542 that Wittgenstein believes we can understand thought by analogy with the sentences of language: just as the sentences of language are facts with a definite structure, thoughts are facts with a definite structure. Furthermore, the goal of the analysis of language is to uncover its true logical form, and this will show us the logical form of the underlying thoughts. However, this is all compatible with my thesis. While we may be able to come to know the logical form of our thoughts via an analysis of language, there must be thoughts with a determinate logical form in order for there to be significant language capable of a logical analysis which has not yet been carried out.

CONCLUSION

The interpretation of the *Tractatus* offered in this essay carves out a position intermediate between two extremes, and thus, points towards a resolution of ongoing disputes among Tractarian commentators about the relation between thought, language, and reality, enabling us to recognize what is important and correct about each of the alternative interpretations, as well as where each is incomplete.[20] At the same time, if the interpretation is correct, the *Tractatus* contains arguments for a language of thought whose "sentences" have original, but not intrinsic, intentionality; thus, the *Tractatus* is both more sophisticated and more similar to contemporary theories of representation than has commonly been recognized.[21]

Notes

References to Wittgenstein's writings are incorporated in the text. *BB* is *The Blue and Brown Books*; *NB* is *Notebooks 1914–1916*; *PI* is *Philosophical Investigations*; *PT* is *Prototractatus: An Early Version of Tractatus Logico-Philosophicus*; *Z* is *Zettel*. All unmarked references (e.g., 3.14) are to the *Tractatus Logico-Philosophicus*, Ogden translation, unless otherwise indicated.

1. Norman Malcolm (1986, 75) writes: "If a physical sentence becomes a projection of a possible situation by virtue of the *thinking* of that situation, then the thought of that situation did not *become* a thought of that situation by virtue of the work of a previous thought—for this would result in an infinite regress. The view that physical sentences get their sense from thoughts seems to require that the latter do not *get* their sense from anything!" Of course, a contemporary philosopher of mind would insist, if thoughts have original intentionality,

that means that thoughts do not get their sense from something else that has intentionality, but that is not the same as saying that their intentionality cannot (or need not) be explained.

2. Fodor's explanation appeals to nomic relationships between token representations in the language of thought, e.g., "cow" and properties instantiated in the thinker's environment, e.g., the property of being a cow. For related attempts to develop (broadly) causal or covariance theories of content determination, see also Dennett, 1987; Dretske, 1981, 1983a, 1983b; Israel, 1987; Stalnaker, 1984; Stampe, 1975, 1977. Other contemporary philosophers of mind attempt to explain the intentionality of the mental in other ways, e.g., by appeal to the functional role of sentences in the language of thought.

3. For more on the parallels between the *Tractatus* and contemporary theories, see Summerfield, manuscript.

4. Notice that, in both the *Notebooks* and *Prototractatus* passages, Wittgenstein gives derivation rules only as an example. This is presumably because there will have to be rules that govern the way names combine to form propositions as well as rules that determine what propositions follow from a given proposition.

5. Malcolm argues in favor of the second interpretation, on the grounds that in the statements following 3.2 Wittgenstein speaks of 'the objects', and clearly means the objects composing the situation which the thought is about. See, e.g., 3.21: "The configuration of objects in a situation corresponds to the configuration of simple signs in the propositional sign" (Malcolm 1986, 68). However, "die Konfiguration der Gegenstände in der Sachlage" is not clearly a matter of reality/the world/the facts /what is the case rather than a matter of possibilities presented in thought. See Garver, 1990 and Summerfield, in preparation.

6. Though he may not agree with the use to which I am putting it, I owe this point to Robert J. Fogelin. See Fogelin 1976, 24.

7. Very early on, Ramsey gave this Fregean interpretation: "As to the relation between a proposition and a thought Mr. Wittgenstein is rather obscure; but I think his meaning is that a thought is a type whose tokens have in common a certain sense, and include the tokens of the corresponding proposition, but include also other non-verbal tokens" (Ramsey 1966, 13).

8. Note that, whereas this passage counts against interpretations, such as Malcolm's, according to which thoughts in the *Tractatus* have intrinsic intentionality, it does not count against my interpretation. Thoughts, in my view, are a kind of language, and thus their elements "have the same sort of relation to reality as words."

9. (*NB*, pp. 129–30). In "Wittgenstein's Early Philosophy of Mind," Anthony Kenny points out that this passage follows "an exegesis of the meaning of 'Sachverhalt' and 'Tatsache' which is notoriously difficult to reconcile with the actual text of the *Tractatus*" (Kenny 1984, 141). Still, other things being equal, we ought to try to reconcile Wittgenstein's various remarks wherever possible. It would be extremely odd if Wittgenstein in the *Tractatus* never, or almost never, uses 'Gedanke' to mean what he tells Russell it means. I do not need to claim that the *Tractatus* never uses 'Gedanke' in any other sense, only that he frequently uses it in the way he says.

10. Anthony Kenny has suggested that, according to Wittgenstein in the *Tractatus*, thoughts are facts whose *only* form is logical form: "it is quite natural, and was long traditional, to regard the mental and the physical as distinct realms whose inhabitants had no properties in common: so that a psychic fact and the physical fact it depicted could have nothing in common beyond the bare logical form" (Kenny 1984, 141–42).

11. Notice that, given my interpretation of 3.263, Wittgenstein's argument in the *Tractatus* for a language of thought parallels Jerry Fodor's argument in *The Language of Thought* for such a language: "we have no notion at all of how a first language might be learned that does not come down to some version of learning by hypothesis formation and confirmation" (Fodor 1975, 58).

12. This explanation of intentionality solves a longstanding puzzle of representation: How can a sign point to what is not there? See section IV below.

13. See Malcolm, 1986; McDonough, 1986; and Miner, 1980.

14. Whether I am right about this is not essential to my main argument that the *Tractatus* presupposes a language of thought.

15. See Summerfield, 1990a, and in preparation. See also Ishiguro, 1969, and McGuinness, 1981.

16. On the other side, many reputable commentators have read the *Tractatus* as presupposing that word-world connections are set up, citing passages such as the following: 2.1513–2.1515; 3.13; 4.024–4.026; 6.124. See also *NB*, 31.5.15, p. 53, p. 60–61. However, I believe these passages are all at least consistent with the view that only connections between representations are presupposed.

17. Tautologies are propositions, but they lack sense and fail to express any thoughts. Thus, Wittgenstein is not being redundant by writing "proposition with a sense." The translation given here is that of Pears-McGuinness.

18. Notice that these passages, read as literal identifications, are puzzling on nearly any view of the relation of thought to language in the *Tractatus*. Even Winch, for example, wants to say that "the word 'thought' expresses a more general concept than does 'proposition' in that there may be thoughts which are *not* 'expressed perceptibly through the senses' and for which, therefore, no corresponding proposition is uttered" (Winch 1987, 12). But if 4 literally identifies thoughts with propositions with a sense, it is difficult to see how to avoid the opposite conclusion. For other attempts to wrestle with these passages, see Griffin, 1964 and Kenny, 1984.

19. Moreover, I have explicitly rejected the view that the simple elements of thoughts are called upon to link names with mind-independent objects. Whereas Malcolm is committed to this thesis as well as to the thesis that thoughts give all propositions sense, I am not.

20. For example, Malcolm argues not only that the *Tractatus* presupposes a language of thought, but also that such a language is required to forge a link between names and mind-independent objects, and that the link between thought-elements and reality must differ radically from the link between names and objects. Winch argues against Malcolm, largely on the grounds that no such links between representation and reality are required. Given my interpretation, we can appreciate the importance of a language of thought in the *Tractatus* without getting embroiled in controversies about whether or not Wittgenstein was a realist in the *Tractatus*.

21. Thanks are due to Penelope Maddy, Pat Manfredi, and David Stern for comments on a draft of this essay.

References

Black, M. 1964. *A Companion to Wittgenstein's 'Tractatus'*. Ithaca, N.Y.

Dennett, D. 1987. *The Intentional Stance*. Cambridge, Mass.

Dretske, F. I. 1981. *Knowledge and the Flow of Information*. Cambridge, Mass.

———— 1983a. "The Epistemology of Belief" *Synthese* 55:3–19.

———— 1983b. "Précis of Knowledge and the Flow of Information." *Behavioral and Brain Sciences* 6:55–90.

Favrholdt, D. 1964. *An Interpretation and Critique of Wittgenstein's Tractatus*. Copenhagen.

Fodor, J. A. 1975. *The Language of Thought*. Cambridge, Mass.

———— 1987. *Psychosemantics: The Problem of Meaning in the Philosophy of Mind*. Cambridge, Mass.

———— 1990a. "Information and Representation." *Information, Language and Cognition*. Edited by P. P. Hanson, Vancouver.

———— 1990b. *A Theory of Content and Other Essays*. Cambridge, Mass.

Fogelin, R. J. 1976. *Wittgenstein*. Boston.

Garver, N. 1990. "The Metaphysics of the *Tractatus*." In *Wittgenstein—Towards a Re-Evaluation: Proceedings of the Fourteenth International Wittgenstein-Symposium, Centenary Celebration*, edited by R. Haller and J. Brandl, Vienna.

Griffin, J. 1964. *Wittgenstein's Logical Atomism*. Oxford.

Ishiguro, H. 1969. "The Use and Mention of Names." In *Studies in the Philosophy of Wittgenstein*, edited by P. Winch. London.

Israel, D. 1987. *The Role of Propositional Objects of Belief in Action*. Palo Alto, Calif.

Kannisto, H. 1986. *Thoughts and Their Subject: A Study of Wittgenstein's Tractatus*. *Acta Philosophica Fennica* 40. Helsinki.

Kenny, A. 1984. "Wittgenstein's Early Philosophy of Mind." In *The Legacy of Wittgenstein*. Oxford.

Malcolm, N. 1986. *Nothing is Hidden: Wittgenstein's Criticism of his Early Thought*. Oxford.

McDonough, R. M. 1986. *The Argument of the 'Tractatus': Its Relevance To Contemporary Theories of Logic, Language, Mind, and Philosophical Truth*. New York.

McGuinness, B. 1981. "The So-called Realism of Wittgenstein's *Tractatus*." In *In Perspectives on the Philosophy of Wittgenstein*, edited by I. Block. Oxford.

Miller, R. W. 1980. "Solipsism in the Tractatus." *Journal of the History of Philosophy* 18:57–74.

Mounce, H. O. 1981. *Wittgenstein's Tractatus: An Introduction*. Chicago.

Ramsey, F. P. 1966. "Review of 'Tractatus'." In *Essays on Wittgenstein's Tractatus*, edited by I. M. Copi and R. W. Beard, New York.

Rhees, R. 1970. *Discussions of Wittgenstein*. New York.

Stalnaker, R. 1984. *Inquiry*. Cambridge, Mass.

Stampe, D. 1975. "Show and Tell." In *Forms of Representation*, edited by B. Freed, A. Marras and P. Maynard. New York.

——— 1977. "Towards a Causal Theory of Linguistic Representation." In *Midwest Studies in Philosophy*, edited by P. French, T. Uehling, and H. Wettstein. Minneapolis.

Summerfield, D. M. 1990a. "Logical Form and Kantian Geometry: Wittgenstein's Analogy." In *Wittgenstein—Towards a Re-Evaluation: Proceedings of the Fourteenth International Wittgenstein-Symposium, Centenary Celebration*, edited by R. Haller and J. Brandl. Vienna.

——— 1990b. "Wittgenstein on Logical Form and Kantian Geometry." *Dialogue* 29:531–50.

——— In preparation. *Wittgenstein, Mental Representation, and Covariance Theories of Content*.

——— Manuscript. "Contemporary Theories of Content Determination and the Rule-following Paradox."

Winch, P. 1987. *Trying to Make Sense*. Oxford.

Wittgenstein, L. 1922. *Tractatus Logico-Philosophicus*. Translated by C. K. Ogden. London.

——— 1958. *Philosophical Investigations*. New York.

——— 1961. *Notebooks 1914–1916*. New York.

——— 1961. *Tractatus Logico-Philosophicus*, Translated by D. F. Pears & B. F. McGuinness. London.

——— 1965. *The Blue and Brown Books*. New York.

——— 1971. *Prototractatus: An early version of Tractatus Logico-Philosophicus*. London.

——— 1970. *Zettel*. Berkeley, Calif.

Does Philosophy Only State
What Everyone Admits? A Discussion
of the Method of Wittgenstein's
Philosophical Investigations

FELICIA ACKERMAN

A striking feature of the method of Wittgenstein's *Philosophical Investigations* (henceforth *PI*) is its anti-theoretical stance. Thus, he says

> we may not advance any kind of theory. There must not be anything hypothetical in our considerations. We must do away with all *explanation*, and description alone must take its place. (*PI* ¶109, italics in original[1])

> Philosophy simply puts everything before us, and neither explains nor deduces anything. (*PI* ¶126)

> In philosophy we do not draw conclusions. (*PI* ¶599)

> If one tried to advance *theses* in philosophy, it would never be possible to debate them, because everyone would agree to them. (*PI* ¶128, italics in original)

As a description of how philosophy is in fact done, these remarks are obviously false. Philosophers are continually explaining things, deducing things, drawing conclusions, advancing and debating theses, and very rarely agreeing on them. But these remarks are intended to tell us not what philosophical practice is, but what it ought to be. Do they have any merit?

Armstrong thinks not. He offers the following criticism of the Wittgensteinian anti-theoretical conception of philosophy.

> Since the work of Wittgenstein, it has been fashionable to maintain that philosophy does not issue in any theories at all about the nature of reality ... this doctrine has proved intellectually corrupting, for in fact it is quite impossible to be in such a theory-free state if you think at all extensively on philosophical topics. Those philosophers who believe they

are in such a theory-free state are really being moved by obscure and ill-formulated theories which escape any criticism or correction because they are never brought out into the open where they can be clearly considered.[2]

Is Armstrong right? In order to discuss this, we need to get clear about what counts as a "theory" here. The Wittgenstein material quoted above characterizes a theory as something hypothetical, that explains rather than merely describes. But these Wittgensteinian characterizations are not equivalent. Something can be explanatory (e.g., a mathematical proof that there is no greatest prime number, which in a sense gives a mathematical explanation of why there is no greatest prime number) without being hypothetical. Armstrong's own conception of a philosophical theory seems to take a philosophical theory to be a general view about some large-scale philosophical area; his above-quoted passage concludes the chapter in his *A Materialist Theory of the Mind* where he compares and contrasts such theories of the mind as bundle dualism, Cartesian dualism, the central-state theory, etc. Wittgenstein's second and third passages quoted above introduce a further element by saying philosophy does not involve deduction or the drawing of conclusions. But if something is to count as theoretical if it involves deduction or drawing conclusions rather than just description, it seems impossible to do philosophy without theorizing, for philosophy does seem to involve deductive reasoning and the drawing of conclusions. When we consider theories as non-deductive explanations, hypotheses, or general views about large-scale philosophical problems such as the mind-body problem, however, whether one can do philosophy without "theorizing" seems less clear. Certainly Armstrong is right to point to the dangers of relying on unrecognized and unexamined theories when claiming that one is not "theorizing" at all. But this danger does not preclude the possibility of drawing some philosophical conclusions based merely on one's intuitions about described hypothetical cases; such intuitions may be said to function as "philosophical observations," in a way analogous to the way sensory observations provide data in science. The obvious question is whether such "observations" can ever be genuinely theory-free, either in philosophy or in science.

I will not try to answer this question here, because even an affirmative answer would not help the basic problem with the method of *Philosophical Investigations*. This problem goes deeper than Armstrong seems to recognize. Wittgenstein seems to reject not only the possibility of philosophical "theories," but even the possibility that philosophy can issue isolated "nontheoretical" insights that are both true and informative. Thus, he holds that

Philosophy may in no way interfere with the actual use of language; it can in the end only describe it. . . . It leaves everything as it is. (*PI* ¶124)

Philosophy only states what everyone admits. (*PI* ¶599)

Again, of course, these remarks are intended to be an account of philosophy not as it is actually done, but as it ought to be. But this account is inconsistent with Wittgenstein's own philosophical practice. *Philosophical Investigations* does not state only what everyone admits; its views are at odds, and are intended to be at odds, with the views of Descartes, Russell, and Wittgenstein's own earlier self. So the "everyone" in ¶599 presumably is all non-philosophers, whose intelligence has not been "[bewitched] . . . by means of language" (*PI* ¶109), who have not "become calloused by doing philosophy" (*PI* ¶348). But this still does not make ¶599 reflect Wittgenstein's actual practice. For one thing, he advances views on subjects which the average non-philosopher has not thought about at all, such as "Hence it is not possible to obey a rule 'privately'" (*PI* ¶202), "To use a word without justification does not mean to use it without right" (*PI* ¶289), and " 'letting myself be guided' [by letters in reading] . . . only consists in my looking carefully at the letters— and perhaps excluding certain other thoughts" (*PI* ¶170). And contrary to his own precepts, Wittgenstein often supports these esoteric views by means of reasoning (and in effect admits this in the quoted passage from ¶202, which uses the word 'hence', a word indicating that despite his stricture in ¶599, he is drawing a conclusion).

Wittgenstein might reply here by again stressing what he takes to be the descriptive nature of philosophy. Since philosophy "simply puts everything before us, and neither explains nor deduces anything.—Since everything lies open to view, there is nothing to explain" (*PI* ¶126), philosophy thus can seem surprising to "unbewitched" people only because it consists of "observations which no one has doubted, but which have escaped remark only because they are always before our eyes" (*PI* ¶415). But in what sense is Wittgenstein's argument for the *conclusion* that "it is not possible to obey a rule privately" (*PI* ¶202) an instance of calling attention to what is "always before our eyes" rather than an instance of reasoning?

Moreover, it is false that once Wittgenstein "simply puts everything before us," everyone who has not "become calloused by doing philosophy" will agree with him. I have tried Wittgenstein's views on non-philosophical acquaintances, as well as on students encountering philosophy for the first time. Thus, I have substantial informal evidence that Wittgensteinian views do not strike the non-philosopher as correct or natural.[3] If the objection is made here that the people I deal with are not truly "unbewitched" by "language," it is incumbent upon the Wittgensteinian to give a non-question-begging way of deciding who is and who is not so "bewitched."

In fact, there are hints in *Philosophical Investigations* of what such a way is supposed to be. Thus, Wittgenstein says

philosophical problems arise when language *goes on holiday*. (*PI* ¶38, italics in original)

When philosophers use a word—"knowledge," "being," "object," "I," "proposition," "name"—and try to grasp the *essence* of the thing, one must always ask oneself; is the word ever actually used in this way in the language-game which is its original home.—

What *we* do is to bring words back from their metaphysical to their everyday use. (*PI* ¶116, italics in original)

[I]t is . . . of the essence of our investigation that we do not seek to learn anything *new* by it. We want to *understand* something that is already in plain view. (*PI* ¶89, italics in original)

—When . . . we disapprove of the expressions of ordinary language (which are after all performing their office), we have got a picture in our heads which conflicts with the picture of our ordinary way of speaking. Whereas we are tempted to say that our way of speaking does not describe the facts as they really are. . . . (*PI* ¶402)

Thus, one is "bewitched" by language when one uses words other than in an "ordinary," "everyday" way. And what might be some examples of such bewitchment?

For *this* [referring to the material in the last quoted paragraph above] is what disputes between Idealists, Solipsists, and Realists look like. The one party attack the normal form of expression as if they were attacking a statement, the others defend it, as if they were stating facts recognized by every reasonable human being. (*PI* ¶402, italics in original)

If I were to reserve the word "pain" solely for what I had hitherto called "my pain" and others "L.W.'s pain," I should do other people no injustice, as long as a notation were provided in which the loss of the word "pain" in other connexions were somehow supplied. Other people would still be pitied, treated by doctors, and so on. It would, of course, be *no* objection to this mode of expression to say: "But look here, other people have just the same as you!"

But what should I gain from this new kind of account? Nothing. But after all neither does the solipsist *want* any practical advantage when he advances his view! (*PI* ¶403, italics in original)

"I can only *believe* that someone else is in pain, but I *know* it if I am."—Yes: one can make the decision to say "I believe he is in pain" instead of "He is in pain." But that is all.—What looks like an explanation here, or like a statement about a mental process, is in truth an exchange of one expression for another which, while we are doing philosophy, seems the more appropriate one. (*PI* ¶303, italics in original)

Objections quickly arise here. First, to the extent that the skeptic doubts that others are really in pain, he will, of course, not pity them. Second, it seems to be a use-mention confusion to hold that the skeptic is merely proposing that new expressions be introduced to replace old ones, the way people might propose that the word 'disabled' be used instead of 'handicapped' or that 'POSSLQ' be used to abbreviate 'person of the opposite sex sharing living quarters'. Instead, the skeptic has an *argument* for his skepticism about other people's pains, an argument that draws upon our ordinary concepts to argue that

    (1) The only possible evidence I can have that someone else is in pain comes from his body, behavior, and circumstances, and from analogy with my own mental states, body, behavior, and circumstances.

    (2) But this evidence is inadequate; other human beings may have no mental states at all, or they may be deliberately deceiving me about which mental states they have, or their natural bodily and behavioral correlates and expressions of mental states may just be different from mine, and I have no way of ruling out this possibility, or even showing it to be less likely than not.

    (3) Therefore, I can never know or even reasonably believe that someone else is in pain.

Why does Wittgenstein discount this argument and instead hold that the skeptic, rather than giving an *a priori* argument involving concepts we already have, is really just proposing a new way of speaking? The answer reflects the deepest way in which Wittgenstein's methodology is anti-theoretical: It repudiates the synthetic *a priori*. This is evident in his view that what purport to be philosophical discoveries about ordinary concepts can really be no more than suggestions of new ways of speaking (see *PI* ¶s 24, 303, 401–403), rather than philosophical conclusions reached by *a priori* reasoning, since "In philosophy we do not draw conclusions" (*PI* ¶599) or "deduce anything" (*PI* ¶126). Consider also this remark.

And this too is clear: if as a matter of logic you exclude other people's having something, it loses its sense to say you have it. (*PI* ¶398)

This passage may make it look as though Wittgenstein holds that statements purporting to ascribe necessary properties are meaningless. But a more representative passage is as follows.

It can't be said of me at all (except perhaps as a joke) that I *know* I am in pain. What is it supposed to mean—except perhaps that I *am* in pain? (*PI* ¶246, italics in original)

See how much more drastic Wittgenstein's rejection of the synthetic *a priori* is than the anti-theoretical position Armstrong attributes to him. Not only does Wittgenstein repudiate philosophical "theories" or "theses," but he repudiates any kind of philosophical remark that teaches us anything new at all. (See the passage quoted above from *PI* ¶89.) Note also how much more drastic this makes Wittgenstein's view than Moore's defense of common sense. Moore,

who of course does not repudiate the synthetic *a priori*, has no interest in denying the possibility of philosophical discoveries about the many philosophical
problems where common sense does not dictate any particular position.

The view that there is no synthetic *a priori* can be attacked on the grounds
that it allows no acceptable account of what we learn when successfully doing
philosophy or mathematics. Logical positivists as well as Wittgenstein face this
problem. For example, Ayer says that "The power of logic and mathematics to
surprise us, depends, like their usefulness, on the limitations of our reason,"[4]
thereby going against his own empiricist rejection of "the fundamental tenet of
rationalism [which] is that thought is an independent source of knowledge."[5]
I have argued above that Wittgenstein's attempts to reconcile his own practice
with a view that repudiates philosophical reasoning, deduction, and conclusion-
drawing are no more successful.

It can be further argued that, like the verification criterion of meaningfulness, Wittgenstein's ordinary language methodology is self-refuting, although
the argument is more convoluted in Wittgenstein's case because of his aversion
to advancing general principles. But general principles can be gleaned from his
arguments. Thus, consider his claim that the skeptic who advances a skeptical
argument about other minds is not using language in its usual sense. Why
not? Because these words are not "ever actually used in this way in the
language-game which is [their] original home" (*PI* ¶116); the skeptic's use
is a "metaphysical" rather than an "everyday use" (*PI* ¶116) because "When
you . . . [l]ook at the blue of the sky and say to yourself 'How blue the sky is!'
. . . spontaneously—without philosophical intentions—the idea never crosses
your mind that this impression of color belongs only to *you*" (*PI* ¶275, italics
in original)

Thus, Wittgenstein rejects counterintuitive philosophical positions such
as skepticism because these views "*go against ordinary language*,"[6] i.e., these
views go against the way the ordinary person uses such terms as 'know', as
the ordinary person would reject the view that he can never know that anyone
else is in pain. So, on this view, the skeptic who thinks he is putting forth a
skeptical argument actually means something different by 'know' from what the
ordinary person means by it, since they use the terms differently and meaning
is use. Thus, his view holds that skeptics and anti-skeptics no more have a
nonlinguistic disagreement about knowledge than someone who says, 'Banks
are financial institutions' and someone who says, 'Banks are the shores of
rivers' have a nonlinguistic disagreement about banks.

An obvious objection here is that many factors besides meaning help
determine use. For example, two people who disagree about whether the
world is round use the word 'round' differently in that one applies it to
the world while the other does not; yet they do not thereby mean different
things by 'world' or 'round'. Ordinary language philosophy allows that this
aspect of use is not part of the meaning, since it rests on a disagreement about
empirical facts. But in relegating all nonempirical disagreements to differences
in linguistic meaning, the ordinary language philosopher denies the possibility

of substantive, nonlinguistic disagreement over *a priori* facts and thus, like the logical positivist, disallows the synthetic *a priori*.

This ordinary language view can now be seen to be self-refuting, as follows. The view that all nonempirical disagreements are linguistic disagreements entails that if someone believes the sentence '*a* is *F*' when this sentence expresses the *a priori* proposition that *a* is *F*, then having the property he takes '*F*' to express is part of what he means by '*a*'. But this goes against the "ordinary use" of the term 'meaning', i.e., what ordinary people, once they understand the term 'meaning', believe on *a priori* grounds about the extension of the term 'meaning'. For example, the ordinary man would deny that an inept student of arithmetic cannot be using his words with our usual meaning when he makes an error of addition and says, '33=12+19'. So by his own lights, Wittgenstein's views about "meaning" have no more bearing on what the ordinary man means by 'meaning' than sentences using 'bank' to mean 'riverbank' have on commercial banks.

There is an obvious parallel between this objection to ordinary language philosophy and the classic anti-verificationist objection that the verification criterion of meaningfulness is self-refuting. Both objections may seem almost like tricks, but they reveal deep methodological problems with the approaches in question. The verification criterion of meaningfulness is intended to delegitimize all controversy that is not resolvable either empirically or by recourse to definitions. This verification principle itself, however, cannot be established either empirically or by recourse to definitions. The principle is an attempt to rule out synthetic *a priori* controversy; yet the principle itself is both synthetic *a priori* and controversial. Similarly, ordinary language philosophy seeks to bar all *a priori* counterintuitiveness on the grounds that it goes against ordinary language, but the ordinary language technique itself is *a priori* counterintuitive and hence "goes against ordinary language."

Even leaving aside the general method of ordinary language philosophy, the question can still arise of whether the skeptic is in fact using the word 'know' in a sense different from that of the ordinary man who sincerely says, 'I know that Laura has a toothache'. A plausible strategy for answering this question is to look at the marks for deciding whether a word is being used in two different senses, and to see what result they yield in this case.

What are such marks? One natural candidate is intelligibility. If I were to say, 'I had a bowl of knowledge for breakfast', my remark would not be intelligible to someone who had to draw upon his ordinary sense of the word 'knowledge'. I could provide additional information to make the remark intelligible, for example, by explaining that I was speaking metaphorically and really meant that instead of eating breakfast, I read Descartes (thereby acquiring knowledge and nourishing myself intellectually rather than physically), or by explaining that I was eating a new breakfast cereal called "Knowledge" (which perhaps is advertised as "The Breakfast of Philosophers" the way Wheaties is the breakfast of champions). But in the absence of a special explanation, the remark is unintelligible. Contrast this with the skeptical argument about other minds, which, whatever its ultimate soundness, gets its initial force precisely because it is so intelligible and gripping to someone who has only his ordinary sense of 'know' to go on. In eighteen years of teaching skeptical arguments to students new to philosophy, I have gotten many different sorts of reactions, including highly critical ones and flat-out rejections. But I have never had a student say, "That makes no sense. What on earth do you mean by 'know'?"

Still, the fact that people do not need to have a new sense of 'know' explained to them in order to understand skeptical arguments does not guarantee that the term is being used in its usual sense. Another possibility is that the skeptical arguments use the term metaphorically, since metaphors often can be understood by drawing on one's usual understanding of the terms in question.[7] For example it might be argued that a literal way of expressing what the skeptic means by 'know' is 'have evidence that strictly implies'. But this fails on two grounds. First, it is not what the skeptic believes he means, and it is poor methodology to suppose that someone is wrong about what he means, or about whether he is using a team metaphorically, when the only justification for this supposition is a philosophical theory with little independent support. Second, the skeptical problem reappears if we eliminate the disputed word 'know' from the conclusion of the above skeptical argument and reformulate the conclusion as "Therefore, I can never have evidence that gives me good reason to believe that someone else is in pain."

Another test is what I call the ease-of-settling-disputes test. Suppose I were to ask a class of ten students, 'How many palms are there in this room?' If some students were to answer 'none' while others answered 'twenty-two', all it would take to resolve this dispute would be to point out that the former students took my use of 'palm' to mean 'palm tree' while the latter took it to mean 'palm of the hand'. Once this point was made, it would be obvious that there was no remaining nonlinguistic dispute over the "true" nature of palms. Skeptics, however, will of course not accept the Wittgensteinian view that they are not using 'know' in the usual sense, so the dispute between skeptics and anti-skeptics remains. In discussing what he takes to be Moore's method of refuting skepticism, Malcolm holds that the reason the skeptic "will not feel refuted" by this method is largely that "Moore's reply fails to bring out the linguistic ... nature" of the skeptical view and also fails to "get at the source of the philosophical troubles which produce" the skeptical view.[8] Yet Wittgenstein provides an account that purportedly does both these things, and the skeptic still does not feel refuted. It is, to put it mildly, methodologically problematic to hold a view of philosophy that maintains not only that one's apparent opponents ought to agree with one, but that they actually do or will. And I have argued that it is not only the methodology underlying Wittgenstein's views about when words are being used in a special sense that is open to objection. The conclusions this methodology leads him to draw about the skeptic's use of language also seem wrong.[9]

Notes

1. All passages from *Philosophical Investigations* are in L. Wittgenstein, *Philosophical Investigations*, 3rd edition, translated by G. E. M. Anscombe (New York, 1968).

2. D. Armstrong, *A Materialist Theory of the Mind* (London, 1968), p. 14.

3. At one university I attended, a prominent Wittgensteinian was notorious for teaching an introductory course in which students' success reportedly depended upon their spontaneously coming up with, or at least readily accepting, Wittgenstein's views as the natural, commonsense views—which, also reportedly, students rarely did.

4. A. J. Ayer, *Language, Truth, and Logic* (New York, 1952), p. 85.

5. Ibid., p. 73.

6. N. Malcolm, "Moore and Ordinary Language" in *The Linguistic Turn*, edited by R. Rorty (Chicago, 1967), p. 113. This article deals explicitly with Moore and does not even mention Wittgenstein, but whatever its deficiencies as an interpretation of Moore, it seems reasonably accurate as an account of the Wittgensteinian ordinary language philosophy that Malcolm himself adheres to.

7. See W. Alston, *Philosophy of Language* (Englewood Cliffs, N.J., 1964), ch. 5.

8. Malcolm, "Moore and Ordinary language," p. 123.

9. I am indebted to many people for helpful discussion of issues in this essay, especially John Bellwoar, Dexter Flowers, Shannon French, Yuanchung Lee, Ernest Sosa, and James Van Cleve.

The Second Person

DONALD DAVIDSON

...meaning something is like going up to someone.
—Wittgenstein, *Investigations, §457.*

How many competent speakers of a language must there be if anyone can be said to speak or understand a language? As a matter governed by the crooked course of evolution, I have no idea what the answer is; perhaps it takes quite a crowd. But as philosophers we can ask the question in a more theoretical vein. In this essay I shall be concentrating on the role—the role in principle—of the second person. My subject is not, I should perhaps add, the grammatical second person, the "you" or "thou," the "tú" or "vosotros"; I shall be talking about real second people, not the words we use to address them.

A language may be viewed as a complex abstract object, defined by giving a finite list of expressions (words), rules for constructing meaningful concatenations of expressions (sentences), and a semantic interpretation of the meaningful expressions based on the semantic features of individual words. I shall not be concerned in this essay with the details of how such objects should be described or defined.

Thought of this way, a language is abstract in the obvious sense that it is unobservable, changeless, and its components are for the most part also unobservable and changeless. Expressions may, if we wish, be viewed as acoustical or two-dimensional spatial shapes that could, on occasion, inform actual utterances or inscriptions, but expressions themselves remain abstract and their existence independent of exemplification.[1] The functions that interpret some expressions by mapping them on to objects or classes of objects are also, of course, abstract. The only concrete particulars that enter into the characterization of a language are some of the objects onto which some expressions are mapped (for example, by the naming relation or Tarski's satisfaction relation).

The abstract character of language is nothing to wonder at. The concept of a language is of a sort with, and depends on, concepts like name, predicate, sentence, reference, meaning, and truth. These are all theoretical concepts. We do not need them in order to use or learn a language; obviously they are not available to us when we are learning a first language. Where we want these concepts is in talking about speech behavior. Philosophers, psychologists, and linguists need these theoretical terms if they want to describe, theorize about, and explain verbal activities. The rest of us also have occasion to talk about talk, or write about writing, so these theoretical concepts have their place in the loose informal "theories" we all have about language. Indeed, we all talk so freely about language or languages that we tend to forget that there are no such things in the world; there are only speakers and their various written and acoustical products. This point, obvious in itself, is nevertheless easy to forget, and it has consequences that are far from universally recognized.

A feature of the concept of a language as I have described it is that there must be an infinity of "languages" no one ever has spoken or ever will speak. To say someone speaks a particular language, for example Spanish, is just to say that his or her datable utterances and writings are tokens of Spanish expressions. To be the token of a Spanish sentence an utterance or inscription must instantiate a Spanish sentence, that is, have one of the shapes defined to be a Spanish sentence; and the utterance must have the semantic features the definition of Spanish assigns to the shape. (Other, probably unspoken, languages will assign other semantic features to these same shapes.) The existence of the Spanish language does not, then, depend on anyone's speaking it, any more than the existence of shapes depends on there being objects with those shapes.[2]

It follows that there is nothing about the existence of a particular language which imbues it with anything more than the sort of interest any abstract object may have; as logicians we can study it as one example among countless others of a formal pattern. There is nothing wrong with such research, but it is only distantly related to our normal concern with understanding the speech of others, or learning to make ourselves understood by them. Our practical, as opposed to our purely theoretical, interest in linguistic phenomena is this: we want to understand the actual utterances of others, and we want our utterances to be understood. What has language to do with this interest?

The answer is that it is only by employing such concepts as word and sentence that we can give a systematic description of the linguistic aspects of linguistic behavior and aptitudes. We could not, for example, say what we have learned when we learn that "mañana" means tomorrow in Spanish if we could not speak of words—those mysterious abstract shapes which utterances of "mañana" share. Thus an utterance of the word "mañana" refers to the day after the day of the utterance. There is no easy way we could specify which sequences of utterances constitute utterances of sentences, and therefore constitute intelligible utterances, if we could not refer to words and sentences.

The point of the concept of a language, then, and its attendant concepts like those of predicate, sentence, and reference is to enable us to give a coherent description of the behavior of speakers, and of what speakers and their interpreters know that allows them to communicate. I do not suggest that speakers and those who understand them must themselves be able to provide such descriptions of their abilities and behavior. A competent speaker of a language (and a competent interpreter) knows the truth conditions of an indefinitely large number of sentences. Thus an English speaker knows that an utterance of the sentence "Madrid is in Spain" is true if and only if Madrid is in Spain; and the speaker knows an analogous fact about endless other sentences. The speaker does not need to be able to put this knowledge into words. But *we* cannot describe the totality of this knowledge possessed by the speaker or interpreter of the language without ourselves having a theory—a theory of truth, or something like it—which is part of the description of English. (This description of what an English speaker knows does not have to be stated in English, and if it is not it does not sound so trivial.)

To return, now, to the question with which I began: how many speakers or interpreters of a language must there be for there to be one speaker of that language? Let me start with an apparent difficulty. To speak a language, one must speak from time to time, and these utterances must be consistent with the definition of some language. The trouble is that utterances are finite in number, while the definition of a language assigns meanings to an infinite number of sentences. There will therefore be endless different languages which agree with all of a speaker's actual utterances, but differ with respect to unspoken sentences. What makes a particular speaker the speaker of one of these languages rather than of another? And the problem may be worse still. For even if a speaker were (impossibly) to utter every sentence in some one language, many other languages would be consistent with all his behavior, as Quine has maintained; and I agree.

The fact that even all possible evidence with regard to the question what language a speaker or group of speakers is speaking might be consistent with many languages (in the sense of "language" we have locally ordained) ought not in itself to worry us. For we can agree that it is enough to know that a speaker speaks any of a set of empirically equivalent languages; indeed there is nothing to stop us from calling this set "the" language of the speaker.[3] This strategy is good enough for empirically equivalent languages if the evidence is imagined to be infinite, or to contain an utterance of every sentence an utterance of which we would count as belonging to the language. But of course such evidence is never available. So there will be endless languages consistent with all the actual utterances of a speaker none of which is "the" language he is speaking.

The problem can be stated in a temporal mode and addressed to an interpreter. If you (the interpreter) do not know how a speaker is going to go on, you do not know what language she speaks, no matter how much she has said up until now. It will not help to mention the fact that the speaker has performed according to expectation so far, or that she went to the same school you did, or belongs to the same culture or community, for the question does not concern the past but the future. Nor can we appeal to the idea that the speaker has mastered a set of conventions (which conventions?), or has learned a set of rules (which ones?). The concepts of conventions or rules, like the concept of a language, cannot be called on to justify or explain linguistic behavior; at best these concepts help describe (i.e., define) linguistic behavior.

This particular difficulty, though it may have troubled Wittgenstein, and certainly troubled Kripke,[4] seems to me to have a relatively simple answer. The longer we interpret a speaker with apparent success as speaking a particular language the greater our legitimate confidence that the speaker is speaking that language, or one much like it. Our strengthening expectations are as well founded as our evidence and induction make them. (Needless to say, we can worry about the justification of our inductive procedures, but this is not a worry specific to language.) These expectations are in the main conditional. We do not usually know what someone will say, but we are prepared to interpret any of a very large number of things he might say. These dispositions on his part and ours are not shadowy or mysterious: they are real features of our brains and muscles. Of course our beliefs about what is true of another person, and therefore what we expect that person to mean by what he does or might say, may easily be wrong. I think such beliefs often are wrong. But far more often they are right, and the things we have right usually put us in a position to correct our understanding of an utterance which does not belong to a language we thought was being spoken. To the extent that we are right about what is in someone's head, and therefore are right about what he would mean by endless things he does not say, we are right about "the" language he speaks.

This very partial answer to the question what reasons an interpreter can have for believing that a person is speaking one language rather than another that is equally compatible with his observed speech behavior does not depend heavily on the details of how we explain successful interpretation. The point of the answer is that there are not *two* questions, one about reasons for believing that a speaker is speaking one language rather than another, and a second question about the validity of induction; the first question is simply a case of the second.

There is another aspect of interpretation, however, that is essential to our concerns: an interpreter (correctly) interprets an utterance of a speaker only if he knows that the speaker intends the interpreter to assign certain truth conditions to his (the speaker's) utterance.[5] A full account of this thesis would require an explanation of the idea of "assigning truth conditions" to an utterance, and this idea is no doubt as difficult to understand in relevant respects as the concept of meaning itself. But my present aim is not to solve that problem; it is only to emphasize, following Grice, the central role of intention in communication. If, with Grice, we are sure that in order to mean something a speaker must intend to have a certain effect on a specific hearer or hearers, then language might already have been shown to be social to the extent of requiring the existence of at least two people (since it is arguable that one could not intend to have an effect on a specific person unless such a person existed). I shall not take this direct and tempting line here. Nevertheless, we are in a position to say that if communication succeeds there must be these intentions on the part of the speaker, and therefore *if* successful communication is essential to meaning, these intentions are essential to meaning. The necessary presence of intentions would be significant, since it would give content to an attribution of error by allowing for the possibility of a discrepancy between intention and accomplishment. Intention, like belief and expectation, does not require attention or reflection, and intentions are not usually arrived at by reasoning. Intentions are not normally attended by any special feelings, nor is our knowledge of our own intentions usually supported by inference or observation. Yet intention has an indefinitely large scope, for intentions depend on the belief that one can do what one intends, and this requires that one believe nothing will prevent the intended action. Thus intention would seem to have just the properties needed to make sense of the idea that a speaker has failed to "go on as before."[6]

The view I have just sketched deals only with interpretation, and so presupposes a social environment rather than providing an argument for it. Nevertheless, it will be useful at this point to consider certain aspects of the view I think Kripke attributes to Wittgenstein. (For expository purposes I shall call this Kripke's view. In fact Kripke does not clearly say he endorses it; and I am uncertain that it is Wittgenstein's view. So it may be no one's view.) Kripke concentrates on the idea of following a rule. According to this idea, to speak a language is to follow rules. The rules specify what it is to go on "in the same way," how, for example, to use a word. There is, however, no inner mental act or process of "grasping" or of "following" the rule, so no study of what is inside the speaker will reveal whether she is following one set of rules or another. The criterion that decides what rule someone is following is just how she actually does go on, and the only test of whether she has it right is whether she goes on as I (her interpreter) would. Put in terms of meaning: we judge that a speaker means what we would if we were to utter the same words. She speaks the same language we do if she goes on as we would.[7]

We ought to question the appropriateness of the ordinary concept of following a rule for describing what is involved in speaking a language. When we talk of rules of language we normally have in mind grammarians' or linguists' descriptions (generalized and idealized) of actual practice, or (often) prescriptions grammarians think we should follow. Rules can be a help in learning a language, but their aid is available, if at all, only in the acquisition of a second language. Most language learning is accomplished without learning or knowing any rules at all.[8] Wittgenstein does, of course, treat meaning something in much the same way he treats following some procedure, such as adding in arithmetic. But there is a clear distinction between the cases, which explains why we ordinarily use the word "rule" in one case and not in the other. In the case of adding, there is an explicit procedure for arriving at an answer; we can learn and describe the procedure, and it is appropriate to call the procedure or its description a rule. We normally follow no procedure in speaking; nothing in the everyday use of language corresponds to taking the sum in adding. If the concept of following a rule is not quite appropriate to describe meaning something by saying something, it is also questionable whether, even if we agree that the use of a language requires a social setting, we should accept without question the idea that meaning something demands a convention, custom, or institution.[9]

A more important question concerns the idea that linguistic communication requires that a speaker go on in the same way as others do—that to mean something in speaking, one must mean the same thing by the same words as others do. The account I gave above of the sort of expectations that must be satisfied if one person is to understand a second did not suggest that the two would have to speak the same language. Nor is it clear why this is necessary. Perhaps language would never have come into existence unless it could depend on the natural tendency of animals to imitate each other. This may be so, though I have my doubts; but surely it could have been otherwise. If you and I were the only speakers in the world, and you spoke Sherpa while I spoke English, we could learn to understand one another, though there would be no "rules" that we jointly followed in our speech. What would matter, of course, is that we should each provide the other with something intelligible as a language. This is, as we saw, a condition speakers must intend to satisfy; but carrying out the intention, while it may require a degree of what the other perceives as consistency, does not involve following shared rules or conventions. It might even be that because of differences in our vocal chords we could not make the same sounds, and therefore could not speak the same language. I know of no argument that shows that under such circumstances communication could not take place. So, while it may be true that speaking a language requires that there be an interpreter, it does not follow that more than one person must speak the same language. This is fortunate, since if we are precise about what constitutes a language, it is probably the case that no two people actually do speak the same language. I conclude that Kripke's criterion for speaking a language cannot be right; speaking a language cannot depend on speaking as someone else does (or as many others do).[10]

Let us suppose, then, that the test for speaking a language is modified to accommodate this point: speaking a language, we will now claim, does not depend on two or more speakers speaking in the same way; it merely requires that the speaker intentionally make himself interpretable to a hearer (the speaker must "go on" more or less as the interpreter expects, or at least is equipped to interpret).

This is certainly a necessary condition for successful *communication*. But why is it a condition that must be satisfied in order to speak a language at all? Why couldn't someone go on in the same way—satisfy all the conditions for being *interpretable*—without actually being interpreted?[11]

It is true that our *evidence* that someone speaks a particular language is mainly based on the fact that he goes on as we expect a speaker of that language to go on. There are, of course, many other sorts of evidence; the speaker's clothes, his companions, his location on the face of the earth, may all be clues to his language. Still, we can agree that pinning matters down must in the end depend on the details of speech behavior. The trouble is that the original question concerned neither the conditions for communication nor the question what evidence one person could have that another was speaking a particular language; the issue was why a speaker's sole or first language could not be private.

Our discussion has led to a modification or elucidation of the concept of a private language: I am taking this to mean, not a language only one person speaks, but a language only one person understands. The question now is, why can't there be a language only one person understands?[12] The answer Wittgenstein seems to offer is: without an interpreter no substance can be given to the claim that the speaker has gone wrong—that he has failed to go on in the same way.

But haven't we, by eliminating the condition that the speaker must go on as the interpreter (or others) would, at the same time inadvertently destroyed all chance of characterizing linguistic error? If there is no social practice with which to compare the speaker's performance, won't whatever the speaker says be, as Wittgenstein suggests, in accord with some rule (i.e., in accord with some language)? If the speech behavior of others does not provide the norm for the speaker, what can? The answer is that the intention of the speaker to be interpreted in a certain way provides the norm; the speaker falls short of his intention if he fails to speak in such a way as to be understood as he intended. Under usual circumstances a speaker knows he is most apt to be understood if he speaks as his listeners would, and so he will intend to speak as he thinks they would. He will then fail in one of his intentions if he does not speak as others do. This simple fact helps explain, I think, why many philosophers have tied the meaning of a speaker's utterances to what others mean by the same words (whether "others" refers to a linguistic community, "experts," or an élite of one sort or another[13]). On my account, this tie is neither essential nor direct; it comes into play only when the speaker intends to be interpreted as (certain) others would be. When this intention is absent, the correct understanding of a speaker is unaffected by usage beyond the intended reach of his voice. (A failed intention to speak "correctly," unless it foils the intention to be interpreted in a certain way, does not matter to what the speaker means.[14])

What these considerations show, if they are right, is that there is a weaker and more plausible alternative to Kripke's proposed account of what is required in order to mean something by what one says. For while Kripke's account makes the test of whether a speaker means something depend on his doing what others do, the same distinction between thinking one means something and actually meaning it can be made in terms of the success of the speaker's intention to be interpreted in a certain way. Both ways of making the distinction depend on a social setting, but the second makes less conservative demands on the speaker.[15]

Have we now shown that there cannot be a private language? Surely not. If we assume that Kripke's proposal is correct, then it is true that one way of distinguishing between thinking one means something and actually meaning it requires that language be public; mutatis mutandis, the same can be said for the alternative I have suggested. But nothing definitive has been said to show there may not be some other way of drawing the distinction, even a way that does not depend on a social environment.

If we are to establish the essentially public character of language, we need an entirely different sort of argument. In the remainder of this essay I suggest such an argument, an argument that applies not only to speech but also to belief, intention, and the rest of the propositional attitudes. The argument that follows does not start with a skeptical doubt to which an answer is sought, but it does end with what many philosophers consider Wittgenstein's conclusion: language is necessarily a social affair.

Consider first a primitive learning situation. Some creature is taught, or anyway learns, to respond in a specific way to a stimulus or a class of stimuli. The dog hears a bell and is fed; presently it salivates when it hears the bell. The child babbles, and when it produces a sound like "table" in the evident presence of a table, it is rewarded; the process is repeated and presently the child says "table" in the presence of tables. The phenomenon of generalization, of perceived similarity, plays an essential role in the process. One ring of the bell is enough like another to the dog to provoke similar behavior, just as one presentation of food is enough like another to engender salivation. If some such discriminative mechanisms were not built in, none could be learned. The same goes for the child: we can class the child's stimuli by the similarity of the responses those stimuli elicit in the child.[16]

This seems straightforward, but as psychologists have noticed, there is a problem about the stimulus. In the case of the dog, why say the stimulus is the ringing of the bell? Why couldn't it be the vibration of the air close to the ears of the dog—or even the stimulation of its nerve endings? Certainly if the air were made to vibrate in the same way the bell makes it vibrate it would make no difference to the behavior of the dog. And if the right nerve endings were activated in the right way, there still would be no difference. In fact, if we must choose, it seems that the proximal cause of the behavior has the best claim to be called the stimulus, since the more distant an event is causally from its perceiver the more chance there is that the causal chain will be broken. Why not say the same about the child: that its responses are not to tables but to patterns of stimulation at its surfaces, since those patterns of stimulation always produce the behavior, while tables produce it only under favorable conditions?

What explains the fact that it seems so natural to say the dog is responding to the bell, the child to tables? It seems natural to us because it *is* natural—to us. Just as the dog and the child respond in similar ways to certain stimuli, so do we. It is we who find it natural to group together the various salivations of the dog; and the events in the world that we notice and group together that are causally linked to the dog's behavior are ringings of the bell. We find the child's mouthings of "table" similar, and the natural (to us) class we find in the world that accompanies those mouthings is a class of tables. The acoustical and visual patterns that speed at their various rates between bell and dog ears, tables and child eyes, we cannot easily observe, and if we could we might have a hard time saying what made them similar. (Except by cheating, of course: they are the patterns characteristic of bells ringing, of tables viewed.) Nor do we observe the stimulation of nerve endings of other people and animals, and if we did we would probably find it impossible to describe in a non-circular way what made the patterns relevantly similar from trial to trial. The problem would be much the same as the (insoluble) problem of defining tables and bell-ringings in terms of sense data without mentioning tables or bells.

Involved in our picture there are now not two but three similarity patterns. The child finds tables similar; we find tables similar; and we find the child's responses in the presence of tables similar. It now makes sense for us to call the responses of the child responses to tables. Given these three patterns of response we can assign a location to the stimuli that elicit the child's responses. The relevant stimuli are the objects or events we naturally find similar (tables) which are correlated with responses of the child we find similar. It is a form of triangulation: one line goes from the child in the direction of the table, one line goes from us in the direction of the table, and the third line goes from us to the child. Where the lines from child to table and us to table converge "the" stimulus is located. Given our view of child and world, we can pick out "the" cause of the child's responses. It is the common cause of our response and the child's response.[17]

Enough features are in place to give a meaning to the idea that the stimulus has an objective location in a common space; but nothing in this picture shows that either we, the observers, or our subjects, the dog and the child, have this idea. Nevertheless, we have come a good distance. For if I am right, the kind of triangulation I have described, while not *sufficient* to establish that a creature has a concept of a particular object or kind of object, is *necessary* if there is to be any answer at all to the question of what its concepts are concepts of. If we consider a single creature by itself, its responses, no matter how complex, cannot show that it is reacting to, or thinking about, events a certain distance away rather than, say, on its skin. The solipsist's world can be any size; which is to say, from the solipsist's point of view it has no size, it is not a world.

The problem is not, I should stress, one of verifying what objects or events a creature is responding to; the problem is that without a second creature responding to the first, there can be no answer to the question. And of course if there is no answer to this question, there is no answer to the question what language a creature speaks, since to designate a language as one being spoken requires that utterances be matched up with objects in the world (and not, in general, events on the surface of the skin). So we can say, as a preliminary to answering the question with which we began, that if anyone is to speak a language, there must be another creature interacting with the speaker. Of course, this cannot be enough, since mere interaction does not show how the interaction matters to the creatures involved. Unless the creatures concerned can be said to react to the interaction, there is no way *they* can take cognitive advantage of the three-way relation which gives content to *our* idea that they are reacting to one thing rather than another.

Here is part, I think, of what is required. The interaction must be made available to the interacting creatures. Thus the child, learning the word "table," has already in effect noted that the teacher's responses are similar (rewarding) when its own responses (mouthing "table") are similar. The teacher on his part is training the child to make similar responses to what he (the teacher) perceives as similar stimuli. For this to work, it is clear that the innate similarity responses of child and teacher—what they naturally group together—must be much alike; otherwise the child will respond to what the teacher takes to be similar stimuli in ways the teacher does not find similar. A condition for being a speaker is that there are others enough like oneself.

So far I have left out of explicit account the concepts of belief and intention which are clearly essential to speaking a language. I have no thought of trying to introduce these concepts in terms of the simple conditioning situations I have been describing; the concept of thought is not reducible to anything else, much less to these simple concepts. All I have tried to show so far is that interaction among similar creatures is a necessary condition for speaking a language.

Now to put two points together. First, if someone is the speaker of a language, there must be another sentient being whose innate similarity responses are sufficiently like his own to provide an answer to the question of what the stimulus is to which the speaker is responding. And second, if the speaker's responses are linguistic, they must be knowingly and intentionally responses to specific stimuli. The speaker must have the concept of the stimulus—of the bell or of tables. Since the bell or a table is identified only by the intersection of two (or more) sets of similarity responses (lines of thought, we might almost say), to have the concept of a table or a bell is to recognize the existence of a triangle, one apex of which is oneself, another a creature similar to oneself, and the third an object (table or bell) located in a space thus made common.

The only way of knowing that the second apex of the triangle—the second creature or person—is reacting to the same object as oneself is to know that the other person has the same object in mind. But then the second person must also know that the first person constitutes an apex of the same triangle, another apex of which the second person occupies. For two people to know of each other that they are so related, that their thoughts are so related, requires that they be in communication. Each of them must speak to the other and be understood by the other. They do not, as I said, have to mean the same thing by the same words, but they must each be an interpreter of the other.

The remarks of the last two paragraphs indicate the sort of work that would be necessary to give an account of meaningful speech. But such an account was not my aim; I was looking only to find an argument why a language cannot be private.

This argument shows that there cannot be a private language, that is, a language understood by only one creature, and to this extent it is in clear agreement with Kripke's Wittgenstein. But the argument takes a different course, and the flavor it gives the social aspect of language is different. Kripke depends on the second person, or a community, to embody a routine which the speaker can share. In contrast, the argument I have outlined does not require (though of course it allows) a shared routine, but it does depend on the interaction of at least two speaker-interpreters, for if I am right, there would be no saying what a speaker was talking or thinking about, no basis for claiming he could locate objects in an objective space and time, without interaction with a second person.

The considerations I have put forward do not apply to language only; they apply equally to thought in general. Belief, intention, and the other propositional attitudes are all social in that they are states a creature cannot be in without having the concept of intersubjective truth, and this is a concept one cannot have without sharing, and knowing that one shares, a world and a way of thinking about the world with someone else.[18]

Notes

An earlier version of this essay appeared in *Wittgenstein et la philosophie aujourd'hui*, edited by J. Sebestik and A. Soulez (Paris, 1992) under the title "Jusqu'où va le caractère public d'une langue?" Some of the final pages are taken (with minor modifications) from "The Conditions of Thought," *Le Cahier du Collège International de Philosophie* (Paris, 1989), 165–71.

1. Or, to take equally abstract entities, expressions may be thought of as classes of utterances or inscriptions. But if we take expressions to be classes of utterances or inscriptions, all unuttered and unwritten expressions, and hence all expressions of unused languages, will be identical. In some cases there are awkward ways around this. (See W. V. Quine and Nelson Goodman, "Steps Toward a Constructive Nominalism," *Journal of Symbolic Logic* 12 (1947): 97–122.) For our purposes it will be better to take expressions to be shapes, i.e., properties that utterances and inscriptions can have.

2. This concept of a language is essentially that of David Lewis, "Languages and Language," in *Language, Mind and Knowledge*, edited by K. Gundersons (Minneapolis, 1975).

3. I regard the existence of empirically equivalent languages (that is, languages equally consistent with all possible empirical evidence) as no more threatening to the reality or objectivity of the correct understanding of utterances and their accompanying mental states than the existence of various scales for recording temperatures or lengths is to the reality or objectivity of temperature or length.

4. Saul Kripke, *Wittgenstein on Rules and Private Languages* (London, 1982). Further references to Kripke are to this book.

5. This is clearly inadequate as it stands. It can be improved by adding the Gricean condition that the speaker intends the interpreter to arrive at the right truth conditions through the interpreter's recognition of the speaker's intention to be so interpreted. I do not argue here for the very large assumption that knowledge of truth conditions is adequate for interpretation.

6. Essentially these points about intention are made by Crispin Wright in attempting, as I do here, to defuse Kripke's view that he has extracted an essentially insoluble "skeptical

paradox" from Wittgenstein's treatment of meaning. See Crispin Wright, "Kripke's Account of the Argument Against Private Language," *Journal of Philosophy* (1984): 759–78

7. "... what do I mean when I say that the teacher judges that, for certain cases, the pupil must give the 'right' answer? I mean that the teacher judges that the child has given the same answer that he himself would give ... if, in enough concrete cases, Jones's inclinations agree with Smith's, Smith will judge that Jones is indeed following the rule ..." (Kripke, pp. 90, 91). The following from Wittgenstein may bear out this interpretation: "... a person goes by [is guided by] a sign-post only in so far as there exists a regular use of sign-posts, a custom.... Is what we call 'obeying a rule' something that it would be possible for only *one* man to do, and to do only *once* in his life? ... —To obey a rule, to make a report, to give an order, to play a game of chess, are *customs* (uses, institutions)" (*Investigations*, §§198, 199). I have ignored a very important aspect of Kripke's discussion, his claim that Wittgenstein's "solution" to the problem of meaning is "skeptical."

8. It should be obvious that the claim that there are internalized or genetically implanted rules of *grammar* is irrelevant here; Wittgenstein's and Kripke's "rules" concern what the words of particular languages mean.

9. I have expressed my skepticism about the explanatory power of the concepts of rule-following and convention in the study of language at greater length in "Communication and Convention," in *Inquiries into Truth and Interpretation* (Oxford, 1984).

10. My mother kept a record, as fond mothers will, of the language I spoke when I was two years old. It certainly was not the language spoken by others in the family—or by anyone else, I imagine. But she claimed, rightly, that she understood me and I her. And it is common for people who cannot or will not speak or write French to answer letters written in French in English.

I have argued that communication does not demand that languages be shared in "A Nice Derangement of Epitaphs," in *Philosophical Grounds of Rationality*, edited by R. Grandy and R. Warner (Oxford, 1986). The same position is endorsed by Noam Chomsky, *Language and Problems of Knowledge* (Cambridge, Mass., 1988), 36–37. For a more extended treatment of this subject, directly aimed at Kripke, see Chomsky, *Knowledge of Language: Its Nature, Origin and Use* (Chicago, 1986), 223–37.

11. Kripke seems to allow that Robinson Crusoe might be judged to be speaking a language, as long as he *could* be included in a society, even if he is not in fact (ever?) in a social setting. There would still have to be a society (or at least another person) legitimately to judge that Robinson Crusoe meant something by his noises. Chomsky thinks that by allowing the Robinson Crusoe case Kripke contradicts his main thesis. Perhaps so; but I think Chomsky is wrong in thinking the pure Robinson Crusoe case possible. By the pure case, I mean a Robinson Crusoe who has never been in communication with others.

12. Of course there can be a "language" only one person understands, for example a secret code used in a diary. The claim would be more accurately stated: a first language, or the only language of a speaker if she has only one, must be understood by someone else. Having a private language depends on having a public language.

13. For examples, see Hilary Putnam "The Meaning of 'Meaning'," in *Philosophical Papers, Vol. II: Mind, Language, and Reality* (Cambridge, 1975); Michael Dummett, "The Social Character of Meaning," in *Truth and Other Enigmas* (London, 1978), and " 'A Nice Derangement of Epitaphs': Some Comments on Davidson and Hacking," in *Truth and Interpretation: Perspectives on the Philosophy of Donald Davidson*, edited by E. LePore, (London, 1986; and Tyler Burge, "Individualism and the Mental," in *Midwest Studies in Philosophy, Vol. 4*, (Minneapolis, 1979).

14. This issue is further pursued in my "Knowing One's Own Mind," in *Proceedings and Addresses of the American Philosophical Association*, 1987.

15. There is a delicate point here that I have not accommodated. A speaker fails in an intention if he is not interpreted as he intends. But it would be wrong to say that such a failure is necessarily a failure to give the meaning to his words that he intended the interpreter to

catch. The latter failure depends (in ways that ordinary usage may not definitively settle) on such questions as whether the speaker was justified in believing his interpreter could, or would, interpret him as he intended.

16. Nothing here depends on the amateur psychology involving babbling, differential rewards, or proverbial induction. All that matters is the fact that generalization takes place in one way rather than another.

17. I first used the triangulation metaphor in "Rational Animals," *Dialectica* 36 (1982): 318–27. The idea of the "common cause" is developed in my "A Coherence Theory of Truth and Knowledge," first published in *Kant oder Hegel?* edited by Henrich, (Stuttgart, 1983) and reprinted in *Truth and Interpretation: Perspectives on the Philosophy of Donald Davidson*, edited by E. LePore (London, 1986).

18. That thought is a social phenomenon is stressed in "Thought and Talk," in *Inquiries into Truth and Interpretation*, and in "Rational Animals."

The present essay owes much to the suggestions, comments, and criticisms of Akeel Bilgrami, Marcia Cavell, Michael Dummett, Warren Goldfarb, and Carol Rovanne.

Contributors

Felicia Ackerman, Department of Philosophy, Brown University
Anthony Brueckner, Department of Philosophy, University of California, Santa Barbara
Arthur Collins, Department of Philosophy, CUNY Graduate Center
Donald Davidson, Department of Philosophy, University of California, Berkeley
Carl Ginet, Sage School of Philosophy, Cornell University
Warren Goldfarb, Department of Philosophy, Harvard University
Lars Hertzberg, Department of Philosophy, Åbo Akademi, Finland
S. L. Hurley, St. Edmund Hall, Oxford University
Peter van Inwagen, Department of Philosophy, Syracuse University
Alasdair MacIntyre, Department of Philosophy, University of Notre Dame
John McDowell, Department of Philosophy, University of Pittsburgh
Ian Niles, Department of Philosophy, University of California, Irvine
D. Z. Phillips, Department of Philosophy, University College of Swansea, Wales
Donna M. Summerfield, Department of Philosophy, Southern Illinois University
Peter Winch, Department of Philosophy, University of Illinois, Urbana
Nick Zangwill, Magdalen College, Oxford University

Peter A. French is Lennox Distinguished Professor of Philosophy at Trinity University in San Antonio, Texas. He has taught at the University of Minnesota, Morris, and has served as Distinguished Research Professor in the Center for the Study of Values at the University of Delaware. His books include *The Scope of Morality* (1980), *Collective and Corporate Responsibility* (1980), and *Responsibility Matters* (1992). He has published numerous articles in the philosophical journals. **Theodore E. Uehling, Jr.,** is professor of philosophy at the University of Minnesota, Morris. He is the author of *The Notion of Form in Kant's Critique of Aesthetic Judgment* and articles on the philosophy of Kant. He is a founder and past vice-president of the North American Kant Society. **Howard K. Wettstein** is chair and professor of philosophy at the University of California, Riverside. He has taught at the University of Notre Dame and the University of Minnesota, Morris, and has served as a visiting associate professor of philosophy at the University of Iowa and Stanford University. He is the author of *Has Semantics Rested on a Mistake? and Other Essays* (1992).